Naval Warfare, 1815–1914

From the era of Napoleon and Lord Nelson to the Anglo-German naval race before the First World War, naval warfare underwent a slow transition from the age of the wooden sailing fleet to the modern steel navy. *Naval Warfare, 1815–1914* covers major clashes such as the Crimean War and American Civil War, as well as lesser-known regional conflicts, colonial empire-building and exercises in "gunboat diplomacy".

The greatest coverage is given to the leading naval powers, including the rise of the German, Japanese and American navies towards the end of the era. In addition, *Naval Warfare, 1815–1914* also includes accounts of lesser-known conflicts, such as those during the Latin American wars for independence, for which there are no readily available English-language accounts.

The technological breakthroughs of steam power, armor, artillery and torpedoes that brought changes not only to warship design, but also to naval strategy and tactics are fully surveyed, and the rivalries of the naval powers, their wars and expeditions are considered with special attention to the evolving state of naval technology. It is this relationship between the industrialization of a country and the advancement of its naval strength which is a key to understanding this important period of world history.

Naval Warfare, 1815–1914 is a concise overview of global naval developments between the Napoleonic era and the First World War and will be invaluable to students and enthusiasts alike.

Lawrence Sondhaus is Associate Professor of History at the University of Indianapolis. He is author of five books including *Preparing for Weltpolitik: German Sea Power before the Tirpitz Era* (Naval Institute Press, 1997) and two volumes on the Austrian navy.

Warfare and History
General Editor
Jeremy Black
Professor of History, University of Exeter

Naval Warfare, 1815–1914

Lawrence Sondhaus

London and New York

First published 2001
by Routledge
11 New Fetter Lane, London EC4P 4EE

Simultaneously published in the USA and Canada
by Routledge
29 West 35th Street, New York, NY 10001

Routledge is an imprint of the Taylor & Francis Group

Typeset in Bembo by Keystroke, Jacaranda Lodge, Wolverhampton
Printed and bound in Great Britain by St Edmundsbury Press, Bury St Edmunds, Suffolk

British Library Cataloguing in Publication Data
A catalogue record for this book is available from the British Library

Library of Congress Cataloguing in Publication Data
Sondhaus, Lawrence, 1958–
    Naval warfare, 1815–1914 / Lawrence Sondhaus.
        p. cm. — (Warfare and history)
    Includes bibliographical references and index.
    1. Naval art and science—History—19th century. 2. Naval art and
    science—History—20th century. 3. Naval history, Modern—19th century.
    4. Naval history, Modern—20th century. I. Title. II. Series.
V51 .S66 2000
359′.009034—dc21   00–034464

ISBN 0–415–21477–7 (hbk)
ISBN 0–415–21478–5 (pbk)

Contents

List of plates

Preface

From the era of Napoleon and Lord Nelson to the naval arms races before the First World War, naval warfare underwent a slow transition from the era of the wooden sailing fleet to that of the modern steel navy. Certain developments during the century of change are fairly well known to scholars and students of history, such as the emergence of the "monitor" design in the American Civil War and the "dreadnought" battleship during the eight years before the First World War. Yet, for most, the evolution of warships and naval warfare from 1815 to 1914 (or at least to 1906) remains shrouded in mystery, along with most of the naval engagements of the period.

This study will attempt to leave the reader with a better appreciation of the technological breakthroughs in steam propulsion, armor plate, artillery, and torpedoes that brought changes not only to warship design, but also to naval strategy and tactics. The rivalries of the naval powers, their wars and expeditions, will be investigated with special attention to the evolving state of naval technology. The three leading naval powers of the century – Britain, France, and Russia – naturally will receive the greatest coverage, but the study will also address the decline after 1815 of the Spanish and Dutch navies, as well as the rise before 1914 of German, Japanese, and American sea power. Smaller navies such as the Italian and Austrian, which in 1866 fought the only fleet-scale action of the century between 1805 and 1905, will receive attention where appropriate, along with the navies of the Ottoman empire, China, and the leading South American countries.

The task of writing a general history of this length compels the author to make hard choices as to what not to include, as it is, of course, impossible to provide exhaustive coverage of the entire period. The mandate being one of writing a work on naval warfare, discussion of matters related to naval personnel, including comparisons in training, education, promotion policies, and so forth, has been reduced dramatically or omitted altogether, unless it has such a direct bearing on the performance of a navy in war as to warrant inclusion as part of the explanation of the outcome of that conflict. Description of factors in the economy, industry, domestic politics, and international diplomacy bearing upon naval developments likewise has been kept to the minimum necessary to orientate the reader. An effort has been made to include summary narratives of those naval campaigns – for example, during the Latin American Wars for Independence – for which there are no published English-language accounts, or at least none readily available to the reader of today. In the same spirit, relatively fewer pages have been devoted to aspects of the period already well covered in the Anglo-American literature.

I would like to thank Professor Jeremy Black, general editor of the *Warfare and History* series, for giving me the opportunity to write this volume, and for his support and encouragement over the years. I am grateful to the interlibrary loan staff of Krannert Memorial Library at the University of Indianapolis for processing my many dozens of requests promptly and efficiently. I owe a great debt of gratitude to Jack Green of the Curator Branch, Naval Historical Center, Washington, DC, for his help in securing the photographs. Of course, in a work of this nature almost any number of illustrations would be inadequate. For warship profiles and more detailed technical specifications, readers are advised to consult *Conway's All the World's Fighting Ships*, volumes for *1860–1905* (London, 1979) and *1906–21* (London, 1985), which are the source for technical data except where overruled by more specialized works on individual navies.

I dedicate this book to my son, Paul, whose first weeks of life coincided with the final preparation of the manuscript.

CHAPTER ONE

The twilight of sail,
1815–30

Contrary to popular belief, Napoleon Bonaparte's naval challenge to Britain did not end with Lord Nelson's victory at the Battle of Trafalgar (1805). Indeed, during the last decade of the Napoleonic Wars, an ambitious French shipbuilding program drove the British to construct unprecedented numbers of ships of the line and frigates in order to maintain a safe margin of superiority. When the fighting ended in 1815, the British and French navies had many more warships than they needed for peacetime, but many had been hastily constructed from unseasoned timbers and would have short service lives. Both countries also had a backlog of warships on the stocks, many of which would remain there for years until being finished or scrapped. Because Napoleon had attempted to mobilize the resources of the shipyards in his satellite kingdoms, beyond Britain and France the maritime countries of postwar Europe inherited a variety of warship projects, built and building, in yards from the Baltic to the Adriatic. Meanwhile, across the Atlantic, the United States – the only naval power beyond Europe – after 1815 proceeded with a naval program begun during the War of 1812 against Britain.

By the time of Trafalgar some of Nelson's ships of the line (*Victory* included) had seen forty years of service, reflecting the relative lack of innovation in battleship building during the preceding decades. Throughout the years 1815–30 the wooden sailing ship still ruled the waves, and the wooden ship of the line underwent improvements which prompted the leading navies to consider the traditional third-rate vessel of 74 guns no longer fit for the line of battle. At the same time, most navies acquired their first steamships, and some visionaries prophesied a day in which the capital ships of a fleet would move by steam. The development of the first shell guns likewise led some to question the future viability of wooden ships in close action or against coastal fortifications.

The sailing fleets after 1815

Assessing the numerical strength of any sailing fleet after 1815 is problematic, as different sources provide a variety of figures for each ship type. Even in Britain the navy list included a number of ships so old or in such disrepair that they could not have put to sea under any circumstances. Further confusion arises when the researcher attempts to evaluate the condition of ships ostensibly on the active list, to include or exclude ships in reserve ("in ordinary") or still on the stocks, or the receiving ships and other vessels disarmed for auxiliary duties. By the most generous estimate, in 1815 the British navy had 218 ships of the line, 309 frigates, and 261 sloops or brigs, but at least one recent source gives figures barely half as high. In 1830, when Britain had 106 ships of the line, only seventy-one were considered "in good order" and fit for service.[1]

In the immediate postwar years the British foreign secretary, Viscount Castlereagh, called for the British navy to remain superior to the combined force of the next two naval powers, France and Russia. In addition to the need for vigilance against a possible Franco-Russian alliance, in the dawning era of the Pax Britannica the navy needed forces sufficient to police the world's oceans in support of the moral and legal positions Britain had taken and was persuading others to take. These included stopping the slave trade, which the British parliament in 1807 had abolished throughout the empire, and keeping commercial sea lanes safe against piracy, which had flourished, especially in Mediterranean waters, during the Napoleonic Wars. Yet the official peacetime standard of the British navy after 1815 did not take into account the strength of any other fleet or the forces needed to pursue any particular policy. It was the same as that of 1792, the last prewar year: 100 ships of the line and 160 frigates. At least on paper, Britain had a navy twice as large as it needed for peacetime service. Hundreds of officers and thousands of seamen were furloughed, while the rapid deterioration of ships hastily built during the war years forced the fleet to shrink dramatically, at a time when relatively few new ships were being launched. By 1820 Britain had 146 ships of the line and 164 frigates. A decade later the force had dwindled to 106 ships of the line and 144 frigates; the latter figure fell significantly below the peacetime standard, despite the fact that some third-rate (74-gun) ships of the line had been cut down and converted to fourth-rate (50-gun) "razee" frigates.[2]

Between 1815 and 1849, the British navy launched a total of fifty-eight new ships of the line. Eleven were launched in 1815 and 1816 alone; these, and another ten completed by 1828, were under construction when the Napoleonic Wars ended. In the postwar era the 120-gun three-decker and the 84-gun two-decker were the most popular designs. The 74 came to be considered unfit for the line of battle, and Britain launched its last vessel of the type, the *Carnatic*, in 1832. The postwar construction program, under covered slips and using seasoned, salt-treated lumber, produced ships that lasted a half-century or more without significant dry rot. Years of accelerated wartime construction left British navy timber stocks seriously depleted by 1815, but contrary to a long-accepted myth there remained plenty of oak forests in the British Isles. The needs of civilian shipbuilders and other domestic consumers forced up the price of British oak, however, making foreign timber less expensive for the navy. British shipyards imported Italian oak as well as Indian and African teak, and the East

India Company continued its earlier practice of building teak warships for the navy in Indian shipyards. After the Napoleonic era, Indian construction projects included seven ships of the line completed at Bombay and one at Calcutta. The last of the Bombay ships was the 80-gun *Meeanee*, launched in November 1848 as the last British sailing ship of the line.[3]

The British navy's declining numbers of larger warships more than sufficed to keep it ahead of potential rivals. France acknowledged that it had no hopeof mounting a battle fleet challenge against Britain and made no effort to do so. In 1815 France had sixty-nine ships of the line, and, by 1830, just fifty-three. As early as 1819 only thirty-one were considered fit for duty. In case of war the French planned to rely on a commerce raiding *guerre de course* and challenge the British worldwide with frigates. During the years 1815–30 a program of frigate construction raised the total of that type from thirty-eight to sixty-seven, still barely half the British total. King Louis XVIII attempted to place royalists in charge of the postwar navy, but Napoleonic veterans quickly regained control. An investigation of the stranding of the frigate *Méduse* on the coast of West Africa in 1816 exposed the incompetence of its captain – a former royalist exile who had not been to sea in a generation – and prompted the dismissal of hundreds like him whose commissions had been recently restored.[4]

Russia emerged from the Napoleonic Wars as the dominant Baltic naval power, with the third-largest battle fleet overall. The Russian navy did not follow the British and French pattern of growing in size after 1800, then declining dramatically after 1815. Instead, the Russian fleet peaked at the turn of the century, at over eighty ships of the line and forty frigates – figures second only to the British – then declined by the end of the war to an active strength of no less than forty-eight ships of the line and twenty-one frigates, a level of strength maintained into the postwar years. In 1830 the Russians had at least forty-seven ships of the line and twenty-six frigates, with roughly two-thirds of each type stationed in the Baltic and the remaining third in the Black Sea.[5] In contrast to the French, the Russians did not embrace the *guerre de course* as a strategy in the event of war with Britain. As early as the 1830s, almost a half-century before summer maneuvers became customary for all navies, the Russians mobilized unusually large fleets every summer in both the Baltic and the Black Sea. It was almost as if the navy wished to use its ships before they deteriorated, which happened fast enough to hulls built primarily of fir. Ships of the line and frigates built of fir typically lasted only eight to ten years, although the Russian navy often sought in vain to keep vessels seaworthy long beyond that.[6]

The War of 1812 against Britain instilled a great sense of confidence in the United States and its navy. Victories of the *Constitution* and other formidable American frigates in ship-to-ship actions against smaller British frigates stirred patriotism and created a new generation of heroes, overshadowing the fact that between 1812 and 1815 the British navy had all but destroyed US overseas trade, attacked or blockaded every important American seaport, landed a force which burned the newly constructed capital city, Washington, and destroyed roughly half of the US navy, including five frigates.[7] In 1813 the US Congress authorized the construction of six ships of the line. Five had been laid down by March 1815, when word arrived that the Treaty of Ghent (24 December 1814) had ended the war with Britain. Only one, the *Independence*, was completed before the war ended; it served from the summer of 1814 to the end of the war as a harbor watch in Boston. In 1816 the Congress authorized nine ships of the line to supplement the five laid down during the War of 1812. Of the total of fourteen begun between 1813 and 1822, seven eventually served as warships, three only as receiving or store ships. The remaining four were never completed.[8]

At least until the mid-1820s, when the French navy revived sufficiently to attract British attention, the Admiralty considered the US navy its principal future rival. But the American ships of the line, unusually heavily armed, were valued primarily as blockade breakers in case of war with a greater naval power and, as such, spent most of their days in reserve at Boston, New York, and Norfolk. Except for a brief hiatus in 1830–33, at least one was in active service at any given time, yet the seven combined spent just forty-seven years in commission. The largest American ship of the line, the three-decker *Pennsylvania*, was launched in 1837 after sixteen years on the stocks, spent five years in reserve, then became a receiving ship at Norfolk. The first battleship, the *Independence*, served continuously from 1814 to 1822, then remained in reserve until 1836, when it was cut down to a 56-gun razee frigate. As such it was far more useful to the US navy, which relied on frigates and sloops to cover its foreign stations. The navy ended the War of 1812 with nine frigates, ranging in displacement from the 2,200-ton* *Constitution* (50 guns) to the prizes *Macedonian* and *Cyane*, the latter formerly a British sloop of 540 tons, armed with 32 guns in American service. During the next forty-five years twenty sailing frigates served in the fleet, with no more than eleven being on the navy list at any given time. The old *Constitution* and *United States* were repaired repeatedly and kept in service, and starting with the *Potomac* (launched 1822), new frigates were modeled after them, displacing over 1,700 tons and carrying 50 guns.[9] Although American leaders were loath to admit it, after 1815 British and American interests usually coincided, and the United States had no complaint with the Pax Britannica. Border disputes in Maine and Oregon ultimately were resolved by treaty in the 1840s, far short of war; meanwhile, the shared values and ideals of the two countries were reflected in their deployment of naval forces against the slave trade and piracy, and in their common front against the reimposition of colonial rule in Latin America. A British overture for a joint declaration on the latter question prompted the United States to issue its own unilateral statement, the Monroe Doctrine of 1823, which reflected both the American government's agreement with the British position and the political necessity, in the wake of the War of 1812, to maintain the appearance of a foreign policy independent of Britain's.

---

* In most cases, displacement figures will be rounded off to the nearest 10 tons.

At the beginning of 1815 Spain had the world's fourth-largest battle fleet with twenty-one ships of the line. The newest of these were four French vessels captured by Spanish loyalists at Cadiz in 1808; Spain had not built a ship of the line of its own since 1798, and still counted in its total three that dated from the 1750s. After 1815 the US navy easily surpassed the Spanish, as Spain went more than a half-century without laying down a ship of the line. In 1818–19 Tsar Alexander I sold five ships of the line and six frigates to Spain for use in the effort to reconquer the rebellious states of Latin America, but their rotten fir hulls made them a poor bargain. All of the battleships were stricken within four years, and only one of the frigates, the 50-gun *María Isabel*, ever made it to the New World. Counting the Russian purchases, Spain had fifteen ships of the line in 1820, but the number dwindled to four by 1830 and just two a decade later. The number of Spanish frigates fell from fifteen in 1815 to five in 1830.[10]

The minor northern European naval powers likewise did not attempt to maintain formidable battle fleets after 1815. The Dutch navy of 1815 included nineteen ships of the line, some inherited from Napoleon's shipbuilding efforts at Antwerp, but fifteen years later just five remained. The Netherlands had a large merchant marine, a global trading presence, and a colonial empire in the East Indies, and thus maintained a respectable fleet of frigates – fourteen in 1815, seventeen in 1830 – for cruising duties. Sweden had thirteen ships of the line and seven frigates in 1815, eight ships of the line and five frigates in 1830. In the immediate postwar years Denmark still suffered the effects of having had its navy twice destroyed by Britain (in 1801 and again in 1807) during the Napoleonic Wars, but by 1830 the Danish navy had been rebuilt to a strength of three ships of the line and seven frigates.[11] Both Sweden and Denmark considered Russia their most likely future adversary and developed elaborate coast defense systems, including dozens of small one- and two-gun boats that could be either rowed or sailed, on the model of the oared gunboats used by Denmark against Britain after the destruction of the Danish battle fleet in 1807. After 1815 King Frederick William III and some of Prussia's leading military men favored the creation of a Prussian navy, but until the early 1840s the country's largest armed vessel was a lone schooner employed mostly as a training ship for the merchant marine academy at Danzig.[12]

Among the minor Mediterranean naval powers, the Ottoman empire after 1770 had rebuilt its navy along European lines, with the help of foreign (mostly French) shipbuilders. By the end of the reign of the pro-navy Sultan Selim III in 1806, the Turkish fleet included twenty ships of the line and fifteen frigates. Naval conscription in the Aegean region brought a large number of Greeks into service aboard the sultan's warships, but after 1821 the Greek War for Independence brought an end to this practice.[13] In North Africa the Muslim rulers of Morocco, Algiers, Tunis, Tripoli, and Egypt, although nominally vassals of the Ottoman sultan, maintained their own naval forces, some of which had taken advantage of the Napoleonic Wars to engage in a lucrative piracy. None had a warship larger than a frigate. In 1814 Austria inherited the predominantly Venetian navy of the Napoleonic kingdom of Italy, including ten ships of the line and eight frigates built or building. Under the direction of Prince Clemens von Metternich, the financially strapped Habsburg government sought to sell most of this fleet, but found no buyers. By 1830 eight of the ships of the line had been broken up or burned in dockyard accidents; the remaining two were commissioned as razee frigates. Meanwhile, all eight of the frigates eventually were commissioned but no more than four served at any given time. Those still on the stocks in 1815 were not completed until needed as replacements for their sister ships, the most extreme example being the 44-gun *Venere*, laid down in 1813 and launched in 1832, which served (after 1849 as *Venus*) until 1860.[14] Between 1815 and 1830 the leading Italian kingdoms far surpassed Austria in naval power. Thanks largely to warships inherited from the regime of Napoleon's brother-in-law Joachim Murat, the Neapolitan navy of 1815 had two ships of the line and six frigates. In the immediate postwar years Sardinia–Piedmont had no warship larger than a 20-gun corvette, but under the patronage of King Charles Felix and the direction of Admiral Giorgio Des Geneys the Sardinian navy grew by 1829 to include eight frigates, among them three powerful 60-gun warships.[15]

North African piracy and southern European revolutions

Having acted decisively against North African piracy a decade earlier, the United States was the first country after the return of general peace in 1815 to deploy naval forces against the so-called "Barbary" pirate states. In June 1815 Captain Stephen Decatur's frigates *Guerriere* and *Constellation* defeated the Algerian frigate *Mashuda*, the most powerful warship on the North African coast, then dictated a peace under which the Bey of Algiers agreed to pay compensation for earlier acts of piracy against American merchantmen. The following month Decatur proceeded to Tunis and, in August, to Tripoli, both of which capitulated without resistance, completing the mission before Commodore William Bainbridge arrived in the Mediterranean with a much larger force led by the ship of the line *Independence*. A late-summer rendezvous at Gibraltar included Bainbridge's flagship, five frigates, and a dozen smaller warships, the greatest American fleet ever assembled in European waters up to that time. The show of force marked the onset of an American naval presence in the Mediterranean uninterrupted until the outbreak of the Civil War in 1861.[16]

The following summer the British sent a far more powerful fleet to the North African coast, consisting of five ships of the line, five frigates, seven sloops and four bomb vessels, supplemented by a Dutch force of five frigates and one corvette, all under the command of Admiral Edward Pellew, Lord Exmouth. Britain had hoped for broader international participation but at least one other country, Austria, declined the invitation to participate because of the cost.

Exmouth's attack on Algiers in August 1816 may be considered the first exercise of the postwar Pax Britannica. Historian Andrew Lambert has called it "a spectacular reassertion of power in support of European ideals." In a nine-hour action the Anglo-Dutch force destroyed the Algerian fleet at anchor, silenced shore batteries, and bombarded the city, prompting the Bey of Algiers to accede to allied demands the following day. The allies lost no ships, but their crews took over 800 casualties. Following the same itinerary as Decatur the previous summer, Exmouth proceeded to Tunis and Tripoli, which likewise capitulated.[17] The North African pirate states traditionally had profited from the slave trade as well, their leading ports being the northern termini of centuries-old caravan routes that crossed the Sahara from Timbuktu and other northern outposts of black Africa. This, too, violated values promoted by the British and embraced by Europeans in general, and in 1819 a squadron called at Algiers, Tunis, and Tripoli to persuade local leaders to suppress the slave trade. In the first case of postwar Anglo-French naval cooperation, France contributed a ship of the line and a frigate to this British operation.[18]

By the 1820s the leading naval powers and the Netherlands no longer had to worry about North African corsairs attacking their merchantmen, but the lesser maritime states were not so fortunate. Even though Exmouth's 1816 expedition had secured promises of good behavior *vis-à-vis* the merchantmen of weaker states, such as Naples, that were not represented in the allied fleet, the North Africans took those commitments less seriously. Ships flying the flags of the Italian states and Austria were especially vulnerable, and the depredations continued until the victims mustered the naval force to confront the pirates. Even then, the first expeditions of the Italian navies hardly inspired fear among the North African states. Des Geneys led Sardinian squadrons against Morocco in 1822 and Tripoli in 1825, with little success, and in 1825 a Neapolitan expedition to Tripoli failed so miserably that Naples subsequently had to pay a tribute double the previous rate.[19] Austria fared somewhat better. In the summer of 1828 Morocco abrogated an earlier treaty and seized a merchant brig, prompting the Habsburg government to send Captain Francesco Bandiera to the Moroccan coast with two corvettes, a brig, and a schooner. After a landing party located and freed the crew of the captured brig, in July 1829 Bandiera bombarded the port of El Araisch (Larache). Reinforced with a frigate, Bandiera remained offshore until the autumn of 1830, when the sultan of Morocco agreed to reinstate the broken treaty.[20] Taking heart from the Austrian success, in 1833 Sardinia–Piedmont and Naples concluded a five-year alliance against the North African menace. That spring they deployed a joint squadron led by one Neapolitan and three Sardinian frigates, which forced Tunis to pay compensation for attacks on Sardinian merchantmen. In 1834 a squadron of three Neapolitan warships secured a great reduction in the tribute paid to the sultan of Morocco.[21]

During the same years the leading powers failed to adopt a common policy to deal with a wave of liberal revolution, even though under the Concert of Europe all had made solemn commitments to preserve the order established at the Congress of Vienna (1814–15). In the first months of 1820 constitutionalist uprisings challenged absolute monarchies in Spain, Portugal, and Naples, and, the following March, in Sardinia–Piedmont as well. Britain, sympathizing with movements in favor of constitutional monarchy, interpreted its Vienna obligations to include only the preservation of national borders, not necessarily the governments within them, while Metternich's bloc of eastern absolute monarchies – Austria, Russia, and Prussia – considered the commitment also to include preservation of the systems of government. The eastern powers clamored for military intervention but Britain would have no part of it, and in the case of Portugal deployed warships to deter any attempt by continental armies to march on Lisbon. The other three revolutions were crushed in the name of the Concert, or at least the Concert minus Britain. In March 1821 an Austrian army routed a Neapolitan rebel army and occupied Naples. The Austrian navy was supposed to support the invasion but its two active frigates made it only halfway down the Adriatic, as far as the island of Lissa, where the Neapolitan ship of the line *Capri* and a frigate blockaded them until word arrived that the Austrian troops were in the city of Naples. During the Austrian march on Naples, revolution broke out in Sardinia–Piedmont. With an eye toward blockading Genoa, the Austrian government authorized the arming of two of the ships of the line then idle at Venice, but the plans were cancelled after Austrian troops easily crushed the revolt in April 1821.[22] The liberal regime in Spain survived longer, until a France eager to return to full participation in the affairs of Europe volunteered to intervene there in the name of the Concert. The French army crossed the Pyrenees in April 1823, met with little opposition, and took Madrid a month later. After the liberal Cortes fled to Cadiz, taking King Ferdinand VII along as hostage, three ships of the line and ten frigates under Rear Admiral Guy Duperré blockaded the port until French troops arrived to lay siege to the city. Unlike in neighboring Portugal, here the British chose not to deploy warships in solidarity with the constitutionalist cause. In September the last of the rebels surrendered, and the French restored Ferdinand VII to absolute power.[23]

The Latin American Wars for Independence

In 1808 Napoleon conquered Spain and installed his brother Joseph Bonaparte as king in Madrid, providing the country's American colonies with a convenient excuse to declare independence: they no longer had a legitimate king. By the time King Ferdinand VII was restored to power in 1814, some Latin American republics already were in their fourth year, supported by merchants and landowners glad to be rid of Spanish mercantilism. In the vacuum created by the wartime collapse of the Spanish navy and merchant marine, Britain dominated trade with the region and, along with the United States, opposed efforts to restore Spanish colonial rule. After 1815 only Alexander I of Russia lent more than moral support to Ferdinand's attempt to recapture the colonies, and of the eleven warships he sold to Spain just one made it to the New World. Spain's liberal revolution of 1820–23, coinciding with the last years of the Latin American Wars for Independence, all but guaranteed the failure of its efforts to retain its mainland American colonies.

Naval power played almost no role in the initial fighting after the revolutions of 1810. Local patriots engaged Spanish garrisons and local royalists in relatively small battles. Spain's makeshift naval presence included armed merchantmen and privateers commissioned by the viceroy in Peru, a royalist stronghold; several of the new republics likewise issued letters of marque and armed some merchant vessels. The first naval action on the Pacific coast came in May 1813, when the Peruvian corsair *Warren* blockaded Valparaíso, a port defended by the Chilean armed merchantmen *Perla* and *Potrillo*. Spanish merchants in Valparaíso persuaded the officers and men of the *Perla* to defect to the royalists, and at the onset of the ensuing battle the *Perla* joined the *Warren* in forcing the *Potrillo* to surrender. Spanish forces then occupied Valparaíso and used it as a base to supply their reconquest of Chile.[24] In exile across the Andes in Argentina, bitter Chilean patriots were impressed with their need for a navy and convinced that, to operate it, hired foreigners would be more trustworthy than veterans of the Spanish navy or merchant marine.

The Argentinians subsequently commissioned a small navy led by William Brown, a former officer of the British navy. In the summer of 1815–16 Brown took two corvettes and two smaller warships around Cape Horn and up the Pacific coast, attacking Callao and Guayaquil. He did little real damage, but did demonstrate the vulnerability of Spanish commerce and communications. In the summer of 1816–17 generals José de San Martín and Bernardo O'Higgins crossed the Andes with an Argentinian–Chilean army that defeated the Spanish at Chacabuco in February 1817, opening the way for the restoration of the republic in Chile under the presidency of O'Higgins. On the field at Chacabuco, O'Higgins remarked that "this triumph and a hundred more will be insignificant if we do not control the sea." He soon sent agents to Britain and the United States, countries where the return to a peacetime footing after 1815 left naval personnel seeking employment abroad.[25]

By 1818 hundreds of foreign seamen had entered Chilean service, many of them aboard ships purchased for the new navy. These included a corvette, two brigs, and the former British East Indiamen *Cumberland* and *Windham*, refitted as the 60-gun ship of the line *San Martín* and 46-gun frigate *Lautaro*, respectively. To command the navy a Chilean agent hired Thomas, Lord Cochrane, later 10th Earl of Dundonald, a decorated veteran British officer living in exile in France after being disgraced in a stock market scandal in 1814. Cochrane left for Chile in August 1818, three months after the former Russian frigate *María Isabel* left Spain for Chile at the head of a force including eleven transports carrying 2,000 troops. The Chileans received word that the Spanish reinforcements were on the way and resolved to interdict their convoy rather than wait for Cochrane to arrive. Command of the Chilean squadron went to Manuel Blanco Encalada, a 28-year-old artillery officer from Buenos Aires who had served the previous seven years in the armies of Argentina and Chile. O'Higgins appointed him because he had been an ensign in the Spanish navy for four years before that, and thus had more naval experience than any other patriot officer. In October 1818 he left Valparaíso with the five warships, to search the seas for the approaching Spanish force. The *María Isabel* managed to evade him, making it through to the port of Talcahuano with two transports, only to be trapped there on 27 October by Blanco's flagship *San Martín*, to which the Spanish frigate surrendered after a brief duel. The remaining Spanish transports were captured as they straggled in, completing the triumph.[26]

Thus Chile was secure by the time Cochrane took over the navy, in December 1818, with the rank of vice admiral. Blanco agreed to become his subordinate as rear admiral, impressing Cochrane with his "patriotic distinterestedness" in the matter of command. They turned their attentions to an assault on royalist Peru, which had to be conquered to secure the independence of both Chile and Argentina. Because the coastal Atacama Desert separating Peru from Chile posed an obstacle more formidable than the Andes, naval power was essential to transport the patriot army northward for the attack. First, however, Cochrane had to establish Chile's command of the sea off the western coast of the continent. In the summers of 1818–19 and 1819–20 he imposed blockades on Callao and seized Spanish-flagged ships on the high seas, using the captured *María Isabel* (renamed *O'Higgins*) as his flagship. But the Spanish were more afraid of the *San Martín*, the only ship of the line in the theater; they refused to come out of Callao to fight, even though the two navies had equal numbers of frigates and smaller warships. In May 1819 Spain dispatched two ships of the line and a frigate as reinforcements, but only the frigate made it to Callao. The leaky *Alejandro I*, formerly a Russian battleship, had to turn back to Cadiz, and the *San Telmo* was lost with all hands in a storm off Cape Horn. Further additions to the Chilean navy included a corvette built in the United States, two more brigs and a schooner. In February 1820 Cochrane briefly turned his attention to Valdivia, a Spanish outpost in southern Chile, which he captured with the *O'Higgins*, a brig and a schooner, in the process losing the brig.[27]

The invasion of Peru finally began in late August 1820. Cochrane, in the *O'Higgins*, led a force of one ship of the line, two frigates, one corvette, three brigs, and one schooner, escorting seventeen transports carrying San Martín and 4,000 troops. The fleet included every available Chilean warship less one corvette, which was deployed to keep watch over the last royalist stronghold in the south, the island of Chiloé. The Spanish squadron in Callao did nothing to challenge the Chilean landings. The frigates *Prueba* and *Venganza* departed before the invaders arrived, to avoid being blockaded, and the hopelessly outnumbered force they left behind suffered a crippling blow on 5 November 1820, when Cochrane captured the remaining Spanish frigate, the *Esmeralda*, in a bold raid on the harbor. The aggressive Cochrane clashed with the cautious San Martín throughout the campaign. Cochrane wanted the navy to assault Callao while the army marched on Lima, but San Martín preferred to negotiate his way into the Peruvian capital. The viceroy in Lima finally agreed to an armistice in April 1821, and three months later San Martín declared himself "protector" of an independent Peru.[28]

Many years passed before Spain recognized the independence of any of the Latin American republics, and Cochrane correctly refused to consider the war ended. Rejecting San Martín's offer to become admiral of a new Peruvian navy, he remained loyal to Chile and put to sea in search of the last significant Spanish warships in the eastern Pacific, the two frigates that had escaped capture at Callao the previous year. Several of Cochrane's British officers and seamen declined to go with him and instead entered the service of Peru, in part because San Martín refused to pay them as long as they remained in Chilean service. After a pursuit of five months, ranging as far north as Baja California, in March 1822 Cochrane finally blockaded the *Prueba* and *Venganza* at Guayaquil. There the two frigates surrendered to local authorities loyal to San Martín and thus ended up in the Peruvian navy. The *Prueba*, renamed *Protector*, became the flagship of one of Cochrane's former captains, George Martin Guise, now serving as Peruvian naval commander. Denied these ultimate prizes of war, in June 1822 Cochrane returned to Valparaíso with the remaining ships of the fleet. By then the Chilean navy showed the strains of years of continuous operations. The numerous desertions at the end of the campaign in Peru forced Cochrane to abandon the ship of the line *San Martín*, and a brig badly in need of repair was given up for lost. This left the fleet with a core of three frigates, three corvettes, and two brigs.[29]

Thereafter, Cochrane's bickering over pay and prize money, combined with his refusal to take sides in domestic political intrigues, left him with few friends in Chile. In November 1822 he responded to an overture from Brazil: "The war in the Pacific having been happily terminated by the total destruction of the Spanish naval force, I am . . . free for the crusade of liberty in any other quarter of the globe." As in the Spanish colonies, in Brazil the Napoleonic Wars had provided the context for independence. In 1807 King John of Portugal fled to Rio de Janeiro, then after the war declined to return to Lisbon. The liberal leaders of Portugal's 1820 revolution insisted upon the return of the king, who complied in 1821, leaving behind his son, Dom Pedro, as regent of Brazil. Merchants and landowners who had prospered under a free trade policy granted in 1808 did not want a resumption of rule from Lisbon, and the regent astutely assumed leadership of their movement. In October 1822 an assembly in Rio de Janeiro proclaimed him Dom Pedro I, emperor of an independent Brazil. From the start the new regime had a powerful friend in Britain, which, despite its general support of the Lisbon revolution, did not want to see Brazil once again under Portuguese mercantilism. There, as elsewhere in Latin America, British merchantmen took full advantage of the weakening of Iberian colonial control, and by 1822 British ships handled half of Rio de Janeiro's commerce.[30]

In a vast country where all population centers lay along the coast and the interior had no roads, naval force became the key to Dom Pedro I's consolidation of power. He formed a navy from Portuguese warships in Brazilian ports, which by November 1822 included three frigates, two corvettes, and two dozen smaller warships, but by January 1823 a frigate and a schooner had mutinied and made for Montevideo, then in Portuguese hands. While over 80 percent of Portuguese naval officers stationed in Brazil in 1822 declared their loyalty to the new regime, most of the common sailors had no desire to change allegiances. Their unreliability paralyzed the new navy and kept Dom Pedro from asserting authority over distant provinces, prompting him to follow the Spanish American example of hiring officers and seamen from friendly foreign nations, in particular Britain. Cochrane, taking command in March 1823, supplemented these with "several highly meritorious" British veterans of Chilean service who followed him to Brazil.[31]

Initially the northern provinces of Brazil remained loyal to the Portuguese, who established a royalist stronghold at Salvador da Bahia, 900 miles northeast of Rio de Janeiro. By the end of 1822 Portuguese naval forces there included the 74-gun ship of the line *Dom João VI*, one frigate, four corvettes, and several smaller warships. The Brazilians improved their chances against them by repairing an abandoned Portuguese ship of the line in the Rio de Janeiro naval arsenal. Cochrane used the 64-gun *Pedro I* (ex-*Martim de Freitas*) as flagship of a force of two frigates, two corvettes, and two brigs in an attack on Salvador, where he met with defeat on 4 May 1823, in part because of pro-Portuguese treachery aboard some Brazilian ships. Complaining that "one half of the squadron is necessary to watch over the other half," Cochrane returned to Rio de Janeiro and put ashore his Portuguese-born sailors. They were replaced by Brazilians and hired foreigners, the latter arriving in ever-greater numbers. Cochrane then sailed back to Salvador and blockaded the port. On the night of 12 June he attempted a daring sortie into the harbor with the *Pedro I*, a frigate and a corvette. Calm winds foiled the attack, but Cochrane's bravado intimidated the Portuguese naval and royalist leaders, whose confidence had been waning. In early July they abandoned Salvador and headed for home.[32]

Cochrane refused to let the Portuguese go in peace, preferring to deliver a crippling blow to ensure they would never return. Fortunately for the Brazilians the retreating squadron was preoccupied with a long convoy of troop transports and merchantmen, and in no shape to fight. With the *Pedro I*, two frigates, and two smaller warships, Cochrane harassed the retreating column, taking sixteen prizes and 2,000 prisoners. After the rest of the squadron returned to Brazil, the frigate *Niterói* took the war to the coast of Portugal, seizing another seventeen prizes between July and November 1823. Meanwhile, Cochrane and the rest of the navy ranged along the Brazilian coast, forcing the surrender of isolated Portuguese and royalist garrisons. The *Pedro I* returned to Rio de Janeiro in November 1823, at the head of a triumphant squadron that had facilitated the capture of Maranhão (São Luis), Pará (Belém), and Montevideo while taking another seventy-three prizes.[33]

For Cochrane, victory once again bore the seeds of discontent. He was, after all, a mercenary, and as with the Chilean government, his relations with the regime of Dom Pedro I soured over issues of pay and prize money. While haggling with the emperor over such matters, Cochrane continued to serve loyally, cooperating with the Brazilian army to suppress a serious revolt in Pernambuco province. In September 1824 his ships blockaded the rebel capital, Recife, forcing its surrender. Using the frigate *Piranga* as his flagship, he went on to help subdue rebellions in other northern provinces. In mid-1825, as British mediation finally secured Portuguese recognition of Brazilian independence, Cochrane abruptly took the *Piranga* from Maranhão directly to Britain. He justified the cruise on the grounds that his ship needed repairs and the health of his crew required "a more bracing northerly atmosphere" after months of operating along the Equator. Upon his arrival, he negotiated a new post as commanding admiral of the navy of Greece, then embroiled in a war for independence from Turkey. The *Piranga* sailed home without Cochrane later that year.[34] The colorful admiral spent just over two years in the service of Brazil, but without him the country may never have established its independence. Furthermore, in light of the fragmentation of the former Spanish America (ultimately into sixteen independent countries on the mainland alone), it was not a foregone conclusion that the former Portuguese America would remain united as a single state. Without the efforts of the Brazilian navy, and in particular, the leadership of Cochrane, several Portuguese-speaking countries likely would have emerged, reducing Dom Pedro I's "empire of Brazil" to Rio de Janeiro and the adjacent provinces.

During the struggle for Brazilian independence a royalist rebellion reignited Peru, where Simón Bolívar had taken over as dictator following the departure of San Martín. After the garrison of Callao mutinied in February 1824, raising the Spanish flag, Spain sent troops convoyed by the ship of the line *Asia* and the brig *Aquiles*. The burning of the frigate *Venganza* during the mutiny left the Peruvian navy with just the frigate *Protector* and a few smaller warships, yet Vice Admiral Guise challenged the Spanish warships after they arrived at Callao in September. They came out only once, fighting an inconclusive battle off Callao on 8 October. Chile reinforced the Peruvian effort with the frigate *O'Higgins* and three smaller warships, under the command of Cochrane's successor, Blanco Encalada. During a brief campaign in November and December, Blanco destroyed royalist installations at Arica before learning that the war had ended in the royalist army's defeat at the Battle of Ayacucho (9 December 1824). Afterward the two Spanish warships were allowed to leave Callao, but during 1825 the *Asia* mutinied and surrendered to Mexican authorities at Monterey, while the *Aquiles* mutinied and entered the service of Chile. In the summer of 1825–26 Blanco commanded an operation to take the last royalist stronghold in the Latin American republics, the island of Chiloé in the south of Chile, which finally surrendered in January 1826. The victory completed the liberation of mainland Spanish America. Two months before the loss of Chiloé the Spanish had surrendered San Juan de Ulúa, the fortress guarding Veracruz harbor, which they had held since Mexico became independent in 1821. Naval power played a role there, too, as a small Mexican navy consisting mainly of former British ships, commanded mostly by former British officers, in October 1825 drove off a Spanish squadron attempting to resupply the beleaguered garrison. The disappearance of the Spanish threat was no blessing for the navies of the former colonies. Demobilizations depleted the navies of Peru and Mexico, but the most dramatic reductions came in Chile. In April 1826 O'Higgins' successor, Ramón Freire, sold the three largest remaining ships of the Chilean navy, the *O'Higgins* and two corvettes, to Argentina, and reduced the active force to a single brig.[35]

Meanwhile, after Cochrane returned to Britain, the Brazilian navy continued to grow. In 1826 two 62-gun sailing frigates arrived from shipyards in the United States, and other new warships were purchased in Britain. From December 1825 to August 1828 the navy played a central role in a war against Argentina, which broke out over Uruguay, a Spanish-speaking province Portugal had annexed to Brazil just before the latter became independent. Dom Pedro I resolved to keep the province, but most Uruguayans favored Argentinian rule or independence. After Argentina attempted to annex Uruguay in 1825, a Brazilian squadron under Admiral Rodrigo Lobo blockaded the mouth of the River Plate, where most of the subsequent fighting occurred. Argentina's commanding admiral, William Brown, proved to be a resourceful opponent, conducting frequent sorties with his outnumbered force and commissioning privateers to raid Brazilian commerce. Brown's largest warship, the corvette *25 de Mayo*, finally sank in July 1826 after a duel with the frigate *Niterói* and two smaller Brazilian warships. Thereafter, of the three ships Argentina purchased from Chile, only the corvette *Chacabuco* made it safely around Cape Horn, to be used by Brown as flagship for sorties along the Brazilian coast later in 1826 and during 1827. Neither Brown nor his flagship were present at the decisive Battle of Chico Bank (23 August 1828) off the coast of Rio Grande do Sul, in which a Brazilian corvette and two smaller warships defeated an Argentinian force of the same size. Afterward Brazil and Argentina signed a preliminary peace treaty. With the leading European powers protesting the rigor of the blockade of the River Plate (a French squadron under Rear Admiral A. R. Roussin arrived in 1828, to underscore his country's displeasure), Brazil chose not to press on for a complete victory. A compromise settlement left Uruguay independent.[36]

Counting warships still under construction, by 1828 the Brazilian navy had two ships of the line, eleven frigates, and seventy-two smaller vessels. The dismantling of Chile's navy in 1826 and the destruction of Argentina's by 1828 left Brazil as the only significant naval power in Latin America. Its fleet had been the decisive factor in the war against Argentina, but the outcome of that conflict underscored the dilemma faced by naval powers of its rank. Brazil had many more warships than it needed to defeat any naval rival on the continent, yet its fleet was far too small to challenge a naval great power, and thus it had prudently made peace when a squadron of one of those powers appeared. After Dom Pedro I abdicated in 1831, to fight for the claim of his daughter Maria to the Portuguese throne, ministers ruling for his son, child-emperor Dom Pedro II, slashed naval spending. By 1833 most warships were laid up, including both the ships of the line and all but one frigate. As elsewhere in Latin America, the reductions prompted an exodus of foreign personnel, and by 1835 less than two dozen British officers remained.[37] The fate of the Chilean navy in 1826 and the Brazilian navy in the early 1830s set a precedent for the entire region. Throughout the rest of the nineteenth century and into the twentieth, no Latin American country would maintain more of a naval force than it needed to defend its interests within Latin America.

The Greek War for Independence (1821–30)

As early as 1822 Cochrane had declared his sympathy with "the struggle for the liberties of Greece,"[38] which had begun in April 1821 with a revolt in the Morea. Unlike the other European revolutions of 1820–21, the uprising in Greece did not divide Britain from the rest of the Concert of Europe. The philhellenism of the Romantic era made the Greek cause very popular in Britain as well as in France, while Russia supported the movement in its role as traditional patron of Orthodox Christians in the Ottoman empire. In the first years of the war the three powers did not actively help Greece but also did nothing to stop arms, money, and volunteers from flowing there. Among the major European powers only Austria lent active support to the Ottoman empire, in part because the new Greek navy, a force little more disciplined than a pirate fleet, preyed upon the merchantmen of Austria and the Italian states in addition to those of Turkey. Metternich deployed a squadron which skirmished with Greek ships, arranged to have the Venice Arsenal build a frigate for Sultan Mahmut II's ally Mehemet Ali of Egypt, and also offered to sell the Egyptians some warships of the Austrian navy.[39]

Early in the conflict, neither side used naval power decisively. The Greek fleet, under the nominal command of Admiral Andreas Miaoulis, in fact was a consortium of private shipowners from the various islands and coastal ports, inspired as much by plunder as patriotism. With individual captains free to come and go as they pleased – and often hesitant to participate in operations where the risk was high and the potential for booty low – Miaoulis resorted to hit-and-run tactics which disrupted Turkish trade and naval operations but left the Turks in overall command of the sea. Greek desertions crippled the Ottoman navy at the start of the conflict, hampering the sultan's efforts to reinforce his garrisons in Greece, which fell one by one to the rebels. As the Turkish fleet began to recover, it failed to bring its superiority to bear, in part because of an exaggerated fear of fireships, which the Greeks used with some success against Ottoman naval formations early in the war. Mahmut II appealed for the assistance of Mehemet Ali out of desperation, for the sultan had no desire to strengthen the already ambitious pasha of Egypt. Over the previous decade, while the other Ottoman North African vassals contented themselves with profiting from piracy and the slave trade, Mehemet Ali had hired foreign (mostly French) advisors to build and train his own formidable army and navy. Egyptian forces first saw action in the war in 1824, crushing the Greek revolt on the island of Crete. In February 1825 Mehemet Ali's navy landed troops on the Morea, where they quickly won a series of victories against the undisciplined rebels.[40]

The success of the Egyptian intervention touched off the crisis which led the Greeks, in August 1825, to hire Cochrane to command their navy. A year earlier Greek agents had gone to western Europe with instructions to purchase eight frigates and hire a foreign admiral. Finding no suitable ships for sale, they ordered the construction of two 64-gun frigates in the United States and six paddle steamers in Britain, Cochrane insisting upon the latter as a condition of his employment. Cochrane's decision to remain in Britain until the ships were ready kept him out of action for over a year-and-a-half after his first contact with the Greeks. The first of four steamers arrived in Greek waters in September 1826, the frigate *Hellas* that December, but the remaining two steamers were never completed, and the second American frigate had to be sold to the US navy to cover the cost of the first. Cochrane finally took command of the Greek navy in March 1827, with Miaoulis staying on as his second-in-command. Some of his British subordinates from Chile and Brazil followed him to Greece; like their commander, they found it difficult to get along with fiercely independent Greek ships' captains accustomed to an undisciplined existence. Their outnumbered navy continued to be little more than a nuisance to the overwhelmingly superior Turkish and Egyptian fleets, and Cochrane's best efforts could not salvage the Greek cause. His boldest stroke, a raid on Alexandria in June 1827, failed when the only available steamer suffered engine trouble, the rest of his force was becalmed by dying winds, and some of his Greek captains refused to obey orders.[41]

Two weeks before the raid on Alexandria a Turco-Egyptian force took the Acropolis, arousing pro-Greek public and political opinion throughout Europe. The governments of Britain and France felt compelled to intervene in the conflict, to save the Greeks from total defeat and also to forestall a unilateral intervention by Russia, more likely under the new tsar, Nicholas I, who had succeeded Alexander I at the end of 1825. In the Treaty of London (7 July 1827), Britain, France, and Russia agreed to send squadrons to Greek waters to force an end to the conflict. The Russian navy's first ships to enter the Mediterranean since 1807 had to come from the Baltic, as the Black Sea fleet could not pass through the Turkish straits. Upon arrival the allies blockaded the coast of the Morea and demanded an Egyptian evacuation. When the Egyptian commander, Mehemet Ali's son Ibrahim, refused to capitulate, Vice Admiral Sir Edward Codrington led an allied force into Navarino Bay, chief anchorage of the Turco-Egyptian fleet. Russia and France each contributed four ships of the line, Britain three, while Russia and Britain each sent four frigates, France one. Six smaller warships rounded out Codrington's formidable fleet. Accounts of Ibrahim's order of battle vary dramatically but, counting ships as small as brigs, he had around sixty-five warships, including seven ships of the line and fifteen frigates. His fleet was anchored along the shore in three concentric semicircles, against which Codrington's ships formed a semicircle of their own, blocking the entrance to the bay. Codrington had no instructions to destroy the Turco-Egyptian fleet, but a battle erupted as the allies entered the bay on 20 October 1827, just before the last of the Russian ships had taken their positions. Under circumstances that remain unclear, Ibrahim's warships apparently opened fire on small boats sent out by the British and French, prompting the entire allied fleet to return fire. In two-and-a-half hours of battle the allied superiority in ships of the line proved decisive, as their broadsides did most of the work in sinking one ship of the line, twelve frigates, twenty-two corvettes, and nineteen brigs, in the process killing 7,000 of Ibrahim's sailors. The allies lost no ships but suffered casualties of 177 killed and almost 500 wounded.[42]

As a naval battle, Navarino was notable for two reasons: for the first time since the 1670s, the British and French navies fought on the same side, and for the last time in history, a major engagement included sailing ships alone. The allies also succeeded where Miaoulis and Cochrane had failed, crushing the naval power essential to the sultan's reconquest of Greece. In January 1828 Count Ioannis Capodistrias, former foreign minister of Russia, assumed the presidency of a Greek republic whose independence was recognized by international treaty two years later. Cochrane clashed almost immediately with Capodistrias and grew disenchanted with the Greek leaders in general, characterizing them as "double-dealing knaves." He resigned in November 1828 and sailed home to Britain.[43] The return to power of the Whigs in 1830 paved the way for his political rehabilitation, and two years later the British navy restored his commission. Meanwhile, in Greece, Miaoulis resumed the post of commanding admiral but also had difficulty getting along with the new president, and unfortunately involved the navy in intrigues against him.

While Britain and France repaired their relations with the Ottoman empire in the months after Navarino, in April 1828 Russia declared war on Turkey. At the onset of hostilities the Russian Black Sea fleet included nine ships of the line and four frigates; the Turks, meanwhile, had only the six ships of the line and three frigates that had escaped destruction at Navarino.[44] For the first time in history Russia enjoyed complete command of the Black Sea, something Peter the Great and subsequent tsars had only dreamed of in their many wars with Turkey. Aboard the three-decker *Parizh*, Nicholas I personally directed the blockade and siege of Varna, which fell in October 1828. The following spring and summer, the navy kept the army supplied from captured coastal ports during its march southward to Constantinople. The larger warships of the Ottoman fleet remained in the Bosporus except for two sorties, in May and June of 1829, the first of which succeeded in capturing the Russian frigate *Rafail*. A wartime building program intended to compensate for the losses at Navarino included the three-decker *Mahmudiye*. Upon completion in 1829 it was the world's largest sailing warship, a distinction it held through the rest of the age of sail.

Meanwhile, in the war on land, the Russian offensive reached Adrianople before it finally fizzled. In September 1829 a peace treaty extended Russia's border to the mouth of the Danube.[45]

The future: paddle steamers and shell guns

During the final months of the War of 1812 against Britain, the United States made the first use of a steamship in a military campaign and also laid down the world's first steam-powered warship. In January 1815 General Andrew Jackson used the Mississippi river steamer *Enterprise* to transport troops and supplies and to carry dispatches before the Battle of New Orleans. Meanwhile, the American steamship pioneer Robert Fulton, whose earlier river boat *Clermont* (1807) was the first commercially successful merchant steamer, in June 1814 laid down the steam warship *Demologos* at New York. The innovative 1,450-ton vessel was designed to defend New York harbor against British ships of the line and frigates. It had a centerline paddle wheel between twin hulls, engines placed below the waterline capable of 5.5 knots, wooden "armor" five feet thick, and thirteen 32-pounders in each broadside. Fulton died shortly before the *Demologos* made its first sea trial in June 1815; by then the War of 1812 was over, and it was never commissioned. The last of three trials took place that September, after which it was laid up in reserve. The *Demologos* made only one further voyage under its own power, in 1817, when it ferried President James Monroe from New York to Staten Island. Its engines were removed in 1821 and it served as a receiving ship until it blew up in an accident in 1829.[46]

Secure in its faith in safety in numbers, the British Admiralty remained open to technological change but gladly permitted Britain's vibrant private sector to make most of the early breakthroughs in steamship design and propulsion. Thus, in an era of great technological change the navy's share of the annual British budget declined from just over 20 percent in 1815 to less than 10 percent by the 1830s. In contrast, some within the French naval leadership saw in modern industrial technology the key to their future ability to challenge the overwhelming superiority of the British fleet. Thus, when the United States abdicated its initial position of leadership in attempting to apply steam propulsion to warship design, France became the hotbed of innovative naval thinking, with virtually all experimentation coming at public expense.[47]

The British and French navies first considered steamships for river service in western Africa. In 1816 the British tested a paddle steamer which they hoped to use for an expedition up the Congo River, but the trials were unsuccessful and the ship was rebuilt as a sailing vessel. Two years later the French commissioned two small paddle steamers for use on the Senegal River.[48] The technology quickly spread to other countries and navies, but most initially retained only one small steamer, more as a novelty pleasure boat for dignitaries than as a practical naval vessel that would have been used in the event of war. Many countries purchased steamers from private British shipyards, then provided the

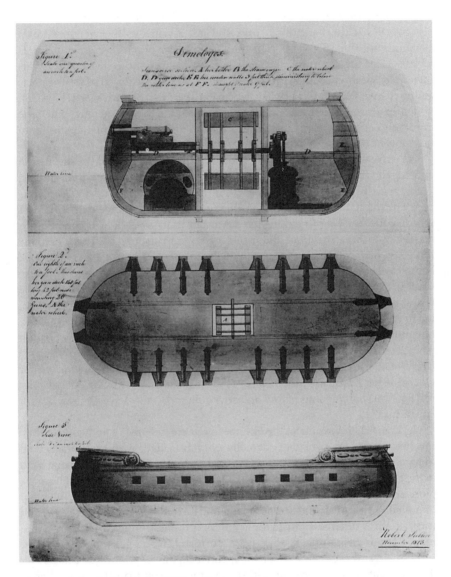

Plate 1.1 Fulton's *Demologos* (1813 preliminary design).
Naval Historical Center, Basic Collection

vessels with a nominal armament; those building their own steamships ordered their engines from British firms. Russia built its first small river steamer in 1815, and the Russian navy commissioned its first steamer two years later. In 1818 Naples launched the Mediterranean's first steamship, but it remained in service just two years; the Neapolitan navy did not acquire its first genuine steam warship until the 1830s. In 1819 the Danish navy purchased James Watt Jr's *Caledonia* for use as a royal steam yacht, but added no more steamers for years thereafter. Meanwhile, the British East India Company acquired its first steamers and used two of them as auxiliaries during the First Burma War (1822–25), which extended British control over Burma. Evidence is sketchy, but some historians consider the company's armed transport *Diana* the first steamship to fire shots in battle.[49]

In the New World, the 100-ton paddle steamer *Sea Gull* had the distinction of being the first steamship actually commissioned in the US navy. Built in 1818 as a merchant steamer, it was purchased in 1822 and served until 1825 on anti-piracy patrols in the Caribbean. As with the *Diana*, there is some confusion over whether the *Sea Gull* functioned as a warship in its own right, in addition to serving as a dispatch vessel and a tug for sailing warships.[50] Lord Cochrane instigated the acquisition of British paddle steamers by both Chile and Brazil, but in each case they arrived too late to see action in the Wars for Independence. Chile's *Rising Star*, a fully rigged corvette-sized steamer, had a centerline paddle wheel like Fulton's *Demologos* and carried a conventional battery of 20 guns, ten in each broadside, on its open spar deck. It arrived in Valparaíso in July 1822, one month after Cochrane returned from his last campaign against the Spanish navy, and later served as a British merchantman in South American waters.[51] Brazil's *Correio Imperial* reached Rio de Janeiro in September 1825, shortly after Cochrane left Brazilian service. Brazil purchased a second British paddle steamer in 1826, but neither ship played an active role in Brazil's 1825–28 war against Argentina.[52]

Cochrane then introduced steamships to Greece, where the 400-ton *Karteria*, the first of the four steamers actually commissioned, is generally accepted to have been the first steam-powered vessel to engage in combat. Starting with its first action in February 1827 its British captain, Frank Abney Hastings, pioneered the use of red-hot shot in skirmishes with Turkish and Egyptian opponents, firing 18,000 rounds of it in 1827 alone. But the *Karteria* and its sister-ships suffered from chronic engine trouble, and even with an armament of four 68-pounders they were no match for larger sailing warships. Nevertheless, the Greek War of Independence was important to the further development of steam warships, if for no other reason than that a number of British officers serving aboard warships on station in the eastern Mediterranean became steamship proponents after observing the four vessels in action.[53] The Ottoman empire received its first paddle steamer too late to use against the Greeks. The 140-ton *Sürat* (ex-*Swift*), a gift from Britain during the fence-mending that occurred after Navarino, remained unarmed for a quarter-century before receiving two guns at the outbreak of the Crimean War. The first armed steamer in the Ottoman navy was the former British packet *Hylton Joliffe*, commissioned as *Sagir* in 1829.[54]

After conducting trials in which private steamers were used to tow sailing warships, in 1822 the British navy activated the brig-sized tugboat *Comet*. It spent virtually all of its time towing ships into and out of ports in times of calm wind or unfavorable tides. The expense of contracting out such duties to private steamship companies compelled the navy to build several more steam tugs of its own, but none was armed or commanded by a naval officer, and none appeared on the navy list. The navy's first use of a steamship beyond home waters came in 1824, when the unarmed paddle steamer *Lightning* went to Algiers to serve as towboat for mortar vessels included in a British squadron tasked with reminding the local ruler of his 1816 treaty commitments. King George IV's brother the Duke of Clarence, the future King William IV, used the *Lightning* as a yacht for dockyard tours after being appointed Lord High Admiral in 1827. Later that year Clarence decided that steamers henceforth would be included in the navy list and commanded by naval officers. In 1828, when Britain intervened in Portugal after the start of the Miguelist War, the navy used the paddle steamer *Echo* as a dispatch boat. The following year the 500-ton *Columbia* was fitted with two light cannon, becoming the first armed steamer in the British navy. In 1830 Britain commissioned its first purpose-built steam warship, the 900-ton *Dee*. By the following year many older steamers, including the *Comet* of 1822, had been armed with at least two guns, and work was underway on four paddle steamers modeled after the *Dee*, all of which were completed by 1833. Though built as naval vessels, the *Dee* and its half-sisters reflected the Admiralty's deference to the civil sector in steamship development. Their liabilities included side lever engines, which featured a large and heavy power plant unsuitable for warships.[55]

As early as 1824, steam became a factor in the calculations of naval leaders on both sides of the Channel, as Britain and France each began to fear the new technology would give the other a great advantage. The British navy's use of the *Lightning* against Algiers in 1824 attracted the attention of the French navy, which later the same year placed the armed steamer *Caroline* on its navy list, three years before the *Lightning* received the same distinction in Britain. During 1824 the First Lord of the Admiralty, Lord Melville, alerted the Duke of Wellington to the danger a French steam-powered navy would pose to the security of Britain.[56] But France's first successful steam warship, the 910-ton paddle steamer *Sphinx*, was not built until 1828–29, and like many early French steamers, it was equipped with imported British engines. The *Sphinx* and another steamer, the *Nageur*, participated in the French invasion of Algiers in June 1830, undertaken by the government of King Charles X, in part to distract public opinion away from pressing domestic issues. Years of disrespect to French merchants and consular personnel served as the pretext for the attack, which the Algerians – and the rest of the world – assumed would have a customary short-term punitive character. Instead France sent Vice Admiral Duperré with a fleet of 103 warships of various sizes to convoy 575 transports with 35,000 troops, enough to seize and occupy Algiers. The *Sphinx* and the *Nageur* participated in the bombardment, then ferried messages to and from Toulon. Five other new steamers slated to participate in the expedition were not ready in time.[57] The conquest of Algiers, achieved in less than a month, provided the beachhead which France eventually expanded into a vast North African empire. The Algerian adventure failed to serve its domestic political purpose, however, as a revolution three weeks later replaced Charles X with his more liberal cousin Louis Philippe. Initially, Britain and the other naval powers with Mediterranean interests had no complaint with France's actions, especially as the new king hesitated to make the conquest permanent, waiting four years to establish formal colonial rule. Meanwhile, the occupation of Algiers encouraged better behavior by the neighboring North African regimes.

In the years after 1815, a slow and subtle revolution in naval ordnance coincided with the gradual acceptance of the steamship as a potential warship. Except for Fulton's *Demologos* and Cochrane's *Rising Star*, the first generation of armed steamers consisted entirely of vessels with side paddles. Because such ships could not accommodate a standard broadside of guns, navies from the start compensated for this deficiency by arming them with a smaller number of heavier guns, as in the case of the 68-pounders aboard Cochrane's Greek navy steamers. The move toward larger guns also affected the armament of sailing ships, albeit not so dramatically. In the War of 1812 the British had been impressed with the use of 24-pounders by large American frigates such as the *Constitution* and the *United States*, which easily defeated British frigates armed primarily with 18-pounders. In 1826 the British navy abandoned the mixed battery of the Napoleonic period in favor of a uniform broadside of 32-pounders for all of its ships of the line. The same year, the news that the American ship of the line *Ohio* had been equipped with a lower-deck battery of 42-pounders caused alarm in Britain but failed to spark a move to embrace a similar armament. The British navy kept faith with the 32-pounder, installing it in 1830 aboard its first gunnery training ship, the razee frigate *Excellent*. The 32-pounder soon became standard for British frigates and paddle steamers as well as ships of the line. Eventually Russia joined the United States in introducing some 42-pounders, and the French navy developed a 36-pounder, but as late as 1843 Britain resolved anew to keep the 32-pounder as its standard gun. Experience, rather than blind conservatism, dictated the British decision. At Navarino, Codrington's flagship *Asia* opened gaping holes in the hull of its Turkish opponent with close-range broadsides from its 32-pounders. Trials confirmed that a battery of well-handled 32-pounders firing solid shot at close range with the latest improved powder more than sufficed to destroy a wooden warship.[58]

The direct connection between the development of the paddle steam warship and the introduction of heavier naval artillery was clearest to the French, who came to consider steamers the ideal platform for revolutionary shell guns. French artillerist Henri-Joseph Paixhans had begun experimenting with shell guns as early as 1809, and early on concluded that the new ordnance required a new type of ship to carry it. In 1821 he wrote *Idées pour le blindage du batteries flottantes*, a visionary work calling for warships to carry a small number of heavy guns in hulls plated with iron armor. Paixhans soon dropped the idea of armor plating but in *Nouvelle force maritime* (1822) argued that a steam-powered French fleet armed with shell guns would overcome British naval superiority by rendering all sailing battle fleets irrelevant.[59] The French naval leadership did not heed his advice but in 1824 placed at his disposal the old ship of the line *Pacificateur*, for trials which demonstrated the destructive power of his new guns.[60] Afterward the navy agreed to buy its first Paixhans shell guns, for the new paddle steamer *Caroline*. Unfortunately for Paixhans, his early guns were unreliable, as were the first French-built steam engines. In the latter case, the deficiencies of French industry left the navy in the embarrassing position of relying upon machinery imported from Britain to mount its challenge to British naval supremacy. Paixhans marketed the steamer and the shell gun as parts of the same package, but in the 1820s the French navy was in no position to embrace his notion that the two technologies could be combined in a capital ship of the future, making the sailing battleship a thing of the past.[61]

Outside of France, the shell gun found its earliest acceptance in the United States, where George Bomford, chief of army ordnance, during the War of 1812 produced the first Columbiad, a chambered cannon capable of firing either shells or solid shot. For a half-century the Columbiad remained the standard heavy gun for American harbor defenses. Far fewer Columbiads were produced for the US navy, and none were mounted aboard ships after the early 1830s.[62] The British navy first introduced shell guns in 1838, fourteen years after the French, but the Admiralty remained as skeptical of Paixhans guns as it was of the American 42-pounder and other heavy solid-shot ordnance. For shell guns, range was the greatest liability, as shells were lighter than solid shot and thus could not be fired as far by the standard smooth-bore guns of the time. For example, a conventional 32-pounder had a range of 1,300 yards, an 8-inch shell gun just 800 yards. After 1838 British ships of the line, frigates, and paddle steamers mounted a few 68-pounder shell guns to supplement their primary armament of 32-pounders.[63]

Conclusion

In the 1820s the French navy did not build the steam fleet Paixhans advocated, but many of its officers accepted the notion that France could best challenge Britain's position as the leading naval power through a decisive move to embrace the latest technology. Paixhans' greatest legacy was that such thinking became a hallmark of the French navy, later reflected in its pioneering of the screw-propelled battleship in the late 1840s, the ironclad warship in the late 1850s, the torpedo boat in the early 1880s, and the submarine in the late 1890s. But France lacked the industrial base to sustain any of these challenges to the status quo, and in each case Britain's stronger industry assured that it would emerge from the competition with its superiority intact. Nevertheless, as the age of sail gave way to a period of intensified technological change, to a significant degree French innovations became the engine which drove the modernization of naval warfare.

Notes

1 Cf. Hans Busk, *The Navies of the World; Their Present State, and Future Capabilities* (London, 1859), 75, and Richard Harding, *Seapower and Naval Warfare, 1650–1830* (London, 1999), 294. See also Andrew Lambert, *Battleships in Transition: The Creation of the Steam Battlefleet, 1815–1860* (Annapolis, Md., 1984), 26.

2 Andrew Lambert, *The Last Sailing Battlefleet: Maintaining Naval Mastery, 1815–1850* (London, 1991), viii, 5; Busk, *Navies of the World*, 75. Harding, *Seapower and Naval Warfare*, 294, gives figures of 82 ships of the line and 100 frigates in 1830.

3 Lambert, *The Last Sailing Battlefleet*, viii–ix, 12, 108–10, 180–9.

4 Michèle Battesti, *La Marine au XIXe siècle: Interventions extérieures et colonies* (Paris, 1993), 16–17; Busk, *Navies of the World*, 75; Lambert, *The Last Sailing Battlefleet*, 10, 142–3, and *Battleships in Transition*, 97. Harding, *Seapower and Naval Warfare*, 294, gives figures of thirty-three ships of the line and forty frigates in 1830.

5 Fred T. Jane, *The Imperial Russian Navy*, 2nd edn ([London, 1904] reprinted London, 1983), 114; Harding, *Seapower and Naval Warfare*, 293–5.

6 George Sydenham Clarke, *Russia's Sea-Power Past and Present, or The Rise of the Russian Navy* (London, 1898), 80; Lambert, *The Last Sailing Battlefleet*, 12, 143; Jane, *The Imperial Russian Navy*, 133.

7 Lambert, *The Last Sailing Battlefleet*, 11–12; Harding, *Seapower and Naval Warfare*, 277.

8 http://www.uss-salem.org/danfs/line (accessed May 1999)

9 Donald L. Canney, *The Old Steam Navy*, 2 vols (Annapolis, Md, 1993), 1: 43; Lambert, *The Last Sailing Battlefleet*, 11–12, 143, 151–2; C. I. Hamilton, *Anglo-French Naval Rivalry, 1840–1870* (Oxford, 1993), 3; Busk, *Navies of the World*, 97; http://www.uss-salem.org/danfs/line; http://www.uss-salem.org/danfs/frigates (accessed May 1999)

10 John D. Harbron, *Trafalgar and the Spanish Navy* (London, 1988), 169–73; Francisco Ghisolfo Araya, "Situación estratégica naval," in *El Poder Naval Chileno*, 2 vols (Valparaíso, 1985), 1: 283; Harding, *Seapower and Naval Warfare*, 294. The latter gives slightly lower figures for Spanish ships of the line.

11 Harding, *Seapower and Naval Warfare*, 294.

12 Lawrence Sondhaus, *Preparing for Weltpolitik: German Sea Power before the Tirpitz Era* (Annapolis, Md, 1997), 4–8.

13 Stanford J. Shaw, "Selim III and the Ottoman Navy," *Turcica* 1 (1969): 221, 226; Bernd Langensiepen and Ahmet Güleryüz, *The Ottoman Steam Navy, 1828–1923*, ed. and trans. James Cooper (Annapolis, Md, 1995), 1.

14 Lawrence Sondhaus, *The Habsburg Empire and the Sea: Austrian Naval Policy, 1797–1866* (West Lafayette, Ind., 1989), 40–6, 275–6.

15 Carlo Randaccio, *Le marinerie militari italiane nei tempi moderni, 1750–1850* (Turin, 1864), 26–34, and *passim*, 86, 90; Lamberto Radogna, *Storia della Marina Militare delle Due Sicilie, 1734–1860* (Turin, 1978), 78, 90–3.

16 Edward L. Beach, *The United States Navy: 200 Years* (New York, 1986), 135–6; http://www.uss-salem.org/danfs/frigates

17 Lambert, *The Last Sailing Battlefleet*, 8, 99.
18 Hamilton, *Anglo-French Naval Rivalry*, 3.
19 Randaccio, *Le marinerie militari italiane*, 28–32, 90–2; Radogna, *Storia della Marina Militare*, 93–5.
20 Sondhaus, *The Habsburg Empire and the Sea*, 74–5.
21 Radogna, *Storia della Marina Militare*, 97–100.
22 Sondhaus, *The Habsburg Empire and the Sea*, 59–61.
23 Hamilton, *Anglo-French Naval Rivalry*, 3; Maurice Dupont and Étienne Taillemite, *Les guerres navales françaises: du Moyen Age à la guerre du Golfe* (Paris, 1995), 227.
24 Araya, "Situación estratégica naval," 1: 276; Ricardo Valenzuela, *Cochrane: Marino y Libertador* (Valparaíso, 1961), 25–6.
25 Araya, "Situación estratégica naval," 1: 278–81; O'Higgins quoted, 1: 279.
26 Ibid., 1: 283–7; Rodrigo Fuenzalida Bade, *Marinos Ilustres y Destacados de Pasado* (Concepción, 1985), 21–2, 38; Thomas [Cochrane], Earl of Dundonald, *Narrative of Services in the Liberation of Chili, Peru, and Brazil, from Spanish and Portuguese Domination*, 2 vols (London, 1859), 1: 3–4.
27 Araya, "Situación estratégica naval," 1: 288–96; Cochrane quoted in Dundonald, *Narrative of Services*, 1: 5.
28 Araya, "Situación estratégica naval," 1: 296–300.
29 Ibid., 1: 296–301; Bade, *Marinos Ilustres*, 39, 265; Dundonald, *Narrative of Service*, 1: 128–82 *passim*.
30 Brian Vale, *Independence or Death! British Sailors and Brazilian Independence, 1822–25* (London, 1996), 3–17. Quote from Cochrane to Don Antonio Manuel Correa da Camara, Valparaíso, 29 November 1822, in Dundonald, *Narrative of Services*, 2: 8.
31 Vale, *Independence or Death!*, 10–21, 32, 40, 43; Cochrane quoted in Dundonald, *Narrative of Services*, 1: 250.
32 Trajano Augusto de Carvalho, *Nossa Marinha: Seus Feitos e Glórias, 1822–1940* (Rio de Janeiro, 1986), 12, 14, 16; Vale, *Independence or Death!*, 11–15, 46–7, 52–5, 59–61. Quote from Cochrane to José Bonifacio d'Andrade y Silva, aboard *Pedro I*, 5 May 1823, in Dundonald, *Narrative of Services*, 2: 31.
33 Vale, *Independence or Death!*, 63–9, 95–6.
34 Ibid., 137–9, 152, 159, 162, 171; Cochrane quoted in Dundonald, *Narrative of Services*, 2: 247.
35 Araya, "Situación estratégica naval," 1: 302–4; David F. Long, *Nothing Too Daring: A Biography of Commodore David Porter, 1780–1843* (Annapolis, Md, 1970), 260; Edward Baxter Billingsley, *In Defense of Neutral Rights: The United States Navy and the Wars of Independence in Chile and Peru* (Chapel Hill, NC, 1967), 181–4, 198–9, 241.
36 Carvalho, *Nossa Marinha*, 22–44, and *passim*; Vale, *Independence or Death!*, 168–9, 172; Hamilton, *Anglo-French Naval Rivalry*, 3.
37 Vale, *Independence or Death!*, 173–5.
38 Cochrane to Don Antonio Manuel Correa da Camara, Valparaíso, 29 November 1822, in Dundonald, *Narrative of Services*, 2: 8.
39 Sondhaus, *The Habsburg Empire and the Sea*, 70–1.
40 Douglas Dakin, *The Greek Struggle for Independence, 1821–1833* (Berkeley, Calif., 1973), 74–7, 123, 132–8.
41 Ibid., 169–72, 202–3, 215–17.
42 John C. K. Daly, *Russian Seapower and "the Eastern Question", 1827–41* (Annapolis, Md, 1991), 1–13; Anthony J. Watts, *The Imperial Russian Navy* (London, 1990), 11–12; Jane, *The Imperial Russian Navy*, 128–30.
43 Dakin, *The Greek Struggle for Independence*, 255–6.

44 F. N. Gromov, Vladimir Gribovskii, and Boris Rodionov, *Tri Veka Rossiiskogo Flota*, 3 vols (St Petersburg, 1996), 1: 172–3.

45 Daly, *Russian Seapower and "the Eastern Question"*, 18–34; Clarke, *Russia's Sea-Power*, 76–7; Langensiepen and Güleryüz, *The Ottoman Steam Navy*, 1–3.

46 Andrew Lambert, "The Introduction of Steam," in Robert Gardiner, ed., *Steam, Steel and Shellfire: The Steam Warship 1815–1905* (London, 1992), 19–20, 29; Canney, *The Old Steam Navy*, 1: 3–4, 2: 1.

47 Lambert, *The Last Sailing Battlefleet*, 1–2; idem, "Introduction of Steam," 14–15; John F. Beeler, *British Naval Policy in the Gladstone–Disraeli Era, 1866–1880* (Palo Alto, Calif., 1997), 58.

48 Lambert, "Introduction of Steam," 15–19.

49 Ibid., 19–20, 27; V. M. Tomitch, *Warships of the Imperial Russian Navy* (London, 1968), 101; Radogna, *Storia della Marina Militare*, 85; David K. Brown, *Paddle Warships: The Earliest Steam Powered Fighting Ships, 1815–1850* (London, 1993), 19.

50 Canney, *The Old Steam Navy*, 1: 4; Lambert, "Introduction of Steam," 20.

51 Bade, *Marinos Ilustres*, 38, 40; Lambert, "Introduction of Steam," 19.

52 Vale, *Independence or Death!*, 168.

53 Douglas Dakin, *British and American Philhellenes during the War of Greek Independence, 1821–1833* (Thessaloniki, 1955), 124–6, 137; Lambert, "Introduction of Steam," 19–20.

54 Langensiepen and Güleryüz, *The Ottoman Steam Navy*, 171.

55 Lambert, "Introduction of Steam," 17–23, 29; Busk, *Navies of the World*, 37–9; Denis Griffiths, "Warship Machinery," in Robert Gardiner, ed., *Steam, Steel and Shellfire: The Steam Warship 1815–1905* (London, 1992), 170. According to Brown, *Paddle Warships*, 12, *Dee* was completed in 1832.

56 Lambert, "Introduction of Steam," 18–21.

57 Ibid., 19; Dupont and Taillemite, *Les guerres navales françaises*, 227–33; François Ferdinand d'Orléans, Prince de Joinville, *De l'état des forces navales de la France* (Frankfurt, 1844), 29.

58 Lambert, *The Last Sailing Battlefleet*, ix, 23, 98, 102, 106; idem, "Iron Hulls and Armour Plate," in Robert Gardiner, ed., *Steam, Steel and Shellfire: The Steam Warship 1815–1905* (London, 1992), 50.

59 Canney, *The Old Steam Navy*, 2: 2; James J. Tritten, "Navy and Military Doctrine in France," in James J. Tritten and Luigi Donolo, eds, *A Doctrine Reader: The Navies of United States, Great Britain, France, Italy, and Spain* (Newport, R.I., 1995), 52.

60 Lambert, "Iron Hulls and Armour Plate," 50; John Campbell, "Naval Armaments and Armour," in Robert Gardiner, ed., *Steam, Steel and Shellfire: The Steam Warship 1815–1905* (London, 1992), 158.

61 Lambert, "Introduction of Steam," 19–20; idem, *The Last Sailing Battlefleet*, 105.

62 Canney, *The Old Steam Navy*, 2: 2–3.

63 Lambert, *The Last Sailing Battlefleet*, 105; Hamilton, *Anglo-French Naval Rivalry*, 24; D. Bonner-Smith and A. C. Dewar, eds, *Russian War, 1854, Baltic and Black Sea: Official Correspondence* (London, 1943), 211.

CHAPTER TWO

Continuity and change, 1830–50

Fifteen years after the end of the Napoleonic Wars, the introduction of steam propulsion promised to change the future of naval warfare, but as yet there was no consensus on the nature and degree of the change. By 1840 the establishment of the first transatlantic steam packet lines demonstrated the commercial value of regularly scheduled transoceanic service, impossible under sail, but the requirements of merchant shipping lines offering point-to-point service were far different from those of the leading navies, which had to be able to cruise anywhere in the world as needed.

The introduction of the paddle wheel, and its eclipse by the screw propeller during the 1840s, left the typical mid-century fleet with a hodgepodge of vessels (sail, paddle, and screw) of all sizes. In the absence of naval conflict among the great powers, the state of naval warfare was illustrated in minor Mediterranean clashes, the skirmishes between Austria and the Italian states in the Adriatic in 1848–49, and Prussian–German attempts at naval warfare against Denmark in the Baltic and the North Sea during the same years. While the age of great colonial expeditions had passed and the heyday of "gunboat diplomacy" was yet to come, naval actions such as the First Opium War (1839–42) reflected the growing naval superiority of the West over the non-Western world.

The dawning age of steam (1830s)

France's partnership with Britain, forged in support of Greek independence, continued after 1830 under the government of Louis Philippe. For almost a decade the French were willing collaborators in the enforcement of the Pax Britannica around the maritime fringe of western Europe. After Belgium seceded from the Netherlands in 1830, they agreed to support an independent and neutral Belgian kingdom. When the Dutch invaded Belgium, the British and French navies cooperated in a blockade while French troops intervened to force a retreat of the Dutch army. The allies calculated, correctly, that the Netherlands would not risk its navy. All seven Dutch ships of the line and several of their twenty-five frigates remained safely at anchor in the Scheldt while the British and the French, with a force smaller than that, maintained the blockade of the coast. The operation, which continued into 1833, featured the first deployment of armed British paddle steamers in a war zone. Meanwhile, in the Iberian peninsula, the British intervention at Lisbon in 1828 against the conservative usurper Dom Miguel was supported by the French and followed three years later by the forcing of the entrance to the Tagus by six ships of the line and nine smaller sailing warships under Rear Admiral Roussin. The operation coincided with the return from Brazil of Dom Pedro I, to support the rights to the throne of his daughter Maria. The Iberian partnership continued after the defeat of the Miguelists, when the death of Ferdinand VII in 1833 created a similar situation in Spain, in which the ambitious Don Carlos, brother of the late king, aligned himself with conservatives in a civil war against liberal supporters of the legitimate heir, the king's daughter Isabella. In 1834 Britain and France formalized their cooperation in the Iberian peninsula in a "Quadruple Alliance" with the legitimate governments of Spain and Portugal. The civil wars, coming in the wake of the loss of the Spanish and Portuguese Latin American colonies, left the navies of the Iberian countries in a shambles. While Portugal never recovered its status as a naval power of the second rank, Spain took a step in that direction when loyalist forces purchased and armed several merchant paddle steamers for service against the Carlists, including the British Atlantic packet *Royal William*, which was renamed *Isabel II*.[1]

Britain accepted France's 1830 conquest of Algiers but clearly did not want all of North Africa to fall into French hands. Louis Philippe initially showed no interest in expanding the coastal foothold, but the first step in that direction – an incursion inland from Philippeville (Skikda) which succeeded in taking Constantine in 1837 – demonstrated the limits of Anglo-French friendship. In 1836–37 two British naval demonstrations off Tunis were calculated as much to deter France from seizing the territory as to bully the local Muslim governor. At the same time that France developed a vital interest in controlling the western Mediterranean from north to south, Britain – which as early as 1836 mapped the path of a canal across the isthmus of Suez – sought to secure the Mediterranean from west to east, as part of its lifeline to India. Reflecting the growing significance of these Mediterranean interests, both navies stationed their strongest fleets there throughout the 1830s.[2] France maintained a presence in the Adriatic throughout the 1830s, initially without steamships, after challenging Austria's incursions into the Papal States in 1831–32 to suppress liberal revolutions. Britain, which also opposed Austria's Italian policy, did not object.[3]

Partnership with Britain and France at Navarino brought a Russian naval presence to the eastern Mediterranean which did not disappear once Greek independence was achieved. Ironically, the Russians were responsible for the destruction of much of the Greek navy left behind by Cochrane, when Admiral Miaoulis supported a rebellion against Capodistrias. After most of the navy backed Miaoulis, in August 1831 the Greek government called upon the Russian squadron to suppress the revolt. In the ensuing action at Poros, warships not sunk or burned by the Russians were destroyed by their own crews to prevent capture, including the American-built frigate *Hellas*, the largest unit of the Greek navy.[4] Later in 1831 the pasha of Egypt, Mehemet Ali, rebelled against the sultan, and over the next year his navy supported his army as it moved up the Levantine coast toward Asia Minor. Britain's foreign secretary, Lord Palmerston, refused Ottoman appeals for help, reasoning that the British navy was occupied enough with operations off the coasts of the Netherlands and Portugal, where their partners were the French, who in the Near East supported the Egyptians. The desperate sultan turned to Russia, which in March 1833 sent Admiral Mikhail Lazarev to the Bosporus with most of the Black Sea fleet: ten ships of the line, four frigates, transports carrying 11,000 troops, and a host of smaller warships, among them the paddle steamer *Meteor*, the first Russian steamship to participate in a naval operation. The show of strength deterred Mehemet Ali from marching on Constantinople, but the Turks paid a heavy price for Russian assistance. The Treaty of Unkiar–Skelessi (Hünkar–Iskelesi), in theory a Russo-Turkish defensive alliance, in reality was a one-sided arrangement giving Russia exclusive rights as "protector" of the Ottoman empire. The Russian navy was granted free passage of the straits, which the Turks were to close whenever Russia was at war. The Russian navy took advantage of the treaty immediately, reinforcing the Black Sea fleet with two frigates and four brigs that had been stationed in the eastern Mediterranean. British and French warships demanding the same right of passage were refused.[5]

Under the terms of Unkiar–Skelessi, the Russian fleet could pass from the Black Sea into the Mediterranean whenever it wished, and in case of danger retreat to the safety of the Black Sea, with the Turks obligated to close the door behind them. During the 1830s the Black Sea fleet normally had a core of twelve ships of the line, operating out of Sevastopol, which British engineers helped upgrade to a fortified naval base. The primary navy yard at Nicolaiev, forty miles up the Bug River, could build warships but, lacking a drydock until the end of the 1840s, could not conduct major repairs. During the 1830s the Russians laid down eleven ships of the line and three dozen smaller sailing warships, all of the former at Nicolaiev, some of the latter at Sevastopol. Six small steamers were built at Nicolaiev, all with imported British machinery, and another eight steamers were purchased in Britain for Black Sea service. Before the end of the decade Lazarev ordered the first shell guns for the Black Sea fleet. But the attempt to project power at sea in the region was limited by the lack of a full range of supporting facilities and by the limits of Russia's own strategic vision. The tsar's advisors considered the Black Sea fleet's primary role to be one of providing local transport and supply for the troops of the Russian army, as it had against the Turks in 1828–29, in their defense in 1833, and against rebels in Georgia throughout the decade. By accident rather than by design, Lazarev's force became a classic "fleet in being," its very existence requiring Britain and France to maintain more warships in the eastern Mediterranean.[6]

While the Russian navy acquired both steamships and shell guns, it had no equivalent to the followers of Paixhans in France or the circle of progressive pro-steam navy men in Britain. The latter included Lord Cochrane, who returned to British service in 1832, and the colorful Sir Charles Napier, a fellow adventurer who had lost a fortune investing in a failed steamship company before moving on to command loyalist Portuguese forces in the recent Miguelist War. In the late 1830s paddle steamers were still valued for their ability to serve as tugs or towboats for large sailing ships, or as fast dispatch vessels, but larger types were designed to function primarily as warships. Rating such ships proved problematic, and the British navy adopted the practice of classifying steamers primarily by their size rather than the traditional method based on number of guns. Thus the 1,610-ton *Gorgon* (commissioned in 1837) was rated a first-class sloop and the 1,960-ton *Cyclops* (1839) a second-class frigate, despite the fact that both carried just six guns.[7] The French navy, meanwhile, reacted to the success of the 910-ton *Sphinx* at Algiers in 1830 by building twenty-two paddle steamers of the same design by the end of the decade. Though small and clearly designed for auxiliary roles, these vessels ranged far and wide in support of the French sailing fleet. In 1838 the *Phaeton* and *Meteore* accompanied Rear Admiral Charles Baudin's four frigates and ten smaller sailing warships to Veracruz to demand compensation from Mexico for depredations against French citizens. Because the aggrieved parties included a baker whose shop had been pillaged by Mexican soldiers, critics lampooned the campaign as the "Pastry War." After Mexico greeted French demands with a declaration of war, Baudin landed troops and seized the fortress of San Juan de Ulúa, closing the port of Veracruz. His bombardment of Veracruz sufficed to secure promises of reparations, but not before a French cannonball shattered the leg of General Antonio López de Santa Anna, galvanizing his status as a Mexican national hero.[8]

With anti-Mexican sentiment running high in the wake of Texas' successful war for independence (1836), the United States chose not to invoke the Monroe Doctrine in defense of Mexico. If it had, the American navy may have been hard-pressed to do battle on even terms with Baudin's squadron. After the engines were removed from the *Demologos* in 1821, the US navy was without an armed steamship until the 1,010-ton *Fulton* of 1837. This unsuccessful ship was in commission just five years before being laid up for a decade and eventually re-engined. Its failure may have set back the introduction of steam in the US navy if not for the sensation created by the maiden voyage of Isambard Brunel's *Great Western*, which arrived in New York in April 1838. The 2,370-ton Atlantic liner was an excellent advertisement for steam power, built to naval standards and equipped with powerful engines, capable of steaming continuously for three weeks. It influenced the construction of large paddle steamers in the British, French, and American navies, the latter leading the way with the *Missouri* and the *Mississippi*, 3,220-ton warships designed by a committee chaired by the captain of the *Fulton*, Matthew C. Perry. Reflecting Paixhans' concept of the future capital ship, upon their completion in 1842 they were armed with two 10-inch and eight 8-inch guns. The engines, a British-style side lever plant in the *Mississippi*, an American design in the *Missouri*, were built by Merrick and

Towne, and were capable of almost 9 knots. The vessels were monuments to the progress of American industry but their domestic construction and components made them the most expensive warships of their era. Tragically the *Missouri* had a very short service life, burning accidentally at Gibraltar in 1843.[9] The loss left the *Mississippi* as the navy's only active steamer. Later in 1843, amid rumors of an impending British annexation of Hawaii, the United States defended its interests there by sending the *United States* and the *Constellation*, sailing frigates completed in 1797.[10]

The first steamer completed in the Ottoman empire, the *Eser-i Hayir* (commissioned 1838), was built under the supervision of John Reeves, one of several American shipbuilders serving the sultan during the decade, but the Turkish program depended mostly upon Britain for its foreign materiel and expertise. At the end of the 1830s the Ottoman navy had six small paddle steamers, three built in Turkish shipyards, all equipped with foreign machinery. In 1840 the Turks ordered their first larger steamer, the paddle corvette *Eser-i Cedid*; six years later, as the leading navies were abandoning the paddle in favor of screw-propelled steamers, they laid down four large paddle frigates in Constantinople, which were completed with British engines and ordnance, then operated by British personnel under contract to the sultan.[11] Elsewhere in the Mediterranean, the Neapolitan navy commissioned its first paddle steamer in 1833, but a strong commitment to steam came only a decade later. Under the rule of naval enthusiast King Ferdinand II, between 1842 and 1847 six paddle steamers were built in Naples and thirteen purchased in Britain and France. The navy of Sardinia–Piedmont languished after the death, in 1831, of pro-navy King Charles Felix. The Sardinians purchased their first paddle steamer from Britain in 1834 and had five by 1847. The Austrian navy launched its first naval steamer at Porto Ré (Kraljevica) in 1836 but commissioned only one more before 1848. Meanwhile, after 1839 the Spanish navy supplemented the paddle steamers purchased during the Carlist War with additional British and American purchases, and in 1843 commissioned its first domestically built naval steamer. Like that of the Ottoman empire, the steam warship programs of all minor Mediterranean navies depended heavily upon Britain and other leading naval powers, whether for engineers, engines, or entire warships. In some countries the capabilities of domestic industry remained primitive for decades to come; Spain, for example, did not even build a railway locomotive of its own until 1884.[12]

Among the northern European maritime countries, the Netherlands possessed a significant marine engineering industry which both the French and Russian navies used as a resource, yet the Dutch government chose not to build a large steam fleet. After Belgium achieved its independence Anglo-Dutch relations quickly normalized, and in a world in which Britain ruled the waves, the Dutch took heart in the fact that the British would not tolerate another naval power attacking either the Dutch coast or the Dutch East Indies. Thus, the Netherlands made a conscious decision not to waste money attempting to preserve its status as a second-rate naval power into the new era. Sweden likewise had the industrial base and the expertise to build a modern navy and, unlike the Netherlands, had a clear potential enemy – Russia's Baltic fleet – to build against. Yet the Swedish navy commissioned only three paddle steamers, which were valued mostly as towboats for the old sailing warships and the fleet of oared gunboats that formed the core of the country's maritime defense system. Denmark, with a similar system of naval defense, also acquired only a limited number of paddle steamers, commissioning four by 1848. Meanwhile, prior to the deterioration of relations that led to the Crimean War, Russia continued to purchase British-built paddle steamers for both the Baltic and the Black Sea fleet. The latter included the 1,500-ton *Vladimir*, the largest and best of the lot, completed in 1848 by C. J. Mare, with machinery from George Rennie.[13]

During the 1830s the introduction of increasing numbers of armed paddle steamers did nothing to change the balance of power among the leading navies. Steamers continued to be valued mostly for their ability to tow larger sailing warships and carry dispatches. In the late 1830s British experts estimated that, in battle, a steamship – with its machinery above the waterline, large side paddles, and a limited number of guns – would be vulnerable to destruction if it came within 3,000 yards of a ship of the line.[14] Even when one factors in the number and value of armed steamers, Britain remained the first naval power, France the second, and Russia the third. The United States had few naval steamers but, unlike the European sea powers, had no immediate need for them to defend home waters, while on overseas stations, big American sailing frigates still sufficed to command respect. Only among navies of the second and third ranks did steam hold the immediate promise of a change in status. For example, by the mid-1840s the Neapolitan navy far surpassed the Spanish, Dutch, Swedish, and Danish navies thanks to an investment in steamships. Late in the same decade, the hasty acquisition and arming of steamers would be a factor in Sardinia–Piedmont's pretensions to be the catalyst for a united Italy, in the Frankfurt parliament's dream of a fleet for a united Germany, and in Austria's survival as a regional naval power.

The Near Eastern crisis (1839–41)

In April 1839 a Turkish army attempted to retake Syria, only to be crushed by the Egyptians, who counterattacked in force. The Egyptian advance caused both Britain and France to fear that Russia would invoke its 1833 treaty rights and intervene to "save" the Turks, extending Russian domination throughout the region, but the Western powers responded to the crisis in very different ways, Palmerston reaffirming Britain's support of the Ottoman government, France deepening its sympathy for the Egyptians. After Sultan Abdul Mecid inherited the Turkish throne in June 1839, a rift at court led to the desertion of the derya kaptan (fleet commander) Firari Ahmet Fevzi Pasha, who took with him a fleet of eight ships of the line, twelve frigates, and several smaller vessels. The defectors further strengthened the impressive Egyptian fleet, which included eleven ships of the line built at Alexandria since 1831. The derya kaptan's British naval advisor Captain Baldwin Walker remained loyal to the sultan, becoming *de facto* commander of what was left of the Ottoman navy and a key figure in Britain's subsequent rescue of the Turks. Anglo-French relations deteriorated further when France supported Egypt's refusal of a British demand that Syria be returned to the Turks. Both powers rushed fleets to the eastern Mediterranean, and Louis Philippe heightened the general war scare by fanning the flames of French nationalism. In November 1839 he reinforced his fleet in the eastern Mediterranean to thirteen ships of the line. The same month he ordered the renaming of several ships of the line then under construction to commemorate French victories in the Napoleonic Wars – *Wagram, Eylau, Austerlitz*, and so forth – and the following year sent a French frigate to bring back the body of Napoleon from St Helena. Early in 1840 French policy became still more aggressive, under the direction of Adolphe Thiers, and the French fleet in the Levant grew to include twenty battleships.[15]

By the summer of 1840 the war scare reached from the Near East to the Rhine, prompting the revival of the allied coalition of the Napoleonic era as a check to French ambitions. In the Treaty of London (15 July 1840), Britain, Russia, Austria, and Prussia agreed to pursue an armed mediation of the Turco-Egyptian conflict. Their terms called for Mehemet Ali to become hereditary pasha of Egypt and ruler for life over southern Syria (Lebanon) but to return to the sultan the rest of Syria, various Arabian conquests, Crete, and the mutinous Ottoman fleet. At the peak of mobilization the British had twenty-six ships of the line in commission, the most since 1815, but owing to the antiquated system of manning the fleet it took six months to raise the additional 4,000 seamen and the force did not achieve its maximum strength until early 1841, after the crisis had passed. Nevertheless, British naval power in the eastern Mediterranean in the summer and autumn of 1840 more than sufficed to neutralize the French. A loyal Ottoman force under Baldwin Walker (now a Turkish rear admiral) included the ship of the line *Mukaddeme-i Hayir* and several smaller vessels. Austria added two frigates, two corvettes, and several brigs, under Rear Admiral Bandiera. Russia, preoccupied with the ongoing rebellion in Georgia, kept its Black Sea fleet in that sea; Prussia had no naval forces to contribute but its army assumed primary responsibility for the watch on the Rhine.[16]

In defiance of the allies, in July 1840 Mehemet Ali used his fleet off the Levantine coast to sustain the Egyptian occupation of Palestine and Syria. When the pasha rejected a British ultimatum to withdraw, in August 1840 an allied (mostly British) fleet under Admiral Robert Stopford arrived to force him out. One by one, coastal strongholds were bombarded by the fleet, then taken by landing parties of British, Turkish, and Austrian marines. On 26 September Archduke Frederick, 19-year-old captain of the Austrian frigate *Guerriera*, personally led the party that stormed the citadel at Sidon. Beirut fell on 10 October, and the following week the Austrian corvette *Clemenza* secured the surrender of Tripoli. Thereafter Haifa and Tyre fell in turn, leaving Acre as the only Levantine port still occupied by the Egyptians. In the bombardment of Acre (3 November 1840) winds favorable to the allies freed Stopford's steamers from their usual duty as towboats. Functioning as warships in their own right, *Gorgon*, *Vesuvius*, *Stromboli*, and *Phoenix* added their heavy guns to the broadsides of thirteen British sailing warships, Walker's *Mukaddeme-i Hayir*, and an assortment of Austrian and Turkish frigates and corvettes in firing 40,000 rounds into the city. Stopford used the *Phoenix* as his flagship for the duration of the battle. After most of the Egyptian garrison withdrew from Acre under cover of darkness, the following morning a small Anglo-Austrian landing party under Archduke Frederick raised the British, Austrian, and Turkish flags over its citadel.[17]

In the wake of the defeat Mehemet Ali agreed to give up all of Syria, reduce the size of his army, return the mutinous ships of the Ottoman fleet, and build no additional warships without the sultan's permission. His only consolation was recognition as hereditary pasha of Egypt. In July 1841 the four allied powers joined France in signing the Straits Convention, closing the Dardanelles and the Bosporus to all foreign warships during times when the Ottoman empire was at peace. The agreement in effect made the sultan a collective ward of the great powers, revoking Russia's claims dating from 1833. The outcome was a triumph for Palmerston, who had successfully invoked his country's naval power to force a solution to a Near Eastern crisis on his terms. Britain had maneuvered Russia out of its position as protector of the Ottoman empire and compelled France

Plate 2.1 HMS *Thunderer* (left) and Austrian frigate *Guerriera* (center) in allied attack on Sidon (26 September 1840)
Naval Historical Center, Basic Collection

to abandon its policy of supporting Egyptian ambitions, without firing a shot against either power. The brief naval campaign was also a boon to the prospects of some of the officers involved. Walker was knighted by Queen Victoria and remained in Constantinople as *de facto* commander of the Turkish fleet until returning to British service in 1844. That same year, Archduke Frederick became commander of the Austrian navy after a serious mutiny by Venetian Italian junior officers, led by two sons of Francesco Bandiera, ruined the career of Austria's most prominent admiral.[18]

The First Opium War (1839–42)

During the height of the Near Eastern crisis the British navy was also involved in a conflict in the Far East. The First Opium War was far more controversial than the intervention against Mehemet Ali, perhaps the most internally divisive foreign conflict pursued by Britain up to that time. Hotly debated in parliament and in the press, the decision to fight a war for the sake of the opium trade drew the criticism especially of religious leaders and missionaries, many of whom were involved directly or indirectly in China. Apologists, then and later, claimed that trading rights in general had been the issue at stake, not opium, but it was difficult to deny the fact that the might of the British empire had been brought to bear against China in order to ensure the continuation of that lucrative trade. The episode demonstrated the ease with which the same naval power that upheld the Pax Britannica, policing the general peace, guarding British interests and enforcing British values worldwide, could be deployed in the cause of a morally indefensible commercial interest.

Ever since the British East India Company completed its *de facto* conquest of the Indian subcontinent, Britain had been the leading importer of opium to China. As early as 1729 the Chinese government attempted to ban the addictive drug, and in 1821 China even temporarily stopped the export of tea in an effort to halt the influx of opium, but to no avail. Instead, during the 1820s the annual level of opium imports quadrupled, then in the 1830s almost doubled again. In May 1839 the Chinese emperor finally ordered his high commissioner at Canton to seize and destroy over 20,000 chests of opium, valued at over £2 million (or $20 million) in the currency of the day. As the crisis deepened the British ordered their merchants to leave the city of Canton for the safety of their ships, only to have the Chinese deny them supplies from shore. In late August the first British warships – the small 28-gun frigate *Volage* and the 18-gun sloop *Hyacinth* – arrived on the scene, and in early September the first shots were exchanged. In the Battle of Chuenpi (3 November 1839) the two British warships all but destroyed a fleet of fifteen armed junks under Admiral Kuan T'ien-p'ei. Afterward China broke off all trade with Britain.[19]

There was no further action until the following summer, when Rear Admiral George Elliot arrived off Canton with three ships of the line, eight frigates, eight sloops and brigs, and twenty-seven transports carrying an Anglo-Indian expeditionary force of 3,600 troops. Elliot's force also included four paddle steamers belonging to the East India Company's Indian navy. The latter, formerly known as the Bombay Marine, in 1837 had become the world's first all-steam navy when it dispensed with the last of its sailing ships.[20] In addition to blockading Canton, in July 1840 some of Elliot's ships bombarded and seized Chusan Island, near the mouth of the Yangtze River. In January 1841 the British again attacked at Chuenpi, guarding the mouth of the Pearl River approach to Canton. Leading the way was the newly arrived Indian paddle steamer *Nemesis*, technically "a private armed steamer . . . although commanded principally by officers belonging to the Royal Navy."[21] The 700-ton iron-hulled vessel alone destroyed eleven armed junks and helped reduce a fort at Chuenpi, in the words of its commander causing "astonishment [among] the Chinese, who were unacquainted with this engine of destruction."[22] Afterward troops were landed to storm the ruins at Chuenpi, and in the subsequent defense of Canton Admiral Kuan was killed. The British did not occupy Canton, instead seizing Hong Kong, at the time a sparsely populated island with an attractive anchorage. In August 1841 Rear Admiral Sir William Parker arrived to take command of the operation. Later that month he led a successful assault on Amoy, where two ships of the line led a three-hour bombardment which silenced the guns of Chinese shore batteries and destroyed twenty-six armed junks. In October a bombardment and landing secured Chen-hai, at the mouth of the Yangtze River, after which the adjacent city of Ningpo also fell.[23]

During the spring of 1842 the expeditionary corps was reinforced to 12,000 men; the fleet likewise was strengthened to include twenty-five sailing warships, six troopships, and fourteen steamers, with twelve of the latter provided by the East India Company. Parker landed troops at several other coastal cities, including Shanghai. In mid-July, flying his flag in the newly arrived ship of the line *Cornwallis*, he led a fleet of eleven frigates and sloops, ten paddle steamers, and several transports up the deep waters of the Yangtze River as far as Nanking, where they anchored in early August. Parker threatened to destroy the city unless the Chinese came to terms. The Treaty of Nanking (29 August 1842), signed aboard the *Cornwallis*, gave the British possession of Hong Kong, trading rights in Canton, Shanghai, and three other ports, and an indemnity more than compensating for the opium destroyed at Canton in 1839. The Chinese agreed to limit their import duty on British goods but refused to concede a formal legalization of the opium trade, leaving that issue unresolved.[24] Taking advantage of Chinese weakness, in 1844 both France and the United States secured similar terms in their own treaties with China.

The outcome of the war also served as a sobering sign of the extent to which the industrial revolution had widened the gap in military and naval technology between Europe and the non-Western world. While the broadsides of sailing ships of the line still sufficed to reduce fortifications ashore, most of the operations undertaken in the campaign, including the decisive expedition up the Yangtze to Nanking, would have been impossible without the *Nemesis* and the other steamships. After the First Opium War, the paddle steamers of the Indian navy reverted to their customary peacetime duty of operating the mail service of the East India Company in Asian waters. As warships, they later saw action in the Second Burma War of 1852, the Persian War of 1857, and the Indian Mutiny of 1857–58. After India became a crown colony the British navy assumed full responsibility for its maritime defense, and in 1863 the Indian navy was disbanded.[25]

From paddle to screw: Britain, France, and the United States (1841–50)

The idea of equipping a ship with a screw propeller dated from antiquity, and the concept reappeared at the onset of the age of steam, only to be overshadowed for three decades by the paddle. The American John Stevens in 1804 and the Austrian Josef Ressel in 1827 were among a half-dozen inventors to build ships with screw propellers which either failed in their initial trials or failed to attract financial support for further experimentation. In 1837 Sweden's John Ericsson gave British naval leaders the first demonstration of a screw-powered vessel, using his steam launch *Francis B. Ogden* (named after his patron, the US consul in Liverpool) to tow the Admiralty barge. A year earlier Britain's Francis Pettit Smith had secured a patent to place a screw propeller between the sternpost and the rudder; in 1838 he established the Ship Propeller Company, which built the 200-ton demonstration vessel *Archimedes*. Like most pioneering screw steamers, the *Archimedes* (with a top speed of 7.75 knots) was slower than the paddle steamers of the time. The first generation of screw steamers also vibrated more than did paddle steamers and tended to leak at the stern. Nevertheless, at least some British naval observers recognized the potential of screw propulsion as an auxiliary to sail. Meanwhile, the technology soon caught on in the civilian realm where, in October 1840, Isambard Brunel decided to complete his iron-hulled *Great Britain* as a screw steamer rather than a paddle steamer.[26]

Before building their first screw warships, the leading navies continued to experiment with wooden- as well as iron-hulled paddle steamers. In 1843 the British navy completed the conversion of the sailing frigate *Penelope* to a paddle steamer, a radical reconstruction which lengthened the ship by 65 feet. The Dutch navy had begun a similar project seventeen years earlier but abandoned it as impractical; the completion of the *Penelope* temporarily dispelled such doubts and spawned similar projects in other navies. The US navy developed plans to convert sailing frigates to paddle steamers, including one, in 1845, for the venerable *Constitution*, then almost a half-century old, but the experiment was never repeated.[27] The desire to build greater numbers of larger armed steamers was especially strong in France, where the influential son of King Louis Philippe, François Ferdinand d'Orléans, Prince de Joinville, became their leading proponent. In 1844 Joinville published *De l'état des forces navales de la France*, in which he argued that steamships were the capital ships of the future and the true gauge of naval strength in the present. He pointed out that, as of 1844, the British navy had just three ships of the line in the Mediterranean but eleven steamers, including nine of a *"grande dimension,"* which were the key to its regional power. Joinville called for a battle fleet in European waters consisting of steamers, supplemented by a fleet of sailing frigates to defend French interests worldwide. If the armed steamer indeed became the new capital ship, Britain's two-to-one advantage over France in ships of the line (eighty-eight to forty-six, as of 1845) would become irrelevant, giving the French navy an opportunity to catch up with its traditional rival. Joinville explained away the fact that the British already had a three-to-one advantage over the French in naval steamships (125 to 43) by pointing out that only seventy-six of the British steamers were armed, and that France had another eighteen under construction. With the proper redirection of resources and the development of appropriate strategies once new steamships were constructed, he believed the French "would reign as masters" in the Mediterranean.[28]

Against critics of the expense of maintaining steamers, Joinville argued that four paddle steamers could operate for a year for the same price as a 74-gun ship of the line.[29] But Britain's experience with its own larger steamers showed otherwise. The largest paddle steamer of the British navy, the 3,190-ton *Terrible* of 1845, cost £94,650 to build – ten times more than the *Comet* of 1822 – and was expensive to operate. Its first-generation twin-cylinder ("Siamese") engines, developed in 1839 by Maudslay, made it capable of almost 11 knots but at a tremendous cost in coal. Furthermore, even though its dimensions were greater than those of a 74-gun ship of the line, it had the same problem as all paddle steamers: its paddle boxes took up much of the broadside and limited the number of guns mounted, in *Terrible's* case to nineteen.[30] Thus, as long as steamers had paddles, the British navy refused to consider the type a potential capital ship. Instead, in 1846 its leaders decided to compensate for the lack of maneuverability of sailing ships of the line by pairing each with a paddle steamer, which could serve, when needed, as a towboat or tug for its partner. By 1847 the thirteen British ships of the line stationed in European waters each had a paddle escort; only the *Collingwood*, Britain's flagship in the Pacific, did not.[31]

By 1845 Joinville concluded that the screw propeller would be the key to the realization of his dream of a steam battle fleet.[32] The new technology could be installed in ships not differing dramatically in design from conventional sailing frigates and ships of the line. The elimination of side paddles made it possible to install a traditional broadside of guns, and the screw – unlike cumbersome paddles – would not seriously hamper a ship's ability to move under sail. Ironically, however, France lagged behind not only Britain but even the United States in introducing the new technology. The British navy's first screw-propelled warship, the 1,110-ton sloop *Rattler*, was launched in April 1843 and topped 9 knots in its trials that autumn. The *Rattler's* success opened the way for more screw steamers, but through the mid-1840s the British navy continued to build sailing ships of the line and sailing frigates, and as late as 1846 laid down a paddle frigate. Finally, in the spring of 1848, after the new screw schooner *Renard* sailed in its trials as well as a sailing ship of the same type, the Admiralty accepted the screw as an supplemental source of propulsion for warships that would sail whenever possible.[33] Meanwhile, after his lukewarm reception by the British Admiralty in the summer of 1837, John Ericsson went to the United States, where he gained the support of Captain Robert F. Stockton in his campaign to sell the idea of screw propulsion to the US navy. The 1,050-ton screw sloop *Princeton* was laid down in 1841 and launched in September 1843, five months after the British *Rattler*. It was the first steamship equipped with a telescopic funnel, eventually a standard feature of all screw steamers. Unfortunately, in 1844 the explosion of Stockton's experimental 12-inch wrought iron "Peacemaker" gun aboard the *Princeton*, an accident which killed two members of the cabinet, generated enough negative publicity to overshadow the ship's success as a screw steamer.[34]

A competing technology unique to the United States further delayed the American navy's transition from paddle to screw steamships. Stormy relations with Ericsson, who zealously defended the patent rights to his version of the screw propeller, made the navy receptive to W. W. Hunter's concept of horizontal underwater paddle wheels, arranged on either side of the keel amidships. These "Hunter's wheels" were introduced in the 960-ton *Union* (commissioned 1843) and later installed in the 255-ton *Water Witch* (1844) and the 1,020-ton *Allegheny* (1847). The *Union* served for five years, the *Water Witch* for seven, and the *Allegheny* for four, the latter including duty in the Mediterranean during the revolutions of 1848–49. The navy considered the experiment a failure; the *Water Witch* eventually was rebuilt as a paddle steamer and *Allegheny* as a screw sloop.[35] During the same years, Robert L. Stevens' project for an armor-plated screw steamer to defend New York harbor created further distraction and a diversion of funds. The "Stevens Battery," a warship 250 feet long, displacing 1,500 tons, was redesigned several times after the contracts were signed in 1843. By the time Stevens died in 1856, it had grown (on paper) to 400 feet but was nowhere near completion even though over $700,000 had been spent. Ultimately $2.2 million was devoted to the unfinished hull, which was broken up in 1885.[36] Meanwhile, for defense of the Great Lakes the navy built another paddle steamer rather than a screw warship. The *Michigan*, commissioned in 1843, was the first iron-hulled ship in the US navy. Built at Pittsburgh and assembled in Erie, Pennsylvania, it remained on the active list for eighty years.[37]

The French navy's first screw steamer, the despatch vessel *Napoléon* (later renamed *Corse*), was built by Normand in 1841–43. By the time it entered service a deteriorating Anglo-French relationship provided the navies of both countries with the incentive to further explore the new technology. In 1842 Admiral A. A. Dupetit-Thouars proclaimed the annexation of Tahiti, after which French shore parties briefly imprisoned the local British consul. To appease Britain the French government repudiated his actions, and in 1843 Queen Victoria made a successful state visit to France. But in 1844 the appearance of Joinville's *De l'état des forces navales de la France* rekindled the fire. That summer the British deployed a squadron to Tahiti, led by the new ship of the line *Collingwood*, and Joinville (who had captained a corvette off Veracruz during the "Pastry War") personally commanded a force, including three ships of the line and six paddle steamers, which bombarded Tangier. The British protested the bombardment, which forced Morocco to conclude a treaty recognizing French sovereignty over Algeria. Amid the rising tensions, the first cracks appeared in the post-Napoleonic hubris of British sea power, albeit among the public and politicians, not in the British navy itself. As the war scare grew, in July 1845 Palmerston gave a speech in the House of Commons characterizing the Channel as a "steam bridge" rather than a barrier to French invasion. In 1846 Anglo-French relations deteriorated further after Louis Philippe violated a prior agreement by arranging the marriage of one of Joinville's brothers to a Spanish princess. Reflecting a rising mood of anglophobia, the French chamber approved a naval program including 93 million francs for new construction.[38]

Anglo-French tensions were reflected in the race to apply the screw propeller to warship designs. The French navy's first larger screw warship, the 2,010-ton converted sailing frigate *Pomone*, was launched in October 1845, some two-and-a-half years after the British *Rattler* and over two years after the USS *Princeton*. During 1845 the French ordered the full-powered screw frigate *Isly* and the paddle frigate *Mogador* (named after French victories in the brief Moroccan War) with an eye toward comparing performance of the two types. The program of 1846 included more sailing ships than steamers and most of the latter were still paddle steamers, but funding was included for the installation of screw propellers in existing ships of the line and for the world's first purpose-built screw ship of the line, the future *Napoléon*, ordered on Bastille Day 1847. The 5,120-ton warship was designed by Stanislas Dupuy de Lôme, son of a former naval officer, who at the age of 30 had emerged as the foremost French naval architect.[39]

The British navy responded to the French *Pomone* by ordering its first screw frigate, the *Amphion*, launched in 1846. The Admiralty laid down additional screw frigates, some as full-powered steamers, others with auxiliary propulsion. In 1846 the paddle steamer *Phoenix* was converted to a screw sloop, and starting in 1847 sailing frigates still on the stocks were completed as screw steamers. The British initially did not consider building screw ships of the line but in 1845 the navy began the conversion to screw of four old 74s built in the Napoleonic era. The first of these slow-moving "blockships," the *Blenheim*, was completed in 1847, the last in 1852. They carried a reduced battery of 60 guns, were capable of 7 knots, and intended to play a role in the British navy's new "Cherbourg strategy," as part of a special force assembled to attack France's major Channel base in the event of war. This "Cherbourg" force was to include dozens of screw gunboats, but other than the iron-hulled prototype *Fairy*, a 310-ton vessel completed in 1845, none was built. The Admiralty assumed large numbers could be constructed in a matter of months in the event of war, as they were, ultimately, for use against Russia during the Crimean War.[40]

In 1848 Captain Sir Baldwin Walker, recently appointed surveyor of the navy, called for a new British standard of fifty ships of the line with another thirty building, supported by thirty-six frigates with fifteen building. The proposal included no specific provision for numbers of steam or screw warships, but Walker soon became known as the father of Britain's wooden screw battle fleet. In April the Admiralty ordered work suspended on the sailing ship of the line *Agamemnon*, just laid down, and proceeded with plans to redesign it as Britain's first purpose-built screw liner. Work resumed only in July 1849, two years after the French ordered their *Napoléon*. The 5,080-ton design emphasized sailing qualities, while *Napoléon* was designed as a steamer; nevertheless, when completed the *Agamemnon* would be capable of 12 knots under steam. By 1850 Britain had laid down a second screw battleship, the *James Watt*; a third ship of the line, the *Sans Pareil*, laid down in 1845 as a sailing ship, was converted on the stocks starting in 1849. In 1850 Walker's powers were expanded to include those of the office of comptroller of steam, leaving no doubt about the navy's future direction. Meanwhile, the fall of Louis Philippe in the February Revolution of 1848 also forced Joinville into exile and killed the ambitious French program of 1846. In January 1849 the financially strapped government of the Second Republic offered to reduce naval spending if Britain reciprocated with cuts of its own. No agreement was reached, and British naval expenditure in 1848 and 1849 barely fell from its peak of 1847, when the navy took over 13 percent of the total budget, the most in thirty years. Across the Channel, unilateral budget cuts delayed projects already underway. The *Napoléon*, laid down at Toulon in February 1848, seventeen days before the Revolution began, was finally launched in May 1850. France laid down no other screw battleships until 1853, limiting its modernizing efforts to the conversion of sailing ships of the line. Despite its problems, the French navy remained far ahead of all but the British, as no other country laid down a screw ship of the line or began a conversion project until 1852.[41]

After 1847 the US navy completed no warships with "Hunter's wheels." A modest expansion program begun during the war with Mexico included two very large paddle frigates, the 3,550-ton *Susquehanna* and 3,600-ton *Powhatan*, along with the 2,200-ton paddle steamer *Saranac* and a screw steamer of the same displacement, the sloop *San Jacinto*, the latter two built for purposes of direct comparison. Meanwhile, the screw sloop *Princeton* was doomed to a short life. As in many wooden ships of the American navy, the use of white oak rather than live oak left its hull rotten after just a few years in service, and it was broken up in 1849. Thus the US navy, after playing an important role in pioneering the new technology, was left with no screw steamers until the completion of the *San Jacinto* in 1851. In their armament, most American steamers continued to reflect the preference for very heavy guns, which European navies found intriguing but ultimately did not copy. The *Powhatan*, when completed, carried three 10-inch and six 8-inch guns.[42]

Initially the British navy armed its screw-propelled warships with heavy-caliber upper-deck guns as if they were paddle steamers, the only difference being that the absence of side paddles allowed the lower deck or decks to carry a conventional broadside battery. But tactical considerations soon brought the adoption of a conventional armament for all decks, as British naval leaders, like their French counterparts, assumed that screw liners would fight in line-ahead formation along with sailing ships of the line. With telescopic funnels down, screw liners could be distinguished from their sailing counterparts only by their greater length. In the *Agamemnon*, the *Sans Pareil*, and two of the original four British blockships, the machinery and funnels were located behind the main-mast, an exception to the general rule that the machinery was always placed ahead of the mainmast. For the typical screw warship, the greater distance between the fore and the mainmast betrayed the fact that it was a steamer even when the funnel was lowered.[43] The first screw engines for British warships were two-cylinder machines provided by Maudslay. Engine builder John Penn produced the first trunk engine, one of which was installed in the screw frigate *Arrogant* in 1848. Critics of the screw frigate design had argued that the place-ment of the mainmast in relation to the length of the ship compromised sailing qualities, but in trials held in 1850 the *Arrogant*, like the screw schooner *Renard* two years earlier, silenced critics by sailing as well as any sailing ship of its type. The sailing abilities of screw steamers, which no paddle steamer could match, clinched the victory of screw propulsion over the paddle wheel.[44]

The New World through the Mexican–American War (1846–48)

After supporting the establishment of independent states in Latin America, Britain and the United States became rivals for influence throughout the region. During the Wars for Independence Americans served alongside British personnel in the Brazilian navy and especially the Chilean. Afterward, US citizens active in Latin American navies included Commodore David Porter, a hero of the War of 1812, who served as commander of the Mexican navy from 1826 to 1829, after Cochrane declined to take the post. Latin American navies also were more likely to turn to the United States for their foreign-built sailing warships; for example, during the 1820s New York shipbuilders provided Colombia with its first two frigates and Mexico with a brig.[45]

For two decades after issuing the Monroe Doctrine, the United States did not use its naval power to meddle in Latin American affairs or expand its interests at the expense of its neighbors to the south. American warships were mere observers during the landings of Spanish troops at Tampico in 1829 and of French troops at Veracruz in 1838. The United States also remained scrupulously neutral when Bolivian dictator Andrés Santa Cruz formed a confederation with Peru, threat-ening Chile, which declared war on its northern neighbors in 1836. Throughout the three-year conflict that followed, the schooner *Enterprise* remained the only

American naval vessel in the war zone, reflecting the fact that neither side deployed many larger warships. The Chilean navy started the war with just a brig and a schooner, the Peruvian navy with eight small warships, but Chile's Commander Pedro Angulo captured half of the latter in August 1836, in a bold raid on Callao harbor. The Chilean navy then added the frigate *Monteagudo* and two corvettes, while the Peruvians reinforced their fleet to a strength of three corvettes and five smaller vessels. Neither side had a steamship. Chile's initial attempt to repeat the successful 1820–21 strategy of Cochrane and San Martín failed miserably, as an 1837 expedition under Vice Admiral Blanco Encalada was forced to withdraw troops landed on the Peruvian coast. Before launching a second invasion the Chilean navy captured a Peruvian corvette, raising its own strength to one frigate, three corvettes, and six smaller vessels. Late in 1838 these warships escorted a larger expedition under the overall command of General Manuel Bulnes, carrying 5,000 troops aboard twenty-six transports. During the landings the Peruvians captured a brig and two of the transports, but the rest of the Chilean squadron, under Captain Robert Simpson, secured command of the sea in the decisive Battle of Casma (9 January 1839). Days later Bulnes vanquished the confederate army at Yungay, prompting the fall of Santa Cruz and the dissolution of the confederation. After the triumph Chile, as in 1826, all but disbanded its navy, maintaining just two schooners for peacetime service.[46]

The United States did take sides in Argentinian dictator Juan Manuel de Rosas' attempt to conquer Uruguay, joining France and Britain in sympathizing with the tiny republic. After the war began in 1838, the aging Admiral William Brown led Argentina's small navy in blockading Montevideo and raiding Uruguayan commerce, in the process disrupting international trade on the River Plate. From 1838 to 1840 the sloop *Fairfield* defended American interests while a French squadron openly supported the Uruguayans, ultimately blockading Buenos Aires. In September 1844 an American squadron led by the new frigate *Congress* attacked and seized an Argentinian navy flotilla which had been blockading Montevideo, then remained on the scene until early the following year to ensure the free flow of American trade. In October 1845 an Anglo-French squadron forced Rosas to stop blocking trade on the Paraná River, then imposed another blockade on Buenos Aires, remaining until revolution broke out in Europe in 1848.[47] In at least one respect, Rosas was the prototypical Third World dictator: his popularity at home only grew as he maintained a defiant stance against the decade of interventions by the three foreign powers. During that time the cause of Uruguay attracted foreign volunteers, including Giuseppe Garibaldi, who spent the years 1841–48 commanding first its tiny navy and Italian Legion, then eventually all Uruguayan armed forces.[48] The war dragged on until 1852, when the Brazilian navy supported the Uruguayans and an Argentinian rebel faction in overthrowing Rosas.

The United States became more directly involved in Latin America thanks to the land hunger of pioneers from the southern states, who moved westward into Mexico's northeastern province of Texas. The creation of an independent

Texan republic in 1836 poisoned Mexican–American relations and led to greater expenditure on armaments south of the border, but the army received almost all of the defense outlay. Under Commodore Porter's command, the Mexican navy had included just one frigate and three brigs; later, during the brief War for Texan Independence, Mexico deployed six brigs against a Texan navy of brigs, schooners, and small privateers. The French seized the Mexican brigs at Veracruz in 1838 and never returned them, hampering Mexico's subsequent efforts to suppress a rebellion in Yucatan and protect its merchantmen against the commerce raiding of a revived Texan navy. In 1842 the Mexican navy acquired two paddle steamers in Britain, the 775-ton iron-hulled *Guadalupe* and the 1,110-ton wooden-hulled *Moctezuma*, and purchased two 68-pounder Paixhans guns for each ship. At the Battle of Campeche (16 May 1843) they became the first warships ever to fire shell guns in action, against a Texan squadron supporting the Yucatan rebels. The British officers and seamen of the steamers did not serve well under the Mexican Commander Tomas Marin, enabling the Texan Commodore Edwin Moore, with an all-sail squadron led by the sloop *Austin*, to fight them to a bloody draw. Both sides claimed victory, the Texans because the Mexican steamers withdrew following the battle, the Mexicans because the Texans withdrew several days afterward. When the United States granted statehood to Texas two years later, the *Austin* and three smaller warships were incorporated into the American navy.[49]

Having never acknowledged the independence of Texas, Mexico considered its annexation by the United States an act of war. At the onset of the fighting in the spring of 1846, the frigates *Raritan* and *Potomac* supported an American army under future president Zachary Taylor, landing troops at Port Isabel, Texas. At Palo Alto (8 May) Taylor won the war's first battle, opening the way for an invasion of Mexico from the north. In March 1847 the navy bombarded Veracruz before landing General Winfield Scott and an army of 10,000 men, which marched on Mexico City from the east. Commodore David Conner planned and executed the landings, which were long studied as a model amphibious operation. His warships included the two sailing frigates, two sloops, a brig, five schooners, the paddle frigate *Mississippi*, three paddle steamers purchased from the merchant marine, and the screw sloop *Princeton*. Another five steamers leased by the army served as transports. Among the steamships the *Princeton* was the most impressive, demonstrating the dimension of flexibility afforded by screw propulsion by easily changing from steam to sail as the situation dictated. Captain Matthew C. Perry commanded the *Mississippi*, which became flagship later in March 1847 after Perry assumed leadership of the squadron from the ailing Conner, who had used the *Raritan*.[50]

The 84-gun *Ohio* joined the fleet off Veracruz and participated in the last days of the bombardment before landing sailors and marines to supplement the army's successful assault on the city. Afterward the ship remained at Veracruz for two months, while 300 of her crew boarded the steamer *Mississippi* for an expedition up the Túxpan River as the army under General Scott moved inland toward

Mexico City. The capture of Tabasco, in June 1847, ended American naval operations on the Gulf coast. Scott's army took Mexico City two months later. Thereafter, word of Mexican efforts to commission privateers kept American warships occupied, but all such rumors proved false, as Mexico from the outset recognized the futility of attempting any sort of naval activity. Nevertheless, allegations of Mexican privateering in the Mediterranean justified a cruise there by the *Princeton*, which remained on the Mediterranean station until 1849.[51]

On Mexico's long Pacific coast, the US navy assembled a force from ships already assigned to the Pacific and the Far East, supplemented by vessels sent from the Atlantic. Some of the latter carried troops; future general William Tecumseh Sherman made the long passage around Cape Horn to California aboard the sloop *Lexington*, a voyage which lasted from July 1846 to January 1847. By the time he arrived, landing parties from the naval forces already on hand, led by Commodore Robert F. Stockton, had secured the lightly defended Californian ports and established a base of operations at Monterey. Ironically, the outspoken proponent of screw propulsion commanded a force that included no steamers at all. Initially his largest warship was the 56-gun razee frigate *Independence*, but in March 1847 the ship of the line *Columbus*, just returned from the Far East, arrived to join the American blockading force. The *Columbus* left in July, returning to Norfolk to be decommissioned, and was replaced by the *Ohio*, no longer needed in the Gulf after the summer of 1847. While awaiting the arrival of the *Ohio*, Stockton's successor Commodore William Shubrick used the *Independence* and the frigate *Congress* to capture Guaymas in October 1847 and Mazatlan the following month. After rounding Cape Horn the *Ohio* finally arrived in the Pacific early in 1848, on the eve of the Treaty of Guadalupe Hidalgo (2 February 1848) which officially ended the war. The agreement confirmed American possession not only of Texas but also of California and the lands in-between.[52]

The activation of the *Ohio* in December 1846, long preceding the deactivation of the *Columbus* in March 1848, left the United States with two ships of the line in commission simultaneously for the first time since 1822. It would never happen again. The *Ohio* remained in service until May 1850, the last American ship of the line to sail as a commissioned warship. Its final cruise fittingly fore-shadowed future American dreams of an empire in the Pacific. After the end of the war against Mexico it visited both Hawaii and Samoa, island groups that became American possessions at the end of the century.[53]

Naval warfare in the revolutions of 1848–49

Three weeks after the formal end of the Mexican–American War, Louis Philippe fell from power in the French Revolution of 1848, touching off a series of liberal revolutions across Europe. By the end of the year presidential elections in the new Second Republic brought to power Louis Napoleon Bonaparte, nephew of the late emperor. Meanwhile, in the German states, the Frankfurt parliament convened, hoping to legislate national unity under a constitutional monarchy. The multinational Austrian empire was threatened by the movement to unify Germany but also by a concurrent drive for Italian unification, a serious revolution in Hungary, and other lesser revolts.

The revolution in Italy posed a danger to Austria's predominantly Italian navy. A serious mutiny in 1844 foreshadowed things to come, and before his death in 1847 the navy's commander, Archduke Frederick, had ordered the transfer of active warships away from the main base at Venice to Trieste, Pola, and other safe anchorages on the Dalmatian coast. In mid-March 1848 the revolution spread from Vienna to Venice, where almost all Austrian naval personnel deserted to the newly revived Venetian republic. Hoping to become the catalyst for Italian unity, Sardinia–Piedmont declared war on Austria, and Naples soon joined the cause. The Austrian navy lost four corvettes, five brigs, and one steamer to the Venetians but saved all three of its frigates, two corvettes, six brigs, and one paddle steamer, in some cases only because non-Italian officers promised immediate discharges to their Italian sailors.[54]

As the Austrian army began the reconquest of northern Italy, the campaign at sea unfolded more slowly. While the Austrian navy had kept most of its ships but lost most of its personnel, the Venetian navy had more than enough officers and seamen but fewer ships, many of which were in reserve or in disrepair in the Venice Arsenal. In late April an Austrian squadron under Captain Ludwig Kudriaffsky blockaded Venice with two frigates, two brigs, the navy steamer *Vulcano*, and three armed paddle steamers leased from the Austrian Lloyd. Kudriaffsky gave up the blockade and withdrew to Trieste a month later, after the arrival of a Neapolitan squadron including two frigates, one brig, and five paddle steamers. The Sardinian navy soon added three frigates, one brig, and one schooner; after the Venetians contributed a corvette and another two brigs, the combined Italian fleet imposed a blockade on Trieste. Fortunately for the Austrians, Neapolitan Admiral Rafaele de Cosa had two sets of orders, one from the revolutionary government in Naples authorizing offensive operations, and another from his monarch, Ferdinand II, temporarily a hostage of the rebels, urging caution. In June 1848 a counter-revolution in Naples restored the absolute monarchy, and Ferdinand II ordered de Cosa to return home. The departure of the Neapolitans left the combined Italian fleet barely stronger than the loyal remnant of the Austrian navy, but Sardinia–Piedmont soon compensated for the loss by sending every available ship of its navy to blockade Trieste. By mid-summer the Sardinian navy had four frigates, two corvettes, two brigs, and eight steamers on the station, under Vice Admiral Giuseppe Albini. But after the Sardinian army lost the Battle of Custoza in late July, an armistice required Albini to withdraw his squadron from the Adriatic. By early August the Austrian army had reoccupied all of Lombardy and Venetia except for the city of Venice, protected by its broad lagoon.

The timely arrival of Neapolitan and Sardinian warships after the revolution had given the defenders of Venice such a sense of security that they had fitted out only a corvette and two brigs, leaving the rest of the ships in no condition to fight and the majority of the seamen idle. Kudriaffsky easily reimposed the blockade of Venice, only to be foiled by a French squadron dispatched to the upper Adriatic in September 1848, as a gesture of sympathy to the Venetians after they had been abandoned by the Sardinians. Their appearance encouraged Albini to bring the Sardinian squadron back into the Adriatic, where it spent the winter at Ancona in the Papal States, which had also succumbed to revolution. Over the winter of 1848–49 the Austrians purchased warships and hired officers abroad. The new units included the British yacht *Waterlily*, which became Austria's first screw-propelled warship; the foreign officers were led by the Danish navy's Hans Birch von Dahlerup, the new naval commander. Dahlerup considered it his patriotic duty to enter the service of Austria, as Denmark at the time was at war with the German states over Scheswig–Holstein and sought to drive a diplomatic wedge between the Austrians and the northern Germans. He assumed command in March 1849, just as Sardinia–Piedmont resumed its war against Austria. In a matter of days Austrian troops defeated the Sardinian army at the Battle of Novara, before Albini could move his squadron northward from Ancona. Under the terms of the new armistice Albini again had to withdraw his ships from the Adriatic.

The French squadron remained in the Adriatic, but after the French election of December 1848, President Bonaparte sought to placate conservative Catholic opinion at home by changing France's Italian policy. Instead of sympathizing with liberal nationalists he opposed them, especially in the Papal States, where Giuseppe Garibaldi's Roman republic had replaced the regime of Pope Pius IX. In the first significant use of a steam-powered fleet to transport troops, in April 1849 the French navy transported over 7,500 men, almost 350 horses, three batteries of artillery, and three weeks' rations from Toulon to Civitavecchia, just ten days after Bonaparte had ordered it. The intervention led to the demise of the republic and the restoration of the pope's temporal powers, the latter guaranteed by a French garrison that would remain in Rome for over two decades. The operation also revived fears in Britain of a French invasion using the "steam bridge" of the Channel.[55] At the same time, however, Britain supported France in protesting the Austrian blockade of Venice, which Dahlerup resumed later in April. As Austrian troops moved southward into the Papal States, the navy also blockaded Ancona, which fell in June. Before the Austrian army positioned siege guns around the Venice lagoon in July, Dahlerup attempted to bomb the city from balloons launched from his warships, with no success. The army's bombardment, averaging 1,000 shells per day, made the rebels desperate enough to pin all hopes on the Venetian navy breaking the blockade. Captain Achille Bucchia, formerly an Austrian officer, led four corvettes, three brigs, and one steamer on a series of unsuccessful sorties against Dahlerup's force, which included the frigates *Guerriera*, *Venere*, and *Bellona*, three steamers, a corvette and two brigs. The Venetians had nothing to match the firepower of the Austrian frigates, and Dahlerup enhanced their mobility by pairing them with his steamers, in imitation of the British practice of pairing steamers with sailing ships of the line, to serve as tugs or towboats when needed. The tactic proved to be especially useful in maintaining a blockade against an enemy force actively seeking to break it. By mid–August cholera had ravaged both Venice and its navy, and the Austrian army, with Russian help, had crushed the revolution in Hungary, leaving Venice as the last outpost of resistance to Habsburg rule. On 22 August 1849 the city surrendered.[56]

The other naval action of 1848–49 came in the Baltic and the North Sea, matching the German states against Denmark. In January 1848 Frederick VII of Denmark proclaimed the union of his predominantly German possessions of Schleswig and Holstein with the remainder of his kingdom. The duchies resisted, and patriotic indignation over their fate swept the German states, coinciding with the wave of liberal revolution. When the Prussian army intervened in the duchies, Denmark countered with its superior naval power, imposing a blockade of the German coast. The Danish blockade became a symbol of the impotence of a divided Germany, and in the months that followed, the creation of a German navy became intertwined with the quest for national unity.[57]

The core of the German navy of 1848 consisted of three paddle steamers and the sailing frigate *Deutschland*, all merchantmen armed by the city of Hamburg. For months it did not grow beyond that, as the politicians of the Frankfurt parliament, after convening in May, divided along regional lines in debating the long-term naval needs of a future united Germany. When the majority refused to allocate funds for a "German" squadron in the Adriatic (Trieste, blockaded by the Italian navies, lay within the borders of the German Confederation), Austria refused to contribute money to the navy. Some inland states joined the boycott, eliminating half the potential funding. The Austrians, battling several revolutionary threats, could hardly afford to help finance the defense of the north German coast, but the boycott embarrassed Austria's Archduke John, recently chosen as imperial regent (*Reichsverweser*) by the Frankfurt parliament. His friend Prince Adalbert of Prussia, already active in preparing Prussian coast defenses, came to Frankfurt in November 1848 to devise a German fleet plan. His collaborators included Saxon-born Captain Karl Rudolf Bromme (or Brommy), a veteran of fourteen years of Greek naval service. The Armistice of Malmö (26 August 1848) gave the Germans a temporary reprieve, but the war was to resume seven months later if the Schleswig–Holstein question remained unresolved. To supplement the ships assembled at Hamburg, north German shipyards began work on small sailing gunboats eventually commissioned in the German navy; by early 1849 twenty-seven entered service.

In February 1849 Prince Adalbert presented the Frankfurt parliament with a plan for a sailing fleet of fifteen frigates and five schooners, a steam fleet of five frigates and twenty corvettes, and another ten steamers to tow eighty small coastal gunboats. The report also cited the need for bases in both the Baltic and the North Sea, and the "indispensability" of a canal across Holstein able to handle seagoing warships. The Eider Canal, completed by the Danes in 1784, already linked Kiel on the Baltic with the Eider River, which flowed west-ward into the North Sea, but it had an average depth of just 3.5 meters, which restricted its use to light vessels. The canal described in the commission's report would not open until 1895. Bases likewise were forgotten while attention turned to assembling ships and personnel. By March 1849 the German navy had eight armed paddle steamers at Bremerhaven, its main anchorage. The *Barbarossa* and *Erzherzog Johann*, former Cunard passenger liners, each displaced 1,300 tons, but the largest of the remaining six displaced 580 tons. All carried British guns from the Woolwich Arsenal.

Adalbert acknowledged that a German navy would have to depend upon foreign officers until it established its own naval academy. He focused first on the United States, other than Belgium the only country to extend formal recog-nition to the Frankfurt parliament. During the winter of 1848–49 the sailing frigate USS *St Lawrence* took on Prussian midshipmen, and Commodore Foxhall Parker visited Frankfurt to discuss the hiring of American officers by the German navy and his own appointment as its commander. But by the time Parker arrived in January 1849, the revolution had been crushed in both Berlin and Vienna, and the forces of reaction were gaining strength at the expense of the parliament. Parker opted not to enter German service and advised American officers to follow his example. After two Austrian naval officers refused the post of German navy commander, Captain Brommy received it almost by default. Brommy hired several former Belgian and British officers to hold the highest ranks, below which the officer corps consisted of veteran merchant mariners and patriotic schoolboys. The seamen were German volunteers or foreigners who passed into the service by staying aboard the ships the Frankfurt parliament purchased abroad. Owing to the British origin of five of the eight steamers, most of the foreign seamen were British subjects.

Shortly after hostilities resumed, Brommy acquired another ship thanks to the work of Schleswig–Holstein forces. On 5 April the Danes attacked the Schleswig port of Eckernförde with the 84-gun ship of the line *Christian VIII*, the 48-gun frigate *Gefion*, two small paddle steamers, and three troop transports. A ten-hour artillery duel between the warships and shore batteries ended in disaster for the Danes when a strong east wind carried the *Christian VIII* and *Gefion* too close to the shore and into the crossfire of two of the batteries. By dusk the *Christian VIII* fell victim to red-hot shot; it ran aground on the beach, a total loss. The *Gefion* surrendered to avoid a similar fate. The victors renamed the frigate *Eckernförde* and presented it to the German navy. It remained in the port as a harbor watch ship, manned by a skeleton crew. In the battle the Danes lost 131 men killed, 80 wounded, and 943 taken prisoner; German losses were four dead and seventeen wounded. On 4 June Brommy finally put to sea, using his flagship *Barbarossa* and two smaller steamers to disperse the Danish vessels standing guard at the mouth of the Weser. Brommy succeeded in cutting off the *Valkyrien*, a sailing corvette that lagged behind the rest of the fleeing Danes. The Germans were moving in for the kill when the corvette headed for the safety of Helgoland (then a British possession, acquired by Germany in 1890). After a British battery on the island fired a warning shot at Brommy's ships, they broke off the chase and returned to port. On 14 June the same three German steamers chased off the Danish paddle steamer *Hekla* and two frigates that had been blockading the Elbe. Brommy's forces then remained idle until the Prusso-Danish Armistice of Berlin (19 July) brought a return to peace. Ironically, the largest ship acquired by the German navy reached Bremerhaven after the end of hostilities. The 1,650-ton transatlantic paddle steamer *Hansa* (ex-*United States*), purchased in February 1849 from the Black Ball Line, arrived in August after being armed in Britain.

The resumption of warfare in 1849 coincided with the demise of the Frankfurt parliament, casting doubt over the future of Germany and its navy. In late March, Frederick William IV of Prussia rejected the offer of the German crown, and in June, the assembly finally disbanded. Archduke John remained in Frankfurt as *Reichsverweser*, pending the restoration of the German Confederation. Brommy continued to take orders from the archduke as the idle German navy, anchored at Bremerhaven, became a pawn between Prussia and Austria in their battle for hegemony over Germany. In the autumn of 1850 the two German powers mobilized their armies, but a strong showing by the Austrian army, backed by the diplomatic support of Russia, brought an end to Prussia's plans to unify the smaller German states around itself. In May 1851 Prussia and its north German allies returned to the German Confederation. Amid this ultimate triumph of the conservative reaction, Prussian Minister–President Otto von Manteuffel demanded the dismantling of the German navy, calling it the "illegitimate child" of the Frankfurt parliament, a ramshackle remnant of the liberal upheaval of 1848. The Prussians put in bids for the frigate *Eckernförde* and the steamship *Barbarossa*, as compensation for financial contributions to the navy between 1848 and 1851. In April 1852 Brommy turned over these ships to the Prussian navy. Bremen firms purchased the *Hansa*, the *Erzherzog Johann*, and the frigate *Deutschland*, and the General Steam Navigation Company of London bought the six smaller steamships. Brommy finally struck his flag in March 1853, when the new owners claimed the last steamers.

The brief life of the first German navy featured far more political action in Frankfurt than naval action in the Baltic and the North Sea. But during the same years frustrated German patriots could take heart in the performance of the tiny Schleswig–Holstein navy, created in June 1848 by Schleswig–Holstein rebels unwilling to wait for the Frankfurt parliament to establish a fleet. The force, based at Kiel, eventually included one schooner and eleven sailing gunboats, three paddle steamers, and the new screw gunboat *Von der Tann*, the first warship constructed in Germany with a screw propeller. The sixteen vessels mounted forty-one guns and employed 800 seamen. The schooner operated as an autonomous warship along with the steamers, but the latter also towed the gunboats to action in the coastal waters of the Baltic and the North Sea, often using the Eider Canal in-between. Danish ships operating along the coasts of the duchies also had to contend with formidable shore batteries, such as those at Eckernförde, and primitive minefields, most notably one at the mouth of Kiel harbor, laid by future industrialist Werner Siemens, then a Prussian engineer officer. Lieutenant Johann Ernst Kjer commanded the Schleswig–Holstein navy in the most active phases of its brief history, from March to July 1849, and after Prussia concluded the Treaty of Berlin (2 July 1850) with Denmark, when the rebels resolved to continue resistance. The navy lost the *Von der Tann* in July 1850 and one of its sailing gunboats in November, before Schleswig–Holstein finally gave up its hopeless fight in January 1851. In the surrender the Danish navy received the surviving warships of the Schleswig–Holstein navy, and later made its triumph complete by raising and repairing the wrecks of the *Von der Tann* and the lost gunboat. Not unlike the Frankfurt parliament's fleet, the Schleswig–Holstein navy died a slow death. The last officers served until November 1851, and the last ships were towed to Copenhagen in April 1852.[58]

In addition to the naval forces organized by the Frankfurt parliament and Schleswig–Holstein, Prussia maintained its own navy throughout the war against Denmark. Before leaving for Frankfurt to draft the German navy's fleet plan, Prince Adalbert designed a defense force for the Prussian coast including forty-two small sailing gunboats; the first was launched just as the Malmö armistice ended the first round of German–Danish warfare in August 1848. Before then the Prussian navy could do nothing to challenge the Danes. Its lone seagoing vessels were the 350-ton training corvette *Amazone*, which remained in Danzig, and an armed postal steamer, which patroled the coast as far west as Stettin, never engaging the enemy. Meanwhile, the Danes seized so many Prussian merchantmen that the sheer number of prisoners became a burden for them. In February 1849, after his work in Frankfurt came to an end, Prince Adalbert returned to Prussia. The German fleet plan he had helped devise remained a dream, and, worse yet, all of the steamers being purchased for the German navy were going to Brommy at Bremerhaven, leaving the Prussian coast no better defended than before. With the armistice scheduled to lapse in late March, he set about the task of developing Prussia's own naval forces, for the moment avoiding the question of their relationship to the German navy. A flurry of activity followed, as personnel and materiel were assembled for the upcoming campaign. A second postal steamer and an armed merchant paddle steamer joined the rest of the Prussian warships at Stettin, a better base than Danzig for operations against Denmark. Captain Jan Schröder, formerly of the Dutch navy, took charge of training personnel, most of whom were volunteer seamen or soldiers from the Prussian army. But after hostilities resumed, the Danish navy focused its attentions on Brommy's fleet and the Schleswig–Holstein navy, leaving the Prussian navy with little to do. In contrast to the close blockade of the entire Prussian coastline mounted in 1848, this time Danish warships stood farther to sea off the main ports. On 27 June 1849 Schröder took the paddle steamer *Preussischer Adler* out to challenge the blockade and engaged the Danish brig *St Croix* in an inconclusive five-hour artillery duel off Brüsterort. The navy saw no further action before Prussia and Denmark concluded the Armistice of Berlin, one month later.[59]

Another year passed before Prussia, in the name of the German Confederation, concluded the Treaty of Berlin with Denmark (2 July 1850). While waiting for the confederation to be restored and the German navy liquidated, Adalbert and Schröder fulfilled their primary goal of keeping the Prussian navy alive in peacetime, preventing a return to the inactivity and indecision of the years before 1848. The navy added the corvette *Mercur*, which in 1850–51 went on a training cruise to Brazil, and opened negotiations with British firms for the construction of additional steamships. With the demise of the German navy, the 1,400-ton frigate *Eckernförde* (which, in the spirit of the counter-revolution, reverted to its original name *Gefion*) and 1,300-ton paddle steamer *Barbarossa* instantly became the largest active warships in the Prussian navy.[60]

Conclusion

As a technological revolution the transition to steam occurred at a remarkably slow pace, compared to the revolutions to come. Into the late 1840s the leading navies still were building new sail-powered warships, even of the largest types. While the British and the French considered the sailing warship and the paddle steamer "dead" by 1850, others continued to add both types. Sailing ships and paddle steamers already on hand would continue to serve in combat roles during the Crimean War and beyond, even in the British navy, which joined others in continuing to build small paddle steamers for auxiliary purposes. As late as 1860 sailing ships of the line still served as flagships of the British Pacific and South African stations. Into the late 1800s most navies continued to use sailing vessels as training ships for cadets and apprentice seamen, and paddle steamers remained active as fleet auxiliaries.

Notes

1 Hamilton, *Anglo-French Naval Rivalry*, 4, 9; Lambert, "Introduction of Steam," 23, 27; Dupont and Taillemite, *Les guerres navales françaises*, 233–34; Daly, *Russian Seapower and "the Eastern Question"*, 79–81.
2 Hamilton, *Anglo-French Naval Rivalry*, 4–10, and *passim*.
3 Sondhaus, *The Habsburg Empire and the Sea*, 78–9.
4 David Woodward, *The Russians at Sea: A History of the Russian Navy* (New York, 1966), 97; Dakin, *The Greek Struggle for Independence*, 296–7.
5 Daly, *Russian Seapower and "the Eastern Question"*, 66–9, 196–9; Woodward, *The Russians at Sea*, 97; Gromov et al., *Tri Veka Rossiiskogo Flota*, 1: 177.
6 Daly, *Russian Seapower and "the Eastern Question"*, 46, 100–39, and *passim*, 196–8; Jane, *The Imperial Russian Navy*, 134; Andrew Lambert, *The Crimean War: British Grand Strategy against Russia, 1853–56* (Manchester, 1991), 2.
7 Lambert, "Introduction of Steam," 20–1, 29.
8 Ibid., 25–6, 29; Dupont and Taillemite, *Les guerres navales françaises*, 235–6.

9 Lambert, "Introduction of Steam," 19, 25–9; Canney, *The Old Steam Navy*, 1: 8–12, 2: 3.

10 http://www.uss-salem.org/danfs/frigates

11 Langensiepen and Güleryüz, *The Ottoman Steam Navy*, 1–2, 142–3; James A. Field, Jr, *From Gibraltar to the Middle East: America and the Mediterranean World, 1776–1882*, rev. edn (Chicago, 1991), 175.

12 Radogna, *Storia della Marina Militare*, 109–12; Sondhaus, *The Habsburg Empire and the Sea*, 91, 130–1, 173; Lambert, "Introduction of Steam," 28; Randaccio, *Le marinerie militari italiane*, 36–40; Agustín Ramón Rodríguez González, *Política naval de la Restauración, 1875–1898* (Madrid, 1988), 126.

13 Lambert, "Introduction of Steam," 27–8.

14 Ibid., 21, 23.

15 Hamilton, *Anglo-French Naval Rivalry*, 11; Langensiepen and Güleryüz, *The Ottoman Steam Navy*, 3; Daly, *Russian Seapower and "the Eastern Question"*, 143; François Ferdinand d'Orléans, Prince de Joinville, *Essais sur la marine française* (Paris, 1853), 10.

16 Hamilton, *Anglo-French Naval Rivalry*, 21; Sondhaus, *The Habsburg Empire and the Sea*, 102–3; Lambert, *The Last Sailing Battlefleet*, 38; Daly, *Russian Seapower and "the Eastern Question"*, 159–63; Bonner-Smith and Dewar, eds, *Russian War, 1854*, 212.

17 Sondhaus, *The Habsburg Empire and the Sea*, 103–4; Lambert, "Introduction of Steam," 23; Langensiepen and Güleryüz, *The Ottoman Steam Navy*, 3.

18 Daly, *Russian Seapower and "the Eastern Question"*, 171–3; Lambert, *The Last Sailing Battlefleet*, 87; Sondhaus, *The Habsburg Empire and the Sea*, 127–36.

19 Jack Beeching, *The Chinese Opium Wars* (New York, 1975), 84–104, and *passim*.

20 Ibid., 111–12; Lambert, "Introduction of Steam," 28.

21 W. H. Hall, *Narrative of the Voyages and Services of the Nemesis, from 1840 to 1843*, 2nd edn (London, 1845), 2.

22 Hall, *Narrative of the Voyages and Services of the Nemesis*, 121.

23 Beeching, *The Chinese Opium Wars*, 115, 124–35.

24 Ibid., 144–56; Hall, *Narrative of the Voyages and Services of the Nemesis*, 478–549 and *passim*.

25 Lambert, "Introduction of Steam," 22, 29.

26 Andrew Lambert, "The Screw Propeller Warship," in Robert Gardiner, ed., *Steam, Steel and Shellfire: The Steam Warship 1815–1905* (London, 1992), 31–2; Brown, *Paddle Warships*, 80.

27 Lambert, "Introduction of Steam," 21, 28–9; Canney, *The Old Steam Navy*, 1: 43.

28 Joinville, *De l'état des forces navales de la France*, 14–15, 25–6, 38–41; Busk, *Navies of the World*, 75.

29 Joinville, *De l'état des forces navales de la France*, 35.

30 Lambert, "Introduction of Steam," 23–24; idem, *Battleships in Transition*, 19; Brown, *Paddle Warships*, 79; Griffiths, "Warship Machinery," 170.

31 Lambert, "Introduction of Steam," 26; idem, *The Last Sailing Battlefleet*, 54.

32 Lambert, "Introduction of Steam," 26.

33 Lambert, "The Screw Propeller Warship," 35, 43; Brown, *Paddle Warships*, 48.

34 Lambert, "The Screw Propeller Warship," 36; Campbell, "Naval Armaments and Armour," 158; Canney, *The Old Steam Navy*, 2: 25.

35 Lambert, "Iron Hulls and Armour Plate," 59; Canney, *The Old Steam Navy*, 1: 17–29, and *passim*, 168; Field, *From Gibraltar to the Middle East*, 222.

36 James Phinney Baxter, *The Introduction of the Ironclad Warship* (Cambridge, Mass., 1933), 48–51, 214; cf. Canney, *The Old Steam Navy*, 2: 3–5.

37 Canney, *The Old Steam Navy*, 1: 18–21, 173; 2: 3.

38 Hamilton, *Anglo-French Naval Rivalry*, 17–20; Lambert, *The Last Sailing Battlefleet*,

41; Dupont and Taillemite, *Les guerres navales françaises*, 237, 239; Battesti, *La Marine au XIXe siècle*, 29, 33; Baxter, *Introduction of the Ironclad Warship*, 65–7.

39 Hamilton, *Anglo-French Naval Rivalry*, 37, 43; Lambert, "The Screw Propeller Warship," 36–9.

40 Lambert, *Battleships in Transition*, 139; idem, "The Screw Propeller Warship," 38, 42–4; Brown, *Paddle Warships*, 16; Busk, *Navies of the World*, 42.

41 Hamilton, *Anglo-French Naval Rivalry*, 42–3, 51–3; Baxter, *Introduction of the Ironclad Warship*, 67; Beeler, *British Naval Policy*, 58; Lambert, "The Screw Propeller Warship," 40; idem, *Battleships in Transition*, 124, 138, 140; idem, *The Last Sailing Battlefleet*, 90.

42 Canney, *The Old Steam Navy*, 2: 168–73; Lambert, "Introduction of Steam," 27; idem, "The Screw Propeller Warship," 36.

43 Lambert, "The Screw Propeller Warship," 37; idem, *Battleships in Transition*, 32–3.

44 Griffiths, "Warship Machinery," 173; Lambert, *Battleships in Transition*, 31–2.

45 Long, *Nothing Too Daring*, 262–82; Cochrane to O'Higgins, Valparaíso, 8 January 1823, in Dundonald, *Narrative of Services*, 1: 241; Paul Constantine Pappas, *The United States and the Greek War for Independence, 1821–1828* (Boulder, Colo., 1985), 102.

46 Araya, "Situación estratégica naval," 1: 307–12; http://www.uss-salem.org/danfs/sail (accessed May 1999)

47 Dupont and Taillemite, *Les guerres navales françaises*, 236–7; http://www.uss-salem.org/danfs/frigates; http://www.uss-salem.org/danfs/sloops (accessed May 1999)

48 Ivan Boris, *Gli anni di Garibaldi in Sud America, 1836–1848* (Milan, 1970), 161–290 and *passim*.

49 E. M. Eller, *The Texas Navy* (Washington, D.C., 1968), 5–25.

50 Philip Syng Physick Conner, *The Home Squadron under Commodore Conner in the War with Mexico* (Philadelphia, 1896), 9, 66; Lambert, "Introduction of Steam," 27, 36; Canney, *The Old Steam Navy*, 2: 31; Beach, *The United States Navy*, 159; http://www.uss-salem.org/danfs/frigates

51 Field, *From Gibraltar to the Middle East*, 215.

52 John F. Marzalek, *Sherman: A Soldier's Passion for Order* (New York, 1994), 54–61; Beach, *The United States Navy*, 160; http://www.uss-salem.org/danfs/line; http://www.uss-salem.org/danfs/frigates

53 http://www.uss-salem.org/danfs/line

54 Unless otherwise noted, the source for material below on Austria and the Italian navies of 1848–49 is Sondhaus, *The Habsburg Empire and the Sea*, 150–60, 175.

55 Hamilton, *Anglo-French Naval Rivalry*, 53.

56 Sondhaus, *The Habsburg Empire and the Sea*, 160–2.

57 Unless otherwise noted, the source for material below on the German navy of 1848–52 is Sondhaus, *Preparing for Weltpolitik*, 19–32.

58 Gerd Stolz, *Die Schleswig–Holsteinische Marine, 1848–1852* (Heide in Holstein, 1978), *passim*.

59 Sondhaus, *Preparing for Weltpolitik*, 37–41.

60 Ibid., 41–5.

CHAPTER THREE

The 1850s

Technological developments during the crucial decade of the 1850s included the spread of screw propulsion beyond the navies of the first rank, and the death of both the line-of-battle sailing ship and the paddle steamer as warship. The Crimean War (1853–56), a clash involving the three largest naval powers, provided the first clear demonstration of the link between a country's industrial development and capacity to make war at sea. The first experimentation with armor plate, to clad French floating batteries towed into action against Russian forts on the Black Sea, touched off the long cycle of development of ever more powerful guns and ever stronger armor.

The early 1850s

Renewed Anglo-French naval competition, fueled by the maritime ambitions of Napoleon III, eventually led to the first armored warships but initially brought the construction of large wooden screw battle fleets. Following his election as president of the Second Republic in the wake of the French Revolution of 1848, Louis Napoleon Bonaparte at first kept naval expenditure low. After the French assembly, in 1851, recommended an increase in the number of ships of the line, he used a naval build-up to help rally public support for his personal rule; ultimately, he hoped the fleet would become a tool to persuade Britain to support (or at least not to oppose) his diplomatic schemes. As dictator of the republic from December 1851 and emperor from December 1852, he devoted unprecedented sums of money to the navy, yet it would be difficult to overcome the damage wrought by the political uncertainty and reduced funding that had followed the revolution. The world's first screw ship of the line, Dupuy de Lôme's *Napoléon*, was launched in May 1850 but not ready for sea until 1852, five years after it was ordered. Additional warships of the same type were not ordered until the spring of 1852. Thus France, after starting the latest naval arms race in 1847, immediately fell behind in the competition.[1]

By the end of 1853, Britain had completed three new screw ships of the line and converted seven others; France had the *Napoléon* and eight conversions. Russia had two conversions underway in its Baltic shipyards and had laid down two new screw ships of the line for the Black Sea fleet at Nicolaiev. The British would complete another two new screw battleships and eleven conversions during the Crimean War; the French, five of new construction and seven conversions. The four British blockships ordered in 1845 all were destined to serve in the Baltic fleet throughout the conflict; another five old sailing 74s were converted to blockships between the autumn of 1854 and spring of 1855, serving in the Baltic fleet in 1855 and 1856. Aside from the three leading naval powers, only Sweden – which converted the old *Carl XIV Johan* in 1852–54 – had a screw ship of the line in commission during the Crimean War years.[2]

While Britain and France had resolved to build their larger warships as screw steamers, adding only smaller types of new paddle steamers, elsewhere large paddle "frigates" were commissioned throughout the 1850s – in some navies instead of screw steamers, in others alongside screw steamers. In a modernization campaign undertaken after 1850 by Grand Duke Constantine, the Russian navy added a number of steamers of foreign construction or equipped with foreign engines, almost all paddle rather than screw. By 1852 the tsar's fleet included thirty-four paddle steamers of various sizes; the following year the largest Russian screw warships in service were three corvettes, all stationed in the Baltic.[3] Meanwhile, in Austria, Emperor Francis Joseph's brother, Archduke Ferdinand Max, entered naval service in 1851 and became navy commander three years later. Enjoying a far more generous budget than in past years, the Austrian navy ordered the paddle frigate *Kaiserin Elisabeth* and the screw frigate *Radetzky* from British shipbuilders, taking delivery of both ships in 1854. During the 1850s Austria armed another twenty paddle steamers but used the type mostly for auxiliary purposes; meanwhile, by 1855 two screw frigates and two screw corvettes had been laid down in Austrian shipyards.[4] Prussia's navy likewise made the transition from paddle to screw under the direction of a member of the ruling dynasty. With Prince Adalbert in command, between 1850 and 1852 the Prussian navy purchased two paddle steamers in Britain, laid down a third in Danzig, and acquired a fourth from the defunct German navy of 1848. The first screw warships, two corvettes, were laid down in 1855.[5] Italy's largest navy, the Neapolitan, continued to invest heavily in paddle steamers, launching its last in 1856. By then, Naples had a dozen large paddle frigates and several smaller paddle steamers, all of them obsolete as warships. Naples laid down its first screw frigates in 1857.[6]

The United States alone made a clean break with the old technology. After building just eight paddle steamers between 1837 and 1852, the American navy commissioned none until after the outbreak of the Civil War in 1861, when vessels of all types would be added for the blockade of the rebellious southern states. An early pioneer in screw propulsion, the United States was slow to apply the technology to warships larger than a sloop and stood alone among naval powers of the first and second ranks in never converting a sailing warship to screw. Until the mid-1850s all station flagships were sailing frigates, and during the decade another two were completed, the *Santee* and the *Sabine*, the latter after thirty-three years on the stocks, to supplement the fleet of older frigates. These still included the *Constitution*, launched in 1797, which was flagship of the Mediterranean squadron and of the anti-slave trade patrol off West Africa between 1852 and 1855. For the task of forcing Japan to open trade with the United States, Commodore Matthew C. Perry was given three large and heavily armed paddle frigates – the 3,220-ton flagship *Mississippi*, the 3,550-ton *Susquehanna*, and the 3,600-ton *Powhatan* – supplemented by smaller sailing warships. Perry delayed his scheduled departure by a year, until early 1853, in the hope of taking along the new screw sloop *Princeton (II)*, which ultimately was replaced by the *Powhatan*. The steamers made a far greater impression than a previous unsuccessful American mission with the same purpose, undertaken by the ship of the line *Columbus* and a sloop escort in 1846. Perry first entered Tokyo Bay in July 1853 and the following spring left Japanese waters with a trade treaty. The success of this American exercise in "gunboat diplomacy" attracted the attention of the leading naval powers, but the outbreak of the Crimean War forced them to postpone plans to follow suit.[7]

The Crimean War (1853–56)

As early as 1850 Louis Napoleon challenged Russia's traditional role as protector of Christian shrines in the Holy Land, in order to court conservative Catholic opinion at home. His foreign policy became bolder after December 1852, when he proclaimed himself emperor as Napoleon III. Britain initially opposed France's bid for greater influence in the Near East, but when Russia responded with further diplomatic bullying of the Ottoman empire, Foreign Secretary Lord Palmerston joined the French in supporting the Turks against Russian aggression. In June 1853 British and French fleets arrived off the Dardanelles, and in July Russian forces occupied the Turkish Danubian Principalities (Romania), preparing to cross the Danube into Bulgaria. Palmerston was not eager to involve Britain in the conflict but came to view it as an opportunity to roll back the recent advance of Russian power, which at least indirectly threatened British interests in Persia, the Baltic and the Black Sea. Britain also sought to protect its economic interests in the Ottoman empire, which had increased eight-fold in value over the past quarter-century.[8]

In late October 1853 Russia and the Ottoman empire finally exchanged declarations of war, and the British and French fleets entered the Sea of Marmara. While estimates of the strength of the Russian navy vary dramatically, there were at least twelve seaworthy ships of the line in the Black Sea fleet, several smaller sailing warships and at least twenty paddle steamers, although by some accounts only seven of the latter were armed. The sultan's fleet, reinforced by a squadron on loan from the pasha of Egypt, included five ships of the line, thirteen frigates, eighteen smaller sailing ships, and eight paddle steamers. His only screw warship was the former Egyptian frigate *Mubir-i Sürur*, converted in Britain in 1850. In the first naval action of the war, during November 1853, the British-built Russian paddle steamers *Bessarabia* and *Vladimir* each captured a steamer from the Turco-Egyptian fleet.[9] These minor successes were followed by a decisive Russian victory at the Battle of Sinope (30 November 1853), where six ships of the line and two frigates under Vice Admiral Pavel Nakhimov attacked a Turco-Egyptian squadron of seven frigates and three corvettes under Vice Admiral Osman Pasha. Neither force included a screw warship but each had three paddle steamers, which in the Russian case were used as tugs to move the 120-gun three-deckers *Imperatritsa Maria*, *Tri Sviatitelia*, and *Rostislav*. While the Turks had no shell guns, the Russian warships carried thirty-eight heavy Paixhans. In the six-hour battle Nakhimov destroyed the entire Turco-Egyptian squadron except for the paddle steamer *Taif*, which escaped to Constantinople with news of the disaster. The Russians lost no ships and suffered casualties of less than 300 killed and wounded, compared to almost 3,000 casualties in Osman Pasha's force.[10]

Many contemporary experts considered the outcome of Sinope a triumph of the shell gun, and there is evidence that the battle sowed the seeds of Napoleon III's doubts about the survivability of wooden warships against the latest heavy artillery. But in order to draw such "lessons" one had to ignore that it took six hours for Nakhimov to destroy the Turco-Egyptian squadron, despite the facts that he had six ships of the line with over 600 guns and that Osman Pasha's largest warships were frigates. Competent gunnery using solid shot alone would have achieved the same outcome.[11] Regardless of whether the shell gun had been decisive at Sinope, the loss of Osman Pasha's squadron left Britain and France fearful that the Russian navy would attempt to assault Constantinople. In January 1854 a reinforced Anglo-French fleet passed from the Sea of Marmara through the Bosporus into the Black Sea; two months later the Western powers declared war on Russia and prepared to land an expeditionary force at Varna.[12] In the spring of 1854 the allied fleet in the Black Sea included ten British and nine French ships of the line. Only a few were screw battleships, but these included the *Sans Pareil* and *Agamemnon*, which had been sent to the Mediterranean in 1853 shortly after being completed. The sultan was more than willing to let his allies shoulder the burden of the war at sea. After Sinope his navy still had five ships of the line, six frigates, fifteen smaller sailing ships, and six paddle steamers, but aside from contributing a few units to the allied fleet, it attempted no further operations.

Like their counterparts in the allied army, senior navy commanders in the Crimean War were aged veterans of the Napoleonic Wars: in 1854 68-year-old Vice Admiral James Deans Dundas and 65-year-old Vice Admiral F. A. Hamelin served as allied Black Sea commanders. The victor of Sinope, Nakhimov, was somewhat younger, his earliest combat experience being the destruction of the Turco-Egyptian fleet at Navarino in 1827, which he had witnessed as a junior officer.[13] Relative youth notwithstanding, like Russia's other admirals he remained bold and decisive only as long as he faced just the sultan's navy. Once they found themselves standing against the world's two strongest fleets, with no screw battleships or large screw steamers of any type, Nakhimov and his superior at Sevastopol, Admiral Vladimir Kornilov, limited Russian naval activity to periodic sorties by individual paddle steamers. The most successful of these, the *Vladimir*, sank or captured a number of Ottoman merchantmen during July 1854.[14]

The Anglo-French intervention in the Russo-Turkish war took the tsar's generals and admirals by surprise. 1853 marked the eighth time Russia had gone to war with the Ottoman empire since the time of Peter the Great, in the 1690s. Never before had the Western powers declared war on Russia on behalf of the Turks. The Russians had not intended to provoke a war against Britain and France, and when faced with that war in the spring of 1854 they withdrew their fleet to Sevastopol and, weeks later, also withdrew troops that had entered Turkey's Balkan and Danubian territories the previous year. Russia was content to return to the status quo ante, but Britain and France opted to fight rather than negotiate. Their goal was to eliminate the threat to the Ottoman empire by smashing Russian naval and military power in the Black Sea and its hinterland. Sevastopol, the linchpin of Russia's position in the region, became the primary target.[15]

The first action involving Anglo-French naval forces came off Odessa shortly after the declaration of war, when the British paddle steamer *Furious* was fired upon while attempting to enter the port under a flag of truce, to evacuate the local British consul. Later in April 1854 Dundas responded with a punitive bombardment of Odessa led by five British and four French paddle steamers. Russian harbor defenses survived the raid largely intact, and shore batteries also did little damage to the attackers aside from the French *Vauban*, which was set afire by red-hot shot. The first British ship lost in the war was the paddle steamer *Tiger*, which ran aground off Odessa in May.[16] Meanwhile, in June, the last Russian troops withdrew north of the Danube, ending the threat to Turkish Bulgaria and freeing the allied army at Varna to be shipped across the Black Sea to the Crimea. In September an armada of eighty-nine warships and over 100 transports ferried around 55,000 troops to Eupatoria (Evpatorii) on the Crimean peninsula. The allied fleet was vulnerable to attack throughout the fourteen-day operation, but the Russian navy did nothing to challenge it. Afterward allied troops advanced on Sevastopol, which they never fully besieged, as roads leading northward out of the city remained open throughout the war. At the insistence of the Russian army, Kornilov removed guns and men from idle ships to bolster the defenses of the city. He also scuttled five ships of the line to block the harbor entrance.[17]

The Russian decision to scuttle so many larger warships ended any possibility of another naval battle in the Black Sea. On 17 October 1854, when a fleet led by Dundas bombarded Sevastopol, the only opposition came from shore batteries. His force of some thirty warships, led by five screw and eight sailing ships of the line, mounted 1,100 guns against just 73 Russian fortress guns, but during the six-hour duel the latter inflicted serious damage on Dundas' ships. Red-hot

Plate 3.1 HMS *Agamemnon* in the bombardment of Sevastopol (17 October 1854)
Naval Historical Center, Basic Collection

shot proved more lethal than shells, setting afire the flagship *Agamemnon*, three other ships of the line, and a frigate, all of which were saved, as was the ship of the line *Rodney*, which ran aground and had to be towed to safety. Several other British and French warships sustained lighter damage. The Russians suffered casualties of 50 killed and wounded, the allies 520. The Russian dead included Kornilov, leaving Nakhimov as the senior sea officer in Sevastopol.[18]

A gale on 14 November did more damage to the allied fleet than any naval action of the war, wrecking twenty-six ships at Eupatoria and along the coast, including the French ship of the line *Henri IV*. A Turkish ship of the line and several smaller vessels were lost at sea. The following month, Dundas turned over his command to Rear Admiral Sir Edmund Lyons, whose flagship *Royal Albert* was one of several screw ships of the line sent to the Black Sea over the winter of 1854–55 to replace sailing battleships. In January 1855 political discontent over the conduct of the war brought a change of government in London, with Palmerston taking over as prime minister. During the same month, over 40,000 Turkish troops arrived at Eupatoria and Sardinia–Piedmont declared war on Russia; the Sardinians sent 15,500 troops to the Crimea for the 1855 campaign.[19] In the spring the focus of the naval war shifted to the Sea of Azov. An allied gunboat flotilla secured the sea by July 1855, forcing the surrender of Kertch, at the eastern tip of the Crimea, and closing the supply line from the Don River basin to Sevastopol. While historians disagree over the significance of the campaign, the outcome further isolated Russia's Crimean stronghold.[20]

During the summer of 1855 Russian troops in Sevastopol made a number of unsuccessful attempts to break the lines of the growing allied army. The warships in the harbor remained idle and the likelihood of any further naval action became still more remote after the deaths of Nakhimov and the third senior Russian admiral in the city, Vladimir Istomin, during July. On 7 September the allies began their final bombardment of Sevastopol, which continued the following day, when French and British troops stormed key points in the city's defenses. On the night of 8–9 September the Russian army abandoned the city via the road still open to the north, leaving behind a burning dockyard. Lyons reported that the following morning, "we observed that . . . the six remaining ships of the line had been sunk at their moorings, leaving afloat no more of the late Russian Black Sea fleet than two dismasted corvettes and nine steamers, most of which are very small." The steamers remained manned until 12 September, when they, too, were scuttled, leaving the harbor impassible from the sheer number of sunken ships.[21]

After the fall of Sevastopol, an allied naval force led by Lyons and France's Vice Admiral A. J. Bruat sailed westward to Kinburn, a formidable fort guarding the mouth of the Bug and the Dnieper. On the morning of 17 October 1855, four British and four French ships of the line participated in a bombardment of Kinburn, but in the treacherous shoals surrounding the spit on which the fort was located, most of the effective firepower came from shallow-draught paddle steamers, mortar vessels, and screw gunboats of the type originally intended for Britain's "Cherbourg Strategy" of the mid-1840s. The attacking force also included the *Dévastation*, the *Lave*, and the *Tonnante*, 1,575-ton armor-plated wooden floating batteries ordered by Napoleon III after the Battle of Sinope and the initial bombardment of Sevastopol had exposed the vulnerability of wooden battleships. They were awkward flat-bottomed vessels which could not sail, with engines capable of just 4 knots; indeed, steamships towed them all the way from French shipyards to the Black Sea, to the spot where they were anchored around 1,000 yards from the fort at Kinburn. During the battle, Russian shot and shell deflected or detonated harmlessly against the 4-inch wrought iron plates of the batteries, which poured 3,000 rounds into the enemy stronghold, helping reduce it to rubble by noon. It should be noted that the guns of Kinburn were not as formidable as those of the Sevastopol forts; at one point the ship of the line *Princess Royal* came within 650 yards of the fort but sustained little damage and only two casualties, the same number that died when a Russian shot went through one of the *Dévastation*'s gunports. Historians continue to debate whether the floating batteries were decisive in the victory. What mattered was that the French emperor thought they were, and this fact made the Battle of Kinburn a milestone in the move toward armored warships. After seeing the floating batteries in action, even the skeptical Lyons urged his superiors to make sure the British navy had "as many good ones as the French." In fact, the British already had laid down five floating batteries in 1854 and started work on another three in 1855, to be used in the projected Baltic campaign of 1856.[22]

The destruction of Kinburn left Russia without a significant coastal fortress on the Black Sea and effectively ended the war in the southern theater. Meanwhile, as the Russians weakened, the pressure against them only grew. After entering the war, Sardinia–Piedmont deployed an all-steam fleet in the theater, consisting of the new screw frigate *Carlo Alberto* and several paddle steamers. Austria did not enter the war but in 1854, with Turkish permission and the acquiescence of Britain and France, its troops occupied the Danubian Principalities after Russian troops withdrew. In 1855 Austria deployed a fleet in the eastern Mediterranean under the command of Archduke Ferdinand Max, consisting of two paddle steamers, four sailing frigates, and four sailing corvettes. After the fall of Sevastopol, Austrian diplomacy helped bring Russia to the peace table, paving the way for the settlement that would end the war.[23]

With the fighting in the Black Sea ended and a peace settlement still months away, the focus of the war shifted to the Baltic, where the allies deployed large fleets in 1854 and again in 1855. Vice Admiral Napier, 68 years old when the war began, campaigned actively for the British Baltic command, which he received amid a storm of controversy in February 1854. At the start of the war the Russian Baltic fleet was roughly twice the size of the Black Sea fleet, including twenty-five ships of the line, of which seventeen were fit for action. Britain responded accordingly, initially deploying all but two available screw ships of the line in the northern theater. In March 1854 Napier took a force of nine screw and six sailing ships of the line, four blockships, and a number of smaller warships into the Baltic. Because the French navy had sent its most battle-ready units to the Black Sea, the French Baltic squadron, under Vice Admiral A. F. Parseval-Deschênes, arrived weeks later and initially included only one screw ship of the line. The allies imposed a loose blockade on Russian ports and wisely considered the fortified base at Kronstadt too strong to attack. Supplementing powerful fortress artillery and shore batteries, the Russians sowed the approaches to St Petersburg with primitive Jacobi mines, caulked wooden kegs filled with explosives. As in the Black Sea, in the Baltic the Russians did not attempt to challenge the allies with their ships of the line.[24]

With most of the allied troops assigned to the Black Sea theater, the fleet in the Baltic lacked the manpower to take heavily defended coastal cities. In May 1854 the British occupied Libau (Liepaja) after its Russian garrison withdrew, and in August, following heavy bombardment of enemy fortifications in the Aaland Islands, allied forces secured the surrender of Bomarsund with its garrison of some 2,000 Russians.[25] By late summer new conversions rushed to the Baltic raised Napier's number of screw liners to thirteen, supplemented by sixteen sailing ships of the line, but he still considered the allied force inadequate for an assault on the fortress of Sveaborg, guarding the approaches to Helsinki. In October the onset of winter conditions prompted the withdrawal of the allied fleet from the Baltic. After being sacked in December, Napier defended his record, arguing that he had not sought a decisive battle against "the very powerful fleet of the enemy" because if such an action had ended in defeat, "in three weeks from that time a Russian fleet, full of troops, might be on our coasts. . . . " He overlooked the fact that the enemy had no screw ships of the line, and that Russian commanders had no intention of leaving Kronstadt.[26]

After Palmerston became prime minister early in 1855, Rear Admiral Richard Saunders Dundas succeeded Napier as commander of the Baltic fleet. He reached the Gulf of Finland in early May, where a French squadron under Rear Admiral Charles Pénaud joined him in early June. The Admiralty deployed no sailing ships of the line in the northern theater in 1855, but added five newly converted blockships to the previous four, along with sixteen mortar vessels and sixteen screw gunboats. The French squadron also included ten small gunboats. On 9–10 August 1855 the allies carried out a bombardment of the harbor and fortifications of Sveaborg. Pénaud had to push a reluctant Dundas to proceed with the attack, as the British supplied most of the units for the operation (a screw-propelled fleet of two ships of the line, three frigates, one corvette, one sloop, four blockships, and all of the gunboats and mortar vessels, supplemented by nine paddle steamers) and their commander feared casualties from shore batteries such as those inflicted by the Russians at Sevastopol. His concerns were unfounded. The bombardment destroyed six ships of the line and seventeen smaller Russian warships, inflicting some 2,000 casualties. Allied casualties included one killed and fifteen wounded, and just one British sloop sustained damages. To this day historians disagree over the extent of damage actually done to Russian installations on land. Dundas sent home the mortar vessels in late August, calling them an embarrassment to the fleet, but the screw gunboats were considered a great success. Against Sveaborg – as against Kinburn in the Black Sea, two months later – most of the damage was done by heavy shot from smaller craft, which themselves made small targets for enemy guns. Larger warships attempting the same bombardment surely would have suffered heavy damage, as they had at Sevastopol the previous October. Along with an additional three armored floating batteries of the type deployed at Kinburn, the British navy ordered 200 screw gunboats and 100 mortar vessels for the 1856 Baltic campaign, which was to include an assault on Kronstadt, followed by an attempt to take St Petersburg. During 1855 the Russians completed the conversion to screw of two ships of the line, the *Orel* and the *Vyborg*, and added twenty-three screw gunboats to the fleet at Kronstadt, manning the latter in part by deactivating almost all of their sailing ships of the line. On 2 September 1855 the *Vyborg* attempted to leave Kronstadt harbor but returned to port after being challenged by the British screw liner *Colossus*. Otherwise, as in 1854, the Russian Baltic fleet attempted no sorties against the allied fleet. In 1855 the allied fleets remained on station longer than the previous autumn, withdrawing during November just before the onset of icing. Peace would be concluded before the spring thaw.[27]

In addition to the Baltic and the Black Sea, the British sent warships into the White Sea during the war, to blockade the port of Archangel. The Crimean War also included a limited Pacific dimension. In 1854 Russia's Pacific squadron, under Rear Admiral E. V. Putiatin, included three frigates and four smaller warships based on the Kamchatka peninsula at Petropavlovsk, as the site of Vladivostok was still in Chinese hands until 1860. In August 1854 an Anglo-French force including three sail and one steam frigate, one corvette and one armed transport attacked Petropavlovsk but was repulsed, suffering 200 casualties among the 700 men landed ashore. The ill-fated operation got off to a bad start when the British commander, Rear Admiral David Price, suffered a nervous breakdown and committed suicide the day before the landings. The British ships spent the winter of 1854–55 in Vancouver and the French in San Francisco, before joining forces for another attack on Petropavlovsk in the spring of 1855. On that occasion they found the place abandoned, its fortifications destroyed, with no sign of the Russian squadron. The allies then recrossed the Pacific to Sitka, Alaska, rumored to be under development as a new Pacific base for the Russian navy. Upon arrival there they again found no Russian forces, and the war ended with no further action in the Pacific.[28]

By the autumn of 1855 the Russian Baltic fleet included two screw ships of the line and at least two dozen heavily armed screw gunboats. The fortifications at Kronstadt and along the coast of the Gulf of Finland were far more formidable than those of the Black Sea coast, and the success of the planned allied attack on Kronstadt and St Petersburg was by no means guaranteed, even if it had included armored floating batteries.[29] Yet the prospect of such an assault, along with the possibility that Austria and even Sweden might join the allied coalition, finally forced Alexander II, Russia's new tsar, to sue for peace. Napoleon III hosted the postwar Congress of Paris, which convened on 25 February. An immediate armistice brought a halt to the allied Baltic plans for 1856. Under the Treaty of Paris (30 March 1856) Russia lost no territory other than a small strip of land along the north bank of the Danube River at its mouth, which became part of Turkish Moldavia, but could have neither fortifications nor a fleet in the Black Sea, where Russian naval forces were limited to "six warships of no more than 800 tons and four of no more than 200 tons," precluding anything more than a coast guard. Meanwhile, in the Baltic, Russia was prohibited from having fortifications in the Aaland Islands. Under the terms of the treaty the screw ships of the line Sinop and Tsesarevich, under construction in Nicolaiev at war's end, were removed from the Black Sea to the Baltic as soon as they were launched and fit to sail. The leaky fir-hulled ships survived a stormy passage during the winter of 1858–59, after which they were repaired and fitted with engines at Kronstadt.[30]

The Crimean War was the first conflict among major European powers in which modern industrial technology proved decisive. The war exposed Russian backwardness on land and at sea. Having so few railroads, and none at all south of Moscow, Russia could not keep its coastal strongholds supplied as well as the allies, using steamships, could sustain the forces blockading and assaulting them. In addition to the debut of armored floating batteries, the Crimean War vindicated the concept of the screw gunboat, an inexpensive design that could be built very quickly. By 1859 Britain had 161 screw gunboats, most displacing under 240 tons, carrying two to four heavy guns. Other countries investing heavily in the new type included Prussia, which laid down twenty-three between 1859 and 1861; Austria, which laid down twenty-two between 1857 and 1860; and the United States, which began a screw gunboat program in 1861, after the onset of the American Civil War. Although they were not designed for overseas duty, eventually screw gunboats were employed extensively in colonial operations and "gunboat diplomacy."[31]

Technological backwardness helped make the Crimean War a humiliating experience for the Russian navy, but in two areas – mines and submarine warfare – Russia emerged as a leader in technology. Jacobi mines sank no allied ships, yet the presence of mines caused concern for allied commanders and affected their decisions. In its quest to build an undersea blockade breaker, the Russian navy hired the former Bavarian artilleryman Wilhelm Bauer, inventor in 1850 of the *Brandtaucher*, a 26-foot manually powered submarine designed for use against the Danish blockade of Kiel during the war over Schleswig–Holstein. That conflict ended before the submarine was ready for action, and in any event it sank in February 1851 on a trial run in Kiel harbor. Nevertheless, Bauer's concept appeared sound and in St Petersburg he built a much larger (56-foot) version of the *Brandtaucher*, known to history by the French name *Le Diable Marin*. Bauer's "sea devil" made over 130 dives in trials conducted after its completion in 1856, too late to be used in the war. The submarine was lost when it ran aground after Bauer tried to pass under a Russian ship of the line at anchor. Russian naval and engineering officers likewise experimented with submarine designs during and after the Crimean War. During the same years several primitive submarines were built in other countries, and there remain many competing claims to undersea breakthroughs and accomplishments. Even Spain had a submarine pioneer, Narcisso Monturiol, who built the steam-powered submarine *Ictineo* at Barcelona in 1859–60.[32]

The late 1850s

The Anglo-French rivalry resumed shortly after the Crimean War, but its revival did not prevent the two powers from cooperating against China in the Second Opium War (1856–60). Also known as the *Arrow* War, the conflict stemmed from China's seizure in October 1856 of the British-flagged coastal trader *Arrow*, a 130-ton former pirate boat built in China and manned by a Chinese crew. By the time the incident occurred the Taiping rebellion already had caused extensive turmoil within China and endangered foreign trading interests; when Britain chose to use it as a pretext to intervene, France lent its support. In the first major action of the conflict, Rear Admiral Sir Michael Seymour bombarded Canton in November 1856, with a British squadron including the sailing ship of the line *Calcutta*, a sailing frigate, three screw sloops, and two paddle steamers. But Seymour lacked the troops to follow up, a problem which worsened the following year with the outbreak of the Indian Mutiny. For most of 1857 Britain could get neither British nor Indian troops out of India and even had to send part of the Hong Kong garrison to reinforce Calcutta. In July 1857 Admiral Rigault de Genouilly arrived with a squadron including the sailing frigate *Némésis*, one sailing and three screw corvettes, and seven smaller steamers. That December a joint Anglo-French force pushed up the Pearl River to Canton, which fell the following month. Shifting their focus to the north, the allies anchored off Taku at the mouth of the Peiho, a river leading inland to Beijing. While their larger warships stood far offshore, in May 1858 the allies used shallow-draught paddle steamers and screw gunboats to assault the Taku forts. After taking the forts they pushed up the river to Tientsin, where allied plenipotentiaries negotiated a treaty (26 June 1858) which the Chinese soon abrogated. In April 1859 Rear Admiral James Hope succeeded Seymour, and for the war in the inshore waters Britain deployed more screw gunboats. Hope soon saw sobering evidence of the weakness of these vessels, during a second attack on the Taku forts in June. This time well-prepared Chinese batteries drove back the allied assault, sinking three British gunboats and killing over 400 allied troops. Thereafter the Anglo-French army in China was reinforced to a strength of 30,000, and in August 1860 Taku was attacked a third time. After the forts were taken, the allies proceeded up the Peiho to Beijing, where they sacked and burned the Summer Palace. The terms of the Treaty of Tientsin were reinstated, including the opening of more ports to foreign commerce, the opening of the interior of China to foreign merchants and missionaries, and the legalization of the opium trade. Russia and the United States participated in a postwar peace conference even though they were not formally involved in the war. The Russian plenipotentiary, Rear Admiral Putiatin of the Pacific squadron, secured from the Chinese the province of Amur, including the site of the future port and naval base of Vladivostok.[33]

Long before the end of the war in China, French fascination with the armored warship had touched off a new Anglo-French naval race. Regardless of whether the armored floating batteries were central or peripheral to the allied victory at Kinburn, after October 1855 mainstream French naval opinion considered the ironclad battleship the capital ship of the future. As early as November 1854 Napoleon III proposed to his navy minister the armoring of ships of the line; thereafter the French navy continued work on new screw liners already under construction and converted more sailing ships of the line to steam, but ordered no new ships of the type after 1855.[34] At the same time that France appeared poised to embrace the ironclad warship, the Treaty of Paris of 1856 outlawed privateering and thus compromised the *guerre de course* that had been central to French naval strategy (in particular, for a war against Britain) since the end of the Napoleonic era. In the late 1850s French naval thinkers once again emphasized fleet operations. Vice Admiral Louis Bouët-Willaumez's *Batailles de terre et de mer* (1855) included tactical concepts for screw-propelled warships which were incorporated into French naval doctrine in 1857. In that year and in 1858, the French navy simulated battle maneuvers under steam alone. But no strategy, tactic, or technology would enable France to overcome Britain's naval superiority. As with the steamship and heavy artillery, in the upcoming ironclad race Britain's sheer industrial might would enable its naval leaders to react rather than take the lead, yet still remain comfortably ahead in the long run. Meanwhile, in the long-neglected area of tactics, Bouët-Willaumez was matched by the somewhat more popular writings of Sir Howard Douglas, author of *Naval Warfare Under Steam* (1858). Douglas, a British general, was one of many authors to conclude that because the age of steam allowed a commander greater control over his forces, in the future the basic principles of land warfare would be more applicable to naval warfare. Such publications signaled the onset of a conceptual "militarization" of naval warfare, but the belief that future naval combat would imitate the relative "order" of a battlefield was far from unanimous. Indeed, Bouët-Willaumez and most French thinkers emphasized the flexibility steam provided to the individual ship commander, and envisioned the future naval battle as a mêlée in which *élan* would be decisive.[35]

Britain's 121-gun, 6,960-ton, three-decker *Victoria*, launched in 1859, was the largest and, at just over £150,000, also the most expensive screw ship of the line ever built. By 1861 Britain had completed seventeen new screw liners and converted another forty-one, plus the nine blockships, to screw steamers. Of another nine screw ships of the line laid down in 1859 and 1860, two were cancelled and the remaining seven eventually completed as ironclads. By 1861 France had completed nine new screw ships of the line and converted twenty-eight to screw. The leading naval powers would have ordered more new ships and fewer conversions if not for a shortage of seasoned timber, which became acute by the end of the Crimean War, and a reluctance to build ships out of green wood, the practice which shortened the lives of many vessels constructed during the Napoleonic era. Among the other naval powers, Russia completed the last of four purpose-built screw ships of the line in 1860, and converted another five. The Turkish navy completed two new wooden screw battleships and two conversions. Sweden completed one new screw ship of the line and one conversion, and Austria, one of new construction. Denmark and Naples each had one conversion. The Turkish, Swedish, Danish, and Austrian screw liner projects all involved British machinery or technical support, in the former case to enhance the naval capability of an ally, and for the others, offered within the framework of British wartime efforts to recruit neutral countries for the anti-Russian alliance. British manufacturers also provided engines for three French ships of the line. Ironically, Russia's largest screw ship of the line, the 5,585-ton, 135-gun, three-decker *Sinop*, likewise had British engines, imported after the war from Maudslay. During the Crimean War, the Spanish navy commissioned the 86-gun ships of the line *Reina Isabel II* (launched at Cadiz, 1853) and *Rey Francisco de Asis* (at Ferrol, 1854), the first of the type completed in Spain since 1797. Plans to give them engines were never carried out, leaving the Spanish fleet with the last two sailing ships of the line ever built but no screw liners.[36]

The four Turkish screw ships of the line were the cornerstone of a postwar Ottoman naval revival undertaken with British support. All received their engines in British shipyards, which also converted three Turkish sailing frigates to screw. Between 1858 and 1860, British shipyards also built six screw corvettes for the Ottoman navy, and between 1858 and 1865, another eight screw corvettes were built in Turkish shipyards with imported British machinery.[37] The naval build-up proceeded despite the fact that the elimination of the Russian Black Sea fleet left little need for a strong Ottoman navy; the lack of a clear reason to maintain a powerful fleet likewise would not deter the Turks from acquiring expensive ironclad warships in the 1860s.

Russia's postwar naval revival, confined by treaty to the Baltic, likewise included a heavy investment in wooden screw steamers soon to be rendered obsolete by the ironclad revolution. Under the supervision of Tsar Alexander II's brother Grand Duke Constantine reforms in naval training and education accompanied the program of screw steamers, which as early as 1858 included six ships of the line, five frigates and seventeen corvettes or "clippers" in commission, along with a large flotilla of screw gunboats. The last of the nine screw liners was not completed until 1862.[38] Even though these battleships were considered an important part of the new fleet, Constantine recognized the futility of building too many of them, as they would only be blockaded in the Gulf of Finland in the event of war. Postwar Russian strategy called for the frigates and the even greater number of corvettes or "clippers" to break out of port in the event of war and engage in a worldwide campaign of cruiser warfare against enemy (presumably British) commerce. Several of these smaller screw warships formed a new Russian Pacific squadron, based at Petropavlovsk until work began on the new port of Vladivostok in 1860.[39] Thus, Russian strategists embraced the *guerre de course* at the same time that the French were abandoning it, despite the fact that, after 1856, international law placed unprecedented restrictions on such campaigns. Decades would pass before the Russian navy again invested heavily in capital ships.[40]

The United States was the greatest naval power never to have a screw ship of the line, a reflection of the US navy's earlier conclusion that cruising duties were best handled by frigates and sloops. Having already defined the role of its handful of sailing ships of the line as one of harbor defense and blockade breaking, the US navy was perhaps best positioned to reconceptualize the capital ship as an ironclad. An abortive step in that direction came in 1842, when Congress first funded the armored "Stevens Battery," eleven years before Sinope and Napoleon III's conversion to the ironclad cause. Yet this warship, intended for the defense of New York harbor, was never completed and no similar warship was laid down for another American port. In 1852 artillerist John Dahlgren, keenly aware of the power of the newest heavy guns, proposed the armoring of warships, but nothing came of it.[41]

Instead, in the mid-1850s the US navy decided to make large heavily armed screw frigates the core of its fleet. After the onset of the Crimean War had accelerated the transition to screw propulsion by the world's leading navies, Congress authorized a program of six such vessels in April 1854, all of which were laid down immediately. The 4,635-ton *Merrimack* was the smallest of the six half-sisters and the first to be completed; it was commissioned in the winter of 1855–56 and crossed the Atlantic for a visit to Britain in the autumn of 1856. The 5,540-ton *Niagara*, commissioned in 1857, was the largest of the six and technically a giant sloop, having no guns on its spar deck until a refit in 1862–63 made it a true frigate. The *Wabash*, the *Roanoke*, the *Minnesota*, and the *Colorado* rounded out the group; all were in service by March 1858. A seventh screw frigate, the *Franklin*, received funding as a "reconstruction" of a sailing ship of the line of the same name; it languished on the stocks for thirteen years after being laid down in 1854. Following the authorization of the frigates, Congress sanctioned a large program of screw sloops. During 1858 sixteen were laid down, ranging in size from the 1,230-ton *Seminole* to the 3,290-ton *Lancaster*; eleven of the ships were completed before the onset of the American Civil War, the rest by March 1862. The navy had only one screw gunboat before 1861, the converted merchantman *Pocahontas*, but this 690-ton vessel would be used as a prototype for a large class of warships laid down shortly after the war began.[42]

As ships designed for cruising duties but also to engage enemy ships of the line, the American screw frigates attracted attention in Europe even before the *Merrimack*'s visit of 1856. All six had a greater length and displacement than a standard two-decker; the *Niagara*, at 328 feet, was almost 100 feet longer than the screw ships of the line *Napoléon* and *Agamemnon*. One advantage of great length, of course, was the capacity for a longer broadside on the spar and the gun deck than a typical frigate, but the ships initially were armed with a smaller number of very heavy guns; the *Niagara*, the most extreme case, carried just twelve 11-inch Dahlgrens from 1857 until receiving a standard frigate armament five years later. The concept of a fast battleship–cruiser hybrid with a homogeneous armament of a lesser number of heavier guns may have been visionary, indeed foreshadowing Sir John Fisher's battle cruiser of a half-century later, but as of the mid-1850s the technology did not exist to make the concept truly practicable. There were limits to how fast American-built engines, though respectable by the standards of the time, could move such large ships: the *Niagara*, at 11 knots the fastest of the lot, was slower under steam than most purpose-built screw ships of the line. A wooden ship of such length may have been acceptable as a cargo clipper (the *Niagara*, in fact, was designed by clipper-shipbuilder George Steers) but lacked the structural strength essential to a warship. Furthermore, at a time when the maximum accurate range of smooth-bore shellfire was 1,200 yards, and of solid shot, 2,000 yards, it still made more sense to mount a greater number of smaller guns, for the only way to destroy an enemy frigate or ship of the line was to close in the old-fashioned way and match broadside against broadside.[43]

Nevertheless, Britain and France quickly matched the *Merrimack* and its half-sisters with frigate programs of their own. Surveyor of the Navy Baldwin

Walker laid down six "response" frigates after June 1856, ranging in size from the 3,680-ton *Doris* to the 5,640-ton *Mersey* and *Orlando*. The latter pair would have been more than a match for any of the American frigates, being not only larger but, at 13 knots, faster, and armed with a mixture of twenty-eight 10-inch guns and twelve 68-pounders. France, meanwhile, launched a homogeneous class of six 3,765-ton frigates in 1856–57, each equipped with a conventional armament of fifty-six guns. They were the largest wooden screw frigates ever built by the French, but were considerably weaker than their British and American counterparts.[44]

Conclusion

The big frigate programs of the middle and late 1850s appear to have been a waste of money if one considers that the ships produced were too small for the line of battle and larger than necessary for overseas cruising. Nevertheless, at least one historian views them as an important stage in the evolution of the capital ship, drawing a direct line from the large American screw frigates to their ultimate response, the British *Mersey* and *Orlando*, and on to the *Warrior*, which was an armored version of the long wooden screw frigate, only of more stable iron construction.[45] The wooden ship of the line, evolving since the early-modern period, continued to rule the waves during the 1850s, but the screw propeller had given it only a temporary new lease on life. With the onset of the ironclad revolution, the frigate, in armored form, became the new standard capital ship.

Notes

1 Lambert, *Battleships in Transition*, 99, 140; idem, "The Screw Propeller Warship," 37–40.
2 Lambert, *Battleships in Transition*, 122–47; idem, "The Screw Propeller Warship," 40–1.
3 Lambert, "Introduction of Steam," 27–8.
4 Karl Gogg, *Österreichs Kriegsmarine, 1848–1918* (Salzburg, 1967), 28–33.
5 Sondhaus, *Preparing for Weltpolitik*, 43, 45, 55.
6 Radogna, *Storia della Marina Militare*, 133–40; Lodovico Bianchini, *Della storia delle finanze del regno di Napoli* (Naples, 1859), 504.
7 Canney, *The Old Steam Navy*, 1: 15, 33, 40–1; http://www.uss-salem.org/danfs/line; http://www.uss-salem.org/danfs/frigates; see also Peter Booth Wiley, *Yankees in the Land of the Gods: Commodore Perry and the Opening of Japan* (New York, 1991).
8 Lambert, *The Crimean War*, 3, 9–22; idem, *The Last Sailing Battlefleet*, 8.
9 Gromov *et al.*, *Tri Veka Rossiiskogo Flota*, 1: 190; Langensiepen and Güleryüz, *The Ottoman Steam Navy*, 2, 4.
10 Watts, *The Imperial Russian Navy*, 12–13; Gromov *et al.*, *Tri Veka Rossiiskogo Flota*, 1: 191–2; Woodward, *The Russians at Sea*, 99; Langensiepen and Güleryüz, *The Ottoman Steam Navy*, 4, 193.
11 Lambert, *The Crimean War*, 60; idem, "Iron Hulls and Armour Plate," 52; idem, *Battleships in Transition*, 92.
12 Watts, *The Imperial Russian Navy*, 13.

13 Gromov *et al.*, *Tri Veka Rossiiskogo Flota*, 1: 192; Bonner-Smith and Dewar, eds, *Russian War, 1854*, 206–7; Woodward, *The Russians at Sea*, 100.

14 Woodward, *The Russians at Sea*, 102.

15 Watts, *The Imperial Russian Navy*, 13.

16 Ibid., 13; Gromov *et al.*, *Tri Veka Rossiiskogo Flota*, 1: 192; Woodward, *The Russians at Sea*, 101; Lambert, "Introduction of Steam," 23; idem, *Battleships in Transition*, 95; idem, *The Crimean War*, 102–3.

17 Lambert, *The Crimean War*, 105–6, 130; Watts, *The Imperial Russian Navy*, 13; Woodward, *The Russians at Sea*, 102; Gromov *et al.*, *Tri Veka Rossiiskogo Flota*, 1: 192; Clarke, *Russia's Sea-Power*, 89–90; Bonner-Smith and Dewar, eds, *Russian War, 1854*, 219–20.

18 Bonner-Smith and Dewar, eds, *Russian War, 1854*, 210–27, and *passim*; Lambert, *The Last Sailing Battlefleet*, 105; idem, *Battleships in Transition*, 95–6; idem, *The Crimean War*, 135–40, 146; Watts, *The Imperial Russian Navy*, 13.

19 Bonner-Smith and Dewar, eds, *Russian War, 1854*, 227–8; A. C. Dewar, ed., *Russian War, 1855, Black Sea: Official Correspondence* (London, 1945), 3, 6–8.

20 Cf. Lambert, *The Crimean War*, 230–4; Watts, *The Imperial Russian Navy*, 13; Woodward, *The Russians at Sea*, 109.

21 Gromov *et al.*, *Tri Veka Rossiiskogo Flota*, 1: 195–6; Lambert, *The Crimean War*, 246–8; Watts, *The Imperial Russian Navy*, 13; Woodward, *The Russians at Sea*, 103; Lyons to Secretary of the Admiralty Thomas Phinn, *Royal Albert*, 10 September 1855, in Dewar, ed., *Russian War, 1855, Black Sea*, 291.

22 Lyons quoted in Lambert, *The Crimean War*, 260; Lambert considers the performance of the batteries to have been "much exaggerated." See also Lambert, "Iron Hulls and Armour Plate," 52; Baxter, *Introduction of the Ironclad Warship*, 78–86; Watts, *The Imperial Russian Navy*, 13; Lyons to Secretary of the Admiralty Thomas Phinn, *Royal Albert*, 18 October 1855, in Dewar, ed., *Russian War, 1855, Black Sea*, 346–7.

23 Sondhaus, *The Habsburg Empire and the Sea*, 183–4; Lambert, *The Crimean War*, 218, 296–8.

24 Woodward, *The Russians at Sea*, 103–4; Lambert, *Battleships in Transition*, 41; Campbell, "Naval Armaments and Armour," 167; Clarke, *Russia's Sea-Power*, 93; Bonner-Smith and Dewar, eds, *Russian War, 1854*, 3–5.

25 Captain Astley Cooper Key to Napier, HMS *Amphion*, 18 May 1854, text in Bonner-Smith and Dewar, eds, *Russian War, 1854*, 56–7; see also ibid., 11–12.

26 Napier to W. A. B. Hamilton, Secretary of the Admiralty, Merchiston, 5 January 1855, in Bonner-Smith and Dewar, eds, *Russian War, 1854*, 189–91.

27 Dundas to Secretary of the Admiralty, HMS *Duke of Wellington*, 13 August 1855, in D. Bonner-Smith, ed., *Russian War, 1855, Baltic: Official Correspondence* (London, 1944), 184; see also ibid., 8–12; Hamilton, *Anglo-French Naval Rivalry*, 77; Clarke, *Russia's Sea-Power*, 94; Watts, *The Imperial Russian Navy*, 13; Lambert, *Battleships in Transition*, 50–2, idem, "The Screw Propeller Warship," 44; Dupont and Taillemite, *Les guerres navales françaises*, 241.

28 Hamilton, *Anglo-French Naval Rivalry*, 178; Dupont and Taillemite, *Les guerres navales françaises*, 241. Several other sources have Price committing suicide after the failed attack on Petropavlovsk. See Woodward, *The Russians at Sea*, 105–6; Gromov *et al.*, *Tri Veka Rossiiskogo Flota*, 1: 199; Clarke, *Russia's Sea-Power*, 96–7; Jane, *The Imperial Russian Navy*, 147–8.

29 Lambert, "Iron Hulls and Armour Plate," 52.

30 Watts, *The Imperial Russian Navy*, 14; Lambert, *Battleships in Transition*, 144.

31 Lambert, "Introduction of Steam," 23–5; Busk, *Navies of the World*, 49–50; Gogg, *Österreichs Kriegsmarine*, 30; Sondhaus, *Preparing for Weltpolitik*, 65–6.

32 Michael Wilson, "Early Submarines," in Robert Gardiner, ed., *Steam, Steel and Shellfire: The Steam Warship 1815–1905* (London, 1992), 148–52.

33 J. Y. Wong, *Deadly Dreams: Opium, Imperialism, and the Arrow War (1856–1860) in China* (Cambridge, 1998), 99, 280, 487–9, and *passim*; Beeching, *The Chinese Opium Wars*, 246–325; Dupont and Taillemite, *Les guerres navales françaises*, 244–5.

34 Napoleon III to Théodore Ducos, Paris, 16 November 1854, text in Baxter, *Introduction of the Ironclad Warship*, 342–4; Lambert, "Iron Hulls and Armour Plate," 53.

35 Tritten, "Navy and Military Doctrine in France," 53–4; Hamilton, *Anglo-French Naval Rivalry*, 108–9, 115–16; Lambert, *Battleships in Transition*, 109.

36 Lambert, "The Screw Propeller Warship," 41, 46; idem, *Battleships in Transition*, 65, 122–47; Harbron, *Trafalgar and the Spanish Navy*, 173n.

37 Langensiepen and Güleryüz, *The Ottoman Steam Navy*, 2, and *passim*.

38 Watts, *The Imperial Russian Navy*, 14; Tomitch, *Warships of the Imperial Russian Navy*, 101; Gromov et al., *Tri Veka Rossiiskogo Flota*, 1: 211.

39 Watts, *The Imperial Russian Navy*, 14.

40 Lambert, *Battleships in Transition*, 113–14.

41 Canney, *The Old Steam Navy*, 2: 7.

42 Ibid., 1: 43–89, 168–70.

43 Lambert, *Battleships in Transition*, 114; idem, "The Screw Propeller Warship," 42–6.

44 Lambert, *Battleships in Transition*, 92–3, 114; idem, "The Screw Propeller Warship," 43; *Conway's All the World's Fighting Ships, 1860–1905*, 45, 284.

45 Lambert, "The Screw Propeller Warship," 43.

CHAPTER FOUR

The ironclad revolution

The era of the armored warship began in January 1857, more than five years before the completion of the USS *Monitor* and the CSS *Virginia*, when Napoleon III appointed Dupuy de Lôme director of construction for the French navy. Dupuy de Lôme himself had designed the first purpose-built screw ship of the line, laid down just nine years earlier, but after the deployment of the armored floating batteries at Kinburn (October 1855) he joined other French naval leaders in the conviction that the future belonged to ironclad warships. After his appointment he began work on a design for an armored frigate, and in November 1857 the plans for the *Gloire* were completed. In March 1858 the ship was laid down at Toulon, and Napoleon III authorized construction of another five ironclads of the same type, sparking understandable consternation in Britain and a resolve to respond in kind. Two years after their Crimean War alliance ended in victory over Russia, the leading sea powers were locked in another naval race.[1]

The revolution in Europe (1858–62)

Just as Admiral Tirpitz, forty years later, believed that a strong German fleet could provide the diplomatic leverage to secure Britain's acquiescence in Germany's quest for a share of world power, Napoleon III considered a strong fleet essential to his goal of persuading the British to accept French schemes for a reorganization of Europe according to principles of nationalism. By the time the *Gloire* was laid down, France clearly had lost the race in screw ships of the line. France and Britain each had six purpose-built and twenty-one converted screw ships of the line in service, but France had only three more on the stocks and four conversions underway, while Britain had eight on the stocks and eight conversions underway. The French emperor felt the time was right to raise the competition to a new level. Dupuy de Lôme's *Gloire* was roughly the same length and breadth as a screw liner, with three masts and a barquentine rig (later replaced with a conventional full rig). Its wooden hull was plated with 4.5 inches of armor. The ship carried thirty-six 6.4-inch rifled muzzle loaders, two on the upper deck and the rest below, divided evenly between two broadsides on the lone gun deck. When the 5,630-ton ironclad was fully loaded, its gunports were barely six feet above the waterline. This feature, and bunkers capable of carrying just 700 tons of coal, reflected the fact that the ship was designed not for traditional frigate duties but for line-of-battle service in European waters. The wooden-hulled ironclad was a compromise necessitated by the weakness of French industry, which in the late 1850s produced enough iron for only one *Gloire*-sized hull per year. Of the six ironclads ordered in 1858, two were identical copies of the *Gloire*, another (the *Couronne*) had an iron hull, and the future *Magenta* and *Solferino* were unique 6,715-ton wooden-hulled two-deckers. The *Gloire* was launched in November 1859 and completed in August 1860; the other five did not enter service until 1862. Meanwhile, in November 1860 another ten armored frigates were ordered, all very similar to the *Gloire* and all but one (the *Héroïne*) with wooden hulls. The second group, all laid down during 1861, ranged in size from 5,700 to 6,120 tons, and entered service between 1865 and 1867.[2]

After the Crimean War the British navy saw no need to erase its own lead in screw ships of the line by introducing armored warships, but the Admiralty ordered experiments with armor plate at the Woolwich Arsenal. In February 1858 Baldwin Walker, father of Britain's screw battle fleet, decided to build a corvette-size ironclad as an experiment, but the French order of six armored frigates the following month prompted him to call for six British armored frigates in response. Thus Walker, who remained in office as Surveyor of the Navy until 1861, also became the father of Britain's ironclad fleet; but, unlike Dupuy de Lôme, initially he did not believe the armored frigate would replace the wooden screw ship of the line, because he considered the latest rifled guns to be more than a match for the wrought iron armor of the time. The British navy had experimented with a heavy Lancaster muzzle-loading rifle in the Crimean War, and Walker hoped that a new 7-inch Armstrong breech-loading rifle would become the next standard heavy naval gun. Attitudes changed at the Admiralty only when it became clear that the new Armstrong gun lacked the muzzle velocity to pierce armor. Meanwhile, the Admiralty decided to lay down two armored frigates, followed eventually by four more. At the same time, work continued on wooden screw ships of the line, reflecting British fears of falling behind in vessels of that type. Another twelve screw liners were laid down between 1858 and 1860, of which three were completed, two cancelled, and the rest eventually converted to ironclads; during the same years, twelve more conversions were begun. France, meanwhile, laid down no new screw ships of the line and began only three additional conversions. Britain's last new wooden screw battleship, the 91-gun *Defiance*, was launched in March 1861, one month after the French launched their last, the 90-gun *Ville de Lyon*.[3]

The design of the first British armored frigate was completed in January 1859 by Isaac Watts, assistant surveyor (chief constructor) under Walker. The ship, named *Warrior*, was laid down by the Thames Iron Works of Blackwall in May 1859, fourteen months after the *Gloire*. Like the pioneering French ironclad, it was a three-masted broadside battery frigate with 4.5 inches of armor and thirty-six guns. The similarities ended there. After initial consideration of wood, at Walker's insistence the hull was made of iron. Because Walker conceptualized the armored frigate as a large cruising frigate, an ironclad version of the *Mersey* or the *Orlando*, the *Warrior* was 125 feet longer than the *Gloire*, had bunkers holding almost 200 tons more coal, and could set twice as much canvas to the wind. Its Penn trunk engines were capable of over 14 knots, at least a knot faster than the *Gloire* and still a respectable speed almost twenty years later. The use of iron rather than wood construction, along with the weight of the armor, raised displacement to 9,140 tons, 60 percent more than the *Gloire's*. The *Warrior* was launched in December 1860 and completed in October 1861. By then, Britain had another nine iron-hulled armored frigates under construction and had begun the conversion to armored frigates of six screw ships of the line. The second British ironclad, the *Black Prince*, was a virtual copy of the *Warrior*. Thereafter the smallest British ironclads were similar in size to the largest of the French, leaving the British armored fleet superior in size and firepower if not in numbers of ships, but experimentation in design left the fleet without the relative homogeneity of its French counterpart. While the six wooden-hulled conversions all emerged with displacement between 6,000 and 7,000 tons, the ten iron-hulled frigates ranged in size from the 6,070-ton *Defence* to the 10,780-ton *Northumberland*. The latter, and its half-sisters *Minotaur* and *Agincourt*, had five masts, the 9,830-ton *Achilles* four; like the *Warrior* and the *Black Prince*, they were designed for cruising service but ultimately spent most

Plate 4.1 HMS *Warrior* (laid down May 1859, completed October 1861)
Naval Historical Center, Basic Collection

of their careers stationed in European waters as battleships. The giant *Minotaur* and the *Northumberland* were not completed until 1868; the others entered service by 1867.[4]

In April 1859 France went to war with Austria on behalf of Sardinia–Piedmont and the cause of Italian unity. The following month France sent a large fleet into the Adriatic including six screw ships of the line, which the Austrian navy did not challenge. None of the French armored frigates was completed in time to participate in the war, but the fleet included the three armored floating batteries used during the Crimean War. In July the brief war ended in an Austrian defeat; in the peace settlement Sardinia–Piedmont acquired Lombardy, and though the Austrians retained Venetia, their influence in the Italian peninsula waned considerably. From Modena to Naples, Austrian client states came under increasing pressure from Italian nationalists, and in May 1860 a makeshift fleet of paddle steamers landed Giuseppe Garibaldi's army of "Red Shirts" in Sicily. The *de facto* birth of the Italian navy followed in September 1860 with the wholesale desertion of the Neapolitan fleet, which placed itself under the authority of Admiral Count Carlo Pellion di Persano, commander of Sardinian naval forces off Naples. By the first weeks of 1861 Sardinian troops had advanced down the peninsula to meet Garibaldi's forces moving up from the south. Meanwhile, Persano's expanded squadron blockaded and shelled the citadel at Gaeta, the last outpost held by royal Neapolitan forces, which surrendered in February 1861. The following month Victor Emmanuel II of Sardinia–Piedmont was proclaimed king of Italy, monarch of a country that still lacked Rome and Venetia. Italy was in the ironclad race at the time of its unification, as the Sardinian government had ordered two 2,700-ton corvettes (laid down in June and December 1860) from the La Seyne shipyard in France. In December 1860 Austria responded with two 2,800-ton armored frigates of its own, laid down by the Cantiere Navale Adriatico in Trieste. In August 1861, the American Civil War notwithstanding, Italy contracted William Webb of New York to build two 5,700-ton armored frigates; two months later, Austria countered with three 3,600-ton armored frigates, ordered in Trieste. Aside from the two French-built Italian ironclads, all the ships laid down in the Adriatic naval race had wooden rather than iron hulls.[5]

During 1861 Spain and Russia became the fifth and sixth countries to order armored warships. The Spanish navy laid down two armored frigates, the 7,190-ton iron-hulled *Numancia* at La Seyne and the 6,200-ton wooden-hulled *Tetuán* in the Spanish navy yard at Ferrol. Both were launched in 1863. Meanwhile Russia contracted the Thames Iron Works to build an armored frigate with a ram bow, the 3,280-ton *Pervenetz*, and two wooden screw frigates converted to ironclads in Russian shipyards eventually emerged as the 6,130-ton *Sevastopol* and 6,040-ton *Petropavlovsk*. The *Pervenetz* arrived in Kronstadt in August 1863; the conversions entered service in 1865 and 1867.[6]

Thus, by March 1862, when the news of the Battle of Hampton Roads reached Europe, six European navies already had a total of forty-six armored broadside battery warships built or building. Britain had two completed and fourteen under construction. France had four completed and twelve under construction, supplemented by another seven small armored batteries of 1,400–1,500 tons. Austria had five ironclads, Italy four, Russia three, and Spain two, all still under construction except the Italian *Terribile*, commissioned in September 1861. The *Monitor* and the *Virginia* did not start the ironclad revolution, but their battle, and other American ironclad actions, silenced European critics of armored warships and changed the terms of the debate. Thereafter the question would be not whether to build ironclads, but what type of ironclad to build.

The American Civil War (1861–65)

In November 1860 anti-slavery candidate Abraham Lincoln won the US presidential election, prompting the southern slave states to secede from the Union, starting with South Carolina in December. In February 1861 the rebels formed the Confederate States of America, and on 12 April their shore batteries at Charleston, South Carolina, fired the first shots of the Civil War against Fort Sumter, the island fortress guarding the harbor. While the loyal north had the majority of the US population and industry, the Confederacy held most of the coastline and navigable rivers. But just 30 percent of the navy's officers were southerners and, unlike their counterparts in the army, the majority of them remained loyal to the Union. The navy list included ninety warships, among them six screw frigates and fourteen screw sloops, and another four screw sloops were nearing completion. In 1861 only Britain had a larger merchant marine than the United States, and over 90 percent of American mercantile tonnage was owned by proprietors from the northern states, including scores of merchant steamers suitable for conversion to warships.[7]

The Union navy focused first on establishing a blockade of the 3,500 miles of southern coastline, using screw sloops and armed merchant steamers, eventually supplemented by thirty-five screw gunboats and forty-seven so-called "double-ended" paddle steamers laid down between 1861 and 1864.[8] Initially there was no rush to order ironclads. Meanwhile, the Confederacy planned to break the Union blockade with ironclads and fast unarmored blockade runners. In May 1861 the Confederate congress appropriated $2 million to purchase armored warships in Europe, and that summer a former Mississippi River towboat was converted at New Orleans into the ironclad *Manassas*, featuring a ram bow and a thin "turtle-back" shell housing one gun. On 12 October 1861 the *Manassas* became the world's first armored warship to engage in combat, when it attacked and rammed (but failed to sink) the screw sloop USS *Richmond* near the mouth of the Mississippi. By then the Confederate government had laid down five ironclads in southern shipyards and began building a sixth ironclad on the hull of the former USS *Merrimack*, the remains of which were captured by rebels when Virginia joined the Confederacy in April 1861. The *Merrimack* had been burned to the waterline in the Union evacuation of Norfolk but its machinery remained intact. Over the winter of 1861–62 work progressed on the six ironclads, but the shortcomings of southern industry left those built from the keel up lagging behind the *Merrimack*, which emerged in February 1862 as the CSS *Virginia*.[9]

Meanwhile, in July 1861 the Union navy ordered seven mastless river ironclads, the so-called "city class" gunboats, followed in September by three ironclads suitable for coastal or high seas service: the 4,510-ton frigate *New Ironsides* and the 950-ton sloop *Galena*, both conventional battery warships, and the 990-ton *Monitor*. The latter was essentially an armor-plated raft, mastless, with two heavy guns in a revolving turret plated with 8-inch wrought iron. It was designed by John Ericsson and built by the Continental Iron Works of New York. All three ships were laid down in October 1861 and completed in a remarkably short time; the *Monitor* was commissioned in February 1862, one month after the seven river ironclads.[10] On 4 March the *Monitor* left New York under tow, and four days later joined the Union naval forces in Hampton Roads. Hours before it arrived, the *Virginia* completed its first sortie against the Union blockade of Norfolk, a force led by the screw frigates *Minnesota* and *Roanoke* (half-sisters of the original *Merrimack*), the sailing frigates *St Lawrence* and *Congress*, and the sloop *Cumberland*. The *Virginia* first rammed and sank the *Cumberland*, then used gunfire to destroy the *Congress*. The wounding of rebel Captain Franklin Buchanan, a falling tide, and approaching darkness prompted the *Virginia* to withdraw. When it returned on 9 March, its temporary commander Lieutenant Catesby Jones found the *Monitor* guarding the remaining Union wooden ships. The *Monitor* steamed out to intercept the *Virginia*, and the first battle between ironclads was underway.[11]

The *Virginia*, which fully loaded displaced 3,500 tons, had no masts and carried its ten heavy guns in a casemate amidships, a wooden structure with angled sides plated with 4-inch armor. It rode so low in the water that the deck fore and aft of the casemate was awash. Its ordnance included six 9-inch smoothbore Dahlgrens (part of the old *Merrimack*'s armament) and four muzzle-loading rifles (two 7-inch and two 6.4-inch) designed by Confederate artillerist John Brooke. The 7-inch rifles were mounted as pivot guns fore and aft on the centerline, each being able to fire end-on or to either side through portals in the casemate. The remaining eight guns were mounted four to each broadside. The *Monitor* carried two 11-inch smoothbore Dahlgrens but could fire only one gun at a time, at a rate of one shot every seven or eight minutes. The steam-powered turret could complete a revolution in just under thirty seconds, compensating for the vessel's lack of maneuverability owing to its slow 6-knot speed. The *Virginia* was capable of 7.5 knots but its draught of twenty-two feet, more than double that of the *Monitor*, limited its scope of operations in the waters of Hampton Roads. During the four-hour engagement the two ironclads exchanged shots at a range of less than 100 yards, yet neither inflicted serious damage on the other. Late in the battle the *Virginia* fired a shell which struck the

Plate 4.2 CSS *Virginia* and USS *Monitor*, Battle of Hampton Roads (9 March 1862)
Naval Historical Center, Basic Collection

Monitor's pilothouse, gravely wounding and blinding its commander Lieutenant
John Worden. The *Monitor* then withdrew; with the tide falling, the *Virginia*
likewise withdrew. The only casualty aboard either vessel was Worden, who
survived and even recovered his eyesight.[12] Each side was pleased with the performance of its own ship. Ericsson's "monitor" became the ironclad type of
choice for the Union navy, while all Confederate ironclads were smaller versions
of the *Virginia*.

The *Monitor* overshadowed the other two seagoing Union ironclads laid down
in October 1861. The *New Ironsides* was completed in just ten months, a remarkable feat for a ship of its size. Plated with 4.5-inch armor and armed with
fourteen 11-inch Dahlgrens and two 150-pounders, it was the equal of the
European armored frigates of the era except in speed, which at 6.5 knots
was half that of its peers. Sent to bolster the Union blockade of Charleston,
in October 1863 it fell victim to the first torpedo boat attack in naval history, launched by the Confederate semi-submersible *David*, which detonated a
spar torpedo against its hull. The damage was minimal, however, and the ship
remained on station for another eight months before steaming to Philadelphia
for repairs. The *New Ironsides* later proved useful in the capture of Wilmington,
North Carolina, the last open Confederate port, in January 1865.[13] The *Galena*

was far less successful. After being commissioned in April 1862, the armored sloop joined the *Monitor* in Hampton Roads but was never tested in battle against the *Virginia*, which the Confederates scuttled in May when Union forces took Norfolk. Later in May an artillery duel with enemy batteries along the James River exposed the *Galena's* weakness. Thirteen shots penetrated its 2-inch plating, leaving twenty-four of the crew dead or wounded. Considered a failure, the *Galena* was stripped of its armor in 1863 and recommissioned as a wooden screw sloop.[14]

Late in 1862 the *Monitor* was reassigned to the blockade of Charleston. Under tow en route to its new station, it sank off Cape Hatteras on the night of 30–31 December 1862, with the loss of sixteen men. The incident underscored the obvious weakness of the "monitor" type: its low freeboard left the deck awash on the high seas and the ship in constant danger of sinking. Nevertheless, the Union navy continued with a large program of monitors begun in October 1862, and laid down its first double-turret monitor in March 1863. Ultimately another forty-one single-turret monitors begun during the war were completed by 1866, along with nine double-turret monitors, all of which were in service by the end of 1865. The war's only triple-turret monitor was the former screw frigate *Roanoke*, reconstructed between April 1862 and June 1863. After its conversion it displaced 4,395 tons and carried six heavy guns, including two 15-inch Dahlgrens. The ship was formidable enough to inspire the British navy's leading turret-ship advocate, Captain Cowper Coles, to write a letter to *The Times* of London contending that a multiple-turret ship with 15-inch guns was superior to the *Warrior* and other ironclads of the broadside battery design. The *Roanoke* had a higher freeboard than conventional monitors but rolled so badly that its guns could not have been trained on a target on the high seas. It made only two sea voyages in its career, from New York to Hampton Roads in the summer of 1863 and back to New York in April 1865 to be decommissioned. In the interim, it served as station flagship in a secure harbor. Other than the *Roanoke*, the only Civil War monitors designed for high seas duty were the 4,440-ton *Dictator*, carrying two 15-inch Dahlgrens in a single turret, and the unfinished *Puritan*, a slightly larger version of the *Dictator* slated to carry two 20-inch Dahlgrens. The *Dictator* was commissioned in November 1864 but engine problems kept it out of action, and, like the *Roanoke*, it never fired a shot in anger. Of the fifty-two monitors of all types completed for the US navy between 1862 and 1866, all except the *Dictator* and the double-turret *Onondaga* had wooden hulls, and most would not last long into the postwar years.[15]

Other than the *New Ironsides*, the *Galena*, and the monitors, the only Union ironclad to see coastal action in the Civil War was the 840-ton *Keokuk*, commissioned in February 1863. It looked like a small double-turret monitor but had stationary gunhouses (each with a single pivoting 11-inch Dahlgren) rather than revolving turrets. Its iron hull was plated with a weak iron-and-oak armor (a novelty at the time, foreshadowing the "sandwich" armor of the 1870s) and, like the armored sloop *Galena*, it was riddled with enemy fire in its first action.

On 7 April the *Keokuk* joined the *New Ironsides* and seven monitors in the largest ironclad operation to date, an attack on Charleston. Fire from rebel shore batteries warded off the Union assault, causing little serious damage to the other ironclads but destroying the *Keokuk*.[16] Charleston remained a focal point of Union naval activity throughout the war but was occupied only after being abandoned by the Confederacy in February 1865. Significant rebel actions against the blockade there included the *David*'s unsuccessful attack on the *New Ironsides* in October 1862, followed in February 1864 by the Confederate submarine *H. L. Hunley*'s successful attack on the screw sloop *Housatonic*. Powered by a hand-cranked propeller, the *Hunley* sank its target – the first ship ever sunk by a spar torpedo – but itself sank as a consequence of the attack, drowning all aboard.[17]

For river service, the Union navy converted dozens of side- and stern-wheel steamers into "timberclads," protected by thick wooden planking, or "tinclads," plated with thin iron armor. The most successful was the 1,000-ton stern-wheeler *Essex*, a tinclad with 0.75-inch side armor. The double-hulled *Benton*, fitted with casemate armor 2.5 inches thick, was the only river boat conversion of 1861 to emerge as a true ironclad. It was rebuilt by James Eads of St Louis, famous engineer and bridge-builder, whose seven "city class" river ironclads were completed during the same month, January 1862. Like the *Benton*, the "city class" featured a protected centerline paddle wheel, a displacement of around 1,000 tons, speed of 5.5 knots, and 2.5 inches of casemate armor. The *Benton* carried sixteen guns in its casemate, the "city class" ironclads thirteen. The eight ironclads first saw action on the Cumberland and Tennessee rivers in February 1862. Over the next two years they were joined by another eight river ironclads, all with side-paddles. The Union navy's fleet of monitors included five single-turret and four double-turret vessels constructed for river service. Two of the single-turret monitors had stern paddle wheels rather than screw propellers.[18] The Union navy assigned one ironclad, the monitor *Camanche*, to the Pacific coast, prompted by fears that Confederate raiders would attack the weakly defended California ports. The *Camanche* was built in 1862–63 in Jersey City, then disassembled and shipped around Cape Horn to San Francisco, where it was reconstructed and commissioned in the spring of 1865. For years it remained the only American ironclad permanently stationed on the west coast.[19]

Of the five Confederate ironclads laid down in 1861, one (at Savannah) was completed as a floating battery, and the rest (at New Orleans and Memphis) were destroyed as a result of Union actions on the Mississippi during 1862. On 24 April eighteen wooden steamers under Captain David Glasgow Farragut forced their way upstream from the Gulf of Mexico to take New Orleans. With the two new rebel ironclads there still under construction, Farragut's greatest challenges came from forts ashore and the ironclad *Manassas*, which rammed the paddle steamer USS *Mississippi* and the screw sloop *Brooklyn* but failed to sink either of them. At the end of the battle the *Manassas* was run ashore and wrecked by its crew. Farragut, promoted after the victory, became the first rear admiral in the history of the US navy. The Memphis ironclads likewise were still under construction when a river flotilla under Captain Charles Henry Davis, steaming downstream from St Louis, helped Union forces take the city on 6 June 1862. The retreating rebels destroyed one of their ironclads but saved the other, which entered service in July as the *Arkansas*. After engaging Union vessels on the Mississippi near Vicksburg, in August the *Arkansas* supported an unsuccessful rebel attempt to retake Baton Rouge, Louisiana, where it was scuttled after engaging the Union tinclad *Essex*. The following summer the rebels had no ironclads on the Mississippi to challenge the Union flotilla, by then under Rear Admiral David Dixon Porter, which supported General U. S. Grant's siege of Vicksburg. The fall of Vicksburg on 4 July 1863 left Union forces in control of the entire length of the river, cutting the Confederacy in half.[20]

The loss of the *Arkansas* left the Confederates with no armored warships, but during 1862 and 1863 they laid down smaller versions of the *Virginia* prototype at river shipyards from Tarboro, North Carolina, to Shreveport, Louisiana. The record is incomplete, but at least fourteen of these ironclads saw duty during the last two years of the war. All were of wooden construction. The only iron-hulled rebel ironclad was the *Atlanta*, originally the 800-ton British-built blockade runner *Fingal*, converted to an armored warship at Savannah. It was also the least successful, being captured on 17 June 1863 in Wassaw Sound, near Savannah, by the monitor *Weehawken*. The Union ironclad fired just five times in the battle, including a 15-inch Dahlgren shot which went through the *Atlanta*'s 4-inch iron plating and 18-inch wood backing. This sobering example of firepower prompted the *Atlanta* to surrender on the spot, and afterward the Confederates increased the thickness of armor on some of their ironclads to six inches.[21]

The last major naval action of the war came on 5 August 1864, when Rear Admiral Farragut led a fleet of eighteen ships into Mobile Bay. The port was defended by Rear Admiral Franklin Buchanan (commander of the CSS *Virginia* on the first day of the Battle of Hampton Roads) with three unarmored gunboats and the ironclad *Tennessee*, which had been built at Selma on the Alabama River. The monitor *Tecumseh*, one of four in Farragut's column, led the Union attack but struck a mine and sank as the battle opened. Thereafter the *Tennessee* led the rebel gunboats down the Union line, and a close-range artillery duel eventually degenerated into a mêlée. The screw sloops *Hartford*, *Monongahela*, and *Lackawanna*, the latter two fitted with iron bow plates, each rammed the *Tennessee* but damaged themselves as much as their target. The monitor *Chickasaw* ultimately closed on the *Tennessee* and pounded it into submission. Farragut's victory closed one of the last open Confederate ports and won him promotion to vice admiral. He had lost no warships after the *Tecumseh* but all fourteen of his wooden vessels suffered damage, and Union casualties exceeded 300 killed and wounded.[22]

In the last months of the war the *Albemarle* was perhaps the most successful Confederate ironclad. After being built on the Roanoke River in North

Carolina, it challenged Union gunboats in Albemarle Sound until it was sunk in October 1864 by an enemy steam launch armed with a spar torpedo. As with the submarine *Hunley*'s sinking of the *Housatonic* eight months earlier, the attacker could not withdraw after delivering the blow and was swamped along with its sinking victim.[23] The deficiencies of the spar torpedo notwithstanding, in 1864–65 the Union navy converted four single-turret monitors still under construction to turretless spar torpedo vessels; none engaged an enemy vessel before the conflict ended.[24] Ultimately mines were the Confederacy's most lethal naval weapon, especially against Union ironclads. The most effective resembled the Russian Jacobi mines of the Crimean War.[25] In addition to the *Tecumseh* at Mobile Bay, three monitors and three armored river gunboats were sunk by rebel mines. Meanwhile, the thinly plated *Keokuk* was the only Union ironclad destroyed by fire from shore batteries, and the only others lost – the original *Monitor* and the monitor *Weehawken* – fell victim to storms. Confederate warships failed to sink a single Union ironclad.

All Confederate efforts to buy or build ironclads in Europe ended in failure. General Robert E. Lee's defeat at Gettysburg in July 1863, combined with Grant's victory at Vicksburg the same month, dashed hopes that European countries would formally recognize the Confederacy. In October 1863 the British government seized two 2,570-ton double-turret rams built by Laird, which were eventually commissioned as HMS *Scorpion* and *Wivern*.[26] One of two 1,400-ton rams built by Arman of Bordeaux ended up in the Prussian navy as the *Prinz Adalbert*. Its sister-ship was commissioned as CSS *Stonewall*, too late to see action in the war. En route to American waters when the Confederacy capitulated, it surrendered to Spanish authorities at Havana in May 1865.[27] In addition to British and French shipyards, rebel agents considered ordering ironclads from the Cantiere Navale Adriatico at Trieste, but nothing came of it.[28] All other ironclads laid down for the Confederacy were either sold to European navies or never completed.

Confederate agents enjoyed greater success in securing fast wooden steamers to serve as blockade runners and high seas commerce raiders. Blockade runners were paddle or screw steamers with draught suitable for operating in the shallow coastal waters of the American south. They carried cotton from southern ports to the nearest port under European control, Nassau in the British Bahamas or Havana in Spanish Cuba. Most were private ventures, and the greatest profits came from luxury items imported for the southern élite. Eventually the Confederate government commissioned its own blockade runners to ensure that military supplies would be imported.[29] The commerce raiders were usually screw sloops. The first such ships purpose-built for the Confederate navy in Europe were the *Florida* (by Miller of Liverpool, completed March 1862) and the *Alabama* (by Laird, completed July 1862), which left British waters unarmed, picked up ordnance from tenders in the Atlantic, then operated with Confederate officers and British crews.[30] Another six similar ships were ordered in Britain and France but none was delivered. Other existing vessels were purchased in Britain or France for conversion to commerce raiders. Austria, financially strapped by its ironclad competition with Italy, in February 1863 offered a rebel agent twenty-six steamers for the price of a single armored frigate, but the ships either had too deep a draught or were too slow, and the Confederacy rejected the lot.[31] The best judges of a ship's potential as a commerce raider were the captains of the raiders themselves, who sometimes converted prizes on the spot into "satellite" cruisers manned by prize crews under junior officers.

The *Alabama* was the most successful of the raiders, in two years sinking or capturing sixty-nine ships, including the armed merchantman USS *Hatteras*, the only Union warship sunk by a Confederate raider. In a slightly longer career the *Florida* sank or captured thirty-seven ships, and three "satellite" cruisers it armed took another twenty-one. The Union navy confronted the raiders with screw sloops not assigned to the blockade, accompanied by the deep-draught screw frigates which were ill suited for service along the southern coast. On 19 June 1864 the screw sloop *Kearsarge* sank the *Alabama* at the end of a ninety-minute duel off Cherbourg, and on 31 October 1864 the screw sloop *Wachusett* captured the *Florida* off the coast of Brazil.[32] The most successful converted raider, the *Shenandoah* (ex-*Sea King*), was also the world's first composite (wood-and-iron) hulled cruising warship. The trend toward ever-longer wooden ships, started in the 1850s, had resulted in serious hogging or sagging problems in some designs, prompting British shipbuilders in the early 1860s to begin constructing wooden steamers with iron frames. Initially all were mercantile vessels or transports built to ferry troops to India; the latter included the *Sea King*, built in 1863 and armed after being purchased by the Confederacy the following year. The *Shenandoah* circumnavigated the globe in 1864–65, destroying much of the New England whaling fleet in the north Pacific between April and June of 1865, after Lee had surrendered the last significant rebel army at Appomattox. When its captain and crew learned that the war had ended, the ship cruised another 17,000 miles, rounding Cape Horn and eventually reaching Liverpool, where it surrendered to British officials in November 1865. Confederate raiders combined to capture or destroy 261 vessels, all but two of which were sailing ships. More devastating for the American merchant marine was the flight of shipowners to foreign flags, with 715 ships being transferred to the British alone. The Union navy inflicted even greater losses on Confederate blockade runners, capturing or destroying 295 steamers and 1,189 sailing ships of various types.[33]

The issue of the commerce raiders further strained an Anglo-American relationship already damaged earlier in the war by the "*Trent* affair" of November 1861, in which the American sloop *San Jacinto* stopped the British steamer *Trent* on the high seas and removed two Confederate agents bound for Britain. The prospect of war with the United States prompted the British navy to reinforce its North American and West Indian squadron to a strength of nine ships of the line and seven frigates (including the *Mersey* and the *Orlando*) by early 1862. Britain lost one warship on the station during the American Civil War, the screw ship of the line *Conqueror*, wrecked in the Bahamas in December 1861. Anglo-American relations remained tense until 1871, when Britain accepted the verdict of an arbitration tribunal at Geneva and paid the United States $15.5 million for damage inflicted by the *Alabama* and other British-built Confederate raiders.[34]

At the peak of its strength during the American Civil War, the US navy had 649 warships of 510,396 tons, mounting 4,600 guns, a navy list including 49 ironclads, 113 unarmored screw steamers, 52 paddle steamers, 323 other steamers used for auxiliary purposes, and 112 sailing ships. The numbers would have been even greater if not for a decision, in 1864, to lay down no additional warships. The rebel surrender in April 1865 left little need for such a large navy; much of the fleet demobilized and dozens of warships on the stocks were never completed. Further decommissionings followed Napoleon III's decision, in February 1866, to withdraw French troops from Mexico, where they had supported the regime of Emperor Maximilian.[35]

Even though Napoleon III's policies during the American Civil War severely strained his relationship with the United States, in 1867 the largest American ironclad and perhaps its best double-turret monitor both were sold to the French navy. The giant *Dunderberg*, begun in 1862 by William Webb of New York, resembled the CSS *Virginia* but, at 7,800 tons, was more than twice as large, with a higher freeboard and masts fore and aft of an angled casemate amidships. The ship was completed in 1866 and sold to the French navy in June 1867, where it served under the name *Rochambeau*. One month later the French also bought the *Onondaga*, the Union navy's lone iron-hulled double-turret monitor. The only other American ironclads of the Civil War era sold to foreign navies were the single-turret monitors *Catawba* and *Oneota*, completed in 1865, which were purchased in April 1868 by Peru.[36] By 1866 the US navy had sold or scrapped one river monitor and all other river ironclads. Most of the coastal monitors were kept in reserve. Of the three ironclads designed for high seas duty, only the large single-turret monitor *Dictator* was commissioned in the post-war era, on two separate occasions between 1865 and 1877. The triple-turret monitor *Roanoke* remained on hand in New York, to defend the harbor in case of war. Both the *Dictator* and *Roanoke* survived until 1883, when they were sold for scrap. The armored frigate *New Ironsides* had a much shorter postwar life; laid up at Philadelphia after the war, it was destroyed by fire in December 1866.[37] Few of the other monitors ever ventured beyond the coastal waters for which they were designed. In May 1865 the double-turret *Monadnock* and single-turret *Canonicus* joined the squadron that went to Cuba before the surrender of the Confederate ram *Stonewall*. In 1865–66 the *Monadnock* steamed around Cape Horn to San Francisco. In the summer of 1866 the double-turret *Miantonomoh* became the only American monitor to cross the Atlantic as a commissioned vessel, in the company of two navy paddle steamers. The *Miantonomoh* spent nine months in European waters, most with the

American squadron in the Mediterranean, but also visited Kronstadt in the Baltic, repaying the favor of Russian naval visits made to New York and San Francisco during 1863. Farragut, as the navy's first full admiral, in 1867–68 commanded a squadron in European waters consisting entirely of wooden steamers. By 1869 only six monitors were in active service.[38]

European navies during the American Civil War

Throughout the American Civil War the British navy maintained unusually large squadrons at Halifax and Bermuda but sent no armored warships across the Atlantic. While some private shipbuilders laid down warships for the Confederacy, others joined the royal dockyards in continuing to build ironclads for the British fleet. In Britain, as elsewhere in Europe, news of the Battle of Hampton Roads dispelled the lingering skepticism about armored warships and touched off a debate between proponents of "monitors" and those of armored frigates. Britain built both types, actually ordering its first turret ship in February 1862, before the *Monitor* made its debut at Hampton Roads. The 3,690-ton mastless coastal ironclad *Prince Albert* was fitted with Coles turrets, designed by Captain Cowper Coles and patented in 1859, which turned on rollers below deck-level (in contrast to Ericsson's turret, which was mounted on top of the

Plate 4.3 HMS *Captain* (laid down January 1867, completed January 1870)
Naval Historical Center, Basic Collection

deck and turned on a central spindle). The ship featured an iron hull, seven feet of freeboard, and four centerline turrets each mounting a single 9-inch gun. Laid down in April 1862 and completed in February 1866, it remained on the effective list for thirty-three years. At the same time, the screw ship of the line *Royal Sovereign*, a three-decker built in 1849–57, was converted to a mastless turret ship between April 1862 and August 1864. Like the *Prince Albert* it had four centerline turrets, only with 10.5-inch ordnance and the bow turret mounting a second gun. The next turret ships in the British navy were the Laird ironclads *Scorpion* and *Wivern*, intended for the Confederacy but seized by the British government in October 1863 and commissioned two years later. Other British turret ships of the era included eight large monitors for coastal operations laid down in 1867–70, ranging in size from 2,900 to 4,910 tons. Britain's first high seas battleship with turrets was the 8,320-ton *Monarch* (built 1866–69), a fully rigged warship with the appearance of a large broadside armored frigate. It carried its primary armament, four 12-inch guns, paired in two centerline turrets amidships. The concept was repeated in the 7,770-ton *Captain* (built 1867–70), which featured a lower freeboard of just 6.5 feet; it capsized and sank in a gale off Cape Finisterre in September 1870, while on service with the Channel fleet. Coles was among the 472 men lost in the disaster.[39]

While building a wide variety of turret warships, the British navy also pioneered the central battery ship as a solution to the dilemma posed by the requirements of ever more powerful guns and ever-thicker armor. Under Walker's successor Spencer Robinson, Edward Reed served from July 1863 a s chief constructor. An opponent of Coles and the turret ship concept, Reed produced a design with the superficial appearance of an armored broadside ironclad but a smaller battery of heavier guns concentrated in a heavily armored casemate amidships, which also protected the ship's engines. Otherwise the ship was unarmored except for a waterline belt. Reed experimented with the concept in four smaller ironclads converted from wooden screw warships, the sloops *Research* (completed April 1864) and *Enterprise* (June 1864) and the corvettes *Favorite* and *Pallas* (March 1866). All these ships, along with a fifth small casemate ironclad, the 4,470-ton *Penelope* (June 1868), had recessed freeboard fore and aft of the casemate to allow the end guns to fire ahead and astern. When Reed applied this concept to the 7,550-ton *Bellerophon* (April 1866) he made the belt and casemate armor six inches thick but did not include the recessed freeboard, installing chase guns in the bow and stern guns to supplement the heavy battery of ten 9-inch guns in the reduced broadside. Of twelve subsequent central battery ships, seven had hull embrasures to allow end-on fire from the casemate while five did not. Of the eighteen central battery ships built for the British navy, all but one was laid down before 1870. Two of the six ships of the line designated for conversion to armored frigates in 1861 were completed as central battery ships; these, along with a third ship of the line conversion and the four small experimental ships, were the only ones of the type to have wooden rather than iron hulls.[40]

In addition to central battery ships and turret ships, during the remainder of the decade the British navy continued to build armored warships of other types. Vessels built for coastal operations ranged from the 4,330-ton ram *Hotspur* (built 1868–71) and the 5,440-ton ram *Rupert* (1870–74) to the three 1,230-ton armored gunboats of the *Vixen* class (1864–67). Reed also designed the wooden-hulled armored frigates *Lord Clyde* (1863–66) and *Lord Warden* (1863–67). At 7,750 tons and 7,840 tons, respectively, they joined the French *Rochambeau* (ex-*Dunderberg*) as the largest wooden-hulled warships ever built. They were Britain's last broadside ironclads and last purpose-built wooden-hulled battleships. Reed also designed the last large turret ships of the era, at the request of the First Lord of the Admiralty H. C. E. Childers; it was an ironic development, given Reed's earlier opposition to Coles and the turret concept, and Childers' subsequent loss of a son in the *Captain* disaster. Working from Childers' request for a "monitor" capable of steaming across the Atlantic, Reed produced the revolutionary 9,330-ton mastless battleships *Devastation* and *Thunderer*, laid down in 1869. These were followed by the 10,890-ton *Dreadnought*, laid down after Reed's resignation in 1870. All three featured a relatively low freeboard and a primary armament of four 12-inch guns in centerline turrets fore and aft of a central superstructure. They foreshadowed the battleships of the turn of the century, the "pre-dreadnoughts" of the generation preceding the all big-gun *Dreadnought* of 1906. The *Devastation* and *Thunderer* had twin screws, which had been installed experimentally on some fully rigged ironclads in the 1860s.[41]

After laying down the last of *Gloire*'s half-sisters in 1861, France did not begin another armored battleship for four years. Between 1865 and 1870 seven central battery ironclads were laid down, none of which had recessed freeboard fore and aft of the casemate to allow end guns to fire ahead and astern. Instead, the armored box amidships was topped by two or four heavy pivoting guns in barbettes, an innovation of Dupuy de Lôme combining a revolving turret within a ring of heavy armor. The ships ranged in size from the 7,580-ton *Océan*, the first completed, in July 1870, to the 8,980-ton *Richelieu*. Only one of the seven (*Friedland*) had an iron hull.[42] Rather than employ battle fleet ironclads as overseas cruisers, the French built smaller armored vessels for such duties: the 3,720-ton broadside ironclad *Belliqueuse* (built 1863–66), the seven wooden-hulled central battery ironclads of the *Alma* class, ranging in size from the 3,510-ton *Thétis* to the 3,830-ton *Montcalm* (all laid down in 1865, completed 1867–69), and the three wooden-hulled central battery ironclads of the 4,585-ton *Galissonnière* class, laid down in 1868–69 but not completed until the 1870s. Like its seven casemate battleships, France's ten casemate cruisers did not have recessed freeboard fore and aft of the casemate to allow for end-on fire. Between 1862 and 1868, France built eleven small (1,400- to 1,500-ton), relatively worthless armored floating batteries for coast defense, the first of which was decommissioned in 1869.[43]

From keel-laying to commissioning, both *Gloire* and *Warrior* took two years, five months to complete. As a group, the *Gloire* and the other fifteen broadside armored frigates laid down in 1858–61 took an average of just over four years to complete, the same as the average for the *Warrior* and the fifteen other British ironclads begun in 1859–61. But by the end of the decade an inferior industrial and shipbuilding capacity clearly had doomed the latest French bid to challenge British naval supremacy. For the seven French central battery ships laid down in 1865–70 building times averaged seven-and-a-half years, while the eleven British central battery ships laid down in 1863–68 took an average of just over three years to complete. British armaments manufacturers also led the way in developing armor-piercing naval artillery. Between 1863 and 1865 experimentation led to the adoption of 9- to 12-inch muzzle-loading guns with rifled steel tubes encased in wrought iron. Such guns proved capable of penetrating 9 to 12 inches of wrought iron plate at a distance of 1,000 yards. France, like Britain, had used rifled muzzle loaders as early as the Crimean War, but the 6.4-inch muzzle-loading rifles of the type mounted in the *Gloire* in 1860 could not pierce the armor of most ironclads of the time. By 1870 the French were producing larger rifled muzzle loaders, ultmately a 10.8-inch gun, yet their artillery remained inferior to the latest British guns.[44]

In the construction of unarmored cruising ships Britain likewise remained ahead of France, as a direct consequence of Anglo-American tensions during the American Civil War. In 1864 the United States authorized a group of fast wooden screw steamers designed not for action against the dying Confederacy but as commerce raiders against the British Empire. The 4,215-ton sloop *Wampanoag* was the largest of four that were actually completed. It had powerful engines designed by Benjamin F. Isherwood, and during extensive trials early in 1868 averaged better than 17 knots per hour. Even though the *Wampanoag* was decommissioned less than three months after its trials, and the remaining vessels met similar fates, the American fast cruisers prompted a British program of six screw frigates and six screw corvettes as a response. Edward Reed's prototype frigate *Inconstant* (built 1866–69) was an unarmored iron-hulled vessel of 5,780 tons which made 16.2 knots on its trials. Reed also designed the 3,080-ton unarmored iron corvettes *Volage* and *Active* (built 1867–70). The high cost of these ships (just over £300,000 for the *Inconstant*, compared to £377,000 for the armored *Warrior*) and the evaporation of the American threat brought the cancellation of the last three frigates and three corvettes.[45] Nevertheless, Reed's fast iron-hulled cruisers established a new standard for unarmored cruising warships. Few wooden-hulled frigates were begun after the late 1860s: the 3,200-ton *Endymion* (built 1860–66) was the last laid down by the British navy, the 4,020-ton *Newcastle* (built 1858–74) the last completed. Wooden screw corvettes continued to be built into the 1870s, but no more frigates.[46]

Among the leading naval powers of Europe, only Russia chose to copy the monitor type and build most of its early ironclads strictly for coastal operations, reflecting the fact that at this stage in its history, Russia – like the United States – was an expansionist power on land but not at sea. During a war scare over Poland in 1863, the Russian navy ordered ten single-turret monitors, virtual copies of the USS *Monitor*. Two were built by the Belgian firm of Cockerill, the rest in St Petersburg shipyards; all entered service in 1866. Other warships begun in 1863 included the 1,460-ton coastal turret ship *Smerch* and a 3,340-ton Russian copy of the British-built armored frigate *Pervenetz*, the *Ne Tron Menia*, both of which were completed in 1865. The 4,000-ton battery frigate *Kreml* followed, laid down in 1864 and completed in 1866. Subsequent projects included six more coastal ironclads (two triple-turret and four double-turret monitors), the battery frigates *General Admiral*, *Gerzog Edinburski*, and *Minin*, and the lone casemate ship *Kniaz Pozharski*. The latter four iron-hulled warships eventually joined the wooden ironclad conversions *Sevastopol* and *Petropavlovsk* in the armored cruising fleet. By 1870, counting ships still under construction, Russia had a formidable ironclad force of five large and three small battery frigates, one casemate ship, sixteen monitors, and one coastal turret ship. A twenty-seventh armored warship, the 9,665-ton *Petr Veliki*, was a virtual copy of the innovative British *Devastation*. The mastless turret battleship was laid down in 1869 but not completed until 1876. Owing to Russia's relative technological backwardness, the tsar's navy could boast of few "firsts" during the ironclad revolution. The Russians had the distinction of being the first to have one of their own armored warships inadvertently sink one of their wooden ships, in an accident in August 1869 in which the *Kreml* rammed and sank the frigate *Oleg*. Fitting for its overall defensive focus, the Russian navy remained at or near the leading edge of mine development from 1868, when it developed the first glass-tube battery electrolyte detonation device.[47]

The Turkish navy continued to fill the vacuum left by the dissolution of the Russian Black Sea fleet, developing a formidable ironclad fleet after Sultan Abdul Aziz inherited the throne in 1861. Between 1863 and 1868 the Turks ordered four 6,400-ton armored battery frigates and three casemate corvettes from British shipbuilders. One of the latter vessels, the *Feth-i Bülend*, became the prototype for the first Turkish-built ironclad, the casemate corvette *Mukaddeme-i Hayir*, laid down at Constantinople in 1870. The efforts of Abdul Aziz gave the Ottoman empire a fleet of expensive warships which it could neither man nor effectively use. The sultan acquired still more ironclads courtesy of Ismail Pasha, grandson of Mehemet Ali, who in the 1860s mounted another Egyptian challenge to Ottoman rule. Turco-Egyptian tensions came to a head after Ismail snubbed Abdul Aziz by not inviting him to the opening ceremonies of the Suez Canal in 1869. The crisis was resolved short of war when the pasha agreed to reduce the size of his army and transfer to the sultan the contracts of six armored warships he had ordered in France and Austria. These included a battery frigate, two casemate corvettes, and two coastal turret ships under construction in French shipyards and a battery corvette at Austria's Stabilimento Tecnico Triestino.

Egypt remained nominally a Turkish province until Britain occupied it in 1882. Meanwhile, the former Egyptian ironclads built in France entered Turkish service in 1870, the same year as the last of the sultan's British-built ironclads.

The lone Austrian-built ironclad was delivered in 1871, giving the Ottoman navy a total of fourteen.[48] None of the sultan's ironclads participated in the Greco-Turkish war of 1866–69, which broke out following an uprising on Crete. The Turks used their large wooden steam fleet to beat back the Greek challenge, and diplomatic intervention by the great powers ultimately ended the fighting, confirming the status quo ante. Greece did not attempt to compete with Turkey in naval power but during the war ordered its first ironclads, the 1,770-ton casemate ship *Basileos Georgios* (launched 1867) from the Thames Iron Works and the 2,030-ton armored corvette *Basilissa Olga* (launched 1869) from the Stabilimento Tecnico Triestino. For two decades they were Greece's only armored warships.[49]

Among the other minor European naval powers, the Netherlands had the most armored warships as of 1870: one battery frigate, five turret ships, and seven monitors. The first Dutch ironclad, the armored frigate *De Ruyter*, may hold the record for having undergone more radical transformations than any other of the larger warships in naval history. Laid down at Flushing in 1831 as a 74-gun sailing ship of the line, *De Ruyter* spent nineteen years on the stocks before being cut down in 1850 and launched in 1853 as a 54-gun sailing frigate. After seven years of service the ship was converted to a 45-gun screw frigate, then in 1863 to a broadside ironclad.[50] Sweden and its sister-kingdom Norway each commissioned three monitors by the end of the 1860s. Qualitatively, Denmark assembled the strongest armored fleet of the lot, with three battery frigates, three small turret ships, and two small schooners by 1870; the Danes also became the last of the minor naval powers to take on a great power in war, challenging Austria and Prussia in the War of 1864.[51]

The wars of 1864 and 1866

In November 1863 Christian IX, the new Danish king, approved a constitution incorporating Schleswig into his kingdom. This bold act revived the Schleswig–Holstein question and put Denmark on a collision course with Germany. Despite recent improvements, the Prussian navy remained vastly inferior to the Danish, with a screw-propelled force of just three corvettes, one yacht, and twenty-one gunboats, supplemented by two paddle steamers. Most of the larger vessels had engines imported from Britain; the navy also did not yet trust Krupp to provide its artillery, instead turning to Finspong of Sweden and the Spandau royal foundry.[52] Prussia had no ironclads but did have a keen interest in the smaller types deployed by the Union navy in the American Civil War, requesting plans of James Eads' gunboats after their initial successes in February 1862. Eads provided a description of his gunboat *Benton*, but by the time it reached Berlin the Battle of Hampton Roads (8–9 March) had focused attention on John Ericsson's *Monitor*. The Prussian press hailed monitors as an inexpensive solution to the ironclad question. One commentator concluded that "for the money that the [armored frigate] *Warrior* has cost the English nation, twenty [ironclads] could be built on the model of the *Monitor*."[53] But in the early 1860s no Prussian or German shipyard was capable of building an ironclad, even one as small as a monitor, and an ongoing financial crisis prevented the ordering of armored warships abroad. Denmark's wooden screw-propelled fleet included one ship of the line, four frigates, three corvettes, and ten schooners, supplemented by eight paddle steamers. The Danish navy further enhanced its superiority over the Prussian by purchasing two small armored schooners from the Thames Iron Works during 1862 and Europe's first "monitor," the 1,350-ton Coles turret gunboat *Rolf Krake*, from Napier & Sons of Glasgow in 1863. The Danes also purchased the armored frigate *Danmark* from Thomsons of Glasgow, a 4,800-ton ship originally laid down for the Confederate states. In Copenhagen, the navy yard began converting the wooden ship of the line *Dannebrog* into a 3,100-ton armored frigate and laid down the 3,400-ton armored frigate *Peder Skram*. Fortunately for Prussia, the *Danmark* and *Peder Skram* were not ready in time for the war.[54]

The Schleswig–Holstein crisis escalated to the brink of war too fast for any last-ditch attempts to improve Prussian readiness at sea. On the initiative of Count Otto von Bismarck, the new Prussian minister–president, on 16 January 1864 Austria and Prussia submitted an ultimatum to Denmark, demanding the withdrawal of the constitution of 1863. After the Danes refused to capitulate, a joint Austro-Prussian force assembled in Holstein and, in early February, moved on into Schleswig. Denmark responded as it had in 1848–49, with a blockade.[55] During the war the *Dannebrog* joined the Danish armored force, while Prussia added only a fourth wooden screw corvette. For the German allies the Austrian navy held the balance, with its five armored frigates in service as of 1863 and an unarmored screw-propelled fleet roughly equal to the Danish: one ship of the line, five frigates, two corvettes, and twenty-one gunboats.[56]

The Italian threat in the Adriatic limited the number of warships the Austrians could deploy against the Danes; nevertheless, in February 1864 Captain Wilhelm von Tegetthoff was sent to the North Sea with the screw frigates *Schwarzenberg* and *Radetzky*. Rear Admiral Bernhard von Wüllerstorf followed later with the main Austrian force, consisting of two armored frigates, one paddle steamer, and a screw-propelled contingent of one ship of the line, one corvette, and one gunboat.[57] While the Austrian warships were still en route to northern waters, the Prussian navy initiated the only action of the war in the Baltic. On 17 March 1864 Admiral Prince Adalbert sent Captain Eduard Jachmann with a force of two screw corvettes, six screw gunboats, and one paddle steamer on a sortie against the blockade off the mouth of the Oder. Rounding the island of Rügen, they encountered the Danes off Jasmund: the screw ship of the line *Skjold* with two screw frigates and three smaller steamers. Hopelessly outgunned, the Prussians still managed to fire more than 250 shots before and during their retreat to Swinemünde. The Danes reimposed their blockade of Swinemünde and Jachmann did not venture out again. After that the focus shifted to the North Sea, where warships enforcing the Danish blockade had captured nineteen

German merchantmen early in the war, effectively closing Hamburg and Bremen for German-flagged shipping. The blockade went unchallenged until early May, when Tegetthoff arrived with the *Schwarzenberg* and *Radetzky*. With the Prussian paddle steamer *Preussischer Adler* and two screw gunboats, they ventured out of Cuxhaven on 9 May to meet the Danes off Helgoland. The three small Prussian vessels contributed little to the allied effort; the Austrian frigates bore the brunt of the fighting against a Danish force commanded by Admiral Suenson, consisting of the screw frigates *Jylland* and *Niels Juel* and the screw corvette *Heimdal*. The rivals exchanged shots at a distance for several hours but neither side attempted to close. In the late afternoon the allies returned to Cuxhaven; the Danes ultimately withdrew all the way to the Skagerrak. The Austrians lost 138 men killed and wounded, and both of their ships were badly scarred. The Danes suffered roughly half as many casualties, and their flagship *Niels Juel* sustained moderate damage. The Prussians lost no men and their vessels emerged completely unscathed. Tegetthoff called the battle a draw, but the Danes, despite giving up their North Sea blockade, claimed victory.[58]

Jachmann was promoted to rear admiral for his efforts at Jasmund, while Tegetthoff was advanced to rear admiral as a reward for Helgoland. Meanwhile, the main body of the Austrian fleet under Rear Admiral Wüllerstorf arrived in the North Sea in late May, long after Tegetthoff had dispersed the Danish blockade there. Prussian army leaders hoped he would move against Copenhagen itself or into the Baltic Sea, but the Austrians, fearing British intervention if they pressed the naval war that far, kept all their warships in the North Sea. Apart from two summer sorties, by the *Rolf Krake* in the Baltic and the *Dannebrog* in the North Sea, the Danish navy made no further efforts to engage the allies. No longer in command of the sea or under the illusion that the British would intervene to save them, the Danes sued for peace. In October 1864 Denmark formally ceded Schleswig–Holstein to the joint control of Austria and Prussia.[59] Following the defeat the Danes retained their resolve to be a regional naval power, if only for a few more years, commissioning the *Peder Skram* and *Danmark*, then building another two small turret ships at Copenhagen. Prussia added its first ironclads in the spring of 1865, the 1,600-ton British-built turret ship *Arminius* and 1,400-ton French-built ram *Prinz Adalbert*, after rejecting an Austrian offer to build armored warships for the Prussian navy in Trieste. The Prussians also purchased two screw corvettes from French shipbuilders and completed another two screw corvettes at home; all three French purchases were warships originally laid down for the Confederate navy. In 1865 Krupp finally secured contracts with the Prussian navy for his revolutionary steel artillery, after first selling the product to the Prussian army and to foreign armies and navies.[60]

After the War of 1864 Prussia occupied Schleswig and Austria, Holstein. The Austrians gave the Prussian navy the right to replace the obsolete Eider Canal with a modern canal across Holstein and allowed it to move its Baltic base from Danzig to Kiel; the Prussian army received transit rights across Holstein to Schleswig. These provisions generated considerable tension, while

Austro-Prussian diplomatic relations deteriorated over the issue of reforming the German Confederation. In March 1866 both German powers began preparing for war, and the following month Prussia concluded an alliance with Italy against Austria. In early June Prussia occupied Holstein, then seceded from the confederation. Most of the smaller northern states followed suit, siding with Prussia, while Hanover and the southern German states supported Austria. In late June, the Prussian army invaded Bohemia and the Italian army Venetia. While the Austrians defeated the Italians on 24 June at Custoza, the Prussians crushed the Austrians on 3 July at Königgrätz.

Prince Adalbert's decision to spend the summer with the Prussian army reflected the fact that the Prussian navy had little to do during the war. Most of the Austrian fleet returned to the Adriatic late in 1864, and their last warship left Kiel in March 1866 to avoid possible capture. As in 1864, Jachmann served as Prussian squadron commander. He supported the army's campaign against Hanover, operating ships on the Elbe, Weser, and Ems rivers to help secure the surrender of Emden, Stade, and other cities.[61] The real naval action in 1866 came in the Adriatic, where Tegetthoff received command of a battle fleet at Pola spearheaded by seven armored frigates: the 2,800-ton *Drache* and *Salamander*, the 3,600-ton *Kaiser Max*, *Juan d'Austria*, and *Prinz Eugen*, and the recently completed 5,100-ton *Habsburg* and *Erzherzog Ferdinand Max*, the latter serving as flagship. All were wooden-hulled ironclads built at Trieste, armed by guns from the Imperial-Royal Foundry at Mariazell. Delivery of Krupp artillery ordered for the newest pair of ironclads was blocked by the Prussian government on the eve of the war.[62] Across the Adriatic at Ancona, Admiral Persano commanded a much larger Italian battle fleet. His twelve ironclads included the 5,700-ton American-built frigates *Re d'Italia* (the flagship) and *Re di Portogallo*, the 4,100-ton British-built double-turret ram *Affondatore*, the 3,500-ton Italian-built frigate *Principe de Carignano*, and eight warships built in French shipyards: the four 4,250-ton frigates of the *Regina Maria Pia* class, the 2,700-ton corvettes *Formidabile* and *Terribile*, and the gunboats *Palestro* (2,200 tons) and *Varese* (2,000 tons). Nine of the twelve Italian ironclads had iron hulls.[63]

On 12 June 1866, just before the war began, Austria had agreed to a demand by Napoleon III to cede its remaining Italian province, Venetia, to Italy at the end of the war, in order to buy French neutrality in the upcoming conflict. Austria hoped the gesture would keep Italy neutral as well, but the Italians wanted more than just Venetia and declared war anyway. While their defeat at Custoza had a sobering effect on the Italians, the Prussian victory at Königgrätz (which forced the Austrians to redeploy their southern army northward, for the defense of Vienna) brought a new confidence and also a sense of urgency. Fearful that the war would end before all of Italy's war aims were achieved, on 12 July Prime Minister Bettino Ricasoli outlined plans to destroy the Austrian fleet in a decisive sea battle, then land troops on the coasts of Istria and Dalmatia, historically Venetian Slavic lands coveted by the kingdom of Italy. On 16 July Persano left Ancona with his twelve ironclads and twenty-two unarmored

Plate 4.4 Austrian screw ship of the line *Kaiser*, the day after engaging Italian ironclads at the Battle of Lissa (20 July 1866)
Naval Historical Center, Basic Collection

vessels, including transports carrying 3,000 troops. His first objective was to "take possession of an important station in the Adriatic," the island of Lissa.[64] Persano's fleet shelled the fortified island on 18–19 July but did not land troops for fear that Tegetthoff's ships would appear in the midst of the operation. Upon learning of the location of the Italian fleet the Austrians steamed down the Adriatic from Pola; approaching Lissa on the morning of 20 July, Tegetthoff formed his fleet into three V-shaped squadrons for a line-abreast attack. The first consisted of the seven armored frigates, led by his flagship *Erzherzog Ferdinand Max*; the second, of seven larger screw-propelled warships, led by the ship of the line *Kaiser*; and the third, of thirteen screw gunboats and paddle steamers. Persano formed a line between the approaching Austrians and the island of Lissa with his eleven foreign-built ironclads; the Italian-built *Principe di Carignano* served as flagship for the unarmored vessels, which fell into line far to the rear. The Italian navy had recently adopted French ironclad tactics based upon Bouët-Willaumez's *Tactique supplémentaire à l'usage d'une flotte cuirassée* of 1865, but the Italian fleet – unlike the Austrian – had not conducted maneuvers before the battle. Persano had not even met with his ship captains to translate the new doctrine into an operational plan. To make matters worse, at the last minute Persano switched his flag from the *Re d'Italia* to the *Affondatore*; his captains were unaware of the change and throughout the battle looked to the wrong ship for signals. In the end it mattered little, for as soon as the *Erzherzog*

Ferdinand Max broke through the Italian line, followed moments later by the *Kaiser* and the wave of unarmored ships, the battle degenerated into a chaotic mêlée.[65]

As the two fleets exchanged shots at close range, neither side was able to do much damage: the Austrian warships had inferior guns, the Italians incompetent gunners. While Persano's wooden ships observed the battle from a safe distance, Tegetthoff's remained in the thick of the fight. The *Kaiser*, the only screw ship of the line ever to be involved in a battle between fleets of warships at sea, became a prize target for the Italian ironclads. Heavily damaged by enemy shellfire, it remained afloat to play an important role in the fight; when Persano's own *Affondatore* attempted to ram the *Kaiser*, a timely broadside warded off the attacker and disabled one of its turrets. Because Tegetthoff had planned to use ramming tactics to compensate for his inferior artillery, the confusion was much to his liking; at the climax of the four hours of close combat, his *Erzherzog Ferdinand Max* rammed and sank the *Re d'Italia*. Meanwhile, Persano's ironclads were unable to sink a single Austrian warship, armored or unarmored. A second Italian ironclad, the *Palestro*, was afire by the time the fleets disengaged and exploded as Persano signaled a retreat to Ancona. The Austrian ironclads, too slow to give chase, remained off Lissa temporarily before returning to Pola. The Italians lost 612 killed and 57 wounded or taken prisoner, the Austrians 38 killed and 138 wounded. "The whole thing was chaos," Tegetthoff confided to a friend, "a melee in the fullest sense of the word. . . . It is a miracle that we did not lose a ship."[66]

The Italian fleet did not venture out again, and when Prussia signed a separate peace with Austria on 26 July, Italy had no choice but to come to terms as well. The Treaty of Vienna (3 October 1866) formally ended hostilities, awarding the Italians Venetia but nothing more. Emperor Francis Joseph rewarded Tegetthoff with a promotion to vice admiral. The Battle of Lissa was significant to history not only for foiling Italy's grand design to seize a foothold on the eastern shore of the Adriatic, but also as the first sea battle between fleets of armored warships. If one discounts Navarino in 1827, where the Turco-Egyptian fleet was destroyed at anchor, Lissa rates as the largest naval battle in the century between Trafalgar (1805) and Tsushima (1905), and thus its "lessons" affected both the design of warships and battle tactics. Tegetthoff's line-abreast attack and ramming tactics may have been born of desperation, but both were embraced afterward by influential naval writers and tacticians, including Britain's Vice Admiral Philip Colomb and France's Admiral Jurien de la Gravière.[67] For years to come the line abreast replaced the line ahead as the favored battle formation, and warships would be built with pronounced ram bows.

Naval warfare in Latin America (1858–70)

After the downfall of the Argentinian dictator Rosas in 1852, the next disruption to the peace of South America originated in, of all places, Paraguay, which emerged as a self-confident country under the dictator Carlos Antonio López. After friction with Britain and France over the treatment of their subjects in Paraguay, López closed the Paraguay and Paraná rivers to foreign warships. Enforcing this policy, in 1855 his troops fired on the American naval steamer *Water Witch*, which had ascended the Paraná on a mapping expedition. Commodore Shubrick led a forceful (if delayed) American response, sailing up the Paraná late in 1858 with a squadron led by the 50-gun frigates *Sabine* and *St Lawrence*. López apologized, paid an indemnity, and allowed the mapping expedition to proceed; by the following year the United States had two steamers, two small sailing warships, and two auxiliaries on the rivers of Paraguay.[68]

The outbreak of the American Civil War forced the US navy to withdraw its warships from the waters of Latin America. Of the three wars fought in the region during the 1860s, two were sparked by European powers taking advantage of the temporary paralysis of the United States. In Mexico, France supported conservatives in a war to establish a monarchy under the protection of Napoleon III (1862–67), while Spain's quest to settle old scores led to a war against a Peruvian–Chilean alliance (1864–66). Only Paraguay's war against its larger neighbors (1865–70) did not stem from European machinations.

The crisis in Mexico began in July 1861, when the liberal regime of Benito Juárez defaulted on its international debts shortly after winning a bitter civil war against conservative forces. Spanish, British, and French squadrons anchored off Veracruz in support of the claims of their nationals. The Spanish and British soon left, but Napoleon III gradually increased French involvement in Mexican affairs. Early in 1862 troops were landed, the first of 40,000 eventually ferried to Mexico by the French navy. In June 1863 the French took Mexico City, and four months later a French-backed delegation of anti-Juárez conservatives offered an imperial Mexican throne to Archduke Ferdinand Max, younger brother of Emperor Francis Joseph of Austria and, since 1854, commander of the Austrian navy. The archduke resigned his post to become Emperor Maximilian of Mexico, arriving in the New World in May 1864. Distracted by serious resistance from republican forces loyal to Juárez, Maximilian had to abandon pet projects including the creation of an imperial Mexican navy. The French fleet filled the void, blockading the gulf and the Pacific coasts of Mexico. In the gulf, French warships supported Maximilian mostly by interdicting arms shipments bound for supporters of Juárez. On the Pacific coast, where the cities and towns were out of reach of French troops moving overland, the navy secured Acapulco, Mazatlan, and other ports for the imperial government. The end of the American Civil War marked the beginning of the end of the Mexican empire, as the United States reasserted the Monroe Doctrine. Content at having looted £2.2 million in Mexican silver during their intervention, the French agreed to leave. In March 1867 their last warships steamed away, leaving an Austrian naval steamer at Veracruz as Maximilian's only means of escape. He refused to abandon his adopted country and three months later was captured and executed at Queretaro. During its five-year campaign in Mexican waters the French navy had no opposition at sea; in 1862–63 the armored frigate *Normandie*, the first ironclad to cross the Atlantic, reinforced the squadron off Veracruz, not because it was needed but to prove that the voyage could be made. The 750-ton screw gunboat *Amphion*, wrecked off Veracruz in April 1866, was the only French warship lost in the Mexican operation.[69]

Just as France flouted the Monroe Doctrine in pursuing its Mexican policy, Spain took advantage of the American Civil War first to re-annex the Dominican Republic in 1861–62, then to demand repayment of Peruvian debts dating from colonial times. When Peru refused to comply, in April 1864 landing parties from a Spanish squadron occupied the Chinca Islands, source of half of the guano which provided the Peruvian government with most of its income. In a show of solidarity, Chile joined Peru in declaring war on Spain, but their combined sea power paled in comparison to that of the Spanish squadron. Admiral José Manuel Pareja commanded a force including the first ironclad to circumnavigate the globe, the armored frigate *Numancia*, supplemented by five unarmored frigates and two gunboats. In comparison, the most formidable allied warships were the Peruvian frigates *Apurimac* and *Amazonas* and the Chilean corvette *Esmeralda*, screw-propelled steamers built in European shipyards in the 1850s. Spain's overwhelming naval superiority made it unnecessary to send the armored frigates *Tetuán* (6,200 tons, launched at Ferrol in 1863) and *Arapiles* (5,700 tons, Blackwall, 1864) to the war zone. The conflict quickly stalemated, as Spain dominated the sea but did not attempt to land troops on the mainland. The allies sent agents to European shipyards in search of unsold warships originally laid down for the Confederate states; Peru purchased two screw corvettes in France, and Chile, one in Britain. The Peruvian vessels made it to Latin American waters but the Chilean *Pampero*, a composite (wood-and-iron) hulled vessel, was captured by the Spanish screw frigate *Gerona* while en route to the war zone and subsequently joined the Spanish fleet under the name *Tornado*. In November 1865 the allies claimed their only success of the war when the Chilean *Esmeralda*, under Captain Juan Williams Rebolledo, captured the Spanish navy screw gunboat *Covadonga* off Papudo. Humiliated by the loss of one of his ships, Admiral Pareja committed suicide; Captain Casto Méndez Nuñez of the *Numancia*, promoted to rear admiral, succeeded him.[70]

With the arrival of the Peruvian purchases and the captured *Covadonga* the joint Peruvian–Chilean squadron grew to include eight steamers, a force still too small to challenge the Spanish. Under the command of Williams Rebolledo and, eventually, 77-year-old Admiral Blanco Encalada, the squadron stayed close to its base on the island of Chiloé, well down the Chilean coast. Shortly after the end of the American Civil War, pressure from the United States prompted Spain to withdraw from the Dominican Republic; early in 1866, as France abandoned Mexico, Spain likewise broke off its campaign against Peru and Chile. Having seized and sold enough guano to cover the cost of the two-year operation, the Spanish squadron steamed for home in early May 1866, but not before Méndez Nuñez carried out bombardments of Callao and Valparaíso. The latter was practically undefended, but the shore batteries of the former inflicted serious damage on the Spanish screw frigate *Resolución*.[71] During the war Peru ordered two ironclads in Britain, the 3,500-ton armored frigate *Independencia* and the 2,030-ton turret ship *Huáscar*. Launched in August and October 1865, they departed for the New World early in 1866 but did not reach the allied base on Chiloé until June, one month after the Spanish squadron left South American waters. Because Spain did not agree to a truce until 1871, Peru feared a renewal of the fighting and in April 1868 further strengthened its navy by purchasing the single-turret monitors *Atahualpa* (ex-*Catawba*) and *Manco Capac* (ex-*Oneota*) from the United States.[72]

Thus by the end of the decade the Peruvian navy had four ironclads, including the two most formidable in American waters, yet in overall numbers of armored warships Brazil took the early lead in the regional naval race, building six small ironclads in Britain and France between 1864 and 1866, in the early years of a war against Paraguay. As the naval action of the war was confined to the Paraná and Paraguay rivers, these ironclads all were small enough to be suitable only for river or coastal operations. The same was true of three single-turret monitors assembled in Brazil and commissioned in 1868. The 1,520-ton *Brasil*, which arrived from La Seyne in July 1865, was the first Brazilian armored warship and also the largest of the lot. During the war Paraguayan President Francisco Solano López, son of the previous dictator, countered by ordering five small ironclads in Europe, but by the time the war ended in 1870 his defeated country could not afford to pay for them, and all five ended up in the Brazilian navy. This more than compensated Brazil for the only armored warship lost in the war, the *Rio de Janeiro*, which sank in September 1866 after striking mines in the Paraguay River.[73]

Argentina was an ally of Brazil in its war against Paraguay but, like Chile, had no armored warships in the 1860s. Argentina and Chile each ordered two ironclads in the early 1870s.[74] Meanwhile, the Spanish navy continued to expand, and by 1870 had seven ironclads built or building. After the war against Peru and Chile, the wooden screw frigate *Resolución* was rebuilt as a 3,380-ton central battery ironclad and launched in 1869 as the *Méndez Nuñez*, in honor of the hero of the recent conflict. That same year Spain launched the 7,350-ton wooden-hulled armored frigate *Sagunto*, converted on the stocks at Ferrol after having been laid down as a screw ship of the line. By then the original Spanish ironclads had been joined by the armored frigates *Vitoria* (7,135 tons, launched at London in 1865) and *Zaragosa* (5,530 tons, Cartagena, 1867).[75]

Japan and the War of the Meiji Restoration
(1868–69)

After the Perry expedition of 1853 opened Japan to trade with the United States, other naval powers pressured the Tokugawa shogun with similar exercises in gunboat diplomacy. Countries securing trade treaties in the late 1850s included Britain, France, and Russia, and in 1861, Prussia, the latter after sending its only operational screw corvette and three sailing ships to Tokyo Bay.[76] The shogunate wisely recognized that Japan lacked the technology to resist even a third-rate Western navy, but the concessions to foreigners rankled in a country with a proud warrior tradition. An attempt to return to isolationism in 1863 brought British, French, and American squadrons to Japanese waters, and the British shelling of Kagoshima served notice that the Western powers would use force to maintain their treaty rights. Unable to return to the past, Japan could only move forward.

In 1868, after failing to deal effectively with fifteen years of pressure from foreign powers, the Tokugawa shogunate was overthrown by a coalition of feudal domains which established a new government in the name of the Meiji emperor, the so-called "Meiji Restoration." While the new government would be known in the long run for saving Japan by enlisting foreign experts to help modernize and industrialize the country, earlier in the 1860s both the shogunate and the feudal domains opposing it hired British naval advisors and purchased steam-powered warships. As early as 1866 the Ishiwajima navy yard completed the screw gunboat *Chiyodogata*, the first steam warship built in Japan, but the 140-ton vessel reflected the state of Japanese industry at the time, taking five years to build, with machinery and other components imported from the West. The first Japanese ironclad was the former CSS *Stonewall*, purchased by the shogun in 1867 from the United States. When the 1,360-ton ironclad ram arrived in Japan the following year, it was taken over by the new imperial government. The Japanese initially called the vessel the *Kotetsu*, meaning "iron-covered ship," before renaming it *Adzuma*. After the revolution, or "restoration," of 1868, supporters of the shogunate fought a brief civil war before conceding defeat. The conflict featured naval battles off southern Hokkaido and northern Honshu, in every case chaotic mêlées between ill-trained forces. In June 1869 at the decisive Battle of Hakodate, an imperial squadron led by the *Kotetsu* defeated the shogun's squadron of wooden steamers, destroying the largest of the latter, the 1,450-ton paddle steamer *Kwaiten* (the former Prussian *Danzig*). A second ironclad, the 1,430-ton armored broadside corvette *Ryujo*, did not join the navy in time to participate in the brief war. Originally a speculation ship built in Britain during the American Civil War, it was purchased in 1869 by Prince Hizen, an opponent of the shogun, who subsequently gave it to the emperor as a gift. Following the elimination of internal rivals, the new imperial government proceeded to lay the foundations of Japanese power at sea as well as on land.[77]

The Franco-Prussian War (1870–71)

Prussia's victory over Austria in 1866 had led to the formation of the North German Confederation the following year and, with it, the transformation of the Royal Prussian Navy into the North German Federal Navy. In the summer of 1867 the navy took possession of the armored frigates *Friedrich Carl* (6,000 tons, from La Seyne) and *Kronprinz* (5,800 tons, from Samuda), followed early in 1869 by the 9,800-ton armored frigate *König Wilhelm*, the former Turkish *Fatikh*, which the navy had purchased from the Thames Iron Works in 1867 after the sultan defaulted on its contract. Krupp received the artillery contracts for all three ships, having developed all-steel muzzle-loading rifles superior to the latest Armstrong rifled muzzle loaders.[78] Production problems delayed delivery of the first guns until the summer of 1869, prompting the postponement of a scheduled West Indian cruise by the new "armored squadron" until the following summer. In July 1870 the onset of war with France forced another change of plans.

Wishing to complete the process of German unification with a victorious war against the French, Bismarck succeeded in baiting France into declaring war on Prussia on 19 July 1870. As the Prussian army and its allies from the lesser German states mobilized and crossed onto French soil, the north German navy deployed the small ram *Prinz Adalbert* as harbor watch at Hamburg and concentrated its three armored frigates with the small turret ship *Arminius* at the new North Sea base of Wilhelmshaven; meanwhile most of the unarmored fleet was dispersed to defend the Baltic coast. The French fleet enjoyed a great superiority over the north German navy. Its 400 warships included seventeen seagoing frigates in the same class with the *König Wilhelm*, *Friedrich Carl*, and *Kronprinz*. French navy leaders pondered attacks on Wilhelmshaven and Kiel, the destruction of merchant shipping, and cooperation with the army in landing troops on the north German coast. But the navy and the army had done little prewar planning for amphibious assaults, and the fleet included too few of the small vessels needed for close coastal operations. In any event, French navy leaders concluded that they could execute landings only on the beaches of the Baltic. Such operations were unthinkable without an alliance with Denmark, which resolved to remain neutral following the Prussian army's invasion of France in the first days of the war.[79]

Nevertheless, the northern squadron, under Vice Admiral Bouët-Willaumez, moved from the Channel into the Baltic, while the Mediterranean squadron, under Vice Admiral Martin Fourichon, relocated to the North Sea. Together they seized enough merchantmen early in the war to deter German-flagged vessels from venturing out. At the onset of bad weather the French squadrons withdrew to Cherbourg, but by then the defeat of Napoleon III at Sedan (2 September 1870) had decided the outcome of the war. After the imperial government gave way to a republic over thirty warships were disarmed, their men and guns put to use ashore in the defense of Paris and other northern cities.

Meanwhile, naval units left in the Mediterranean evacuated the French garrison from Rome, abandoning the city to be annexed by Italy. France pursued the war for another five months, sustained in part by American arms shipments that the north German navy could do nothing to stop. The only action beyond European waters came on 9 November 1870, when the 350-ton screw gunboat *Meteor*, commanded by future admiral Eduard Knorr, engaged the 800-ton dispatch steamer *Bouvet* in an inconclusive two-hour duel off Havana.[80]

Throughout the war, the north German navy at best annoyed the French. Admiral Prince Adalbert himself underscored the irrelevance of sea power in the Prussian–German strategy by spending the war with the army, as he had in 1866. At the end of the first week of August 1870, Vice Admiral Jachmann took the *König Wilhelm*, the *Kronprinz*, the *Friedrich Carl*, and the *Arminius* on a sortie all the way to the Dogger Bank but encountered no French warships. The French made their first appearance in the North Sea, off Wilhelmshaven, shortly after Jachmann returned to port. Thereafter, the durable *Arminius* went out on more than forty sorties while the armored frigates were idled by engine trouble. On 11 September Jachmann finally took all three frigates out on a second squadron sortie, but by then the French already had left for home.[81]

After the French navy seized a number of German merchant ships early in the war, Bismarck authorized commerce raiding against the French merchant marine. In November 1870, after most of the French navy had returned home, Captain Johannes Weickhmann took the corvette *Augusta* to the Atlantic coast of France, where he captured three ships at the mouth of the Gironde in January 1871. The action caused alarm in nearby Bordeaux, then serving as temporary capital of the new Third Republic. With several French armored frigates bearing down on him, Weickhmann took the *Augusta* to the safety of Vigo in neutral Spain, where it remained blockaded until the war ended. The *Augusta*'s three prizes were the only French merchantmen taken by the Germans in the war. In comparison, the French navy captured no German warships but seized more than 200 merchantmen, paralyzing German overseas trade for more than half a year.[82]

At its birth the German empire ranked as the foremost military power in Europe, but the negligible role played by the Prussian and the north German navy in the wars of German unification left deep scars on the younger generation of the officer corps. The frustrated young men included Lieutenant Alfred Tirpitz, then 21 years old, who spent most of the Franco-Prussian War at anchor in Wilhelmshaven aboard the *König Wilhelm*. For Tirpitz, the humiliation of 1870 helped shape his later conviction that Germany must have a fleet capable of offensive action.[83]

Conclusion

Perhaps the most remarkable thing about the first decade of the armored warship was that the advent of the revolving turret (in the American *Monitor* of 1862) and the concept of protecting heavy pivoting guns in an armored casemate (in the British *Research* of 1864) did not bring an immediate end to the construction of ironclads capable only of broadside fire. The last such ship commissioned in the British navy would be HMS *Triumph* in 1873, while the Russian navy added battery frigates as armored cruisers throughout the 1870s. No navy developed a coherent doctrine of how to fight a war at sea, then designed its ironclads accordingly; instead, the focus was on accumulating ironclads regardless of type, even if they did not reflect the latest technology.[84] This approach left the typical armored fleet of 1870 with a heterogeneous mix of broadside, turret, and casemate ironclads. Only ironclads displacing less than 2,000 tons, along with some larger monitors and other low-freeboard types designed for coastal operations, were not counted as part of the battle fleet.

Of the twenty-one countries to own an armored warship at any time before 1914, seventeen had at least one by 1870. In sheer numbers of armored units Britain had fifty-four completed or under construction and the United States and France each had fifty-one. They were followed by Russia with twenty-seven, Italy sixteen, Ottoman Turkey fourteen, the Netherlands thirteen, Brazil thirteen, Austria–Hungary eleven, the North German Confederation nine, Spain seven, Denmark six, Peru four, Sweden three, Norway three, Japan two, and Greece two. But in warships of 2,000 tons or more, not designed for coastal operations, the rankings looked somewhat different: Britain had thirty-seven, France thirty-five, Italy sixteen, Ottoman Turkey twelve, Austria–Hungary eleven, Russia ten, north Germany seven, Spain seven, the Netherlands four, Denmark three, Peru two, and Greece one. The United States, Brazil, Japan, Sweden, and Norway had no ironclads truly capable of operating on the high seas.

With the construction of the *Gloire* and the *Warrior*, a competition ensued in which navies sought to develop ever more powerful guns to pierce armor, and ever stronger armor to stop armor-piercing ordnance. The first armored frigates cost six times as much as unarmored screw frigates of the same dimensions; improvements in artillery and armor drove naval estimates still higher, while technological change doomed many expensive ironclads to an early obsolescence.[85] In European waters only the six great powers, along with Spain and the Ottoman empire, appeared to have the resolve to continue to build ever-larger and more powerful armored warships capable of high seas operations. Otherwise, the quest for ironclads would be limited to the Far East and Latin America, where modest numbers of armored warships could redress local imbalances of power or serve as a hedge against great power gunboat diplomacy. Aside from the Netherlands, which launched the 5,315-ton rigged turret ship *König der Nederlanden* in 1874, and Denmark, which launched the 5,330-ton *Helgoland* in 1878, no minor European navy ever again would attempt to build battleships even approaching the dimensions of the newest types of the first- and second-rate navies.

Notes

1 Lambert, "Iron Hulls and Armour Plate," 53.
2 Lambert, *Battleships in Transition*, 101, 122–43, and *passim*; idem, "Iron Hulls and Armour Plate," 53–4; *Conway, 1860–1905*, 286–7.
3 Lambert, *Battleships in Transition*, 71, 122–43, and *passim*; idem, "Iron Hulls and Armour Plate," 54; *Conway, 1860–1905*, 4; Campbell, "Naval Armaments and Armour," 158–9.
4 David K. Brown, *Warrior to Dreadnought: Warship Development, 1860–1905* (London, 1997), 12–13; Lambert, "Iron Hulls and Armour Plate," 55–8; *Conway, 1860–1905*, 7–13.
5 Sondhaus, *The Habsburg Empire and the Sea*, 192, 202, 205, 209–13; Mariano Gabriele, *La politica navale italiana dall'unità alla viglia di Lissa* (Milan, 1958), 30, 89, 129; Franco Bargoni, *Le prime navi di linea della marina italiana, 1861–1880* (Rome, 1976), *passim*.
6 *Conway, 1860–1905*, 173, 380; Tomitch, *Warships of the Imperial Russian Navy*, 98–9.
7 Raimondo Luraghi, "Background," in William N. Still, Jr, ed., *The Confederate Navy: The Ships, Men and Organization, 1861–65* (Annapolis, Md, 1997), 7–8; Canney, *The Old Steam Navy*, appendices.
8 Canney, *The Old Steam Navy*, 1: 91–125, and *passim*, 168–78, and *passim*.
9 Ibid., 2: 7, 14; Robert Holcombe, "Types of Ships," in William N. Still, Jr, ed., *The Confederate Navy: The Ships, Men and Organization, 1861–65* (Annapolis, Md, 1997), 51–3.
10 Canney, *The Old Steam Navy*, 2: 8–10, 54.
11 William N. Still, Jr, "Operations," in *The Confederate Navy: The Ships, Men and Organization, 1861–65* (Annapolis, Md, 1997), 216–17.
12 Still, "The American Civil War," in Robert Gardiner, ed., *Steam, Steel and Shellfire: The Steam Warship 1815–1905* (London, 1992), 74; idem, "Operations," 217; Holcombe, "Types of Ships," 52; Canney, *The Old Steam Navy*, 2: 29–32. Most sources give no displacement figure for the *Virginia*, but Gromov *et al.*, *Tri Veka Rossiiskogo Flota*, 1: 226, lists the ship at 3,500 tons and the *Monitor* at 1,200 tons, most likely figures for full load.
13 William H. Roberts, *USS New Ironsides in the Civil War* (Annapolis, Md, 1999), 18–28, 80–3, 89–91, 99–103; Canney, *The Old Steam Navy*, 2: 15–20. Still, "Operations," 222, alleges that the *David* "badly crippled" the *New Ironsides*.
14 Canney, *The Old Steam Navy*, 2: 21–5.
15 Ibid., 2: 29–30, 33, 59–69, 75, 89–91, 138; *Conway, 1860–1905*, 119–23.
16 Canney, *The Old Steam Navy*, 2: 70–3, 79.
17 Ibid., 1: 97; David Lyon, "Underwater Warfare and the Torpedo Boat," in Robert Gardiner, ed., *Steam, Steel and Shellfire: The Steam Warship 1815–1905* (London, 1992), 135.
18 Canney, *The Old Steam Navy*, 2: 38–55, 95–118, 138. The world's only other turreted stern-wheeler was HMS *Pioneer*, an unarmored iron-hulled warship built at Sydney in 1863 for use against the Maori in New Zealand. See Brown, *Paddle Warships*, 58–9.
19 Canney, *The Old Steam Navy*, 2: 78.
20 Canney, *The Old Steam Navy*, 2: 55; Chester G. Hearn, *Admiral David Glasgow Farragut: The Civil War Years* (Annapolis, Md, 1998), 98–113, 166; idem, *Admiral David Dixon Porter: The Civil War Years* (Annapolis, Md, 1996), 135–237 and *passim*; Holcombe, "Types of Ships," 53; Still, "Operations," 219, 224–8.
21 Holcombe, "Types of Ships," 54–6; Canney, *The Old Steam Navy*, 2: 80.
22 Hearn, *Farragut*, 257–91, 305; Canney, *The Old Steam Navy*, 1: 102; Still, "Operations," 231–2.

23 Still, "Operations," 223; Lyon, "Underwater Warfare and the Torpedo Boat," 135.
24 Canney, *The Old Steam Navy*, 2: 124, 138. *Conway, 1860–1905*, 123, says five monitors became spar torpedo vessels.
25 Campbell, "Naval Armaments and Armour," 167.
26 Canney, *The Old Steam Navy*, 2: 29–30; Warren F. Spencer, *The Confederate Navy in Europe* (Tuscaloosa, Ala., 1983), 111.
27 Holcombe, "Types of Ships," 57–8.
28 Lawrence Sondhaus, "Die österreichische Kriegsmarine und der amerikanische Sezessionskrieg 1861–1865," *Marine–Gestern, Heute* 13 (1986): 81–2.
29 Holcombe, "Types of Ships," 58–61.
30 Spencer, *The Confederate Navy in Europe*, 43, 55, and *passim*.
31 Sondhaus, "Die österreichische Kriegsmarine und der amerikanische Sezessionskrieg 1861–1865," 81–3.
32 Lambert, "The Screw Propeller Warship," 42; Holcombe, "Types of Ships," 50–1.
33 Spencer, *The Confederate Navy in Europe*, 198–200, 216–17; Brown, *Warrior to Dreadnought*, 17–18; *Conway, 1860–1905*, 136.
34 Lambert, *Battleships in Transition*, 84–5; Spencer, *The Confederate Navy in Europe*, 216.
35 Still, "The American Civil War," 61; Canney, *The Old Steam Navy*, 2: 131.
36 *Conway, 1860–1905*, 119; Canney, *The Old Steam Navy*, 2: 64, 86, 126–9, 138.
37 Stanley Sandler, *The Emergence of the Modern Capital Ship* (Newark, Del., 1979), 69; Canney, *The Old Steam Navy*, 2: 15–20, 62, 66–70; Roberts, *USS New Ironsides in the Civil War*, 1–2.
38 Canney, *The Old Steam Navy*, 2: 66–70, 83, 86–8; William N. Still, Jr, *American Sea Power in the Old World: The United States Navy in European and Near Eastern Waters, 1865–1917* (Westport, Ct, 1980), 34; Beeler, *British Naval Policy*, 200; Hearn, *Farragut*, 310–11. On the Russian navy visits of 1863, see Gromov *et al.*, *Tri Veka Rossiiskogo Flota*, 1: 238–40; Naval Historical Foundation, *The Russian Navy Visits the United States* (Washington, D.C., 1969), 10, 18–19.
39 Sandler, *Emergence of the Modern Capital Ship*, 177–233; Brown, *Warrior to Dreadnought*, 41–52; *Conway, 1860–1905*, 19–21; Canney, *The Old Steam Navy*, 2: 25–9, 57. See also Arthur Hawkey, *Black Night Off Finisterre: The Tragic Tale of an Early British Ironclad* (Annapolis, Md, 1999).
40 David K. Brown, "The Era of Uncertainty, 1863–1878," in Robert Gardiner, ed., *Steam, Steel and Shellfire: The Steam Warship 1815–1905* (London, 1992), 76–8; *Conway, 1860–1905*, 4–5, 12–18. On Reed's opposition to Coles on the construction of the *Captain*, see Beeler, *British Naval Policy*, 110–23.
41 Sandler, *Emergence of the Modern Capital Ship*, 24, 171–2, 234–49; Brown, *Warrior to Dreadnought*, 58–63; idem, "The Era of Uncertainty, 1863–1878," 80–3; *Conway, 1860–1905*, 22–4, 111; Griffiths, "Warship Machinery," 175.
42 Baxter, *Introduction of the Ironclad Warship*, 330; *Conway, 1860–1905*, 288–9.
43 *Conway, 1860–1905*, 298, 301–2.
44 Campbell, "Naval Armaments and Armour," 159.
45 Canney, *The Old Steam Navy*, 1: 133, 141–2; Brown, "The Era of Uncertainty, 1863–1878," 89; idem, *Warrior to Dreadnought*, 14, 20; cf. *Conway, 1860–1905*, 47, 50.
46 *Conway, 1860–1905*, 45–6.
47 Watts, *The Imperial Russian Navy*, 14; Tomitch, *Warships of the Imperial Russian Navy*, 1: 96 and *passim*; Campbell, "Naval Armaments and Armour," 168.
48 Langensiepen and Güleryüz, *The Ottoman Steam Navy*, 2–3; *Conway, 1860–1905*, 416.
49 Langensiepen and Güleryüz, *The Ottoman Steam Navy*, 5; *Conway, 1860–1905*, 387.
50 *Conway, 1860–1905*, 374.
51 Ibid., 360–88 and *passim*.

52 Erich Gröner, *Die deutschen Kriegsschiffe, 1815–1945*, 8 vols (Coblenz, 1989), 1: 68–9, 107, 113–14, 160–2. Starting in November 1862, the Swedish firm delivered ninety-four guns to Prussia. See Sondhaus, *Preparing for Weltpolitik*, 73, 259 note 8.

53 Sondhaus, *Preparing for Weltpolitik*, 73; quote from unidentified newspaper clipping enclosed in Ministry for Foreign Affairs to Albrecht von Roon (war and navy minister), Berlin, 14 April 1862, Bundesarchiv–Militärarchiv, RM 1/750, 205.

54 Robert Steen Steensen, *Vore Panserskibe, 1863–1943* (Copenhagen, 1968), 137–8, 146, 148–9, 160–8, 178–83; idem, *Vore Krydsere* (Copenhagen, 1971), 37.

55 There is no recent comprehensive Danish account of the navy's role in 1864. Otto Georg Lütken, *Søkrigsbegivenhederne i 1864* (Copenhagen, 1896), remains the most detailed study.

56 Sondhaus, *The Habsburg Empire and the Sea*, 277.

57 Ibid., 239–41.

58 Sondhaus, *Preparing for Weltpolitik*, 76–7. The Danes apparently still claim Helgoland as a victory. The frigate *Jylland* is preserved in Copenhagen as a national historic monument. See F. H. Kjølsen, "The Old Danish Frigate," *The Mariner's Mirror* 51 (1965): 27–33.

59 Sondhaus, *Preparing for Weltpolitik*, 77–8.

60 Ibid., 80–2.

61 Ibid., 82–4.

62 Sondhaus, *The Naval Policy of Austria–Hungary*, 6.

63 Bargoni, *Le prime navi di linea della marina italiana, passim*.

64 Instructions to Persano summarized in Depretis to Ricasoli, Florence, 17 July 1866, in Sergio Camerani and Gaetano Arfè, eds, *Carteggi di Bettino Ricasoli, vol. 22: 20 giungno–31 luglio 1866*, (Rome, 1967), 298 note 421, which confirms that the Lissa campaign was intended only as a prelude to a direct assault on Istria and Dalmatia.

65 Sondhaus, *Habsburg Empire and the Sea*, 254–55; Luigi Donolo, "The History of Italian Naval Doctrine," in James J. Tritten and Luigi Donolo, eds, *A Doctrine Reader: The Navies of United States, Great Britain, France, Italy, and Spain* (Newport, R.I., 1995), 102–3.

66 Sondhaus, *Habsburg Empire and the Sea*, 255–6; Tegetthoff to Baroness Emma Lutteroth, "At sea," 22 July 1866, text in Maximilian Daublebsky von Sterneck zu Ehrenstein, *Admiral Max Freiherr von Sterneck: Erinnerungen aus den Jahren 1847 bis 1897*, ed. Jerolim Benko von Boinik (Vienna, 1901), 149–50.

67 James J. Tritten, "Doctrine and Fleet Tactics in the Royal Navy," in James J. Tritten and Luigi Donolo, eds, *A Doctrine Reader: The Navies of United States, Great Britain, France, Italy, and Spain* (Newport, R.I., 1995), 21; idem, "Navy and Military Doctrine in France," 54.

68 Busk, *Navies of the World*, 98–9; http://www.uss-salem.org/danfs/frigates

69 Sondhaus, *The Habsburg Empire and the Sea*, 226, 245, 261 note 18; Dupont and Taillemite, *Les guerres navales françaises*, 249–50; Shirley J. Black, "Napoléon III et le Mexique: un triomphe monétaire," *Revue historique* 259 (1978): 63–73; *Conway, 1860–1905*, 286, 320.

70 Araya, "Situación estratégica naval," 2: 402–7; Rodríguez González, *Política naval de la Restauración*, 120; *Conway, 1860–1905*, 380, 383, 419.

71 Araya, "Situación estratégica naval," 2: 407–12; *Conway, 1860–1905*, 381, 419.

72 Pedro Espina Ritchie, *El Monitor Huáscar* (Santiago, 1969), 53–5; Canney, *The Old Steam Navy*, 2: 64, 86, 138.

73 Carvalho, *Nossa Marinha*, 54–86; *Conway, 1860–1905*, 405–6. Carvalho, 78, 82, refers to the monitors *Rio Grande*, *Alagoas*, and *Pará*, which are not listed in Conway.

74 *Conway, 1860–1905*, 401, 410.

75 Ibid., 381.

76 Sondhaus, *Preparing for Weltpolitik*, 67.
77 David C. Evans and Mark R. Peattie, *Kaigun: Strategy, Tactics, and Technology in the Imperial Japanese Navy, 1887–1941* (Annapolis, Md, 1997), 5–7, 11–12; *Conway, 1860–1905*, 219, 235.
78 Campbell, "Naval Armaments and Armour," 160.
79 Sondhaus, *Preparing for Weltpolitik*, 93–4.
80 Ibid., 94, 99; Dupont and Taillemite, *Les guerres navales françaises*, 251–4.
81 Sondhaus, *Preparing for Weltpolitik*, 95.
82 Ibid., 96.
83 Ibid., 96, 100.
84 James J. Tritten, "Revolutions in Military Affairs, Paradigm Shifts, and Doctrine," in James J. Tritten and Luigi Donolo, eds, *A Doctrine Reader: The Navies of United States, Great Britain, France, Italy, and Spain* (Newport, R.I., 1995), 145.
85 Brown, "The Era of Uncertainty, 1863–1878," 75.

CHAPTER FIVE

The 1870s

With the advent of armor, a country's industrial base became even more important to its naval power, and the sheer cost of larger armored warships meant that only those aspiring to great power status would attempt to build them. When the Ottoman empire and Spain failed to sustain their ironclad programs of the 1860s, by the early 1870s the list of naval powers for the first time ever was identical to the overall list of the great powers of Europe: Britain, France, and Russia, joined by Italy, newly united Germany, and Austria–Hungary. The other maritime countries of Europe, the United States, and other naval states beyond Europe fell into a clearly inferior category of sea power. Even among the great powers, those whose fate in war would be determined on land tended to restrain their naval spending. The 1870s also witnessed a clear division of fleets into armored and unarmored components, with the terms "battleship" and "cruiser" coming into use to describe the two groups of vessels. For the European powers the ironclad battle fleet remained in home waters for the event of a war against another great power, while the unarmored fleet showed the flag worldwide in defense of colonial and trading interests.

Naval warfare from the perspective of the 1870s

The battleships of the 1870s were larger than those of the previous decade but also more vulnerable, both to stronger artillery and the new self-propelled torpedo; finally, it became impossible to plate a ship with enough wrought iron armor in sufficient thickness without reducing its speed and seaworthiness to unacceptable levels. The central battery or casemate ship design popular in the 1870s provided for heavy armor on the waterline and around a central casemate, which housed the guns as well as the ship's engines, and left the rest of the ship unarmored. At the end of the decade, after a brief experiment with "sandwich" (iron-and-wood) armor, "compound" (iron-and-steel) armor was developed which proved to be stronger than wrought iron plates of greater thickness. The armored battleship was saved, but the crisis left navies looking for alternative warship designs. In the meantime, improvements in armor and ordnance doomed many of the battleships of the 1860s to an early obsolesence, and some built with armor-plated wooden hulls were scrapped during the decade. In France, two of the *Gloire*'s sister-ships were stricken in 1871–72, followed by the *Gloire* itself in 1879. In Britain, the armored frigate *Lord Clyde* was sold for breaking up in 1875, less than a decade after its commissioning. The same year, Italy discarded two armored frigates completed in 1864 and 1865. Iron-hulled ironclads proved to be far more durable. The *Gloire*'s iron half-sister *Couronne* remained afloat until 1930, and Britain's *Warrior* survived to become a museum ship late in the twentieth century. But the inflexible broadside battery configuration of their guns made these and all other surviving armored frigates obsolescent. Too weak to stand in the line of battle and too expensive to maintain as cruisers (the *Warrior*, which cost £377,000 to build, consumed another £121,000 for repairs in its first seven-and-a-half years in commission), many rusted at anchor as harbor watch ships.[1] Some navies lost other armored warships in accidents rooted in inexperience with the challenges of their maintenance or maneuver. Following the *Captain* disaster of 1870, Britain's 6,010-ton casemate ship *Vanguard* sank in 1875, after it was rammed by its sister-ship *Iron Duke* in a fog in Dublin Bay. The same year France lost the 6,715-ton *Magenta*, which exploded and sank in harbor. In 1878 Germany's brand-new 6,800-ton turret ship *Grosser Kurfürst* sank after it was rammed by the armored frigate *König Wilhelm* in broad daylight in the English Channel.[2]

The unarmored "cruisers" of the 1870s were even more of a hodgepodge than the battleships, as the category included vessels of wood, composite (wood-and-iron), and iron construction. Late in the decade the first all-steel cruisers made their appearance. Some composite-hulled armored ships had been built as early as the 1860s, but other than the Confederate raider *Shenandoah* and the Spanish *Tornado* (ex-Chilean *Pampero*), originally laid down for the Confederacy, there had been no unarmored cruising ships of composite construction. Austria–Hungary led the way with the composite frigates *Radetzky* and *Laudon*, laid down in 1870 and 1871; France followed with its first composite ship in 1872, Britain in 1873, and Russia in 1876. The French and Russian navies continued to build the ships concurrently with iron-hulled unarmored cruisers, the British, alongside iron-hulled and, ultimately, steel-hulled cruisers. Among the leading navies, Italy, Germany, and the United States built no composite warships at all. The Italian and American navies, which began the 1870s with large numbers of wooden cruisers, continued to use these ships into the era of the steel cruiser, while the Germans went straight from wood to all-iron hulls before the introduction of steel.[3]

Naval tactics remained muddled throughout the decade. The naval battles of the 1860s involving the greatest number of warships – Farragut's victory at Mobile Bay in 1864 and Tegetthoff's triumph at Lissa in 1866 – had been mêlées in which the formations of the competing admirals broke down as soon as the action began. Free to take the initiative, the boldest and most resourceful (and one might add, luckiest) ship captains had fared the best, vindicating Bouët-Willaumez's 1855 prediction. Nevertheless, the conceptual "militarization" first apparent in naval tactical works of the late 1850s continued into the 1870s, despite the lack of evidence that steam propulsion would bring military "order" to naval battles. A number of writers continued to emphasize littoral operations, a legacy of the Crimean War. Meanwhile, many observers, ranging from the exiled Prince de Joinville in the late 1850s to the future British admiral John Fisher in the early 1870s, wondered if future fleets would be reduced to mere floating artillery formations. But the British and other navies charged in part with defending colonies and overseas trade came to recognize the inadequacy of such a "military" theoretical framework. J. C. R. Colomb's *The Protection of our Commerce and Distribution of our Naval Forces Considered* (1867), though far from articulating a full-blown Mahanian concept of command of the sea, in many ways laid the foundation of the future "Blue Water" school.[4] Yet even in Britain the "militarization" progressed to a point where most navy leaders lost sight of the connection between the fleet and the commerce it was supposed to protect, and it would take decades for their vision to be restored. During the era of the Jeune École, when commerce raiding again became a fashionable strategy for Britain's naval rivals, no one at the Admiralty advocated a convoy system in response. When such a campaign was finally implemented against Britain, in the submarine threat from Germany during the First World War, the Admiralty would wait almost three years before introducing convoys for the protection of trade.

During the 1870s technologies emerged which, in the 1880s, would cause many navies to question the future of the battleship and the battle fleet concept, in particular, the self-propelled torpedo. In the American Civil War, spar torpedo attacks had claimed the screw sloop USS *Housatonic* and the ironclad CSS *Albemarle*, but in both cases the attacking craft also sank. The first alternative delivery concept, only marginally safer for the attacker, was to tow the torpedo behind a fast-moving smaller vessel, which would steam straight for its target, then turn away at the last moment to avoid collision while the trailing torpedo hit the mark. The self-propelled torpedo was first developed by British expatriate Robert Whitehead, in his factory at Fiume (Rijeka) in Austria– Hungary, following its invention in 1864 by Austrian navy captain Johann Luppis. Whitehead took Luppis' concept of a mechanical surface torpedo and developed a submerged version driven by compressed air. After adding a hydrostatic depth regulator, in 1868 he sold the finished product to the Austro–Hungarian navy. Britain purchased its first Whitehead torpedoes in 1870, France in 1872, Germany and Italy in 1873, and Russia in 1876. By the end of the decade even the Chinese navy had them. Starting with Britain's Woolwich Arsenal in 1872, most naval powers produced their own Whitehead torpedoes under license. But because the self-propelled Whitehead torpedo of the early 1870s had a speed of just 7 knots and carried a charge of less than twenty pounds of dynamite, throughout the decade more lethal spar torpedoes and towed torpedoes remained in the arsenals even of those navies that introduced Whiteheads.[5] Until more reliable, more deadly, self-propelled torpedoes were developed, along with tactics and a strategy for their use, the viability of the battleship and the battle fleet remained unquestioned.

Italy and Austria–Hungary

After the defeat of the Italian fleet at Lissa in July 1866, the Austrian navy at least momentarily could claim to have the fourth most powerful seagoing battle fleet in the world, inferior only to the British, French, and Russian fleets. But the Italians, after failing to defeat the Austrians either at sea or on land, after the war acquired Venetia under an arrangement Austria had made with Napoleon III on the eve of the war, in order to ensure France's neutrality. Even after losing two ironclads at Lissa, the Italian navy still had more than the Austrian (ten, compared to seven) and a future Italian naval base at Venice would pose a threat to Austria's primary commercial port, Trieste. In September 1866 the Habsburg war minister observed that "under the circumstances" the strengthening of Austrian seapower "appears to be of decisive importance."[6]

After the victory at Lissa, Wilhelm von Tegetthoff was promoted to vice admiral, then sent on a tour of naval facilities in Britain, France, and the United States in 1866–67, after which he went to Mexico to retrieve the body of Emperor Francis Joseph's brother, whose unsuccessful reign as Emperor Maximilian had ended with his execution at Queretaro. Upon his return in 1868 Tegetthoff became commander of the navy, by then the Austro–Hungarian, after the constitutional reorganization of the empire in 1867. Unfortunately for the navy, its victory of 1866 had demonstrated that a smaller Austrian force with inferior equipment could defeat a larger Italian rival on the strength of its superior training and tactics. The Austrian army, crushed by the Prussians in 1866, naturally received most of the postwar money and attention. But Tegetthoff's prestige ensured that the navy would continue to receive a respectable share of the defense outlay. In the late 1860s its seven broadside ironclads were rearmed with 7-inch Armstrong guns and work began on three new casemate ships, the wooden-hulled *Lissa* and the iron-hulled *Erzherzog Albrecht* and *Custoza*, as well as the conversion of the ship of the line *Kaiser* into a casemate ship. Like the broadside ironclads, the casemate ships were built by domestic shipyards, but Austria–Hungary depended heavily on British firms for armor plate and iron fittings as well as artillery.[7]

In the early 1870s, the political troubles of the Austro-Hungarian navy paled in comparison to those facing the Italian navy. Neapolitan and Piedmontese cliques (joined, after 1866, by a Venetian faction) left the officer corps less cohesive than that of the multinational Habsburg navy, and the Italian government waited until 1878–81 to phase out the old naval academies at Genoa and Naples in favor of a single academy at Livorno.[8] In 1871 a special commission even rejected a high seas deterrent, instead calling for a coast defense system with thirty-one fortified bases to protect Italy's long and vulnerable coastline. After a bitter debate over defense expenditure during 1870, the navy budget for 1871 was slashed to a mere 26.8 million lire, its lowest allocation ever and the only year in history that the Italian navy budget actually was lower than the Austro-Hungarian. But the fortunes of the two fleets went in opposite directions thereafter. In 1871, Tegetthoff died unexpectedly at the age of 43, while in Italy, Benedetto Brin became chief of naval engineering. Brin became the driving force behind the recovery of the Italian navy.[9]

Amid declining budgets in the years after the death of Tegetthoff, the Austro-Hungarian naval leadership could take comfort, at least until the end of the 1870s, in the fact that their fleet was still superior to the Italian. In 1871 Italy could boast of sixteen seagoing ironclads built or building to Austria–Hungary's eleven, but aside from the twin-turret ram *Affondatore* all were broadside frigates or corvettes. The Austrians, having laid down no new ironclads between 1863 and 1867, had no armored frigates under construction when the leading navies of Europe adopted the casemate ship design; the Italians, however, had six armored frigates still on the stocks as of 1867, and all were destined to be obsolete as soon as they were launched. In an attempt to adjust to the new technology, three of the six were modified while under construction, but only one – the 5,800-ton *Venezia*, completed in 1873 – emerged as a true casemate ship. The four armored frigates built with wooden hulls were decommissioned by 1880.[10]

After taking over as chief engineer, Brin designed an ironclad to be constructed entirely of iron and steel, larger, faster, and more heavily armored than any warship then afloat. Ignoring the casemate design then popular with other naval architects, he revived the turret ship, but in a form barely recognizable, with four very large guns paired in two armored turrets atop a vessel with a much higher freeboard than the *Affondatore*'s or that of any "monitor" of the 1860s. Unlike the casemate ship, Brin's new design eliminated all masts and yards, a break from the past that would place it among the vessels called "pre-dreadnoughts" by the navies of the early twentieth century.[11] The *Duilio*, displacing 11,100 tons, and the *Dandolo*, 11,200 tons, were laid down in January 1873 at Castellammare and La Spezia, respectively. Their speed and power depended upon imported British engines and 17.7-inch Armstrong guns, the latter reflecting a decisive turn back toward faith in the gun and away from the ram. They were the world's first battleships fitted with all-steel armor, purchased from Schneider of Creusot after trials at La Spezia in 1877. Foreign firms also supplied the iron for their hulls. Italy remained heavily dependent upon foreign materials for Brin's next pair of battleships, the 13,900-ton *Italia* and *Lepanto*, laid down in 1876. The design was similar to the *Duilio* and *Dandolo*, only larger, with combination iron-and-steel hulls (all steel, in the case of *Lepanto*), slightly lighter (17-inch) Armstrong guns, relatively lighter armor, and more powerful engines, capable of 18 knots. Owing to the ships' combination of size, heavy primary armament, speed, and weak protection, some historians have characterized the *Italia* and *Lepanto* as forerunners of Sir John Fisher's battle cruiser design of the years before the First World War. In 1880 the Italian parliament authorized another three battleships, but Brin was temporarily out of office at the time and their design reflected the views of his critics, especially Vice Admiral Ferdinando Acton, who felt Brin's most recent pair of ships had been too large. The three units of the 11,200-ton *Ruggiero di Lauria* class were laid down in 1881–82.[12]

Across the Adriatic, Austria–Hungary was in no position to match Brin's battleships. Lacking a charismatic, respected leader after Tegetthoff's death, the navy often saw its budget proposals rejected by both German Austrian and Hungarian political leaders, the latter considering anything maritime to be an exclusively "Austrian" affair. Under the circumstances the navy could do no better than gradually replace its broadside frigates with casemate ships, at times resorting to sleight of hand to secure funding. Starting in 1873 money was budgeted to "rebuild" the 3,600-ton broadside frigates *Kaiser Max*, *Prinz Eugen*, and *Juan d'Austria* as casemate ships, but the navy actually scrapped the old wooden-hulled ships and built new iron-hulled ships of the same general dimensions, salvaging the armor plate and engines. Another of the original seven armored frigates was stricken in 1875 but the remaining three served into the 1880s. The only completely new battleship was the 7,550-ton casemate ship *Tegetthoff*, laid down in 1876. When it entered service in 1882 Austria–Hungary had a fleet of eight casemate ships commissioned within the past eleven years, all but one armed with imported Krupp artillery, supplemented by the three obsolete broadside frigates. The navy remained a respectable rival to the Italian fleet through the 1870s only because of the inadequacies of Italian shipyards, which took seven years to complete the *Duilio* (commissioned in 1880), nine for the *Dandolo* (1882) and *Italia* (1885), and eleven for the *Lepanto* (1887).[13] But the heaviest blow fell in May 1882, when the Dual Monarchy joined Germany and Italy in the Triple Alliance. With the Italians as allies, the Austro-Hungarian navy lost its primary *raison d'être*; meanwhile, having Austria–Hungary as a partner in a German-led anti-French alliance freed the Italian navy from its focus on the Adriatic and justified an even larger battle fleet capable of competing with France in the Mediterranean.

Italy laid down few new cruising vessels during the 1870s, as it continued to use a large fleet of wooden-hulled screw warships dating from the 1850s and 1860s. The brief age of composite-hulled and unarmored iron-hulled cruising ships already had passed by the time work began on the 2,490-ton corvettes *Flavio Gioia* and *Amerigo Vespucci*, fully rigged steel-hulled vessels laid down in 1879.[14] After 1866 Austria–Hungary had a more pressing need to replace its smaller fleet of wooden screw steamers, and between 1869 and 1876 laid down two composite frigates and six composite corvettes. The program was completed before the unarmored iron-hulled cruiser gained popularity, and by the time the ships warranted replacement, two decades later, the brief era of the fully rigged steel cruiser had passed.[15]

Britain and France

Prussia's victory over France in 1870–71 eliminated British fears of a French naval threat for at least a decade, leaving the British confident of their own superiority and security, perhaps as never before. The third naval power, Russia, took advantage of the Franco-Prussian War to abrogate the Black Sea clauses of the Treaty of Paris, and the London Conference of 1871 legalized the remilitarization of the Black Sea, but the overall condition of Russia's fleet and the industrial base supporting it left Britain with little to fear from that quarter. Reflecting its confidence, the navy maintained few active battleships, as of 1874 just four in the Mediterranean squadron and four in the home squadron, supplemented by ten coastal ironclads.[16]

In a world with no credible foreign naval threat, Britain continued to experiment with armor, armament, and steam propulsion technologies but with no sense of urgency. The last central battery ship built for the British navy was the 9,490-ton *Alexandra*, laid down in 1873 and commissioned in 1877. The 8,540-ton *Temeraire*, built during the same years, was a hybrid design, essentially a central battery ship but with two guns mounted on the upper deck in French-style barbettes, one foreward and one aft, thus making it Britain's first barbette ship.[17] The next British capital ship, *Inflexible*, laid down in 1874, bore striking similarities to the Italian *Duilio*, begun the previous year. Historians disagree over whether Nathaniel Barnaby, Reed's successor as chief constructor, designed the *Inflexible* in "response" to the *Duilio* or developed the same design concepts concurrently with Benedetto Brin. The *Inflexible*, at 11,880 tons, was slightly larger than the *Duilio* but its four guns (16-inch) were not quite as heavy. In contrast to its unrigged Italian counterpart, the ship initially had a two-masted brig rig. It was the first battleship equipped with fuel-efficient vertical compound engines and electricity for searchlights and interior illumination. Like the *Duilio* the *Inflexible* took seven years to complete, in part because of a campaign waged against it by Barnaby's predecessor. After a 1875 visit to Italy, Reed condemned the design of Brin's ships as well as the *Inflexible*, arguing that the armored citadel amidships would be dangerously unstable if the unarmored ends flooded. The ship survived further scrutiny, and modified versions of the same design were used for all British battleships laid down in the late 1870s. As the *Inflexible* neared completion, the controversy shifted from its design to its cost, driven up by the incorporation of so much new technology in one ship. At £812,000, the *Inflexible* cost more than twice as much as the *Warrior*, laid down just fifteen years earlier, and remained the most expensive British battleship for another quarter-century.[18]

The 8,510-ton *Agamemnon* and *Ajax* (built 1876–83) and the 9,420-ton *Colossus* (1879–86) and *Edinburgh* (1879–87) were smaller versions of the *Inflexible*. From the drawing board they had no sailing rig. The *Agamemnon* and *Ajax*, laid down during the Near Eastern crisis that preceded the Russo-Turkish War of 1877–78, had a shallower draught (two feet less than the *Inflexible*'s, 3.5

less than the *Temeraire's*) intended to make them more useful in the Baltic and Black Sea, in a war against Russia. Compound (iron-and-steel) armor, developed by the firms of Cammell and John Brown, passed muster at Shoeburyness in 1877 and was ordered for the turrets of the *Agamemnon* and the *Ajax* as well as those of the *Inflexible*. In 1879 the Admiralty decided to order compound armor for the *Colossus*, the *Edinburgh*, and subsequent battleships. Doubts about the basic design of the ships persisted for two decades, until the Battle of the Yalu in the Sino-Japanese War vindicated its soundness.[19] From 1876 Britain laid down no battleships with sailing rig, but the *Inflexible* kept its brig rig until 1885 and older battleships long after that, reflecting a legitimate concern that, in case of war, the navy might need capital ships on distant stations that could not be reached on steam alone. Concerns for coal supply – even for Britain, which had more coaling stations worldwide than any other country – kept most ironclads in European waters. Furthermore, iron warships, armored or unarmored, had to have their hulls cleaned more frequently than wooden ships, and no colonial bases had drydocks capable of accommodating larger vessels.[20]

Thus, there remained a clear need for smaller, unarmored, cruising warships, and maintenance considerations kept the smaller wooden-hulled cruiser alive even after the appearance of the first iron-hulled cruisers. During the 1870s Britain also needed new cruising vessels to replace wooden screw steamers laid down in the 1850s. Even the once-formidable *Orlando* and *Mersey* were decommissioned in 1871 and 1875, respectively, the former after only a decade of service. Of the fifty frigates and corvettes in Britain's wooden screw fleet as of 1860, only twenty-one were still in service in 1875; thirty-five frigates and corvettes were commissioned as replacements between 1860 and 1875. Reed's iron cruising frigate and corvettes of 1869–70 were followed in the 1870s by the frigates *Raleigh* and *Shah* and four iron corvettes, completed long after his retirement. Following the abandonment of all-wood construction, the British navy employed composite construction for its smaller unarmored cruisers. The six 2,120-ton corvettes of the *Emerald* class, completed in 1876–78, and thirty-two smaller sloops of the *Fantome* and subsequent classes commissioned after 1873 eventually replaced the last generation of wooden overseas cruisers.[21]

For service as overseas flagships, in the 1870s Barnaby designed three fully rigged armored cruisers: the 5,670-ton *Shannon* (built 1873–77), the 7,630-ton *Northampton* (1874–78), and the 7,470-ton *Nelson* (1874–81). They were broadside armored frigates except for recessed freeboard, like a casemate battleship, which allowed the forward gun in each broadside to fire ahead. Intended as a counter to the armored cruising ships deployed worldwide by France and the ironclad warships of the minor navies of the Americas and East Asia, theoretically they were also to hunt down commerce raiders but lacked the speed (under sail or steam) for the latter task. They were also too weak in armor and armament to fight a genuine battleship. The *Shannon* served with the fleet only four years but *Northampton* led the North American–West Indian station until 1886 and

Nelson the Australian station until 1889.[22] Reflecting the prejudices of their conceptual "militarization" of warfare at sea, in the early 1870s some British naval leaders concluded that trade protection by cruising warships was impossible. Sailing merchantmen or slow merchant steamers, even if organized in convoys, could be sunk at will by fast steam-powered cruisers. In any event, a country with a large merchant marine, such as Britain, could never build enough cruisers to "protect" its overseas commerce. Like Alfred Thayer Mahan two decades later, Barnaby felt that fast merchantmen could be armed to protect commerce in case of war. The strategy made sense especially for Britain, because at the time most fast merchant steamers were British. On the advice of the chief constructor and the Admiralty, Britain's shipbuilders began to build merchantmen stable enough to carry an armament, with watertight compartments and more of the machinery below the waterline.[23]

The dilemma of how to protect British interests overseas and police the world's sea lanes without armored warships became apparent off the west coast of South America in May 1877, where the 6,250-ton *Shah*, iron-hulled but not armored, served as Pacific flagship at a time when Britain temporarily had no ironclads in the Pacific Ocean. On 7 May naval officers sympathetic to a Peruvian coup seized the 2,030-ton armored turret ship *Huáscar*. After leaving Callao, the *Huáscar* stopped at least four British merchant steamers on the high

Plate 5.1 HMS *Amethyst* (left background) and HMS *Shah* engage the *Huáscar* in the Bay of Pacocha (29 May 1877)
Naval Historical Center, Basic Collection

seas, stealing coal, taking mail addressed to the government of Peru, and tak
some passengers prisoner. These violations of international law were brought
to the attention of the British navy, and on 29 May the *Shah* and its escort, the
1,970-ton wooden screw corvette *Amethyst*, intercepted the *Huáscar* in the bay
of Pacocha. During two hours of combat the *Shah* alone fired 237 rounds and
the two British ships together registered more than 50 hits on the *Huáscar*,
without seriously damaging it. The *Shah* also fired the first self-propelled
torpedo ever used in a naval action, which missed its target. The *Huáscar* carried
two 10-inch muzzle-loading rifles in a Coles turret protected by 8-inch wrought
iron armor, but because its gunners were inexperienced and its turret had to be
cranked by hand (with sixteen men manning the levers, it could make one
revolution in fifteen minutes), it fired only a half-dozen rounds and registered
no hits. That night, the *Huáscar* escaped Pacocha under cover of darkness and
steamed for Iquique, where it surrendered to Peruvian authorities the following
day. The incident demonstrated that even a lone relatively antiquated ironclad could defy the will of the world's greatest naval power if the latter had no
armored warship in the area. Britain responded by sending two ironclads to the
Pacific, and after 1881 maintained at least one there.[24]

The *Shah's* attempted use of a Whitehead torpedo came during a time of
experimentation with torpedo boat designs. Thornycroft's 32-ton *Lightning* of
1876, capable of 19 knots, won out against larger and slower vessels. It was
equipped with an innovative forced draught boiler, designed to draw more steam
from machinery restricted in size by the overall dimensions of the vessel. The
efficiency of the forced draught system soon made it standard for all new warship
boilers.[25] In the late 1870s Thornycroft built twelve of the British navy's first
eighteen torpedo boats and many others for export abroad. Vessels of the
Lightning type were not tested in action, but in the 1880s modified versions of
the design would be mass produced in all major navies.

After concluding peace with Germany in 1871, the French republic under-
standably devoted most of its defense budget to rebuilding its army. In 1870
France's naval outlay was three-quarters that of Britain, by 1872 barely half.[26]
During the decade Schneider of Creusot adopted the open hearth Siemens
Martin process to produce steel suitable for use in warship construction, and
later pioneered the manufacture of all-steel armor plate. Such breakthroughs
enabled the French navy to pioneer all-steel warship construction as well as all-
steel armor, but inadequate budgets and production problems ultimately left it
trailing other navies in both areas. In the 1870s French battleship design evolved
in its own unique direction. The French never built a lower-freeboard battleship
similar to the ill-fated British *Captain* or the German *Grosser Kurfürst*, instead
maintaining high freeboard as a distinctive feature of their designs. Heavy guns
in barbettes above a central battery gradually gave way to heavier barbette guns
on deck and no battery below.[27]

The 9,220-ton central battery ship *Redoutable* (built 1873–78) was the first
battleship laid down by the Third Republic. As the first capital ship constructed

primarily of steel, it attracted the attention of the British; in 1874 Barnaby and his eventual successor, William White, proponents of steel construction, visited Creusot and the slip at Lorient where the *Redoutable* was constructed. The ship did not reflect a complete break with the past, as it had wrought iron armor and, like subsequent French battleships, an exterior hull of mixed iron-and-steel construction. In contrast to the seven central battery ships laid down in 1865–70, the *Redoutable* had casemate guns capable of end-on fire, made possible by an exaggerated tumblehome. It carried eight 10.8-inch guns, one at each corner of the casemate and the rest virtually unprotected: two atop the casemate, one in the bow and one in the stern. The 10,450-ton *Courbet* (built 1875–86) and *Dévastation* (1876–82) followed the *Redoutable*; they were larger versions of the same design and the last of the navy's ten central battery ships. In the years 1873–82 the French also built four large monitors for coastal operations, ranging in size from the 4,635-ton *Vengeur* to the 5,870-ton *Fulminant*.[28]

In most French central battery ships the casemate guns were supplemented by heavy guns on deck, either in lightly armored barbettes or completely unprotected; in the British navy only the *Temeraire* had such a configuration of guns. But the French navy took its faith in the barbette concept to new heights in January 1877, when construction began at La Seyne on the 11,030-ton battleship *Amiral Duperré*. Its primary armament consisted of four 13.4-inch guns, all mounted in barbettes: two abreast forward and two on the centerline, amidships and aft. By the time it entered service in 1883, France had laid down ten additional barbette battleships, ranging in size from the four 7,530-ton vessels

Plate 5.2 French composite corvette *Éclaireur* (laid down 1874, completed 1879) *Naval Historical Center, Basic Collection*

of the *Terrible* class to the 11,720-ton *Amiral Baudin* and *Formidable*. The French barbette battleships had a mixed protection consisting of compound iron-and-steel armor as well as innovative all-steel plate of the type exported to Italy for the *Duilio*. After trials in 1880 the French navy chose compound over all-steel armor but was forced to accept the latter after Schneider of Creusot, eager to continue its development of steel armor, refused to fill orders for compound armor. But Schneider could not produce enough steel armor to meet the navy's needs, and it had to import compound armor from other manufacturers to satisfy its contracts. Between 1877 and 1883 the French built six smaller barbette ships, two for coastal operations and four armored cruisers for overseas service. The latter had composite wood-and-steel hulls.[29]

With the completion of the last of the ten central battery cruisers laid down between 1865 and 1869, by the late 1870s France had more armored cruising ships on foreign stations than any other naval power. In the 1880s the addition of the new barbette cruisers further modernized the armored cruising fleet. Meanwhile, France, like Britain, needed new unarmored cruisers to replace its deteriorating stock of wooden screw steamers. Of the twenty-six frigates and corvettes in the French wooden screw fleet of 1860, just twelve were still in service in 1875. Most of their replacements were also made of wood: twelve sailing frigates converted to screw during the 1860s, and another two frigates and thirty corvettes laid down by 1869 and completed in the early 1870s. Thereafter, France's defeat in the War of 1870–71 and the abdication of Napoleon III brought a hiatus in construction starts until 1873–74, when the iron-hulled cruising frigates *Duquesne* (5,905 tons) and *Tourville* (5,700 tons) were laid down, along with the 3,480-ton *Duguay-Trouin*. These ships were completed in 1877–79. Between 1874 and 1880 the French laid down twenty-eight more composite corvettes, gunboats, and dispatch vessels, all for colonial service. In 1879 one of the dispatch vessels, the *Voltigeur*, became the first warship equipped with the modern Belleville boiler. The superior French water-tube boiler design gained a near-universal acceptance which lasted until 1900, as many naval powers produced their own Belleville boilers under license. Ironically, given its emphasis on torpedo warfare in the 1880s, during the 1870s France produced no innovative torpedo boat designs, ordering most of its initial flotilla from Thornycroft.[30]

The birth of the Imperial German Navy

In 1871 the navy of the North German Confederation became the Imperial German Navy, reflecting the achievement of German unity under Prussia. At its birth the German battle fleet included three broadside ironclads, with a casemate ship (the 3,950-ton *Hansa*) and three large fully rigged turret ships (the 6,800-ton *Grosser Kurfürst* class) under construction. After spending the Franco-Prussian War with the army, Prince Adalbert did not return to the navy before his death in 1873. The operational commander Vice Admiral Jachmann became the scapegoat for the navy's relative inactivity during the war, paving the way for a politically connected general, Albrecht von Stosch, to become chief of the Imperial German Admiralty in 1872.

During Stosch's eleven-year tenure the navy completed the four battleship projects he inherited and added six more: the 7,600-ton casemate ships *Kaiser* and *Deutschland*, designed by Edward Reed and completed by Samuda in 1875, and the four barbette battleships of the 7,600-ton *Sachsen* class, completed between 1878 and 1883. The *Sachsens*, called "sortie corvettes" (*Ausfallkorvetten*) by Stosch, were the first German battleships built without masts or yards. They were designed to conduct sorties from fortified bases, either to break an enemy blockade or prevent enemy landings. For battleships of their size they had a light armament (six 10.25-inch Krupps, compared to eight in the *Kaiser* and *Deutschland*) and an unusually shallow draught of 21.5 feet, reflecting their intended defensive deployment in the shallow North Sea waters off Wilhelmshaven or along the Baltic coast. Their design made them poor high seas warships, and the limited capacity of their coal bunkers precluded extended deployments too far from home. Worse yet, their speed of 13.5 knots was more than a knot less than that of the latest battleships of other leading navies, the British *Inflexible*, the French *Redoutable*, and the Italian *Duilio*. Nevertheless, Stosch defended the design with the argument that Germany's battleships were components of an integrated system of coast defense. Other warships tailored for the system included eleven 1,100-ton armored coastal gunboats, each armed with a single 12-inch Krupp gun, completed between 1876 and 1881. Stosch appreciated the applicability of the new torpedo technology to his coast defense scheme yet commissioned few torpedo boats. Instead, torpedo experiments centered around the 1,000-ton dispatch boat *Zieten*, an iron-hulled vessel built in Britain in 1875–76. The new German empire owned no colonies but had the world's third-largest merchant marine and, thus, needed cruising warships to show the flag overseas. Stosch added eight large iron-hulled corvettes and three iron gunboats to a fleet of twelve wooden screw corvettes built earlier.[31]

Stosch laid the foundation of the naval–industrial complex that helped make Germany a first-class naval power in the years before the First World War. After the *Kaiser* and the *Deutschland*, all German battleships were built in German shipyards; aside from the *Zieten* and some torpedo boats constructed in Britain, all smaller warships likewise were built in Germany. Stosch also took steps to end the navy's dependence on Britain for armor plate. The *Hansa* and the three warships of the *Grosser Kurfürst* class had British armor, as did five of the eleven 1,100-ton gunboats, but the remaining six armored gunboats and the four "sortie corvettes" of the *Sachsen* class had armor from Karl Stumm's foundry at Dillingen on the Saar. The *Sachsens*, caught in the transition between wrought iron and compound (iron-and-steel) armor, received "sandwich" armor of alternating layers of iron and teak, while the gunboats were given obsolete wrought iron armor. The first German warships with compound armor were the 870-ton gunboats *Brummer* and *Bremse*, laid down in 1883, Stosch's last year at the Admiralty. Dillingen provided the plate, after securing a license in 1880 to produce compound armor on the British model.[32]

After conceding defeat in 1865 in its initial attempt to manufacture armor plate, the Krupp works of Essen did not reenter the armor business for a quarter-century. In the meantime, however, Krupp provided all artillery for the German fleet while also supplying the Austro-Hungarian, Russian, and several smaller navies. After introducing the all-steel muzzle-loading rifle in the late 1860s, Krupp pioneered the manufacture of all-steel breech-loading naval guns. In comparison, the leading producers of Britain and France lagged a step behind. Throughout much of the 1870s the Royal Gun Factory at Woolwich and the leading British private manufacturer, Armstrong, both produced steel muzzle-loading guns reinforced by iron hoops. The French navy's factories at Ruelle and Nevers from 1870 produced cast iron breech loaders lined with a steel tube, before switching in 1875 to all-steel breech loaders. In 1878 Armstrong began producing breech-loading guns, which the Italian navy purchased for its new battleships. The British Admiralty rejected the breech loader on safety grounds until an accident aboard the *Thunderer* in January 1879, involving a Woolwich muzzle loader, cast doubt upon the safety of the older technology. Then, between May and August 1879, British representatives joined an international audience (all except the French) observing the performance of Krupp's latest steel breech-loading guns. Suitably impressed, the British navy ordered Armstrong breech-loading guns for the new *Colossus* and *Edinburgh*, and began producing its own breech loaders at Woolwich. The latter would never be able to deliver the new ordnance in the quality or quantity desired by the navy, leading to the gradual eclipse of the Royal Gun Factory by Armstrong during the 1880s.[33] Even then, Armstrong failed to surpass Krupp as industry leader.

Though he was considered a political rival of Bismarck, Stosch agreed with the chancellor on the role of German naval power. Proposing a new fleet plan in 1872, the general argued that the fleet should "not . . . have the task to proceed offensively against the great European states, but . . . extend our power only where we have to represent lesser interests and where we cannot otherwise bring to bear the actual power of our state, our power on land." Bismarck agreed but added that "we must surpass all sea powers of the second rank."[34] By the early 1880s Germany had, indeed, equalled or surpassed all but Britain and France in numbers of battleships, even if the older armored frigates and coastal gunboats were not counted. Its first show of strength came in the waters off Spain, a country in turmoil since the overthrow of the monarchy in 1868. The establishment of a weak republic in February 1873 led to civil war, and that June Vice Admiral Reinhold Werner arrived in Spanish waters with the armored frigate *Friedrich Carl* and two unarmored escorts. Werner joined a squadron of British warships patrolling the southern coast, where four of Spain's seven ironclads had been seized by a rebel faction of the Spanish navy. International custom gave Werner, the senior officer on the station, command of the Anglo-German force, which blockaded two rebel ships in the harbor of Cartagena after they were observed shelling coastal ports. He subsequently seized a Spanish dispatch vessel and briefly held a captured rebel leader aboard his flagship. Bismarck considered Werner's actions excessive, even though he was instrumental in forcing the surrender of the rebels.[35] After calling Werner home to face a court martial, Bismarck kept the navy on a shorter leash, refusing to give its officers similar leeway in future exercises of "gunboat diplomacy."

Stosch remained chief of the Admiralty until 1883, but the last five years of his tenure were overshadowed by the scandal and crisis following the accidental sinking of the new turret battleship *Grosser Kurfürst* in May 1878. The loss of a new battleship, along with 276 of the men aboard, provided plenty of opportunity for recriminations among those involved, and Stosch made matters worse by attempting to protect his own protégés and force the retirement of officers he considered "disloyal." Stosch clung to power even after Bismarck sought to dismiss him, but his tenacity did the navy no good. Between 1878 and 1883 the naval outlay declined by one-third and no new battleships were laid down.[36] It was thanks to projects begun earlier in his tenure that Stosch left Germany with the world's third-largest armored fleet. With no construction starts after 1878, the navy had no hope of maintaining that status long beyond the early 1880s.

The Russo-Turkish War (1877–78) and its aftermath

After the great powers accepted the remilitarization of the Black Sea in 1871, Russia did not proceed immediately with the construction of a new Black Sea fleet, instead concentrating on completing unfinished ironclads laid down in the Baltic shipyards in the 1860s. Monitors and conversions were completed quickly enough, but a weak industrial base slowed the five largest iron-hulled projects, which took an average of eight years to complete. The armored cruiser *Minin*, finally commissioned in 1878, was under construction for twelve years. The 6,140-ton *Minin*, the 5,030-ton *General Admiral* (built 1870–75), and the 4,840-ton *Gerzog Edinburski* (1870–77), were the most highly regarded ships in the Russian navy. All were essentially broadside armored frigates with a few guns in sponsons, allowing some radius of fire. Otherwise, the Russian cruising fleet consisted of wooden screw frigates, corvettes, and clippers (sloops) laid down between the Crimean War and 1862. Skipping the composite ship phase, Russia laid down eight small iron-hulled clippers after 1873, but just two of these were commissioned by 1877. The only armored vessels begun by the Russians between 1870 and 1881 were the circular ironclads *Novgorod* and *Popov*, laid down at Nicolaiev for use in the Black Sea. Easily the oddest looking warships ever built by any navy, the 2,490-ton *Novgorod* (built 1872–74) had a diameter of 101 feet, the 3,550-ton *Popov* (1874–77) 120 feet, and both drew just 13.5 feet of water. Once commissioned, these floating fortresses did not handle well on the open sea; even on rivers and in calm waters their shape left them prone to a spinning motion which rendered them worthless as warships.[37]

In April 1877, after two years of rising tensions in the Balkans, Russia declared war on the Ottoman empire. At the onset of the conflict, the Russian navy had twenty-nine ironclads built or building, but nineteen were designed for coastal operations. Thanks to the efforts of the pro-navy Sultan Abdul Aziz (reigned 1861–76), the Ottoman navy had thirteen seagoing ironclads, two coastal iron-clads, and seven small river monitors. The fleet included the 9,120-ton *Mesudiye*, the largest casemate ship ever constructed. Designed by Edward Reed, it had wrought iron belt and casemate armor as thick as twelve inches; its builder, the Thames Iron Works, was completing a sister-ship, the *Hamidiye*, when hostilities began. Because the Russian Black Sea fleet had just two ironclads (the *Novgorod* and the *Popov*), the Turks had a command of the sea in the war zone as great as that enjoyed by the Anglo-French alliance during the Crimean War. This time the Western powers did not intervene, however, considering Turkey strong enough to stand on its own.[38] As Russian armies advanced on land around both sides of the Black Sea, the hopelessly outnumbered Black Sea fleet resorted to the use of torpedoes, making the war the first in which the new technology played a significant role. The Russians requisitioned nineteen fast merchant steamers of 1,000–1,500 tons and modified them for service as tenders for small steam launches, which they armed with spar torpedoes, towed torpedoes, and eventually self-propelled torpedoes.[39]

To support a Russian army advancing into the Balkans, the navy first targeted the Ottoman Danube flotilla, which included two armored corvettes and several small monitors. Mines sowed at the mouth of the river and fire from Russian army field artillery supplemented the mobile torpedo attacks against the flotilla's warships. On 11 May 1877 Russian army guns sank the 2,540-ton armored corvette *Lüft-ü Celil* at Iriali. Two weeks later, a steam launch armed with a spar torpedo attacked and sank the 400-ton river monitor *Seyfi* at Maçin.[40] In the torpedo campaign, Russian attackers and Turkish defenders both improvised their tactics. Russian lieutenants commanding the launches showed great bravery and ingenuity; among them were Stepan Makarov and Zinovy Rozhestvensky, future admirals of the Russo-Japanese War. Most early Russian attacks failed because of the inability of their launches to steam close enough to deliver a spar or towed torpedo to its target. On 10 June four Ottoman ironclads anchored at Sulina used a floating boom to foil an attack, sinking one of six launches deployed from the tender *Veliki Kniaz Konstantin*. On 23 June, similar anti-torpedo netting again foiled an attack, this time on a Turkish monitor at Nikopol, over 200 miles up the Danube, near the site where the Russian army was preparing to cross the river from Romania into Turkish Bulgaria. Five days later, the bombardment covering the army's crossing damaged two monitors. The Turks withdrew their flotilla after the Russians captured two monitors on 16 July, leaving just two of seven Ottoman river monitors still in service undamaged. The only other Turkish warship lost in the area, a wooden screw gunboat sunk at the mouth of the Danube in October, fell victim to a Russian mine placed months earlier.[41]

Meanwhile, the Turks fared better on the eastern shores of the Black Sea, where Ferik Hasan's armored squadron of five casemate corvettes and one battery corvette shelled Sochi on 14 May 1877, before landing forces which secured the city. The war's only conventional open-sea action followed on 23 July, when the casemate corvette *Feth-i Bülend* chased but failed to catch the Russian armed merchantman *Vesta*. During the pursuit both vessels sustained light damage and casualties. After the fighting at the mouth of the Danube died down, the Russian navy reassigned its most successful tender, the *Veliki Kniaz Konstantin*, to the eastern Black Sea. On the night of 23–4 August four of its launches attacked but failed to sink the casemate ship *Asar-i Şevket* at Sukkum Kale. On the same night three launches from another tender attacked the battery corvette *Asar-i Tevfik* at Sochi. One spar torpedo detonated below the ship's waterline, but it remained afloat and steamed to Batum for repairs. By the time of these attacks the Russians had painted their torpedo launches sea-green, the first known instance of the camouflaging of warships with paint of a color similar to that of the waters in which they operated.[42]

In the late summer of 1877 the Turks abandoned Sochi to an approaching Russian army, using their navy to ferry Muslim refugees down the coast to Batum. By the winter of 1877–78 Russian troops were within striking distance of that city as well, and in attacks on its port the Russian torpedo launches made their first use of self-propelled torpedoes. An unsuccessful attack on the armored frigate *Mahmudiye* and corvette *Asar-i Tevfik* at Batum on 27 December featured the second firing of a self-propelled torpedo in action, after the one by the *Shah* against the *Huáscar* seven months earlier. Finally, in another attack on Batum on the night of 25–6 January, the wooden screw gunboat *Intikbah* became the first warship ever sunk by self-propelled torpedoes, succumbing to torpedoes fired by two Russian launches. The success came with peace talks underway, begun after the Russian army's victory at Plevna, Bulgaria, on 10 December 1877. The war ended in an armistice on 31 January 1878, under which the Turks surrendered Batum.[43]

Fearing a complete Turkish collapse, Britain deployed a fleet in the eastern Mediterranean which steamed through the Dardanelles on 13 February. Russia responded by marching its Balkan army to San Stefano, six miles from Constantinople, and preparing its navy for a full-fledged Anglo-Russian war. By March 1878 the active Baltic squadron at Sveaborg included the turret ship *Petr Veliki*, the armored frigates *Petropavlovsk* and *Sevastopol*, and the casemate ship *Kniaz Pozharski*. The navy mobilized its monitors and screw gunboats for coast defense, and made arrangements with American and German firms to purchase and fuel a fleet of commerce raiding steamers to operate against British shipping worldwide.[44] Britain countered with a tactic used in future crises, in particular on the eve of the First World War, seizing and purchasing warships under construction in British shipyards for foreign powers, both to increase the strength of the British fleet and to prevent them from falling into enemy hands. These included two 4,870-ton armored rams built by Samuda for the Ottoman navy, which entered service as *Belleisle* (1878) and *Orion* (1882); the 9,120-ton *Hamidiye*, constructed by the Thames Iron Works for the Ottoman navy, which was commissioned as *Superb* (1880); and the 9,130-ton masted turret ship *Independencia*, built at Millwall for Brazil, which entered service as *Neptune* (1881).[45] Diplomatic intervention by other great powers averted war, and during the summer Bismarck hosted the Congress of Berlin, which overturned the harsh Treaty of San Stefano (3 March 1878). Russia kept all of its territorial gains, Bulgaria achieved independence (but in a form much smaller than Russia desired), Austria–Hungary occupied the rebellious Ottoman province of Bosnia–Hercegovina, and to protect its lifeline to India via the Suez Canal, Britain occupied Cyprus. In August 1878, after signing the Treaty of Berlin, Tsar Alexander II demobilized the Russian navy.[46]

The net results of the Russian campaign were meager: torpedoes claimed a small monitor and a wooden screw gunboat, while an armored corvette and another wooden screw gunboat were sunk by other means. Nevertheless, the improvised strategy allowed the bravery, daring, and ingenuity of junior officers to shine through, overcoming the cautiousness that had become traditional for Russian admirals. Their efforts succeeded in keeping a vastly superior Turkish fleet on the defensive, fearful of torpedo attacks. The giant new *Mesudiye* remained in port throughout the war, and other than the battery frigates *Mahmudiye* and *Osmaniye*, used mostly to transport troops, the Turks deployed no ironclads displacing over 3,000 tons.[47] In the 1880s proponents of the Jeune École pointed to the war to support their argument that flotillas of inexpensive torpedo boats would have a paralyzing effect on an enemy battle fleet, and thus were a far more effective deterrent than expensive and vulnerable battle-ships. The leading battleship power was the first to copy the Russian example. Later in 1878 the British navy commissioned the *Hecla*, a 6,400-ton vessel built as a merchant liner but modified to serve as a torpedo boat carrier and tender.[48]

In contrast to the effect of the Crimean War, Britain's 1878 intervention to save Constantinople did not bring it greater influence in the Ottoman empire. At the same time, the episode poisoned Anglo-Russian relations for years to come.[49] After taking such a strong stand at the Turkish straits in 1878, for almost two decades the British navy struggled to maintain its ability to do so again, not necessarily to protect the Ottoman empire but to stop a revived Russian Black Sea fleet from breaking out into the eastern Mediterranean, where it could threaten Egypt and the Suez Canal. Britain became even more concerned about the internal situation of Egypt, where the sultan in 1879 sacked Ismail Pasha from his post as hereditary viceroy (khedive) in favor of Ismail's son Tewfik. The new khedive inherited a tremendous debt, owed mostly to Britain and France, which exercised a *de facto* joint protectorate over the country to ensure repayment and to safeguard their mutual investment in the Suez Canal. Having already bolstered its position in the region by occupying Cyprus and purchasing the khedive's share in the Suez Canal Company, Britain played the leading role in preventing Egypt from slipping into chaos when Egyptian army officer Ahmed Arabi (Arabi Pasha) launched a revolt against Tewfik.

Arab massacres of fifty European residents of Alexandria on 11 June 1882 brought warships of all six European powers to the Egyptian port, where they were joined by others from the navies of the United States, Spain, Greece, and Turkey. After the khedive lost control of his own army, the ships provided sanctuary to foreigners evacuating the city, and the British government ordered the commander of its squadron, Admiral Sir Beauchamp Seymour, to block any Egyptian attempt to strengthen Alexandria's harbor defenses. Upon receiving evidence of such preparations, on 11 July Seymour moved his ships into position to bombard the fortifications. The attacking force consisted of the masted turret battleships *Inflexible* and *Monarch*, six casemate ships, ranging in size from the *Superb* to the corvette *Penelope*, and six gunboats. The squadron did not have to contend with mines or torpedo boats, and the Egyptian forces manning the guns of the forts were woefully inexperienced. British landing parties crushed the last opposition ten hours after the operation began. During the height of the action three of the battleships closed to within 400 yards of Fort Meks, but none was seriously damaged. Indeed, the fire of the forts failed to penetrate the armor of any of the attackers, and the squadron suffered casualties of just six killed and twenty-five wounded.[50] In August the navy ferried 15,000 troops to Ismailia, which served as a foothold for a British occupation of Egypt after the French – having just occupied Tunis in 1881 – declined to participate in a joint operation. At Tel-el-Kebir (13 September 1882) General Sir Garnet Wolseley defeated Arabi Pasha, paving the way for the establishment of a formal protectorate.

The decline of the US navy

The American representation off Alexandria in the summer of 1882 consisted of four wooden screw steamers, reflecting the severe limits the US Congress had imposed on the navy since the end of the Civil War. The US navy budget fell from $122 million in 1864–65 to $43 million in 1865–66, then collapsed further to $19 million in 1870–71.[51] Until its revival began in the mid-1880s the navy languished, with no battle fleet and a dwindling stock of wooden cruisers committed to operating predominantly under sail. The burning of the battery frigate *New Ironsides* in December 1866 and the sale of the *Dunderberg* to France in June 1867 left the United States with no rigged seagoing ironclads. After a plan to convert the screw frigate *Niagara* to an ironclad failed to make it off the drawing board, the American armored fleet remained an all-monitor force, almost all of which was laid up in reserve. Among the unarmored warships, innovative projects such as the fast commerce raiding sloop *Wampanoag* had been decommissioned shortly after their completion in the late 1860s. In the higher ranks of the officer corps, traditionalists such as Admiral David Dixon Porter won the favor of Congress by opposing expensive new technologies. As *de facto* navy commander in the late 1860s, he ordered captains to use sail whenever

possible and made them pay out of their own funds for "unnecessary coal use."
But the screw frigates and sloops of the 1850s could not remain in commission
much longer, and many of the vessels begun during the Civil War, hastily built
of white oak, were unseaworthy by the early 1870s. Between 1853 and 1873,
the US navy laid down 54 wooden screw steamers displacing 1,200 tons or
more: eight frigates and forty-six sloops. By the early 1870s roughly half of these
were no longer on the navy list as warships, and four of the frigates (*Wabash*,
Minnesota, *Colorado*, and *Franklin*) were nearing the end of their service lives,
having been laid down in 1854.[52]

Long before the naval demonstration off Alexandria, an incident much closer
to home revealed the weakness of the US navy. On 31 October 1873 the Spanish
composite corvette *Tornado* intercepted the American merchant steamer *Virginius*
off Cuba and found aboard it arms and Cuban revolutionaries. After seizing the
ship, Spanish authorities executed the American captain and fifty-two of his
passengers and crew. The United States responded by assembling at Key West
a wooden screw fleet including five frigates and fourteen sloops, supplemented
by six monitors, under Rear Admiral Ludlow Case. But the senior American
naval officer, Admiral Porter, advocated a diplomatic solution, fearing the
consequences of battle with the superior Spanish fleet. Case's force demobilized
after Madrid offered Washington compensation to the families of executed
Americans. The Spanish subsequently pursued their suppression of the on
again–off again Cuban rebellion without American interference, at least until
the 1890s.[53] Porter advocated diplomacy with good reason, even though the
Spanish navy had its weaknesses. By the time of the *Virginius* affair Spain had
commissioned seven large armored warships, but only the British-built *Numancia*
and *Vitoria* had iron hulls. In 1873 the wooden-hulled armored frigates *Arapiles*
and *Tetuán* left the active list, the former condemned with a rotten hull after less
than a decade in service, the latter blown up by rebels at Cartagena. The following year, just before Spain's civil war ended in a restoration of the monarchy, the
navy added two coastal ironclads: a double-turret monitor and a small floating
battery. Notwithstanding its superiority in ironclads, the civil war made it
unlikely that Spain would fight the United States over the *Virginius* affair.
At the height of the crisis the Spanish navy maintained just one armored frigate
at Havana and avoided any further action that would have required an American
response.[54]

The last naval appropriation granted by the US Congress before the crisis
included the only funding for new construction between 1864 and 1883, but
even if the ships had been ready in time they would not have strengthened the
navy's hand: the 1873 package included the last American wooden screw frigate
USS *Trenton*, five 1,375-ton gunboats of the *Enterprise* class, and three smaller
gunboats. The *Virginius* affair spurred Congress only to increase the repair
budget, appropriating almost $850,000 in 1874 for the "rebuilding" of the
double-turret wooden-hulled monitors *Monadnock*, *Miantonomoh*, *Amphitrite*
(ex-*Tonawanda*), and *Terror*. The navy broke them up, along with the unfinished

Puritan, and used the money to lay down five new iron-hulled monitors. Scandal and indecision delayed the projects; the new *Miantonomoh* was launched in 1876, the others in 1882–83. Improvements in armor and armaments technology during their years under construction delayed their completion and commissioning for several more years (the *Miantonomoh* in 1891, the others in 1895–96), by which time each reflected a mixture of the technologies of the past two decades. In addition to the double-turret monitors broken up for "rebuilding," between 1873 and 1875 the US navy purged its reserve fleet of three double-turret and nineteen single-turret monitors. Fourteen single-turret monitors – of the durable *Passaic* and *Canonicus* classes – remained in reserve. Meanwhile, the navy resorted to politically attractive "rebuilding" projects for its wooden cruisers which often were more costly than new iron or steel construction. The worst case was the frigate *Tennessee*, originally built in 1864–67 as the 4,105-ton commerce-raiding sloop *Madawasca*. Laid up after its sea trials, the ship was renamed in 1869 and over the next six years rebuilt as a 4,840-ton frigate. The *Tennessee* remained in service from 1875 until 1886, mostly as a station flagship. The cost of its construction and subsequent rebuilding totaled $3.8 million, over three times more than the $1.25 million spent to build the 4,500-ton steel cruiser *Chicago* in the mid-1880s.[55]

Thus, congressional limits on new construction and the navy's efforts to circumvent them led to wasteful practices which left the fleet with a strength that did not reflect its cost. Through 1875 the United States spent more money per year on its navy than Russia and, into the early 1880s, more than Austria–Hungary, Italy, or (except for one year) Germany, but ended the period without a single armored warship capable of fighting on the high seas.[56] In unarmored warships, the addition of the *Trenton*, the *Tennessee*, and the unarmored gunboats of the 1870s fell short of meeting the navy's cruising needs. The 3,600-ton wooden paddle-steamer *Powhatan*, part of Perry's expedition to Japan in 1853, served as a station flagship until 1886, and the iron-hulled "double-ended" paddle steamers of Civil War vintage likewise saw considerable postwar duty overseas. The last of these, the 1,170-ton *Monocacy*, served off the China coast until 1903.[57]

Peru, Chile, and the War of the Pacific (1879–84)

With the US navy in serious decline, Chile became arguably the most formidable naval power of the Americas after defeating Peru in the War of the Pacific. The solidarity between Peru and Chile against Spain in the war of 1864–66 ended as soon as the Spanish navy steamed away. In 1866 Chilean miners discovered saltpeter near the port of Antofagasta on the coast of the Atacama Desert, igniting a dispute over nitrate mining rights in a region where the borders of Peru, Bolivia, and Chile had never been clearly defined. In 1872 a Chilean–Bolivian treaty established the border at the 24th parallel, just south of Antofagasta, and two years later Bolivia pledged not to raise taxes on Chilean companies operating between the 23th and 24th parallels for a period of twenty-five years. Meanwhile, Peru entered the picture in 1873, guaranteeing Bolivia's territorial integrity and secretly pledging to support a future expulsion of Chile from the lucrative nitrate fields. Peru also nationalized all nitrate deposits in its share of the Atacama, the provinces of Tacna and Tarapacá, where Chileans had been the most active miners. With the only ironclad warships on the Pacific coast of South America, Peru could afford to behave aggressively, at least until Chile purchased ironclads of its own. Relations promptly normalized in 1875, when the 3,370-ton casemate ships *Almirante Cochrane* and *Blanco Encalada*, designed by Edward Reed, arrived from Britain. The desert remained calm until February 1878, when Bolivia imposed a new export tax on saltpeter, in violation of the 1874 tax-freeze pledge. Chile's leading mining company at Antofagasta refused to pay, and in January 1879 Bolivian authorities there arrested its president. Chile responded the following month by sending Rear Admiral Williams Rebolledo with the *Almirante Cochrane*, the *Blanco Encalada*, and a screw corvette escort to Antofagasta, where they landed 800 troops to seize the city. In March the squadron landed troops north of the 23rd parallel at the smaller Bolivian ports of Cobija and Tocopilla. By early April, Peru had come to the defense of Bolivia, and Chile retaliated with a blockade of Iquique, main port of the Peruvian province of Tarapacá. Most of the action on land and at sea in the ensuing "saltpeter war" centered around the nitrate-rich provinces in the disputed desert territory, but the War of the Pacific is deserving of its formal designation, for the naval action ranged along the entire 4,500-mile Pacific coast of South America. Peruvian warships cruised as far south as Cape Horn to intercept arms shipments bound for Chile from Europe, while Chilean warships ranged as far north as Panama to stop the flow of arms to Peru across the isthmus from the United States and Europe.[58]

At the start of the war the Chilean navy had two casemate ships, five screw corvettes, and two smaller unarmored steamers, against the Peruvian navy's 3,500-ton armored frigate *Independencia*, 2,030-ton turret ship *Huáscar*, the former American monitors *Manco Capac* and *Atahualpa*, one screw corvette, and five other unarmored steamers. Chile kept Argentina from adding its new (1874) Laird monitors *La Plata* and *Los Andes* to the enemy fleet by renouncing long-standing claims to Patagonia, and entered the conflict with a slight advantage because the two Peruvian monitors had not been maintained after their purchase in 1868 and were suitable only for harbor defense. The two navies spent the first month of the war convoying troop transports, the Chileans from Valparaíso north to Antofagasta, the Peruvians from Callao south to Arica, while the Chileans continued to blockade Iquique in-between. After the Peruvian army arrived safely at Arica, the *Independencia* and the *Huáscar* steamed south to challenge the Chilean blockade of Iquique and landings at Antofagasta. At the same time, Williams Rebolledo steamed north with most of the Chilean fleet to contest the transport of the Peruvian army from Callao to Arica, leaving the screw corvette *Esmeralda* and screw gunboat *Covadonga* to maintain the blockade of Iquique. After the two forces passed at sea without encountering one another, the Chileans arrived off Callao to learn that the Peruvian army had already landed at Arica. Meanwhile, the two Peruvian ironclads descended upon the two Chilean wooden steamers at Iquique. Williams Rebolledo hastened back to Iquique but arrived on the morning of 22 May, too late to save the *Esmeralda* and *Covadonga*, which had engaged the Peruvian ironclads in battle the previous day.[59]

Chile still celebrates 21 May as a national holiday, and with good reason. On that morning Captain Arturo Prat of the *Esmeralda* refused to abandon his station at Iquique and engaged the *Huáscar* for over three-and-a-half hours, while the *Covadonga* (Captain Carlos Condell) escaped to the south with the *Independencia* in hot pursuit. The wooden hull of the 20-year-old *Esmeralda* took a terrific pounding but Prat refused to strike his flag. In the climax of the battle shortly after noon, Rear Admiral Miguel Grau of the *Huáscar* dealt the fatal blow to the corvette, ramming it amidships. Prat responded not by surrendering but by leading a charge from the deck of the sinking *Esmeralda* in an attempt to board and take the *Huáscar*. It was perhaps the greatest act of bravado in any naval battle since John Paul Jones took HMS *Serapis* from the deck of the sinking *Bonhomme Richard* a century earlier. This time, however, the bold boarding party failed to take its prize, and Prat was killed on the deck of the *Huáscar*. Minutes later the *Esmeralda* sank with flags flying; of its 200 officers and seamen, 146 perished in the battle. Meanwhile, the *Covadonga* steamed southward, hugging the coast, chased by the *Independencia*. At Punta Gruesa the shallow-draught steamer passed safely over a reef which trapped its far heavier pursuer. Condell then turned on the *Independencia*, positioned the *Covadonga* at its bow, out of reach of either broadside, and raked it until its commander surrendered. The engagements of 21 May made Prat a Chilean national hero and reduced by half the armored strength of the Peruvian navy.[60]

Over the next five months the Chilean navy pursued Grau and the *Huáscar* up and down the coast. The ironclad had some success as a raider, sinking a Chilean army transport and several small coastal merchantmen. At Iquique on the night of 9–10 July, the *Huáscar* encountered just the screw corvette *Magallanes* maintaining the blockade. The ship's captain, future admiral Juan José Latorre, emulated Prat's earlier heroism, deliberately closing with the *Huáscar* and engaging it for forty-five minutes until the *Almirante Cochrane* arrived, prompting Grau to flee.[61] Frustration over the navy's inability to catch the *Huáscar* was at least one factor in the retirement of Williams Rebolledo in early August. In a subsequent shake-up Captain Galvarino Riveros took command of the squadron and Latorre received command of the *Almirante Cochrane*. On the morning of 8 October Latorre finally trapped the *Huáscar* off Punta Angamos, north of Antofagasta. The action featured the first use of armor-piercing Palliser shells, which the *Almirante Cochrane*'s 9-inch Armstrong guns fired with great effect especially after the ships closed to within 2,200 meters. The *Blanco Encalada* arrived on the scene forty-five minutes after the fighting began, and the two casemate ships engaged the *Huáscar* for another forty-five minutes before it finally surrendered. British observers praised the gunnery of the Chileans, who fired a total of seventy-six rounds and scored a remarkable twenty-seven hits; in contrast, the guns in the hand-cranked turret of the *Huáscar* managed just three hits against its two opponents, causing no damage. The battle left Grau and half his crew dead, and Chile firmly in command of the sea.[62] Unlike the *Independencia*, a total loss after running onto the reef at Punta Gruesa, the *Huáscar* was repaired and commissioned in the Chilean navy, and converted to a museum ship after leaving service in 1898. (The *Huáscar* remains the world's only contested museum ship; as recently as August 1999 President Alberto Fujimori demanded its return to Peru.[63])

On 2 November the *Almirante Cochrane* and three unarmored warships escorted transports carrying 9,500 troops northward from Antofagasta to Pisagua, where they landed unopposed after a shelling by the warships. By the end of the month the army had marched inland to defeat an allied Peruvian–Bolivian army at Tarapacá (27 November), securing for Chile the southernmost Peruvian province of the same name. Meanwhile, on the coast, Rear Admiral Riveros deployed the *Blanco Encalada* to blockade Arica, where it captured the screw gunboat *Pilcomayo* (18 November), and the *Almirante Cochrane* to blockade Iquique, where it took the surrender of the Peruvian garrison (23 November). Thereafter, the allies regrouped at Arica, where the immobile *Manco Capac* served as harbor watch. On 27 February 1880 the old Peruvian monitor exchanged fire with the *Huáscar* when the latter arrived to shell the port. Riveros soon arrived with the two Chilean casemate ships, which joined in the bombardment. Chilean troops landed north of the city in March eventually cut off the garrison from resupply by land; they finally stormed Arica and captured it on 7 June. The previous day, the *Manco Capac* was blown up by its own crew to prevent its capture.[64]

In April 1880 Riveros blockaded Callao with a squadron led by the *Blanco Encalada* and the *Huáscar*. After the fall of Arica, the *Almirante Cochrane* and its unarmored escorts joined them. The hopelessly outnumbered Peruvians, taking their cue from the recent Russian campaign against the Turks in the Black Sea, used torpedo boats against the blockaders, the most active of which was the *Independencia*, named for the armored frigate lost the previous May. Peruvian torpedoes sank the armed transport *Loa* in July and the screw gunboat *Covadonga* in September. The Chilean navy soon had five torpedo boats of its own off Callao. The ensuing action in and around the harbor centered around the raids and skirmishes of the two torpedo flotillas, during which each side lost one torpedo boat. In late November Chilean troops landed unopposed at Pisco and began to march up the coast toward Lima. Shelling from Riveros' squadron contributed to a decisive victory at Chorrillos (13 January 1881), after which the army occupied the Peruvian capital. The remnants of the Peruvian navy surrendered at Callao, but not before scuttling their last ironclad, the immobile monitor *Atahualpa*, on 16 January. The Chilean navy then secured the smaller

Peruvian ports north of Callao, an operation completed when the *Huáscar* took the surrender of Paita in June.[65] The naval campaign thus came to an end but not the war, as Peru and Bolivia refused to agree to terms. The Chilean government held the navy in such high esteem that it named a rear admiral, Patricio Lynch, commander of the army in occupation of Peru. Lynch, whose early career at sea had included service in the British navy during the First Opium War, commanded campaigns against pockets of Peruvian resistance in the interior, crushing the last of them in July 1883. Peru finally signed a treaty of peace three months later, ceding the provinces of Tacna and Tarapacá with the ports of Arica and Iquique. The Bolivians continued to hold out, unable to accept the loss of their Pacific coastal province and port of Antofagasta, but an invasion led by Lynch forced them to agree to a truce in April 1884. The Chilean army of occupation left Peru that August; Bolivia, never occupied, did not agree to a definitive peace treaty until 1904.[66]

After the loss of the *Independencia* in May 1879, Peru made strenuous efforts to purchase armored warships in Europe. The fruitless quest came closest to success with the government of Austria–Hungary, whose three 3,600-ton casemate ships of the *Kaiser Max* class – roughly the equivalent of Chile's *Blanco Encalada* and *Almirante Cochrane* – would have filled Peru's needs. The opposition of the Austro-Hungarian naval leadership blocked the deal, and the Peruvian navy ultimately purchased just the 1,700-ton unarmored cruiser *Lima*, a merchantman converted in Britain in 1881, and a few torpedo boats. Only the latter made it to Peru in time to see action in the war. After the War of the Pacific, Peru never again attempted to be a regional naval power; for the next quarter-century the *Lima* remained its largest warship.[67] Meanwhile, the postwar Chilean navy appeared destined for a place in the second rank of the world's naval powers. The *Huáscar* was modernized by the addition of a steam winch for its turret, and all three of the fleet's armored warships received new 8-inch Armstrong breech-loading rifles. Before the capture of the *Huáscar*, when the outcome of the naval war was still in doubt, Chile ordered two cruisers from Armstrong's Elswick shipyard, to be named after its newest naval hero and his gallant lost ship. In early October 1879 work began on the first of the pair, the 1,350-ton *Arturo Prat*, a nominally rigged steel-hulled vessel. Conceptually, the ship was a forerunner of the *Esmeralda*, the world's first modern light cruiser, in combining impressive speed (16.5 knots) and heavy primary armament (two 10-inch guns) in an unarmored warship. After the *Arturo Prat* was launched in August 1880 the *Esmeralda* was laid down by the same builder, but the *Arturo Prat* was not ready for delivery until June 1883, the same month in which the *Esmeralda* was launched. With the naval action of the War of the Pacific having already ended two years earlier, Chile decided to sell the *Arturo Prat* to Japan and await delivery of the larger, more powerful *Esmeralda*.[68]

Japan and China

Thus the *Arturo Prat*, commissioned in 1885 with the name *Tsukushi*, became the first steel cruiser in the Japanese navy. By that time, thanks to steps taken during the 1870s, the foundations of Japan's future naval power had been established. At the end of the civil war of 1868–69 the imperial fleet included the armored ram *Adzuma* (ex-*Kotetsu*), the armored corvette *Ryujo*, and six wooden steamers of various types. In the early 1870s the navy added three screw corvettes purchased from Britain, France, and the Netherlands, and a composite gunboat from Britain. Like its German counterpart of the same decade, the Japanese navy had non-seamen among its leaders, and lacked both a maritime tradition of its own and the infrastructure to support a modern fleet. A British naval mission (1873–79) imported British-style traditions and practices for officers and seamen alike, and established a curriculum for the naval academy in Tokyo.

The navy's next action came in 1874, against Taiwanese pirates. Problems encountered during that operation, coinciding with worsening relations with Korea, sparked a naval build-up during the second half of the decade. The 3,720-ton casemate ship *Fuso*, the 2,200-ton armored corvettes *Hiei* and *Kongo*, and four torpedo boats were ordered from British shipyards, while French advisors arrived to supervise the construction of four wooden screw steamers in the Yokosuka shipyard.[69] By the end of the decade Japan had five armored warships, supplemented by an unarmored fleet of five frigates or corvettes (over 1,000 tons) with two more under construction, and seven sloops or gunboats (under 1,000 tons), but until the arrival of the *Tsukushi* (ex-*Arturo Prat*) in 1885, the casemate ship *Fuso* was the only formidable fighting vessel.

Just as Chile could not aspire to be a second-rate naval power on the world stage until it had surpassed Peru, Japan at this time still measured its naval power against that of its regional rival, China. Unlike Japan after the Meiji Restoration, China never took decisive measures to save itself from Western domination. Nevertheless, during the 1860s China ordered four screw gunboats in Britain and built a screw corvette and two screw gunboats at Foochow. Between 1870 and 1876 the Foochow yard built another eight screw corvettes and three gunboats, all wooden ships, followed between 1877 and 1880 by four composite corvettes. Meanwhile, between 1872 and 1876 the Kiangyan shipyard built two wooden screw frigates and a composite gunboat. China's first armored warships were flatiron gunboats built for coastal and river service. Between 1875 and 1880 British shipyards launched fourteen such vessels for the Chinese navy, displacing between 260 and 440 tons, only four of which had significant armor plating. The 200-ton flush-decked *Tiong Sing*, launched in 1875 at Shanghai, was the only Chinese ironclad built in China.[70]

Thus, by the end of the 1870s China had fifteen armored warships but the largest was less than one-third the size of the smallest of Japan's five ironclads. Whereas none of the Chinese ironclads could operate out of sight of the coast, all of Japan's ironclads, at least theoretically, were high seas warships. The Chinese unarmored fleet was much larger than the Japanese, with fifteen frigates or corvettes (over 1,000 tons) and ten gunboats (under 1,000 tons). Aside from the tiny *Tiong Sing*, all Chinese and Japanese ironclads were ordered abroad, but at a time when most of Japan's unarmored warships were still foreign-built, twenty-one of China's twenty-five unarmored warships had been built in Chinese shipyards. At the end of the decade, however, the shift from wood or composite construction to steel construction posed insurmountable challenges for Chinese domestic shipbuilding. In 1879 China turned to Britain for its first steel-hulled cruising warships, the 1,380-ton *Chao Yung* and *Yang Wei*. These unrigged cruisers, practically identical to the Japanese *Tsukushi* (ex-*Arturo Prat*) only with deck armor, were laid down by Mitchell in January 1880 and completed in July 1881, some four years before the *Tsukushi* arrived in Japan. In addition to the fact that the armored warships of China were of a completely different design than those of Japan, a comparison of the two navies must consider the greater coastal and river defense responsibilities of the Chinese navy and its subdivision into the autonomous northern (Peiyang), southern (Nanking), Fukien, and Kwantung fleets.[71]

Conclusion

By 1882, two decades had passed since the Battle of Hampton Roads silenced the early critics of the armored warship, and the challenge to the battleship posed by the revolutionary ideas of the Jeune École was still a year or two away. Most fleets included a mixture of ironclad types, from the broadside frigates and monitors of the early 1860s to the casemate ships, barbette and turret battleships commissioned in the 1870s, making it difficult to compare the strength of one fleet to another. Nevertheless, by the standards of the early 1880s, navies no longer considered ships capable only of broadside fire as first-rate battleships, regardless of their size; likewise, ironclads displacing less than 2,000 tons, along with some larger monitor types, were considered suitable for coastal operations only and not counted as part of the battle fleet.

Britain ended 1882 with thirty-seven armored warships, built or building, with another fifteen for coastal operations and twenty broadside ironclads. France had thirty-four, along with thirteen coastal and ten broadside ironclads. Germany ranked a distant third with nine, not counting twelve coastal and three broadside ironclads. Italy also had nine, with one coastal and nine broadside ironclads. Russia had seven, along with twenty-two coastal and two broadside ironclads. Austria–Hungary had eight casemate ships, no coastal ironclads, and three battery frigates.

Few other navies in or near European waters had battleships capable of high seas operations. Ottoman Turkey had ten relatively modern armored warships, supplemented by four broadside ironclads and one designated for coast defense, but six of the ten were casemate ships of under 3,000 tons. Spain had one casemate ship, four broadside ironclads, and two small coastal ironclads. Beyond Europe, Chile arguably had the world's strongest navy, emerging from the War of the Pacific with three armored warships capable of high seas operations. Of Japan's five ironclads only the casemate ship *Fuso* was in this category. The United States still had the most armored warships of any non-European navy, with twenty-one built or building, but all were monitors suitable only for coastal operations. Brazil's sixteen ironclads, Argentina's two, and China's tiny gunboats likewise were suitable only for coastal or river operations.

But naval experts soon would no longer measure the strength of a fleet in terms of battleships, for the latest guns and shells had proved to be more than a match for armor previously considered impregnable. In the War of the Pacific, General Sir William Palliser's armor-piercing shells had passed through the 8-inch wrought iron on the *Huáscar*'s turret. Aside from very large casemate ships such as the Turkish *Mesudiye* and British *Superb*, which had 12-inch traditional plate covering parts of their hulls, no battleship could be fitted with wrought iron thick enough to assure its safety, and as yet there was no consensus on the feasibility of compound iron-and-steel or all-steel armor. Meanwhile, the potential of the self-propelled torpedo had been demonstrated in the sinking of one Turkish warship by the Russians in 1878 and two Chilean warships by the Peruvians in 1880. The new weapon had yet to claim an armored vessel, but few believed that devices such as the anti-torpedo booms deployed by the Turks in 1877–78 would make battleships immune to the threat.

Indeed, even before the lethal nature of armor-piercing shells and self-propelled torpedoes was demonstrated in combat, cost alone had sufficed to slow the proliferation of armored warships. Aside from Chile, Argentina, and China, of the countries that had no ironclads in 1870 only one – Portugal – commissioned its first during the following decade. By 1876 every country that would own an armored warship before 1914 already had one, and in 1881 the ranks of the ironclad navies lost a member – Peru – which came to consider armored warships unnecessary to its future security. Fears of losing expensive battleships in attacks by inexpensive torpedo boats only strengthened the hand of the skeptics. During the 1880s, the Jeune École would provide proponents of alternative naval warfare with the organizing principles and ideology needed to displace, at least temporarily, the traditional battle fleet or battleship-centered strategy.

Notes

1 Lambert, "Iron Hulls and Armour Plate," 53; *Conway, 1860–1905,* 13, 286, 338; Beeler, *British Naval Policy,* 91.
2 *Conway, 1860–1905,* 15, 287; Sondhaus, *Preparing for Weltpolitik,* 123–4.
3 *Conway, 1860–1905,* 51, 56, 198, 317, 321; Lawrence Sondhaus, *The Naval Policy of Austria–Hungary: Navalism, Industrial Development, and the Politics of Dualism, 1867–1918* (West Lafayette, Ind., 1994), 26.
4 Hamilton, *Anglo-French Naval Rivalry,* 117, 138, 143.

5 Lyon, "Underwater Warfare and the Torpedo Boat," 136; Campbell, "Naval Armaments and Armour," 166; Antonio Casali and Marina Cattaruzza, *Sotto i mari del mondo: La Whitehead, 1875–1990* (Rome, 1990), 12–13; Brown, "The Era of Uncertainty, 1863–1878," 92.

6 Franck to Wüllerstorf, Vienna, 4 September 1866, Haus- Hof- und Staatsarchiv, AR, F44 – Marinewesen, Carton 3: Generalia 1860–70, quoted in Sondhaus, *The Naval Policy of Austria–Hungary*, 9.

7 Sondhaus, *The Naval Policy of Austria-Hungary*, 9–10, 16–26, 44–5.

8 Donolo, "The History of Italian Naval Doctrine," 105.

9 Sondhaus, *The Naval Policy of Austria–Hungary*, 26–7; Franco Micali Baratelli, *La marina militare italiana nella vita nazionale, 1860–1914* (Mursia, 1983), 237–8; Lucio Ceva, *Le forze armate* (Turin, 1981), 103.

10 Bargoni, *Le prime navi di linea della marina italiana*; Sondhaus, *The Naval Policy of Austria–Hungary*, 48–9.

11 Sondhaus, *The Naval Policy of Austria–Hungary*, 49.

12 Bargoni, *Corazzate italiane classi Duilio–Italia–Ruggiero di Lauria, 1880–1892* (Rome, 1977), *passim*; Conway, *1860–1905*, 341–2; John Roberts, "Warships of Steel, 1879–1889," in Robert Gardiner, ed., *Steam, Steel and Shellfire: The Steam Warship 1815–1905* (London, 1992), 97.

13 Sondhaus, *The Naval Policy of Austria–Hungary*, 45–7; Bargoni, *Corazzate italiane classi Duilio–Italia–Ruggiero di Lauria, passim*.

14 Conway, *1860–1905*, 345.

15 Sondhaus, *The Naval Policy of Austria–Hungary*, 26, 392.

16 Beeler, *British Naval Policy*, 10–11, 19, 202, 209.

17 Brown, "The Era of Uncertainty, 1863–1878," 78; Conway, *1860–1905*, 17–18.

18 Brown, *Warrior to Dreadnought*, 203; idem, "The Era of Uncertainty, 1863–1878," 84–6; Conway, *1860–1905*, 26; Griffiths, "Warship Machinery," 176.

19 Roberts, "Warships of Steel, 1879–1889," 96–7; Brown, *Warrior to Dreadnought*, 167.

20 Beeler, *British Naval Policy*, 21, 215.

21 Conway, *1860–1905*, 43–52, 56–8.

22 Ibid., 63–4; Brown, *Warrior to Dreadnought*, 70; Beeler, *British Naval Policy*, 218.

23 Brown, *Warrior to Dreadnought*, 109.

24 Brown, "The Era of Uncertainty, 1863–1878," 89; idem, *Warrior to Dreadnought*, 21; Ritchie, *El Monitor Huáscar*, 56–63; Beeler, *British Naval Policy*, 25.

25 Brown, "The Era of Uncertainty, 1863–1878," 92; Griffiths, "Warship Machinery," 176.

26 Beeler, *British Naval Policy*, 193, 205.

27 Brown, "The Era of Uncertainty, 1863–1878," 86.

28 Ibid., 86; Roberts, "Warships of Steel, 1879–1889," 96; Conway, *1860–1905*, 289–90, 299.

29 Roberts, "Warships of Steel, 1879–1889," 97–100; Conway, *1860–1905*, 290–2, 300, 302–3.

30 John Roberts, "The Pre-Dreadnought Age, 1890–1905," in Robert Gardiner, ed., *Steam, Steel and Shellfire: The Steam Warship 1815–1905* (London, 1992), 114; Griffiths, "Warship Machinery," 177; Conway, *1860–1905*, 284, 314–21, 323.

31 Sondhaus, *Preparing for Weltpolitik*, 113–15; Gröner, *Die deutschen Kriegsschiffe*, 1: 28–33, 70–1, 117, 164–6.

32 Sondhaus, *Preparing for Weltpolitik*, 136, 140.

33 Roberts, "Warships of Steel, 1879–1889," 97–8.

34 Stosch quoted in Ivo Nikolai Lambi, *The Navy and German Power Politics, 1862–1914* (Boston, Mass., 1984), 4, and Ekkard Verchau, "Von Jachmann über Stosch und

Caprivi," in Herbert Schlottelius and Wilhelm Deist, eds, *Marine und Marinepolitik im kaiserlichen Deutschland, 1871–1914* (Düsseldorf, 1972), 59; Bismarck quoted in Wilhelm Gerloff, *Finanz- und Zollpolitik des Deutschen Reiches* (Jena, 1913), 79.

35 Sondhaus, *Preparing for Weltpolitik*, 120–1; Beeler, *British Naval Policy*, 21–2.

36 Sondhaus, *Preparing for Weltpolitik*, 125–35.

37 Watts, *The Imperial Russian Navy*, 15; Woodward, *The Russians at Sea*, 110; *Conway, 1860–1905*, 174–7, 186, 198.

38 Clarke, *Russia's Sea-Power*, 103–4; Langensiepen and Güleryüz, *The Ottoman Steam Navy*, 5; Jane, *The Imperial Russian Navy*, 180; *Conway, 1860–1905*, 391.

39 Watts, *The Imperial Russian Navy*, 15–16; Woodward, *The Russians at Sea*, 110.

40 Gromov *et al.*, *Tri Veka Rossiiskogo Flota*, 1: 245–6; Langensiepen and Güleryüz, *The Ottoman Steam Navy*, 6, 137, 140; Woodward, *The Russians at Sea*, 112; Watts, *The Imperial Russian Navy*, 15–16.

41 Watts, *The Imperial Russian Navy*, 16; Woodward, *The Russians at Sea*, 113; Langensiepen and Güleryüz, *The Ottoman Steam Navy*, 6, 161.

42 Watts, *The Imperial Russian Navy*, 16; Woodward, *The Russians at Sea*, 115; Langensiepen and Güleryüz, *The Ottoman Steam Navy*, 6.

43 Gromov *et al.*, *Tri Veka Rossiiskogo Flota*, 1: 252–3; Watts, *The Imperial Russian Navy*, 16; Woodward, *The Russians at Sea*, 115; Langensiepen and Güleryüz, *The Ottoman Steam Navy*, 5–6, 162.

44 Clarke, *Russia's Sea-Power*, 107; Gromov *et al.*, *Tri Veka Rossiiskogo Flota*, 1: 254.

45 Langensiepen and Güleryüz, *The Ottoman Steam Navy*, 135–6; *Conway, 1860–1905*, 18, 25.

46 Gromov *et al.*, *Tri Veka Rossiiskogo Flota*, 1: 255.

47 Langensiepen and Güleryüz, *The Ottoman Steam Navy*, 6–7.

48 Brown, "The Era of Uncertainty, 1863–1878," 92; *Conway, 1860–1905*, 106.

49 Clarke, *Russia's Sea-Power*, 110–11.

50 Brown, *Warrior to Dreadnought*, 71–3.

51 Still, *American Sea Power in the Old World*, 83–9; Beeler, *British Naval Policy*, 200.

52 Canney, *The Old Steam Navy*, 1: 145, 168–78, and *passim*, 2: 131–3. For an alternative view of Porter's attitude toward technological change see Hearn, *Porter*, 318–20.

53 Rodríguez González, *Política naval de la Restauración*, 100–1; Field, *From Gibraltar to the Middle East*, 333–4; Still, *American Sea Power in the Old World*, 68–9.

54 *Conway, 1860–1905*, 380–1; Still, *American Sea Power in the Old World*, 69.

55 Canney, *The Old Steam Navy*, 1: 141, 147–51, 154–61, 2: 133–7.

56 Beeler, *British Naval Policy*, 192.

57 Canney, *The Old Steam Navy*, 1: 35, 120.

58 Gonzalo Bulnes, *Resumen de la Guerra del Pacífico* (Santiago, 1979), 15–41, and *passim*; *Conway, 1860–1905*, 410–11; Ritchie, *El Monitor Huáscar*, 85–7.

59 Bulnes, *Resumen de la Guerra del Pacífico*, 43, 45, 51; Ritchie, *El Monitor Huáscar*, 64–7; *Conway, 1860–1905*, 401.

60 Ritchie, *El Monitor Huáscar*, 67–71; Bulnes, *Resumen de la Guerra del Pacífico*, 55.

61 *Conway, 1860–1905*, 413, and some other sources refer to the 950-ton *Magallanes* as a screw gunboat.

62 Ritchie, *El Monitor Huáscar*, 76–84, 94–100; Bulnes, *Resumen de la Guerra del Pacífico*, 63; Brown, *Warrior to Dreadnought*, 24–5; Sandler, *Emergence of the Modern Capital Ship*, 94.

63 "Fujimori Pediría que el Huáscar Sea Devuelto a Perú," *El Mercurio* (Santiago), 13 August 1999, C2.

64 Ritchie, *El Monitor Huáscar*, 86, 103–5; Bulnes, *Resumen de la Guerra del Pacífico*, 79, 91, 95, 99, 107, 121, 131–57; Canney, *The Old Steam Navy*, 2: 86, 138.

65 Ritchie, *El Monitor Huáscar*, 106–9; Bulnes, *Resumen de la Guerra del Pacífico*, 179–88; *Conway, 1860–1905*, 418–19.

66 Bulnes, *Resumen de la Guerra del Pacífico*, 207, 229–264, and *passim*; Bade, *Marinos Ilustres*, 115–17.

67 Sondhaus, *The Naval Policy of Austria–Hungary*, 52–3; *Conway, 1860–1905*, 418–19.

68 Ritchie, *El Monitor Huáscar*, 107–9; *Conway, 1860–1905*, 233, 410–11.

69 Evans and Peattie, *Kaigun*, 7–12; *Conway, 1860–1905*, 216, 219–20, 231–2, 235–6.

70 *Conway, 1860–1905*, 395, 398–9.

71 Ibid., 395–6.

CHAPTER SIX

The Jeune École

The era of the Jeune École, the French "Young School" advocating modern unarmored cruisers and torpedo boats over armored battleships, reached its peak in 1886–87, when the school's founder, Admiral Théophile Aube, served as French navy minister. The ideas of the group were rooted in the technological developments of the mid-1870s; its members drew further inspiration from Russia's use of torpedo launches against the Ottoman navy in the Russo-Turkish War of 1877–78. The school had a near-universal impact by the mid-1880s and remained strong in some navies until the mid-1890s. Aube, whose own service had been largely on colonial stations, rejected ironclads from the start and lamented the evolution of two fleets – one for home waters and one for overseas duties – that had occurred within all navies by the 1870s. The self-propelled torpedo was his weapon of choice and ruthless commerce raiding his tactic. Aube saw the overall Jeune École strategy as a means for France to challenge British naval power worldwide.

During the 1880s, the building programs of most of the great powers included fewer battleships and many more modern unarmored steel cruisers and torpedo boats. In France, the alternating pro- and anti-Aube factions made a shambles of naval construction. Meanwhile, Germany embraced the new school of thought wholeheartedly and fell from third place to fifth in armored tonnage, while Austria–Hungary seized upon the strategy of the Jeune École as an inexpensive counter to the battleship program of its Adriatic rival, Italy. When the United States finally awoke from its naval slumber in mid-decade, its first program included no battleships.

Steel cruisers

In terms of materiel, unarmored steel cruisers and torpedo boats provided the foundation of the new strategy. Torpedo boats developed rather quickly from the torpedo launches of the 1870s, with the British *Lightning* (1876) serving as the general prototype, but the cruiser evolved much more slowly. Two decades had passed since the vision of the battleship first changed from a wooden ship of the line to an armored frigate of some sort, but a redefinition of the cruiser had yet to occur. During the 1870s composite and iron cruisers, then some of the first steel cruisers, still had the traditional look of fully rigged frigates or corvettes.[1] The Jeune École strategy required nothing less than the reconceptualization of the cruiser as a modern warship, with tubes for self-propelled torpedoes and heavy guns capable of firing armor-piercing shells, with speed produced by powerful engines rather than some combination of screw propulsion and a full sailing rig.

Even though France ultimately embraced the modern steel cruiser as an ideal weapon to use against the navy and maritime commerce of Britain, the British actually pioneered the development of the type. After Nathaniel Barnaby and William White returned from their 1874 tour of France, the Landore works in Wales began to produce good quality steel using the same Siemens Martin open hearth process as Schneider of Creusot. Landore provided the steel for Barnaby's 3,730-ton all-steel cruisers *Iris* and *Mercury*, laid down in the winter of 1875–76 and completed in 1879. These three-masted ships had graceful lines and *Iris* had a clipper bow, but their engines were capable of unprecedented speeds: the *Mercury* achieved 18.5 knots in her trials and for years remained the world's fastest warship. Their role remained uncertain, but this did not stop Britain from continuing to lead the evolution of the type. After building their last wooden hull in 1875, the British abandoned the iron hull after 1878, constructing steel cruisers as replacements for all older cruising warships withdrawn from service. While the six *Emerald* class corvettes (completed 1876–78) and seven *Satellite* class corvettes (completed 1882–84) had composite hulls, the ten *Comus* class corvettes (completed 1878–81) and two *Calypso* class corvettes (completed 1883–84) had steel hulls, like the *Iris* and the *Mercury*. The smaller rates of overseas sloops and gunboats made the same transition from wood to composite to steel construction, the sailing rig shrinking with each new design. Along with the *Iris* and the *Mercury*, steel-hulled vessels rated as second-class cruisers included thirteen warships of the *Leander*, *Mersey*, and *Medea* classes, laid down between 1880 and 1887. By 1889 twenty-one third-class steel cruisers were begun.[2]

The real breakthrough in cruiser design came in Britain but not for the British navy, thanks to the entrepreneurial Armstrong firm. In 1881, with the War of the Pacific still underway, Armstrong's Elswick shipyard laid down the 3,000-ton *Esmeralda* for Chile. Designed by the innovator George Rendel, this first "Elswick cruiser" had a truly modern appearance. Constructed entirely of steel with two military masts and no sailing rig, it carried a formidable primary armament of two 10-inch guns, one fore and one aft, with a secondary armament of three 6-inch pivoting guns in each broadside and three torpedo tubes. It had no side armor but the 2-inch deck armor and some plating around its gun mountings made it the first "protected" cruiser. Capable of 18 knots, it was a more formidable warship than any of the second-class steel cruisers begun for the British navy. The ship was launched in June 1883 and completed in July 1884, and thus did not reach South American waters until long after the end of hostilities. Armstrong built similar cruisers for Austria–Hungary (two, completed

1885–86), Italy (three, completed 1885–89), Japan (four, completed 1885–98), China (four, completed 1887–99), and Argentina (three, completed 1891–96). Brazil eventually ordered two, which were purchased by the United States on the eve of the Spanish–American War. Chile's *Esmeralda* also changed owners, purchased by Japan during the Sino-Japanese War. Armstrong built no steel cruisers for the British navy until 1888, when the first two of nine 2,575-ton *Pearl* class cruisers were laid down at Elswick.[3] By then the Elswick cruiser had been imitated worldwide, and proponents of the Jeune École considered the general type to be "the battleship of the future."[4]

France, Britain, and the Jeune École Strategy

France's shift away from the *guerre de course* after the Crimean War lasted only until the fall of Napoleon III. After 1870, with less generous funding under the Third Republic, many French naval officers again became infatuated with commerce raiding as an anti-British strategy. The ideological forefather of the Jeune École, Vice Admiral Baron Richild Grivel, wrote *De la guerre maritime avant et depuis les nouvelles inventions* in 1869. Admiral Aube, leader of the school of thought, further developed its concepts in *La guerre maritime et les ports français* (1882), *A terre et à bord, notes d'un marin* (1884), and *De la guerre navale* (1885). Thereafter, the most significant French works were by journalist Gabriel Charmes, *La reforme de la marine* (1886), and by Commander Gabriel Fontin and Lieutenant Paul Vignot, *Essai de stratégie navale* (1893). But the strategy, and the navy to support it, had anything but a smooth course of development. In its first thirty years the Third Republic changed navy ministers thirty times, with proponents of the *guerre de course* and, from the early 1880s, the comprehensive strategy of the Jeune École often alternating with advocates of a more traditional blue-water navy. This political instability, along with fiscal constraints and the limitations of its industry, held France back in its development of modern cruisers and torpedo boats even as Aube's school led the way in formulating the strategy for their use and the broader ideology to justify it.[5]

The "young school" of naval strategy that emerged in France during the 1880s ultimately produced a philosophical schism within every navy, wreaking havoc with fleet plans and construction programs. Aube, the founder of the Jeune École, actually belonged to the older generation. Almost forty years of service on overseas stations left him with a strategic outlook that focused on the defense of worldwide interests and, in wartime, on a *guerre de course* attacking enemy commerce. He took a dim view of ironclads from the time of their introduction. His "discovery" of the torpedo boat, upon returning to home waters in 1883, confirmed his view that large battleships were worthless. That same year he invited the journalist Charmes to observe maneuvers with the French Mediterranean fleet. During the exercises two 46-ton torpedo boats rode out a heavy storm better than some of the larger vessels, prompting Charmes, as Aube's mouthpiece, to write several articles arguing that torpedo boats could be used as autonomous seagoing warships within a *guerre de course* strategy. According to Aube and Charmes, torpedo boats would join modern steel cruisers in a campaign to cripple enemy commerce. The new school of thought quickly gained the support of younger French officers, and of all those who saw Britain as their country's most likely enemy. Aube and his protégés felt the perfection of the torpedo neutralized Britain's battleship advantage over France. They were also aware of Britain's traditional faith in a seagoing deterrent and its disinclination to invest in coastal defenses. Torpedo attacks on ports and indiscriminate shelling of the enemy coast thus found their place in Aube's strategy, alongside commerce raiding.[6]

For a majority of Aube's critics, the most controversial aspect of the Jeune École strategy was the appeal for ruthless commerce raiding, ultimately for an unrestricted torpedo boat warfare against all enemy shipping. Reflecting a Darwinian contempt for standards of international law at sea (established as recently as 1856), Aube declared that "war is the negation of law. . . . Everything is therefore not only permissible but legitimate against the enemy."[7] In France, the heyday of the Jeune École came in 1886 and 1887, when Aube served as navy minister. Despite protests over the immorality of the strategy, his ideas had a profound and immediate effect on all navies. Shipyards came alive with the construction of torpedo boats, and doubts about the battleship could be heard from every corner. In 1886, during the debate in Britain over the funding of the 12,590-ton *Nile* and *Trafalgar*, even proponents of the two battleships conceded that they probably would be the last of their size ever added to any navy.[8] The following year, 1887, was the only year between the onset of work on the *Gloire* in 1858 and the beginning of international naval disarmament in 1922 in which no country laid down a battleship. The length of the hiatus in battleship construction varied from country to country. France laid down none between the *Magenta* (the last barbette battleship, begun January 1883) and the *Brennus* (the first French turret battleship, laid down January 1889), but French shipyards remained occupied with the eleven barbette ships laid down between 1877 and 1883, which took an average of over nine years to complete.[9]

The first French steel cruiser was the 1,705-ton *Milan*, laid down in 1882, seven years after the British *Iris* and *Mercury*. It had the lines of a clipper like its British predecessors, but its distinctive plow bow became a hallmark of subsequent French steel cruisers. It entered service in 1885, by which time not only Britain but (thanks to Armstrong's Elswick cruisers) Austria–Hungary, Italy, Chile, and Japan all had steel cruisers already in service. The navy's first larger steel warship, the 4,560-ton protected cruiser *Sfax*, was built in 1882–87. Between 1885 and 1887, the peak years of the Jeune École, France laid down another thirteen protected cruisers ranging in size from the 7,470-ton *Tage* to the 1,920-ton *Cosmao*. Smaller warships specifically designed to fit the Jeune École strategy included the four 1,270-ton torpedo cruisers of the *Condor* class and the eight 400-ton torpedo gunboats of the *Bombe* class (all begun in

1883–84).[10] The design for the seagoing torpedo boat so crucial to the Jeune École was a close copy of the 63-ton *Poti*, built by Normand in 1883 for the Russian navy. The French navy ordered three of the boats from Normand in August 1884 and six from other builders in February 1885; all nine were in service by 1886, as the 58-ton *Balny* class. Another nine seagoing torpedo boats were completed by 1889, all roughly twice as large as the *Balny* and its sisters. In the construction of smaller torpedo boats for coastal waters, France took the lead even before the strategy of the Jeune École had crystallized. Between 1876 and 1881 the French navy had commissioned fifty-eight boats displacing 43 tons or less; between 1882 and 1890 another seventy were added, most of which were reproductions of a 45-ton or 53-ton design. By 1889 France also laid down four small armored gunboats of the 1,100-ton *Fusée* class and four of the 1,690-ton *Achéron* class, which in the long run were no more successful than their slightly older German counterparts.[11]

In the midst of the Jeune École era, the British navy built the six barbette battleships of the *Admiral* class, laid down in the years 1880–83 and completed in 1887–89. Aside from the first of the class, the 9,500-ton *Collingwood*, all displaced 10,600 tons. *Collingwood* carried four 12-inch guns and the last of the six, *Benbow*, two 16.25-inch guns; the rest were armed with four 13.5-inch guns. Like the Italian battleships of their time, the *Admirals* had insufficient armor for their hulls and, like the French barbette ships, inadequate protection for their guns. They were roundly criticized on both accounts and these flaws were not repeated in subsequent battleships. The 10,470-ton *Victoria* and *Sans Pareil* (built 1885–91) and the 12,590-ton *Nile* and *Trafalgar* (built 1886–91) marked a return from barbettes to turrets, the former pair with a single forward turret carrying two 16.25-inch Armstrongs, the latter more conventionally with four 13.5-inch guns paired in centerline turrets fore and aft. Other large armored warships of the 1880s included two unsuccessful 6,200-ton turret rams, *Conqueror* (built 1879–86) and *Hero* (1884–88), which were too small for the line of battle but too large to serve as coast defenders. The *Sans Pareil* was the first battleship fitted with triple expansion engines, a technology pioneered in merchant steamers a decade earlier, and first installed in a warship in the torpedo gunboat *Rattlesnake* (1885–87).[12]

Throughout the decade Britain continued to build armored cruisers, beginning with the 8,500-ton *Imperieuse* and *Warspite*, laid down in 1881. The *Imperieuse* was the last large British warship designed with the ability to sail, but it soon lost its brig rig in favor of a single military mast, which the *Warspite* had from the start. The ships were completed in 1886 and 1888, respectively. In part to counter the Jeune École program of fourteen protected cruisers begun in France during the mid-1880s, the British navy added another seven armored cruisers of the 5,600-ton *Orlando* class, laid down in 1885–86 and completed in 1888–89, and the 9,150-ton first-class protected cruisers *Blake* and *Blenheim*, laid down in 1888. The latter were designed by William White, successor to Rendel as senior designer at Armstrong before returning to the Admiralty in

Plate 6.1 Protected cruiser HMS *Blake* (laid down July 1888, completed February 1892)
Naval Historical Center, Basic Collection

the mid-1880s. The *Blake* and *Blenheim* were sleek steel warships capable of over 21 knots. Fleet service alone did not justify their coal capacity, an unprecedented 1,800 tons, which reflected their alternate mission of "long range trade protection." Despite the fact that the *Blake* and *Blenheim* were laid down by a British navy seeking to counter the threat of Jeune École warfare, their successful design was copied until 1900 for first-class cruisers worldwide.[13]

In addition to maintaining its superiority in battleships and large cruisers, throughout the era the British navy also remained safely ahead in the smaller classes of warship commonly associated with the Jeune École. From the pathbreaking *Iris* and *Mercury* through the 1880s, Britain laid down three dozen second- and third-class steel cruisers. After commissioning the pioneering *Lightning* in 1876 and the torpedo boat carrier *Hecla* in 1878, the British navy by 1889 added another 159 torpedo boats – more than the French navy in the same years – and seventeen torpedo gunboats. In 1885, during an Anglo-Russian war scare over Afghanistan, the first annual maneuvers of the British navy simulated a Jeune École scenario of torpedo boats attacking a port defended by an anti-torpedo boom and minefield, most likely a rehearsal for an operation against a Russian harbor in the Baltic.[14]

Austria–Hungary and Germany

While the French developed strategic theories calling for torpedo attacks in a wide variety of circumstances, they left much work to be done in the applied science of tactics. It was here that the Austro-Hungarian navy excelled, indeed impressing the French. The two navies were sharing information long before Aube became navy minister, and the conclusion of the Triple Alliance in 1882, formally aligning Austria–Hungary with an anti-French bloc, ironically did not stop the exchanges. Under the leadership of Admiral Max von Sterneck after 1883, the Austro-Hungarian navy hosted even more French visitors at its base in Pola and at the Whitehead torpedo factory in Fiume, members of the chamber of deputies as well as officers. The latter were impressed with Austro-Hungarian exercises which included the use of torpedo boats in simulated actions against battleships at sea. They adopted the Austro-Hungarian tactic of "hiding" a torpedo boat beside each battleship until smoke provided safe cover for their attacks, and used it until 1902.[15]

Sterneck admired French strategy just as the French were impressed by Austro-Hungarian tactics. Through a nephew serving at the Dual Monarchy's Paris embassy (where Austria–Hungary did not yet have a naval attaché), Sterneck established contact with Gabriel Charmes and received the latest Jeune École literature. It gave him great satisfaction that he had already tried at sea many of the maneuvers that Aube's chief publicist was still discussing in the realm of theory. "It appears as if we have had the same ideas simultaneously, with the difference that I can put them into action immediately." In a time of peace and tight defense budgets, with his country now an ally of its traditional naval rival, lacking the means or a good reason to match the Italian navy in big battleships, Sterneck embraced the Jeune École wholeheartedly. Indeed, the impact of the Jeune École was stronger and lasted longer in Austria–Hungary than anywhere else. Between the casemate ship *Tegetthoff* (1876) and the battleships of the *Monarch* class (1893), the navy laid down just two battleships, the 6,900-ton *Kronprinz Rudolf* and the 5,100-ton *Kronprinzessin Stephanie*, both begun in 1884. The navy had only ten torpedo boats when Sterneck took command but added fifty-three between 1883 and 1891, along with six torpedo gunboats. Austria–Hungary purchased two small Armstrong cruisers, then built a third of the same type in Trieste and, in 1888, laid down two protected cruisers, which Sterneck called "ram cruisers," the 4,000-ton *Kaiser Franz Joseph I* and *Kaiserin Elisabeth*. Like Armstrong's "Elswick" cruisers, the ram cruisers had a heavy primary armament (two 9.4-inch Krupp guns) and no side armor, but also an anachronistic ram bow. The heavy guns were supposed to enable the ram cruiser to exchange fire at a distance with armored enemy battleships and thus cover attacking torpedo boats while serving as a flotilla leader. Marketed by Sterneck as "battleships of the future" and replacements for obsolete casemate ships, the ram cruisers cost half as much as the *Kronprinz Rudolf* and *Kronprinzessin Stephanie*, and thus were attractive to the politicians. Thanks to the virtual abandonment of battleship construction for seventeen years, the early 1890s found Austria–Hungary mired in sixth place among the naval powers of Europe.[16]

Germany, like Austria–Hungary, contributed to the strategy and tactics of the Jeune École. Aube copied freely from the coast defense strategy of General Stosch, chief of the Imperial Admiralty until 1883, in advocating shallow-draught ironclads similar to the German program of "sortie corvettes" (the 7,600-ton *Sachsen* class) and small (1,100-ton) armored gunboats. Dispersed in fortified coastal bases, such warships would conduct sorties to break an enemy blockade or disrupt enemy attempts to land troops on the coast.[17] Like Stosch, Aube believed that shallow-draught battleships and armored gunboats would be able to operate on the high seas and fight on equal terms with enemy battleships. The French admiral clearly was unaware of problems that the German warships of these types experienced after entering service. By the time the last of the four *Sachsens* was commissioned in 1883, their lack of speed and maneuverability were encouraging a growing skepticism within the German navy about their design and the concept behind it.[18]

These early problems with the coast defense aspect of the Jeune École failed to dampen German enthusiasm for the strategy as a whole. Indeed, General Leo von Caprivi, Stosch's successor as chief of the Imperial Admiralty from 1883 to 1888, became a strong proponent of it. Under his direction Germany constructed its first five modern steel cruisers, including the 4,300-ton protected cruisers *Irene* (built in 1886–88) and *Prinzess Wilhelm* (1886–89). Though Caprivi rejected cruiser warfare as irrelevant to Germany's strategic situation (neither France nor Russia, the most likely adversaries, depended heavily on overseas trade), the cruisers laid down on his watch were justified in part by an important change in that situation: the founding of a German colonial empire in Africa and the western Pacific in 1884–85.[19]

Caprivi endorsed Aube's view of the torpedo as the decisive factor in future naval warfare and dramatically expanded the number of torpedo boats in the fleet. After Stosch had ordered seven boats, which entered service in 1883, Caprivi ordered another sixty-five, all commissioned by 1888. In September 1884, at the end of the annual maneuvers, German torpedo boats built by Schichau of Elbing rode out a heavy storm in the North Sea. Just as a similar experience had fired the imagination of Aube and Charmes during the French maneuvers the previous summer, on this occasion the durability of the boats impressed Alfred Tirpitz, then a captain in the torpedo service. From 1885 onward the navy patronized Schichau almost exclusively; in all, forty-two of the boats commissioned under Caprivi came from Schichau. In 1886 Caprivi established the Torpedo Inspection in Kiel, with Tirpitz as its head. The following year he created two torpedo divisions, one based in Kiel, the other in Wilhelmshaven. The navy also established its own torpedo factory at Friedrichsort, to supplement the output of Whitehead and its German licensee, Schwartzkopf of Berlin. Years before Krupp produced world-class armor plate,

Schwartzkopf manufactured first-rate torpedoes, good enough to be ordered in 1885 by the British navy, which had a demand at the time that neither its own Woolwich Arsenal nor Austria–Hungary's Whitehead could fill.[20]

As a soldier, Caprivi could not support a program that would drain resources away from the army, the key to Germany's fate in wartime. His views were reflected in his often-cited remark that the question should be one of "how small our fleet can be, not how large."[21] Attentions thus focused not on creating a larger fleet but on improving the smaller navy's chances against larger potential rivals, especially the Franco-Russian combination Caprivi dreaded. In 1883 he revived a plan for a canal across Holstein, to facilitate the rapid concentration of the fleet in either the Baltic or the North Sea. The Reichstag funded this "Kiel Canal" in 1886, and it opened nine years later. Caprivi eventually acknowledged the need for new armored warships, provided that their design reflected a coast defense mission. The eight ships of the 3,500-ton *Siegfried* class carried three 9.4-inch Krupp guns, two paired in a forward turret and one aft in a turret of its own. Its modest dimensions notwithstanding, the onset of construction on the *Siegfried* in 1888 – the year in which Caprivi left the Admiralty and the staunch navalist William II became emperor – signaled the revival of the German armored program. Aside from the 5,200-ton casemate ship *Oldenburg*, laid down in 1883, Germany had not ordered a new battleship since 1876. Stosch's political problems before 1883 and Caprivi's infatuation with the Jeune École afterward caused the navy to lose the momentum built in the 1870s. In 1883 Germany trailed only Britain and France in armored tonnage, but in 1885 Italy surpassed Germany, and in 1892 Russia did likewise. By 1893 Germany trailed all European powers except Austria–Hungary in both armored and total warship tonnage.[22]

The Russian and Italian anomalies

Germany's relative decline occurred because Italy and Russia continued to build battleships during the era of the Jeune École. The Russian hiatus in battleship construction starts came earlier, between 1870 and 1881, while in Italy it came later, between 1885 and 1893. Indeed, Russia laid down armored warships in all but three years of the decade (1882, 1886 and 1887). While their torpedo strategy against the Turks in 1877–78 inspired other navies to invest in flotillas of torpedo boats, the Russians themselves drew a very different conclusion. The bravado of Makarov and other lieutenants may have kept Turkish commanders in port, fearful of losing their ships, but the absence of fire support from battleships had slowed the advance of the Russian army along both the eastern and western coasts of the Black Sea. After Russia's Balkan army advanced to San Stefano in late February 1878, the lack of a battle fleet at the Black Sea approaches to the Bosporus left its position before Constantinople far less secure. Rather than celebrate the success of the torpedo campaign against the Turks, Russian leaders considered naval weakness the factor that had compelled them to back down after the British fleet passed the Dardanelles.[23]

To remedy the deficiencies of its fleet, in 1882 Russia embarked upon its first long-term program of naval expansion, focusing on the Black Sea. Between 1883 and 1902 a total of fifteen battleships and ten cruisers were to be built, at a cost of 242 million rubles; a subsequent revision added another five battleships and fourteen cruisers, the latter reflecting some degree of influence of the Jeune École. In the first six years of the program, years in which France began no battleships at all, Russia laid down nine: four of the 10,200-ton *Ekaterina II* class and five smaller battleships ranging in size from the 9,480-ton *Navarin* to the 6,590-ton *Gangut*. All were equipped with Krupp guns manufactured under license in Russia; the *Navarin* and the 8,440-ton *Imperator Nikolai I* carried theirs in turrets, while the other ships had barbettes. In addition to being the largest, the *Ekaterina II* and its sisters were also the most heavily armed, with six 12-inch guns paired in three barbettes; at the opposite extreme, the *Gangut* had a lone 12-inch gun mounted in a forward barbette. Of the nine battleships, the five largest were built in Sevastopol or Nicolaiev for the Black Sea fleet. Owing to improvements in the shipyards there and in St Petersburg, they took an average of less than six years to complete. All had compound armor except the *Georgi Pobiedonosets* (laid down 1889), the last ship of the *Ekaterina II* class, which had all-steel armor. In a decade in which all other navies except the British stopped building armored cruisers the Russians added four, the largest of which was the 8,520-ton *Admiral Nakhimov*, a close copy of the British *Warspite* and *Imperieuse*, bristling with eight 8-inch and ten 6-inch guns, capable of 17 knots. Early in the decade the navy commissioned its first unarmored steel cruiser, the 3,000-ton *Pamiat Merkuria*, built at Le Havre. The Russians turned to the same source for the commerce raider *Admiral Kornilov*, delivered in 1888. The largest of three protected cruisers built during the 1880s, the 5,860-ton vessel had engines capable of 18.5 knots.[24]

The use of armed merchantmen in the Black Sea during the Russo–Turkish War inspired Russia to create a "volunteer fleet" of merchant ships which would be converted to commerce raiders in wartime. The fleet consisted entirely of British-built liners, twenty-five as of 1898, which in case of war were to be fitted with 8-inch and 6-inch guns stored at Vladivostok and Sevastopol.[25] The navy's first modern torpedo boat, the 43-ton *Batum*, was built by Yarrow in 1880. Of another thirty-one boats added by 1890, thirteen were built in Russia, the rest in Britain, France, or Germany. The navy commissioned a further fifty-six torpedo boats between 1891 and 1904. Almost all the dozens of torpedo boats and launches built during and immediately after the War of 1877–78 were discarded by 1890. Though the motive behind Russia's naval expansion program was clearly anti-British, its goal was not to surpass the British navy alone, rather to create a navy strong enough to join the French or another fleet in neutralizing Britain's command of the seas. Ironically, if Russia had resorted to a Jeune École strategy against Britain, it would have done so with a British-built "volunteer fleet" and at least a few British-built torpedo boats.[26]

In Italy, the early 1880s brought the completion of Benedetto Brin's *Duilio* and *Dandolo* and the continuation of work on his two *Italia* class battleships, but his rival and critic Ferdinando Acton (navy minister from 1880 to 1883) scaled down the size of the three *Ruggiero di Lauria* class battleships begun in 1881–82 and also sympathized with many of the ideas soon to be identified with the Jeune École. Brin responded with the polemic *La nostra Marina Militare* (1881), defending his belief in a battle fleet of large battleships.[27] After he returned to office the size of Italian battleships increased once again, with the three vessels of the 13,900-ton *Re Umberto* class, laid down in 1884–85. Like their predecessors they carried their primary armament of four heavy guns paired in two French-style barbettes, and had steel armor imported from Schneider of Creusot. Their primary armament of four 13.5-inch Armstrongs (compared with the 17- and 17.7-inch guns of their predecessors) marked the Italian navy's abandonment of very large guns. For Brin and others envisioning Italy as a great naval power, Italian shipyards remained a problem. Their efficiency did not improve and construction times actually increased, the *Ruggiero di Lauria*s taking an average of almost eight years to complete, the *Re Umberto*s nearly ten.[28]

After laying down six large battleships between 1881 and 1885, Italy went eight years without ordering another, as the navy, ironically under Brin's direction, belatedly embraced the Jeune École. In 1885 Armstrong delivered the navy's first protected cruiser, the 3,280-ton *Giovanni Bausan*, ordered by Acton three years earlier. Between 1885 and 1892, another thirteen protected cruisers were laid down for the Italian navy, two by Armstrong, the rest by Italian shipbuilders, and fifteen small protected cruisers of under 1,000 tons, some rated as "torpedo cruisers," were built in Italy.[29] The Italian navy had just four torpedo boats in 1881 but added another 159 by 1888, more than any other navy during the decade.[30] Also in harmony with the Jeune École, Italy developed a naval presence that was, if not global, clearly not limited to the Mediterranean. The navy extended its operations into the Red Sea and western Indian Ocean, providing support to the army during the occupation of Eritrea (from 1882) and Somalia (from 1889). At the same time overseas missions, including more than twenty circumnavigations of the globe, transformed the focus of the Italian navy from the battle fleet to cruising duties.[31]

Nevertheless, as Italy's big battleships inched toward completion the battle fleet continued to consume the greatest share of the naval outlay, and once completed, their large crews accounted for the greatest share of the personnel. Even during the eight-year hiatus in battleship construction after 1885, Italy maintained naval ambitions that required a strong battle fleet. With Austria–Hungary an ally and its navy currently no threat to the security of Italy, Italian strategists focused on France as their leading rival. Franco-Italian relations continued to worsen, poisoned first by France's annexation of Tunis in 1881, then by Italy's accession to Bismarck's Triple Alliance (1882) and the Mediterranean Agreements (1887), the latter linking Britain, Italy, Austria–Hungary, and Spain. After francophobe Francesco Crispi became prime minister in 1887, tensions increased still more. In February 1888, when France broke off negotiations for a trade agreement with Italy, coincidentally at a time when the French navy was testing a new system of mobilization, Crispi concluded that the fleet at Toulon was preparing a preemptive strike and asked Bismarck for support. Appeals to London from Rome and Berlin prompted Britain to send a squadron to Genoa, reflecting British solidarity with the Italians at a time when the threat of the Jeune École had seriously strained the Anglo-French relationship. Afterward, amid talk of increased Anglo-Italian naval cooperation, Bismarck hoped to secure a firmer British commitment to his anti-French system of alliances.[32] But the incident reflected a harsh reality of Italy's strategic position: membership in the Triple Alliance made sense only as long as Britain and France were rivals. Around the turn of the century, a deterioration of Anglo-German relations and subsequent Anglo-French rapprochement would weaken Italy's commitment to Germany and Austria–Hungary.

Japan and China

Britain's influence over the Japanese navy waned temporarily after the end of the British naval mission in 1879. Japan made a conscious effort to maintain good relations with other naval powers, particularly France which had helped establish the Yokosuka navy yard. Many Japanese navy officers embraced the Jeune École, considering torpedo boats uniquely suited to their country's geographical situation and martial traditions, with their low cost being an added bonus. Émile Bertin, one of the leading designers of French Jeune École warships, spent three years in Japan during the 1880s as a consultant on shipbuilding. Reflecting the Jeune École's influence, the Japanese navy spent virtually all of its construction budget on unarmored or protected cruisers and torpedo boats. Between 1878 and 1897 Japan commissioned just one armored warship, the 2,400-ton armored cruiser *Chiyoda*, built by Brown of Clydebank in 1888–90. Japanese fleet plans of the decade included dozens of torpedo boats, but ultimately only twenty-five were purchased or ordered between 1880 and 1890. All were either foreign-built or built abroad, dismantled, and assembled in Japan. Early British and French models gradually gave way to a preference for the German Schichau design. The 1,750-ton unprotected cruiser *Takao*, built at Yokosuka in 1886–89, was the first steel-hulled warship constructed in Japan, followed by the slightly smaller *Yaeyama* (1887–92). Supplementing its fleet of fully rigged cruisers, between 1882 and 1892 Japanese shipyards completed three composite corvettes and five gunboats.[33]

After purchasing the Armstrong-built *Tsukushi* (ex-*Arturo Prat*) from Chile in 1885, Japan bought two 3,650-ton protected cruisers directly from Armstrong in 1885 and 1886, and turned to France for the 3,615-ton protected cruiser *Unebi*, built at Le Havre in 1884–86. The *Unebi* sank in the South China Sea in 1887, in a disaster which may have resulted from a flawed design, but Japanese confidence in French technology remained undiminished. In 1888 Japan ordered two 4,220-ton *Matsushima* class protected cruisers from La Seyne and laid down a third ship of the same class under French supervision at Yokosuka. Designed by Bertin, their armament included one heavy 12.6-inch Canet gun.[34] Thus Japan had eight modern steel-hulled cruisers built or building by 1890, with twenty-five torpedo boats and only one new armored warship, a very small cruiser. A second British naval mission (1887–93) further encouraged the modernization process. Under its influence the navy opened its first staff college, introduced the study of tactics, and began to develop its own doctrine. British advice also brought the deactivation of obsolete ships and the creation of a fleet organizational structure for peacetime as well as wartime. The mission reinforced the British concept of naval professionalism within the officer corps and reaffirmed the primacy of British influence in the midst of Japan's infatuation with the Jeune École, at a time when French and German firms were doing a brisk business with the Japanese navy.[35]

During the 1880s the Chinese navy also had British advisors, did business with British and German firms, and was influenced by the French Jeune École. But the new school affected the Chinese much less than the Japanese, as evidenced by the fact that during the decade China ordered the 7,220-ton battleships *Ting Yuan* (launched 1881) and *Chen Yuan* (1882) and two 2,900-ton armored cruisers (1887), all from Vulcan of Stettin. Vulcan built most of the fifteen torpedo boats commissioned by the Chinese navy between 1881 and 1887; German firms also built a 2,300-ton protected cruiser (launched 1883) and two 2,200-ton unarmored cruisers (1883–84). The rest of China's foreign-built cruisers came from British builders, two 1,380-ton cruisers from Mitchell (launched 1880–81) and two 2,300-ton Armstrong cruisers (1886). China's domestic naval shipbuilding record remained more impressive than that of Japan. The three unarmored cruisers of the 2,100-ton *Kai Che* class (launched 1882–86) were built in Foochow, giving China three domestically built steel cruisers before Japan laid down its first, but in design the barque-rigged trio bore little resemblance to the modern cruisers of the Jeune École. At a time when Japan was building its first steel-hulled warship, China, in 1888, laid down its first domestically built armored cruiser, the 2,150-ton *Ping Yuan*, also at Foochow. Other domestic construction included a 1,480-ton unprotected cruiser launched at Kiangyan in 1883, three 1,000-ton torpedo gunboats launched at Foochow in 1890–91, and a composite-hulled dispatch vessel.[36] Thus the Chinese navy had eleven steel-hulled cruisers built or building by 1890, with eighteen torpedo boats and torpedo gunboats, slightly more cruisers and slightly fewer torpedo boats than its Japanese rival. But while Japan had added only one very small armored cruiser, China's newest warships included two large battleships and three armored cruisers.

The Jeune École had less influence in China (and French shipbuilders secured no contracts there) in part because of a Franco-Chinese war over Indochina, fought in 1884–85. France had first intervened in Indochina during the Second Opium War, and during the 1860s established a colony in southern Vietnam.

In the early 1880s the French invaded northern Vietnam and in 1882 took Hanoi, prompting China to lend its support to anti-French Vietnamese. Treaties signed in the spring of 1884 required the Chinese to withdraw from Indochina and recognize the French colonial establishment, but war broke out anyway after France attempted to seize the stronghold of Lang Son before China was prepared to give it up. French naval forces in the theater of war included Vice Admiral A. A. P. Courbet's 5,915-ton flagship *Bayard*, four other masted armored cruisers, and twenty-six unarmored steamers of various types. Courbet destroyed the Fukien fleet at the Battle of the Min River (23 August 1884), where he compensated for a lack of torpedo boats by using four launches as torpedo craft, to great effect. After the victory he bombarded the Foochow shipyard. Outnumbered French troops did not fare as well in the ground war, however, and ultimately France made no gains other than those China had promised to recognize in 1884. These were reaffirmed in a new treaty concluded in June 1885, under British mediation.[37]

The French navy lost no ships during the brief conflict. Chinese losses reflected the fact that the Fukien was perhaps the weakest of China's four fleets: the wooden screw frigate *Yu Yuan*, three wooden screw corvettes, one composite gunboat, and two shallow-draught flatiron gunboats, all warships dating from the early 1870s. Indeed, the conflict had remarkably little impact on the Chinese naval build-up, as the five German-built warships launched before the outbreak of the war – two battleships and three cruisers – did not arrive in Chinese waters until after the fighting ended. During the war most of the other modern units were safely on the stocks in foreign shipyards, and those in Foochow were not seriously damaged by Courbet's bombardment of the shipyard there. Afterward, the material growth continued at a rate more impressive than that of the Japanese navy, obscuring the fact that the Chinese were doing little right other than acquiring more warships. China kept obsolete vessels in commission, retained its traditional divided structure of four fleets, and did little to encourage the development of a professional officer corps abreast of the latest strategic and tactical thinking. After a British naval mission left in disgust in 1890, the qualitative balance between the two East Asian navies tipped all the more in favor of the Japanese.[38]

The Americas and the rebirth of the US navy

By 1883 ten years had passed since the US Congress last authorized funds for new warship construction. Its navy had no steel-hulled vessels of any type and no torpedo boats. The only armored warships were five large monitors under construction since 1874 and dozens of smaller monitors laid up since the late 1860s, all incapable of action on the high seas. The United States could not have taken the offensive at sea even against the leading powers of South America.

Emerging victorious from the War of the Pacific, in 1883 Chile had three armored warships more powerful than any vessel in the US navy: the casemate ships *Almirante Cochrane* and *Blanco Encalada*, and the turret ship *Huáscar*. The famous *Esmeralda*, just delivered from Armstrong's Elswick shipyard, was the first modern steel cruiser in any Western hemisphere navy. Chile also had eleven small Yarrow torpedo boats.[39] Argentina, like Chile, continued to rely entirely on British builders for its warships. In 1883 Argentina had the 4,200-ton casemate ship *Almirante Brown*, recently built by Samuda, two monitors from Laird, four tiny flatiron gunboats from Laird and Rennie, and six torpedo boats from Yarrow and Thornycroft.[40] Chile, which since independence had owned the Juan Fernandez archipelago (including the Isla Róbinson Crusoe) 400 miles offshore, in 1888 extended its reach far into the Pacific by annexing Easter Island, 2,350 miles west of the Chilean coast. Ambitious Chileans even dreamed of inheriting the Philippines from Spain. Meanwhile, Argentina occupied Patagonia, which Chile had formally conceded in an 1881 treaty, and asserted its claim to the Falklands (Malvinas), 300 miles east of the Patagonian coast, while prudently not contesting Britain's possession of the islands.

In 1883 Brazil took a decisive step toward challenging Chile's position as the leading naval power of South America, taking delivery of its first true high seas battleship, the 5,610-ton *Riachuelo*, from the British builder Samuda. Though of modest size by European standards, the *Riachuelo* would be the largest battleship in the Western hemisphere for almost a decade. Brazil also acquired five Yarrow torpedo boats and, during 1883, ordered a second battleship from Samuda, the 4,920-ton *Aquidaba*.[41] Brazil entered the decade with sixteen small coastal ironclads, of which thirteen dated from the 1860s. They were discarded beginning in 1885, the same year the Brazilian navy conducted its first annual maneuvers. In the inaugural exercises the active squadron consisted of a "battleship division" including the *Riachuelo* and three coastal ironclads completed in the 1870s, a "cruiser division" of screw corvettes, and eight torpedo boats. In an exercise similar to those conducted by European navies under the Jeune École, the squadron conducted a mock assault on the harbor of Rio de Janeiro, where the torpedo boats played the role of the defending force. After launching three of its own monitors in 1868, Brazil remained the only country in the Americas other than the United States to build its own armored or iron-and-steel warships. The 2,170-ton coastal battleship *Sete de Setembro* was launched in 1874, and in the late 1880s four river gunboats were built using iron from the Ipanema foundries in São Paulo and steel imported from Krupp. But the 4,735-ton steel cruiser *Almirante Tamandaré*, laid down at Rio de Janeiro in 1885, strained the limits of the country's industrial capabilities and was a costly failure, spending most of its service life at anchor after being launched in 1890.[42]

The strength of the Chilean navy by the end of the War of the Pacific, and the subsequent delivery of the *Riachuelo* to Brazil and the *Esmeralda* to Chile, underscored the weakness of the American navy and finally drove the United States to action. In 1883 Congress authorized the construction of three protected cruisers, the 3,190-ton *Atlanta* and *Boston* and the 4,500-ton *Chicago*, along with the 1,490-ton dispatch vessel *Dolphin*.[43] These "ABCD ships" were the first American steel-hulled warships, the foundation of the "new navy" which, within fifteen years, enabled the United States to achieve great power status in the international arena. Between 1887 and 1890 the American navy laid down another eight protected cruisers, three unarmored cruisers of the 2,090-ton *Montgomery* class, and four steel gunboats. The first battleships, originally rated as armored cruisers, were the 6,680-ton *Maine* and 6,135-ton *Texas*, laid down in 1888 and 1889, respectively, but not completed until 1895. The 8,200-ton armored cruiser *New York*, laid down in 1890, was the first modern high seas armored warship commissioned by the United States, in 1893. The emphasis on cruisers reflected the Jeune École spirit of the times, but the build-up gained momentum only in the late 1880s, after the torpedo boat craze of mid-decade had subsided. The US navy had only two torpedo boats in commission by 1890.[44]

As the United States began to build a modern steel navy, its interests overseas continued to be represented by wooden steamers built during the Civil War or in the modest program of 1873. During the 1880s the navy finally decommissioned twelve of the remaining eighteen frigates and sloops of Civil War vintage, and in the midst of the Samoan crisis of March 1889 a typhoon symbolically spelled the end of the American wooden ship fleet. Years of tension between the United States, Britain, and Germany over the Samoan islands worsened in 1887, when Germany established a *de facto* protectorate there. It was the last significant international crisis in which the rival powers all sent fully rigged screw steamers to defend their interests: Britain the steel corvette *Calliope*, Germany the iron-hulled corvette *Olga* and two gunboats, and the United States the wooden-hulled frigate *Trenton*, the sloop *Vandalia*, and the gunboat *Nipsic*. On 15 March 1889 nature intervened to defuse the tension, as a typhoon wrecked or grounded all of the warships except the *Calliope*, which had the most modern and powerful engines of the lot. The three navies cooperated to save survivors, but ninety-three Germans and fifty Americans died in the disaster. While the *Olga* and the *Nipsic* were repaired and refloated, the *Trenton*, the *Vandalia*, and the two German gunboats were a total loss. Afterward the three countries agreed to a tripartite protectorate over Samoa, and a decade later to a three-way partition of the island group.[45]

After the Samoan disaster, American steel cruisers assumed responsiblity for overseas stations once manned by wooden ships. In 1889–90 the new cruisers made their first appearances in European waters, and after 1893 at least one could be found there at any given time, manning a revived European station.[46] One of the last wooden screw steamers in commission, the venerable sloop *Kearsarge* – refitted five times at great expense since its victory over CSS *Alabama* in 1864 – fell victim to a storm in the Caribbean in 1894.[47] Later in the 1890s, when the United States went to war with Spain in the Caribbean and Pacific, it deployed an entirely modern fleet of warships.

For the United States, like Japan, the foundations of naval power laid in the 1880s made possible victory in naval warfare in the 1890s, and entry into the ranks of the world's great naval powers by the turn of the century. But in 1890, the United States had a fleet in service inferior in materiel to that of China, with the same number of steel cruisers as Japan, and fewer torpedo boats than any major European, Asian, or South American navy. In refusing to purchase any warship from a foreign builder, the United States provided a powerful stimulus to its own navy yards and private shipbuilders. Meanwhile, Japan and, to a lesser extent, China depended upon foreign shipyards. Other than the United States, Brazil was the only country in the Americas that had built an armored warship or steel cruiser, and after the disappointing *Almirante Tamandaré* Brazil never again attempted to construct a larger warship of its own. For the United States, the long construction times of the battleships *Maine* (seven years) and *Texas* (six years) bore witness to the fact that American shipyards and supporting industries were not yet fully equal to the task at hand.

Submarines: idea and reality

The Jeune École put the torpedo at the center of its tactics and ruthless attacks on enemy shipping at the center of its strategy; in the future, when such campaigns actually were carried out (by Germany in both World Wars, and by the United States against Japan in the Pacific theater of the Second World War), the submarine served the role that Aube and others had envisioned for torpedo boats supporting cruisers. From the late 1870s through the 1880s, the weaknesses of torpedo boats led to a renewed interest in the submarine as a delivery system for torpedoes, but the undersea technology did not develop rapidly enough to replace the torpedo boat as linchpin of the Jeune École. If the evolution of the submarine somehow had been advanced by a quarter-century, the Jeune École would have survived to establish a new paradigm of naval warfare, making cruisers the capital ships of the world's navies. In such a scenario, the battleship renaissance of the years 1890–1914 would never have occurred.

George Garrett of Liverpool, a clergyman by vocation, began experimenting with submarine designs after a visit to Russia during the Russo-Turkish War. While many observers came away from that war convinced of the striking power of the torpedo boat, Garrett drew the opposite conclusion, having been impressed most of all by the futility of Russian torpedo boat attacks against Ottoman warships deploying anti-torpedo netting or surface booms. Whereas early submarines, including Wilhelm Bauer's *Brandtaucher* (1851) and the Confederate navy's *H. L. Hunley* (1864), had been manually powered, Garrett's 30-ton *Resurgam* (1879) had the advantage of being steam-powered. After the boat foundered and sank in 1880, Garrett joined forces with the Swedish armaments manufacturer Thorsten Nordenfelt and constructed four more submarines between 1882 and 1891. Their 60-ton *Nordenfelt I*, built at Stockholm in 1882–85, was the first submarine armed with self-propelled Whitehead torpedoes. A Greco-Turkish war scare during the Bulgarian crisis of 1885–86 provided the context for the sale of this vessel and orders for two more. The great powers of Europe, minus France, cooperated to contain the conflict and, from January to June 1886, used a naval blockade to compel Greece to demobilize. Afterward, the Greek navy purchased the *Nordenfelt I* for £9,000, despite the fact that it had never run submerged for more than five minutes. The submarine made it to Piraeus, where it remained idle until scrapped fifteen years later. After learning that Greece possessed a submarine, the Ottoman empire promptly ordered two *Nordenfelts*, which were built in Britain, dismantled, then shipped to Constantinople. Only one of the boats was actually reassembled to undergo trials in Turkish waters, but to operate it the clergyman Garrett received a commission in the Ottoman navy. He soon left for home along with his British crew, before training any Turks to operate the submarine, which became a worthless relic in a Turkish navy yard.[48]

Undeterred by these failures, Garrett and Nordenfelt completed the 245-ton *Nordenfelt IV* for Russia, but the boat ran aground on the coast of Jutland in November 1888, while en route from Britain to St Petersburg. Nordenfelt built two more submarines without Garrett, both for the German navy, but like their predecessors they were unsuccessful. Meanwhile, in France, the aging Dupuy de Lôme experimented with submarines prior to his death in 1885, after which work continued under the direction of Gustave Zédé. In September 1888 Zédé completed the first truly operational submarine, the 30-ton *Gymnôte*, a vessel powered by an electric battery and manned by a crew of five. The *Gymnôte* made around 2,000 dives during a career of almost twenty years in the French navy. Zédé died in 1891, before his breakthrough was fully appreciated, but by the turn of the century his colleagues made their country the early leader in submarine technology.[49]

Conclusion

Far from falling victim to a mindless reassertion of battleship-centered "naval tradition,"[50] the Jeune École died for good reasons. The French navy's early fascination with the submarine coincided with its loss of faith in the torpedo boat, the centerpiece of the strategy. In January 1890, one year after ending its six-year hiatus in battleship construction by laying down the *Brennus*, the French navy withdrew the nine *Balny* class torpedo boats from high seas service, concluding that the 58-ton vessels were fit only for the coastal *défense mobile*.[51] By then, torpedo nets and electric searchlights were being employed to make stationary battleships less vulnerable to torpedo attack. Furthermore, improvements in propulsion systems and artillery that had been pioneered aboard torpedo vessels or light cruisers were being introduced to larger warships, giving them the speed and rapid medium-range firepower to counter the threat of the torpedo while underway. In 1887 trials an Armstrong 4.7-inch gun fired ten rounds in 47.5 seconds, a dramatic improvement over the standard 5-inch breech-loading rifle of the time, which fired at a rate of one round per 40 seconds. The British torpedo gunboat *Sharpshooter* (commissioned 1889) and the Elswick protected cruiser *Piemonte* (delivered to Italy in 1889) were the first warships to carry the medium-caliber quick-firing gun, which became common in the early 1890s as the secondary armament for battleships and large cruisers. At the same time, the water-tube Belleville boiler technology that had given torpedo boats and smaller cruisers a great advantage during the early 1880s was introduced to larger warships, enabling them also to benefit from the latest increases in speed.[52]

In addition to the Belleville boiler, the French developed two other technologies which sowed the seeds of the demise of their own Jeune École. In 1886 they pioneered the first "smokeless" powder, a nitro-cellulose combination, some four years before the British introduced cordite, a powder with a nitro-glycerine base. Also in 1886, the French shell manufacturer Holtzer produced the first chrome steel shells, paving the way for further improvements which soon led to the armor-piercing shell cap and the production of shells vastly superior to the Palliser type of the 1870s.[53] Even though "smokeless" powder did, indeed, produce some smoke, Jeune École advocates no longer could count on the artificial "fog of war" created by the smoky fire of big guns as a factor that would allow torpedo boats to close on larger warships. At the same time, the improved armor-piercing steel shell gave new life to the big gun and to the larger warships needed as platforms for such ordnance. When revolutionary developments in armor production in 1890–92 resolved the problem of how to provide adequate protection for such vessels, the Jeune École would lose what little life it had left. In addition to Britain and Russia, which had never suspended their battleship construction as a result of the Jeune École, Germany (from 1888), France (from 1889), Italy and Austria–Hungary (both from 1893), and Japan (from 1894) resumed their programs and continued to build ever-larger classes of battleships until the outbreak of the First World War. In the revitalized US navy the last echo of the Jeune École came in 1890, when Congress authorized the 7,375-ton protected cruisers *Columbia* and *Minneapolis*, lightly armed warships designed as commerce raiders. The same budget included three battleships of the 10,290-ton *Indiana* class, reflecting the changing times.[54]

Notes

1 Roberts, "Warships of Steel, 1879–1889," 105.
2 Ibid., 106; Brown, "The Era of Uncertainty, 1863–1878," 89–90; *Conway, 1860–1905*, 51–82, and *passim*.
3 Roberts, "Warships of Steel, 1879–1889," 107; *Conway, 1860–1905*, 82, 154, 226–9, 277, 348–9, 396–7, 402–3, 411.
4 E.g. Austro-Hungarian naval chief, Admiral Max von Sterneck; see Sondhaus, *The Naval Policy of Austria–Hungary*, 99.
5 Tritten, "Navy and Military Doctrine in France," 56–7.
6 Theodore Ropp, *The Development of a Modern Navy: French Naval Policy, 1871–1904*, ed. Stephen S. Roberts (Annapolis, Md, 1987), 132, 155–6, 159–65; Arthur J. Marder, *The Anatomy of British Sea Power: A History of British Naval Policy in the Pre-Dreadnought Era, 1880–1905* (New York, 1940), 86–7.

7 Aube quoted in Ropp, *The Development of a Modern Navy*, 165.
8 Marder, *The Anatomy of British Sea Power*, 125.
9 Roberts, "Warships of Steel, 1879–1889," 95; *Conway, 1860–1905*, 290–2.
10 Roberts, "Warships of Steel, 1879–1889," 96, 109; *Conway, 1860–1905*, 308–10, 320, 324.
11 *Conway, 1860–1905*, 211, 300, 327–8, 330–2.
12 Ibid., 28–31; Roberts, "Warships of Steel, 1879–1889," 101–3; Griffiths, "Warship Machinery," 176; Brown, *Warrior to Dreadnought*, 99.
13 Roberts, "Warships of Steel, 1879–1889," 102–3, 109–10; *Conway, 1860–1905*, 64–6.
14 Brown, *Warrior to Dreadnought*, 84–85; Marder, *The Anatomy of British Sea Power*, 134; *Conway, 1860–1905*, 88–9, 101–6.
15 Sondhaus, *The Naval Policy of Austria–Hungary*, 97.
16 Sterneck quoted in Max von Sterneck to Richard Sterneck, Vienna, 3 March 1886, in Sterneck, *Erinnerungen*, 232; see also Sondhaus, *The Naval Policy of Austria–Hungary*, 97–100.
17 Ropp, *The Development of a Modern Navy*, 28–30, 157.
18 Sondhaus, *Preparing for Weltpolitik*, 136.
19 Ibid., 153–9; Gröner, *Die deutsche Kriegsschiffe*, 1: 120–3.
20 Sondhaus, *Preparing for Weltpolitik*, 161–4; Campbell, "Naval Armaments and Armour," 167.
21 Caprivi quoted in Verchau, "Von Jachmann über Stosch und Caprivi," 67.
22 Sondhaus, *Preparing for Weltpolitik*, 165–6, 168.
23 Clarke, *Russia's Sea-Power*, 108.
24 Gromov et al., *Tri Veka Rossiiskogo Flota*, 1: 259; Woodward, *The Russians at Sea*, 117; Watts, *The Imperial Russian Navy*, 16; Roberts, "Warships of Steel, 1879–1889," 103–4; *Conway, 1860–1905*, 178–9, 186–8, 192–3.
25 Jane, *The Imperial Russian Navy*, 334–5.
26 Watts, *The Imperial Russian Navy*, 16; Woodward, *The Russians at Sea*, 117; *Conway, 1860–1905*, 211–15.
27 Donolo, "The History of Italian Naval Doctrine," 105.
28 Bargoni, *Corazzate italiane classi Duilio-Italia-Ruggiero di Lauria*, passim; idem, *Corazzate italiane classi Re Umberto – Ammiraglio di Saint Bon, 1893–1901* (Rome, 1978); Roberts, "Warships of Steel, 1879–1889," 100–1.
29 *Conway, 1860–1905*, 346–50.
30 Baratelli, *La marina militare italiana*, 259–60; Giorgio Giorgerini, *Almanacco storico delle navi militari italiane: La Marina e le sue navi dal 1861 al 1975* (Rome, 1978), 419–27.
31 Donolo, "The History of Italian Naval Doctrine," 104–5.
32 Ropp, *The Development of a Modern Navy*, 191–2.
33 Evans and Peattie, *Kaigun*, 15; *Conway, 1860–1905*, 223, 233–7.
34 *Conway, 1860–1905*, 226–27.
35 Evans and Peattie, *Kaigun*, 13.
36 *Conway, 1860–1905*, 395–7, 399–400.
37 Dupont and Taillemite, *Les guerres navales françaises*, 246–8, 255–60; Lyon, "Underwater Warfare and the Torpedo Boat," 141–2; *Conway, 1860–1905*, 395.
38 *Conway, 1860–1905*, 395, 398.
39 Ibid., 410–11, 414.
40 Ibid., 401–4.
41 Since its construction the name of this warship has been consistently misspelled in English-language sources, which call it *Aquidaban* (e.g. ibid., 407).
42 Carvalho, *Nossa Marinha*, 98–100, 120, 124; *Conway, 1860–1905*, 405–7, 409. Carvalho, 78, 82, refers to three monitors which are not listed in *Conway*.

43 Benjamin Franklin Cooley, *Gray Steel and Blue Water Navy: The Formative Years of America's Military-Industrial Complex, 1881–1917* (Hamden, Ct, 1979), 50; Roberts, "The Pre-Dreadnought Age, 1890–1905," 121.

44 John D. Alden, *The American Steel Navy*, rev. edn (Annapolis, Md, 1989), 361, 368, 370–4, 376–7, 379; cf. *Conway, 1860–1905*, 139, 147, 150–3, 159, 163–4.

45 Sondhaus, *Preparing for Weltpolitik*, 204–5. See also Paul Kennedy, *The Samoan Tangle: A Study in Anglo-German–American Relations, 1878–1900* (New York, 1974), 87–102, 105–6, 189–239; Alden, *The American Steel Navy*, 313, 318.

46 Still, *American Sea Power in the Old World*, 91–3.

47 Canney, *The Old Steam Navy*, 1: 78.

48 Wilson, "Early Submarines," 149–51; Sondhaus, *The Naval Policy of Austria–Hungary*, 105–6; *Conway, 1906–21*, 387.

49 Wilson, "Early Submarines," 154; *Conway, 1906–21*, 206.

50 As asserted in Robert L. O'Connell, *Sacred Vessels: The Cult of the Battleship and the Rise of the U.S. Navy* (Oxford, 1993), 142.

51 *Conway, 1860–1905*, 327.

52 Campbell, "Naval Armaments and Armour," 163; Griffiths, "Warship Machinery," 177.

53 Roberts, "The Pre-Dreadnought Age, 1890–1905," 113.

54 Alden, *The American Steel Navy*, 362, 374.

CHAPTER SEVEN

The rebirth of the battleship

Strategic considerations joined the technical and technological factors that turned the leading navies away from the Jeune École and back toward the battleship. It became generally accepted that an armored battle fleet provided a better deterrent against attack and could defend home waters reliably regardless of the weather. Furthermore, most countries did not have a rival with a volume of overseas commerce sufficient to justify commerce raiding as a primary strategy. Finally, from the United States, the writings of Alfred Thayer Mahan provided battle fleet proponents with historical arguments to support their points of view. From Emperor William II to Theodore Roosevelt, pro-navy political leaders would treat Mahan's works as holy scripture. Unarmored cruisers and torpedo boats remained an important part of all navies, but no longer were considered a potential main striking force. Out of the confusion of 1860–90 there finally emerged a standard design of battleship, what would later be called the "pre-dreadnought." Masts and yards, still in evidence on the casemate ships of the 1870s, disappeared entirely. In the early 1890s compound armor gave way to nickel–steel plate, perfected by the German firm of Krupp. Increased protection without added weight facilitated a further increase in battleship size, paving the way for the dreadnought design after the turn of the century.

The 1890s and first years of the new century witnessed the emergence of Germany, the United States, and Japan as naval powers of the first rank. In the German empire, Rear Admiral Alfred Tirpitz promoted the fleet as cornerstone of a new *Weltpolitik* that would make Germany a world power. From modest beginnings in the 1880s, the American steel navy grew to include an impressive force of battleships and armored cruisers. In the Far East, the Russo-Japanese War of 1904–5 featured the destruction of the Russian fleet at the Battle of Tsushima (1905), the largest naval engagement since Trafalgar, a century earlier.

Britain and the Naval Defence Act of 1889

Before most naval powers began their turn away from the Jeune École, Britain led the way with a program of battleships laid down under the Naval Defence Act of 1889. The legislation funded a systematic peacetime naval expansion based upon the "two-power standard." Until then the standard had been an informal measure of strength, often cited by British admirals, politicians, and journalists over the seven decades since it was first proposed by Lord Castlereagh as the surest guarantee of the security of Britain, its empire, and the general peace. In fact, the British navy had in commission a number of capital ships equal to or greater than the combined strength of the next two navies only during the remainder of the era of the sailing ship of the line and, in the 1850s, the brief era of the screw ship of the line. Since the introduction of the iron-clad warship, Britain had maintained its position as leading naval power but never approached a two-power standard in armored warships. Thus, in the Naval Defence Act, Britain made a commitment to achieve a level of naval supremacy it had not enjoyed in thirty years.

The new program marked a dramatic departure from the policies of the previous two decades. The defeat of Napoleon III in 1870 had left Britain with an unprecedented sense of security; from then until the onset of the Jeune École, the pace of British naval construction reflected a marked lack of fear of the French navy. During the 1870s Britain laid down less than half as many ironclads as it had the previous decade, and from 1880 to 1888 just ten battleships were begun. Neither political party favored naval expansion as a matter of principle. Liberal leader William Gladstone was famous for his complaint that the design of warships changed as often as the fashion of ladies' hats, and his main political rival, Conservative leader Benjamin Disraeli, often criticized "bloated arma-ments." Yet Britain continued to measure naval strength in battleships even as it built fewer of them; indeed, during the 1880s it was not the French Jeune École alone, but the combination of the new French strategy and the much more comprehensive Russian naval build-up, including battleships, which cast doubt over the British navy's ability to play its traditional role in the world. An Anglo-French war scare during the first months of 1888 escalated the public and parliamentary debate over the strength of the navy.[1] Lord Charles Beresford, naval officer and Member of Parliament, played a leading role in the "navalist campaign," delivering a key speech in the House of Commons in December 1888 in which he insisted upon "a definite standard . . . against the fleets of two powers combined, one of which should be France."[2] During subsequent parlia-mentary hearings the First Sea Lord, Admiral Sir Arthur Hood, invoked the two-power standard as the traditional measure of British naval strength. The bill authorizing the expansion of the fleet would make the standard official.[3]

On 7 March 1889 Parliament passed the Naval Defence Act, providing £21.5 million over five years to construct eight first-class battleships (the 14,150-ton *Royal Sovereign* class), two second-class battleships (the 10,500-ton *Centurion* and *Barfleur*), nine first-class cruisers (the 7,350-ton *Edgar* class), twenty-nine second-class cruisers (the 3,400-ton *Apollo* and 4,360-ton *Astraea* classes), four third-class cruisers (the last four vessels of the 2,575-ton *Pearl* class), and eighteen torpedo gunboats. The program was designed to leave the British navy roughly equal to the combined strength of the French and Russian navies. While the ships constructed included a total of forty-two cruisers and the large number of torpedo gunboats, the *Royal Sovereigns* were the heart of the program. The 14,150-ton battleships were the largest ever built and set the standard for battleship construction for the next seventeen years, until their general concept was rendered obsolete by the all big-gun *Dreadnought*. The design was a modified version of the 12,590-ton *Nile* and *Trafalgar*, retaining the layout of four 13.5-inch guns paired on the centerline fore and aft, only in barbettes rather than turrets, saving weight and allowing a higher freeboard. Against the threat from torpedo boats, they carried a formidable secondary armament of ten 6-inch quick-firing Armstrong guns. One of the eight, the *Hood* (built 1889–93), carried its guns in turrets and had a lower freeboard, but also displaced 14,150 tons and was identical to the other *Royal Sovereigns* in all other respects. Lord George Hamilton, First Lord of the Admiralty, expressed confidence that the sheer size of the program would deter rivals from attempting to match it.[4]

The Naval Defence Act reaffirmed Britain's faith in the primacy of the battleship, at a time when the Jeune École remained strong elsewhere. The *Royal Sovereigns* themselves reflected the fact that some of the technological breakthroughs essential to the battleship renaissance had yet to occur. They carried quick-firing guns as their secondary armament and, once completed, surpassed their designed speed (some making over 18 knots under forced draught), but all except the *Hood* carried their heavy guns in barbettes, and all had compound armor. Perhaps more significant, as of 1889 no one yet had rebutted the overall strategy of the Jeune École as an alternative paradigm of naval warfare. The first of the *Royal Sovereigns* was laid down in the summer of 1889 and the last completed in the summer of 1894. During those five years the battleship-centered fleet gained several influential advocates, of whom Alfred Thayer Mahan was the most important, and was further strengthened by developments in the production of armor and artillery.

Mahan, armor, and artillery

The ideas that shaped Alfred Thayer Mahan's influential work *The Influence of Sea Power upon History, 1660–1783* (1890) and his subsequent books had their roots in the early 1880s off the coast of Peru, where a rather bored Captain Mahan read works of history in preparation for his next assignment, to the faculty of the Naval War College in Newport, while commanding a warship observing the final phase of the War of the Pacific. Reflecting on Theodor Mommsen's classic history of Rome, Mahan concluded that the Romans had defeated the Carthaginians because of their naval strength. Applying the same analysis to the early-modern rivalry between Britain and France, he developed an ideology grounded in the notion that naval power was the most decisive factor in the political and economic rise and fall of nations. While posted to Newport between 1886 and 1889, Mahan developed lectures on the subject which ultimately formed the basis of his first book. After the British Parliament passed the Naval Defence Act, Mahan joined those advocating a similar program for the American navy, adding to the manuscript a lengthy introductory chapter – "Elements of Sea Power" – which underscored the significance of naval strength to the development of countries in general and the United States in particular.[5]

In the words of Jon Tetsuro Sumida, Mahan "invented historically based and broadly focused international security studies." Unlike earlier naval historians, he linked questions of naval policy and operations to their political, diplomatic, and economic context. Especially in countries with representative governments reluctant to spend great sums on defense in peacetime, Mahan believed that a great navy required a coalition of special interests to support it. Politicians and their constituents with a vested interest in an export-oriented manufacturing economy, a strong merchant marine, colonies and colonial markets would also support naval expansion.[6] In this regard he was in tune with the spirit of the dawning decade. During the 1890s politicians in all countries, but especially Britain, Germany, the United States, and Austria–Hungary, began to view peacetime naval programs not as "wasteful spending" but as a means of sub-sidizing domestic industries which provided employment for their working-class constituents. Thus, it would be remarkably easy to build a broad base of political support behind naval expansion, even in countries that had never had a large navy before.[7] In some countries, Germany in particular, merchant shipping magnates and politicians from the leading seaports were late converts to the cause, mostly because they viewed naval warfare as destructive of inter-national trade.[8] Mahan's ideology assuaged their fears, for he believed that commerce raiding had its place in naval warfare, but not a central place. Firm in his belief that command of the sea could be achieved only by decisive naval warfare conducted by blue-water forces of battleships, he stressed the need for naval powers to maintain battle fleets. At the same time he downplayed the need for cruisers, even arguing that their role could be filled by armed merchantmen hastily assembled in times of crisis.[9]

By the time Mahan returned to sea in 1893 as captain of the protected cruiser *Chicago*, his second book, *The Influence of Sea Power upon the French Revolution and Empire* (1892), had appeared, reinforcing the concepts of the first. During the *Chicago*'s European posting Mahan was feted wherever the ship called; in Britain he dined at Buckingham Palace as a guest of Queen Victoria, and he received honorary degrees from both Oxford and Cambridge.[10] In Germany, both William II and Alfred Tirpitz read the original English edition of Mahan's *Influence of Sea Power upon History*, the emperor during 1894 and Tirpitz somewhat earlier. Whereas the emperor remained a cruiser advocate for at least two years after his exposure to Mahan, Tirpitz shared the American captain's faith in the battle fleet as early as 1891, just two years after he left the torpedo service. In his critique of the German navy's autumn maneuvers of 1893, Tirpitz encouraged the "study of naval history," especially "the works of Captain Mahan."[11]

The truly global impact of Mahan's *Influence of Sea Power upon History* was reflected in the number of languages into which it was translated. The first non-English editions appeared in German and Japanese, both in 1896. The German edition was prepared at the request of the chief of the High Command, Admiral Eduard Knorr, and his chief of staff, Alfred Tirpitz. The Imperial Navy Office purchased one-quarter of the initial press run of the German edition for distribution to support Tirpitz during his campaign for the First Navy Law in 1897–98. Meanwhile, the first Japanese edition became required reading at Japan's service academies.[12] By the end of the 1890s Mahan's works had been translated into Russian and French, and shortly thereafter into Italian and Spanish as well. Mahan overshadowed other naval writers of his era, including some whose similar views reinforced the impact of his own publications. The most important of these was retired-admiral Philip Colomb, an instructor at the Royal Naval College in Greenwich, whose *Naval Warfare: Its Ruling Principles and Practice Historically Treated* appeared in 1891. Like Mahan, Colomb considered a fleet of battleships the key to command of the sea and victory in war. They shared an offensive doctrine and a faith in the decisive battle, in both cases mirroring the views of turn-of-the-century advocates of the "cult of the offensive" in land warfare. While these views never became official doctrine in the British navy, they helped shape the outlook of a generation of officers including Sir John Fisher, future father of the dreadnought and battle cruiser.[13]

In order for designs such as the dreadnought and battle cruiser, or even large pre-dreadnoughts, to become feasible, armor manufacturers had to resolve the problem of how to provide adequate protection for such vessels. As with boilers, smokeless powder, and steel shells, a French firm played a key role, but in this case others were responsible for the ultimate breakthrough. Schneider of Creusot pioneered all-steel armor in the 1870s, exporting it to Italy for the *Duilio* and subsequent battleships, but the French navy remained skeptical of the new product, and, in any event, Schneider could not produce enough of it to plate the last group of barbette battleships laid down in France before the onset of the Jeune École. In the late 1880s the firm began experiments with nickel–steel armor, but with mixed results. A breakthrough came in September 1890, at a US navy test in Annapolis: imported Schneider plates, hardened by a process devised by an American, Hayward Augustus Harvey, emerged unscathed while the same fire destroyed the best British compound armor. Harvey nickel–steel armor, treated with carbon and hardened in cold water, seemed indestructible. Nickel ore prices skyrocketed, and the leading naval powers scrambled to duplicate or improve upon Harvey's process.[14]

The focus then shifted to Germany, where the four 10,000-ton battleships of the *Brandenburg* class had been approved by the Reichstag in 1889. Karl Stumm's Dillingen foundry, which had produced compound armor for the German navy under the British "Wilson system" since 1880, expected to receive the armor contracts, but in the hope that competition would bring down prices, the navy invited the Krupp works into the bidding. The two firms each came away with two of the contracts, but, to the dismay of the navy, Stumm and Friedrich Krupp concluded a corporate alliance as soon as Krupp entered the armor business. They agreed to fix prices and divide future contracts. Stumm shared his license to produce compound armor under the "Wilson system," while Krupp became responsible for research and development for both firms. As they started to manufacture compound armor for the *Brandenburgs*, in October 1890 researchers at Krupp's Essen complex began experimenting with plates made with nickel–steel alloys.[15]

In the late 1880s Krupp, like Schneider, had experimented with nickel–steel, only for gun barrels rather than armor; earlier in 1890 these trials resulted in the decision to use nickel–steel in Krupp naval artillery. Experiments with carbon-treated nickel–steel armor, begun in the autumn of 1890, continued through 1891. In tests conducted early in 1892, in the presence of William II, the new plates proved to be 15 percent stronger than compound armor. Still in the midst of fulfilling its armor contracts of 1890, the Krupp works stopped production and retooled for the manufacture of nickel–steel plates, in time to deliver the new armor for the *Kurfürst Friedrich Wilhelm*, a sister-ship of the *Brandenburg* launched in June 1891. The first three *Brandenburgs* to be launched still included a small amount of compound armor, but thereafter all German battleships had Krupp nickel–steel armor. Krupp became the world leader in armor production after it introduced the "gas cementing" process late in 1892, using gas to carburize the face of nickel–steel plates before hardening them in running water. By summer 1894, nickel–steel plates including a small amount of chromium and manganese, carburized with gas and hardened by a high-pressure water spray, proved to have a strength equal to compound armor twice as thick, and outperformed the best Harvey armor. The 11,100-ton *Kaiser Friedrich III* (laid down 1895) was the first ship to receive the new product; after 1895 Krupp produced only plates of this type.[16]

The British ships laid down under the Naval Defence Act were too near completion to be affected by the revolution in armor production. The first British battleship with all-steel armor, the 12,350-ton second-class battleship *Renown* (laid down in February 1893), had Harvey nickel–steel plates, as did all other British battleships through the last vessel of the 14,560-ton *Majestic* class (laid down in March 1895). During that brief period, Harvey dominated the world market. After Harvey plates made by Bethlehem Steel of Pennsylvania passed muster in July 1892, the US navy ordered Harvey armor for its new battleships. Between 1892 and 1895, representatives of the Harvey Steel Company supervised the treatment of plates at European foundries including the Vickers works in Britain, Dillingen in Germany, Witkowitz in Austria, and Terni in Italy. After a brief legal battle, Schneider took a license to manufacture Harvey armor in France. Thereafter, however, the tide turned quickly in favor of Krupp. Britain's 13,150-ton *Canopus* class (laid down from December 1896) had Krupp armor of the latest design, manufactured under license in Britain. Russia made the change in 1898. Japanese battleships built in Britain had Harvey armor until 1899, then Krupp. France and Italy adopted Krupp armor for battleships laid down in 1901. After the turn of the century Harvey armor had a market only in the United States, where the navy used both types for at least a decade after buying its first American-made Krupp plates in 1899.[17]

Extensive tests ultimately showed that 5.75 inches of Krupp armor had the same strength as 7.75-inch Harvey armor, 12-inch all-steel plate, 12-inch compound iron-and-steel armor, or 15-inch wrought iron plate. While Harvey nickel–steel armor was a great improvement over compound armor, it was no match for Krupp gas-cemented nickel–steel armor when tested against the latest Holtzer steel shells.[18] One must bear in mind that the tests of plates during the armor revolution of the 1890s involved the latest guns firing the latest shells, and thus bore witness to the advances in artillery as well. Armstrong, Vickers, Krupp, Canet, and other firms produced heavy breech-loading guns of steel or nickel–steel with a variety of methods of construction, all superior to those of the 1880s, capable of using the new "smokeless" nitro-cellulose or nitro-glycerin propellants to fire their steel shells. After 1890 the 12-inch gun became the standard primary battleship armament, and remained so well into the dreadnought era, as most navies abandoned slightly lighter or heavier guns. It was adopted in France (for battleships laid down after 1891), in Britain (1893), by British shipyards building for Japan (1894), in Russia and Italy (1898), and in the United States (1899). The primary armament of German battleships remained slightly lighter than the new norm, as the 11.1-inch Krupps of the *Brandenburg* class (laid down 1890) gave way to 9.4-inch guns in two subsequent classes before a return to the 11.1-inch gun in the *Braunschweig* class (1901–2). Germany did not adopt the 12-inch gun until 1908, for its second class of dreadnoughts. Austria–Hungary imported 9.4-inch Krupps as primary armament for its battleships until 1901, when the Skoda works began producing its own 9.4-inch guns; the 12-inch Skoda debuted in the *Radetzky* class (1907). During the 1890s quick-firing secondary armament ranged from the 8-inch guns mounted in American battleships to the 5.9-inch Krupps used by Germany and Austria–Hungary, but overall the 6-inch gun mounted in British pre-dreadnoughts was most common.[19] The effective combat range of all ordnance remained a matter of speculation until the guns were tested in action, in the Sino-Japanese, Spanish–American, and Russo-Japanese wars. Because of the similarity, if not homogeneity, of gun types used by the leading navies, the lessons of these conflicts would have a broad and immediate impact on warship design, tactics, and artillery fire control.

The Franco-Russian Alliance and Britain's response

Contrary to Lord George Hamilton's expectations, the Naval Defence Act did not deter France or Russia from pursuing battleship programs of their own. The 11,190-ton *Brennus* (laid down 1889) marked the resumption of French battleship construction after the peak years of the Jeune École. The *Brennus* was the first of a dozen generally similar warships laid down over a ten-year period, all but one displacing between 11,000 and 12,500 tons. In addition to being significantly smaller than the British program of *Royal Sovereigns* begun the same year, these French warships were not built in homogeneous classes. All now carried their primary armament in turrets rather than barbettes, but as in the battleships of the 1870s and early 1880s the layout of heavy guns varied from one ship to another, as did caliber of ordnance. For example, the *Brennus* carried three 13.4-inch guns in a twin turret forward and a single turret aft, while the next three French battleships carried two 12-inch and two 10.8-inch guns, mounted in four single turrets. The only genuine sister-ships of the twelve were the three 11,100-ton *Charlemagnes* (laid down 1894–96), which were also the first French battleships mounting a primary armament of four heavy guns paired in two centerline turrets fore and aft. The *Brennus* was the last French battleship to have compound armor. The next four battleships had nickel–steel plate produced with Schneider's process, but for the *Bouvet* (laid down 1893) and six subsequent projects Schneider provided Harvey armor produced under license. More impressive were the eighteen armored cruisers laid down during the same years, from the revolutionary 6,680-ton *Dupuy de Lôme* (begun 1888) to the five warships of the 9,860-ton *Gloire* class (begun 1899–1901). The largest of these cruisers, the *Jeanne d'Arc* (begun 1896), at 11,090 tons was almost as big as the French battleships of the 1890s and, unfortunately, not much faster, as it never achieved its projected speed of 23 knots.[20]

After the retirement of Bismarck in 1890, Germany cut Russia loose from its system of alliances; Russia and France, both friendless, immediately gravitated toward one another. The French navy visited Kronstadt in 1891, and the Russian navy reciprocated at Toulon in 1893, while the two countries signed a treaty of alliance and military convention in 1892 and 1894. Reflecting the diplomatic realignment, the Russian navy abandoned Krupp artillery for Schneider–Canet guns, the latter, like the former, produced in Russia under license. Eleven battleships laid down by 1895 completed the total of twenty prescribed in the fleet plan of 1882, but these included three 4,970-ton coastal battleships of the *Admiral Ushakov* class and the 8,880-ton second-class battleship *Rostislav*, along with seven respectable first-class battleships ranging in size from the 10,400-ton *Sissoi Veliki* to the first two vessels of the 12,680-ton *Peresviet* class. Armored cruisers included the 11,000-ton *Rurik*, obsolete by the time of its launch in 1895, and the more modern 13,675-ton *Rossia* (laid down 1894) and 13,220-ton *Gromoboi* (1897). Naval spending rose from £4.3 million in 1890 to £7 million in 1898, a year in which Russia's Far Eastern ambitions prompted a new seven-year construction program, providing for another eight battleships, seventeen cruisers, and over fifty smaller vessels. Even though construction times for first-class battleships in Russian shipyards still averaged a respectable six years, the navy placed its first foreign orders for armored warships since the 1860s. The highly regarded 12,700-ton *Retvisan*, built by William Cramp of Philadelphia, was the first Russian battleship protected by Krupp armor.

The 12,915-ton *Tsesarevich*, built in La Seyne, was used as a prototype for four warships of the 13,520-ton *Borodino* class. The *Borodino*s were built in Russian shipyards, along with a third ship of the *Peresviet* class and the 12,580-ton *Potemkin*. The eight battleships of the 1898 program all were in service by the beginning of the war with Japan in 1904. While focusing on capital ships Russia remained a leader in mine warfare, in 1898–99 constructing the world's first purpose-built minelayers, the 3,010-ton *Amur* and *Yenisei*. Russia also purchased the submarine *Protector*, launched in 1902 by the American Simon Lake, built additional submarines in St Petersburg designed by Lake, and ordered three more from Germania of Kiel.[21]

Britain ultimately aligned with France and Russia against Germany in the Triple Entente, but from the perspective of the early 1890s the Franco-Russian Alliance, uniting the second- and third-largest naval powers, posed the greatest challenge to the Pax Britannica since 1815. In Britain the last battleships of the Naval Defence Act of 1889 had been laid down in 1891, and after no first-class battleships were begun in 1892 or 1893, growing concerns about French and Russian naval expansion led the First Lord of the Admiralty, John Poyntz Spencer, to propose another five-year program. Earl Spencer's program, which was passed by Parliament in December 1893, was even larger than that of 1889, including seven battleships, thirty cruisers, and 122 smaller vessels at a cost of £31 million. Further reflecting the drift toward battleships, the program ultimately was revised to include nine battleships (the 14,560-ton *Majestic* class) and fewer cruisers. The *Majestic*s were improved *Royal Sovereign*s, incorporating the Harvey nickel–steel armor first used in the *Renown*. They were the first British battleships to carry their heavy guns in modern turrets rather than the barbettes of recent classes, a "turret" henceforth being defined as a full armored hood covering guns in a barbette mounting. Their four 12-inch guns were paired in centerline turrets fore and aft; the design also featured an increased secondary armament of twelve 6-inch quick-firing guns. The first of the *Majestic*s was laid down just days after Parliament approved the program, the last in 1895. Thereafter annual appropriations for battleship construction became the norm, and by 1901 a further twenty battleships had been laid down. The six 13,150-ton vessels of the *Canopus* class, three 14,500-ton *Formidable*s, five 14,500-ton *London*s, and six 13,270-ton *Duncan*s had the same armament as the *Majestic*s but lighter Krupp armor and Belleville boilers which gave them a speed of 18 to 19 knots, unprecedented for battleships. Meanwhile, the nine *Edgar* class protected cruisers of the Naval Defence Act were followed by another ten first-class protected cruisers and ten first-class armored cruisers, the latter of the 12,000-ton *Cressy* class and the 14,150-ton *Drake* class, all laid down by 1899. In cruisers, as in battleships, the British more than maintained the two-power standard.[22]

Among the smaller vessels included in Spencer's program were thirty-six destroyers, or "torpedo boat destroyers" as they were initially known. The British navy ordered the first six boats of the new type in 1892 and 1893, two each from Yarrow, Thornycroft, and Laird, all displacing 275–80 tons, capable of 26–27 knots. Armed with torpedo tubes and light deck guns, they had the firepower as well as the size and speed to escort larger warships on the high seas and, if necessary, hunt down and destroy enemy torpedo boats. All other major navies quickly added destroyers of their own, with the US and French navies being the last to embrace the new type, both in 1899.[23] By 1914 the newest British destroyers were vessels of around 1,000 tons, capable of 35 knots, but older destroyers half as large saw action in the First World War.

Just as the German army reacted to the Franco-Russian Alliance by devising the Schlieffen Plan, the British navy drafted war plans assuming a coordination of French and Russian efforts at sea. Of the strategic imperatives of the British navy, after 1878 none ranked higher than stopping the Russian Black Sea fleet from breaking out into the eastern Mediterranean, but the diplomatic realignment of the early 1890s strained calculations of how this could be done. As early as March 1894 the prime minister, Lord Rosebery, informed the Austro-Hungarian foreign minister that the navy would not be able to defend Constantinople and the Turkish straits against a Russian attack for fear of having the French fall upon it from the rear. In October 1896 the Admiralty prepared new war plans which assumed the Black Sea fleet would pass through the straits and establish a base in the Aegean. The British navy would then concentrate on holding Gibraltar, Malta, and Alexandria, and preventing a union of the French and Russian fleets in the Mediterranean.[24] In fact, Franco-Russian naval cooperation remained minimal until after 1900, but the revision of Britain's war plans in response to the perceived threat reflected a lack of confidence that defies explanation, especially as its programs of 1889 and 1893 ensured a superiority over France and Russia combined, and the new angst predated the turn-of-the-century rise of the German, Japanese, and American navies. George Goschen, First Lord of the Admiralty from 1895 to 1900, personified the insecurity, fearing that even with the two-power standard the British navy "might be fatally crippled by a single great disaster."[25] For eighty years the Pax Britannica had been upheld by a naval establishment whose hubris reflected its superiority in materiel and personnel; after the mid-1890s the superiority remained, but the hubris faded considerably.

The Sino-Japanese War (1894–95)

Early in 1891 China's Admiral Ting Ju-ch'ang visited the major ports of Japan with the 7,220-ton battleships *Ting Yuan* and *Chen Yuan*, accompanied by four smaller warships. His cruise was a calculated attempt at intimidation, at a time when Sino-Japanese relations were deteriorating. Artillery demonstrations by the battleships off Yokohama and Nagasaki alarmed the Japanese public and political leaders, but despite its material superiority, the Chinese navy did not impress many Japanese officers. In touring one of the Chinese battleships, Captain Heihachiro Togo, future commander of the Japanese navy, noted the disorderly appearance of the ship and the indiscipline of the crew.[26] Admiral Ting, commander of China's northern (Peiyang) fleet, had been a cavalryman in the Chinese army and knew little of the sea. In contrast, Yuko Ito, commander of the Japanese fleet, was the first, since the creation of the navy a quarter-century earlier, to rise to full admiral through the ranks of the officer corps. His second-in-command, Rear Admiral Kozo Tsuboi, was among a number of then-senior Japanese officers who had spent at least some time abroad, his education having included two years at Columbia University, New York, in the early 1870s.[27] By the time of the Sino-Japanese War, the Chinese navy still employed foreign officers and technicians aboard its warships, whereas the Japanese had adopted the practice of limiting foreign advisors to roles ashore. Aside from two Vulcan torpedo boats added in 1894, prior to the war the Chinese had commissioned no new warships other than those already under construction in 1890. Japan, meanwhile, commissioned all projects underway as of 1890 and added two more protected cruisers, the 3,100-ton *Akitsushima*, built at Yokosuka in 1890–94, and the 4,150-ton *Yoshino*, built by Armstrong at Elswick in 1892–93. Another protected cruiser, the *Idzumi* (ex-Chilean *Esmeralda*), was purchased during the war. New smaller units included a steel gunboat built at Kobe but no torpedo boats other than those already on order in 1890.[28]

The first shots of the conflict were fired on 25 July 1894, five days before the formal declaration of war, when a "flying squadron" of four protected cruisers under Rear Admiral Tsuboi intercepted a weaker Chinese force convoying troops to Korea, center of the Sino-Japanese rivalry. The Battle of P'ung Island, off Chemulpo (Inchon), foreshadowed later Japanese navy preemptive strikes against Russia in 1904 and the United States in 1941. Captain Togo's cruiser *Naniwa* sank the troopship *Kowshing*; the Chinese also lost the 1,000-ton torpedo gunboat *Kuang Yi* and suffered damage to one of their cruisers. On 10 August Admiral Ito and the entire Japanese fleet bombarded Chinese bases at Port Arthur and Weihaiwei, but Admiral Ting and the Peiyang fleet remained in port. Meanwhile, the Japanese army took Seoul and in mid-September advanced on Pyongyang. With its position in Korea near collapse, the Chinese government ordered Ting to convoy an army to a point sixty miles down the coast from the Yalu River. On 17 September 1894, while returning to Port Arthur after landing the troops, the Peiyang fleet encountered the Japanese fleet in the northern Yellow Sea, off the mouth of the Yalu.[29]

At the start of the Battle of the Yalu, Admiral Ito's fleet was steaming from south to north in line-ahead formation, led by seven protected cruisers (ranging in size from the three units of the 4,220-ton *Matushima* class to the 3,100-ton *Akitsushima*) and the 2,400-ton armored cruiser *Chiyoda*. The old casemate ship *Fuso*, the old armored corvette *Hiei*, and two small escorts brought up the rear. Admiral Ting's Chinese force, steaming from east to west, attacked the Japanese line in line-abreast formation, with the battleships *Ting Yuan* and *Chen Yuan* at the tip of a jagged "V" that included three armored cruisers, five protected cruisers, and one dispatch vessel. Aside from the battleships, the 2,900-ton armored cruiser *King Yuan* was the largest Chinese warship, the 1,300-ton composite dispatch vessel *Kuang Chia* the smallest. Ting also had one torpedo gunboat and a few torpedo boats, which played no significant role in the battle.[30] Ting's decision to attack in line abreast, as Tegetthoff had at Lissa in 1866, reflected the tactical backwardness of the Chinese navy. Even the Austro-Hungarian navy had abandoned the line abreast in favor of a return to the line ahead a decade earlier, in 1884.[31]

The first four protected cruisers, under Rear Admiral Tsuboi, steamed ahead of the rest of the Japanese line at the start of the battle and maneuvered separately for the remainder of the engagement. The deadliest moments for the Chinese came when the bulk of their fleet was caught between parallel lines of Tsuboi's cruisers and the rest of Ito's column. The Chinese opened fire at 5,000 meters, the more disciplined Japanese at 3,900 meters, but most of the action came at a range of just over 2,000 meters. The battle lasted roughly six hours, from mid-day until dusk, and few Chinese ships survived unscathed. The armored cruiser *King Yuan* and four protected cruisers were sunk. The battleships *Ting Yuan* and *Chen Yuan* sustained damage along with the armored cruiser *Ping Yuan* and one protected cruiser, but the 12-inch guns of the battleships scored several hits on Japanese warships. Ito's flagship *Matsushima* suffered the most damage, coming so close to sinking that the admiral shifted his flag to the protected cruiser *Hashidate*. The obsolete ironclad *Hiei*, too slow to keep up with the rest of the column, likewise took a number of hits; the casemate ship *Fuso* and a second protected cruiser sustained lesser damages. After breaking off the action, Ting headed for Port Arthur with Tsuboi's protected cruisers in pursuit. Still fearing the firepower of the retreating Chinese battleships, Ito recalled Tsuboi and thus failed to achieve a more complete victory. Nevertheless, the Battle of the Yalu gave the Japanese command of the Yellow Sea, enabling their army to land unopposed on the Liaotung peninsula several weeks later. The Japanese besieged Port Arthur, which surrendered on 21 November.[32]

Just before the fall of Port Arthur, Admiral Ting took the remnants of the Peiyang fleet to Weihaiwei, where units from the other three Chinese fleets joined him. Over the winter of 1894–95 the Japanese navy landed army units on the Shantung peninsula which eventually laid siege to Weihaiwei. By early February 1895 they had taken the city and the entire shoreline, leaving the Chinese warships in the harbor all the more vulnerable to the blockading Japanese fleet. Ito's attempt to finish off Ting's warships with torpedo boat raids on the nights of 3 February and 4 February met with limited success, sinking the small armored cruiser *Lai Yuan* and a composite corvette, and forcing aground the battleship *Ting Yuan*. Japanese army artillery proved far more lethal, sinking the battleship *Chen Yuan* and a protected cruiser on 9 February. After the Chinese surrendered three days later, Ting committed suicide. At the end of the month China sued for peace, and afterward Japan commissioned in its own navy the ships captured at Weihaiwei.[33]

The Sino-Japanese War had an impact far beyond East Asia. As the first high seas encounter between fleets of warships since 1866, the Battle of the Yalu attracted worldwide attention. Its clearest lesson was that the line-ahead formation enabled a greater efficiency of fire and gave commanders greater tactical control once a battle began. The Japanese decision to fight in two separate squadrons rather than a single line, like the Austrian deployment in three squadrons at Lissa, supported the argument that a fleet commander should delegate authority to subordinate squadron commanders. Analysts noted that aside from the obsolete *Fuso* and *Hiei* at the rear, the Japanese units were similar in speed and firepower, underscoring the importance of homogeneity in a line of battle. The Battle of the Yalu produced no clear lessons in the key areas of artillery and armor, in part because of the primitive state of fire control in 1894 (the Japanese scored around 10 percent hits, the Chinese 5 percent). The medium-caliber quick-firing guns of Japanese cruisers with unarmored hulls sank or damaged seven Chinese cruisers and killed almost enough men aboard the Chinese battleships to put them out of action. But at a range of 2,000 meters, the 12-inch guns of the battleships blew holes in the *Matsushima*, which the Japanese were fortunate not to lose. The battleships were impressive simply in their ability to survive the battle. Ever since the 1870s some experts had predicted that vessels of their design, heavily armored amidships but unarmored at the bow and stern, would sink under heavy fire, yet the *Chen Yuan* took 150 hits, the *Ting Yuan* 200, and both steamed away. Neither side had a warship equipped with the latest armor, whether Harvey or Krupp. The compound plates of the Chinese battleships held up well enough, but the same could not be said of the wrought iron armor of the Japanese *Fuso* and *Hiei*, underscoring the fact that such obsolete ironclads had no place in a modern naval battle.[34]

The demonstrated firepower of the big guns of the Chinese battleships and quick-firing guns of the Japanese cruisers vindicated the mixed battery (four 12-inch guns, a dozen 6-inch quick-firing guns) typical to the pre-dreadnoughts being built at the time. In the *Brandenburg* class (laid down 1890), armed with six 11.1-inch guns and six 4.1-inch guns, the German navy had almost stumbled on the all-big-gun battleship, but German analysis of the Battle of the Yalu contributed to the decision to give two subsequent classes of battleships a much weaker primary armament of four 9.4-inch guns and a much stronger secondary armament of eighteen(!) 5.9-inch guns.[35] Within the Japanese navy, the Battle of the Yalu discredited the French-designed *Matsushima* class of protected cruisers, ensuring that no more Japanese warships would be built in France or to French designs.[36] The British navy was more concerned about the strategic implications of the Japanese triumph. The six *Canopus* class battleships laid down in 1896–98 were designed with a slightly shallower draught to enable them to pass through the Suez Canal en route to deployment in East Asian waters. The subsequent build-up of both the Japanese navy and the Russian Pacific fleet contributed to the decision to deepen the Suez Canal during 1898.[37]

Japan did not lose a single ship in the Sino-Japanese War, while China lost its twelve best ships. In all, one battleship, two armored cruisers, four protected cruisers, one torpedo gunboat, and one dispatch vessel were sunk; one battleship, one armored cruiser, one protected cruiser, one torpedo gunboat, four torpedo boats, and six flatiron gunboats were captured. The Chinese navy was left with a half-dozen small unarmored cruisers, several torpedo boats and obsolete vessels over two decades old. A rebuilding effort after 1895 yielded results too modest to restore China's position as a regional naval power. By the end of the war, in February 1895, the Japanese navy had landed troops on Taiwan and the Pescadores, which in April were awarded to Japan in the Treaty of Shimonoseki. Japan also received the Liaotung peninsula with Port Arthur but diplomatic pressure from Russia, France, and Germany forced the return of these lands to China.[38] Thus the war left China weaker than ever, yet the intervention of the great powers (notably minus Britain) left Japan dissatisfied in victory. This turn of events established Northeast Asia (Korea and Manchuria) as one of the focal points of international tension in the twentieth century.

The Spanish–American War (1898)

In 1895 Cuba resumed its rebellion against Spain, and as the fighting continued the Cuban cause gained a measure of popularity in the United States. In January 1898 the American consul in Havana requested that a formidable warship show the flag there and, if necessary, serve as a refuge for US citizens endangered by fighting in the city. The battleship *Maine* arrived on 25 January, and the officially friendly visit passed without incident until the night of 15 February, when the ship exploded and sank, killing 254 men. While it is now generally accepted that the *Maine* was destroyed by an accidental ignition of its forward magazines, at the time the US public and government were certain of Spanish treachery, ignoring the obvious fact that it would not have been in Spain's interest to provoke a conflict. On 25 April the US Congress declared war.[39]

Over the fifteen years since its revival in 1883 the navy had grown in popularity with the public as well as the politicians. Attracting ever greater outlays from Congress, the fleet also attracted enough native-born and naturalized American citizens to end its traditional dependence upon foreigners for its common manpower. Whereas in the late 1880s over half of the seamen were foreign-born, by the late 1890s three-quarters were American citizens.[40] In 1898 the warships they manned included the three battleships of the *Indiana* class (completed 1895–96) and the 11,410-ton *Iowa* (1897), which joined the smaller and older *Texas* to give the American navy five battleships after the loss of the *Maine*. But the United States fought the Spanish–American War primarily with its cruiser fleet, consisting of the vessels built or building as of 1890–91 (one armored cruiser and twelve protected cruisers) joined by the 9,215-ton armored cruiser *Brooklyn* (completed 1896) and the 5,865-ton protected cruiser *Olympia*

Plate 7.1 USS *Maine* entering Havana harbor, 25 January 1898
Naval Historical Center, Basic Collection

(1895). The only warships of foreign construction were two 3,770-ton protected cruisers built by Armstrong and destined for Brazil until purchased by the United States in March 1898; only one of the pair, the *New Orleans*, was delivered in time to see action. By the time the war began the navy had commissioned a total of twenty small unarmored cruisers and steel gunboats, along with eleven torpedo boats. The 6,060-ton *Puritan* and the four other large monitors "rebuilt" since the 1870s were in commission during the war, along with the 4,080-ton monitor *Monterey* (completed 1893) and six single-turret Civil War monitors, most of them from the *Passaic* class. They proved to be of value only in bombarding coastal installations.[41]

Spain's formidable ironclad fleet of the 1860s deteriorated in the years that followed. The armored frigates *Numancia* and *Vitoria*, the only iron-hulled warships of the original seven, survived to be modernized in 1897–98 but were ready too late to see action in the Spanish–American War. Thanks to a revival initiated in the mid-1880s, the Spanish battle fleet of 1898 had as its core the French-built *Pelayo*, a 9,745-ton barbette ship commissioned in 1888, the Italian-built *Cristóbal Colón*, a 7,230-ton armored cruiser commissioned in 1897, and the three 6,890-ton armored cruisers of the *Infanta Maria Teresa* class, all launched at Bilbao in the early 1890s. Owing to the slow pace of domestic shipbuilding, three armored cruisers of the *Princesa de Asturias* class, laid down in 1890, were not ready in time for the war. The 9,090-ton armored cruiser *Emperador Carlos V* was completed at Cadiz during 1898, but too late to see action. Thomson of Glasgow built the 4,725-ton protected cruiser *Reina Regente*, lost at sea in 1895 but only after serving as a prototype for two sister-ships built in Spain. Two 1,030-ton Armstrong protected cruisers of the *Isla de Luzon* class likewise had a third sister built in Spain. Spanish shipyards built all but two of the navy's fourteen unarmored cruisers, a hodgepodge of vessels including the wooden-hulled *Aragon* class (three units of 3,290 tons, designed to be plated with armor), the iron-hulled *Velasco* class (eight units of 1,150 tons, one of which was lost off Cuba in 1895), and the steel-hulled *Alfonso XII* class (three units of 3,040 tons). The fleet also included twelve torpedo gunboats, six brand-new destroyers, fifteen torpedo boats, and five small iron-hulled gunboats.[42] Thus, in 1898 Spain had an impressive navy of the second rank, but it was not large enough to defend the country's worldwide empire or to take on the US navy, which was superior to the Spanish in armored warships (five battleships and two armored cruisers to one battleship and four armored cruisers), in protected cruisers (fourteen to five), and in unarmored cruisers or steel gunboats (twenty to thirteen). The Spanish navy had more torpedo gunboats, torpedo boats, and destroyers; the US navy had none of the latter.

The first action of the war came when Commodore George Dewey led the American navy's Asiatic squadron in an attack on the Philippines. Dewey's squadron included four protected cruisers, ranging in size from the 5,865-ton flagship *Olympia* to the 3,180-ton *Raleigh*, and two steel gunboats, the 1,710-ton *Concord* and the 870-ton *Petrel*. The *Olympia* and two other American cruisers carried 8-inch quick-firing guns, and even the *Petrel* carried four 6-inch guns. Steaming from Hong Kong after the declaration of war, Dewey led the squadron into Manila Bay before dawn on 1 May 1898. There he met Rear Admiral Patricio Montojo's squadron of eight warships, six of which were smaller than the *Concord*, none with guns larger than 4.7-inch caliber. The 1,030-ton *Isla de Luzon* and *Isla de Cuba* were Montojo's only protected cruisers; the 3,040-ton flagship *Reina Cristina*, the 3,290-ton *Castilla*, three cruisers of the *Velasco* class, and a 490-ton iron-hulled gunboat were completely unarmored. Keenly aware of his squadron's weaknesses, Montojo anchored his ships in a line off Cavite, under the guns of shore batteries, protected from torpedo attack by a line of barges filled with stone. Dewey opened fire at daybreak from a distance of 4,500 meters and for two hours steamed up and down the Spanish line, pouring fire into Montojo's ships while gradually closing to 2,000 meters. He broke off the engagement from 7:00 until after 11:00, waiting for the badly damaged Spanish units to surrender. When none did, he resumed fire for another half-hour, after which all of Montojo's ships struck their flags. Aside from the flagship *Reina Cristina*, the Spanish fought at anchor; their only other larger warship, the *Castilla*, was suffering engine trouble and could not have moved in any event. The shore batteries were not a factor in the battle, as Dewey's ships remained safely out of their range. They took just fifteen hits from the guns of the Spanish squadron, suffering casualties of none killed and six wounded. Estimates of the number of American hits on the Spanish range from 74 to 170; their casualties included 167 killed and 214 wounded. When the smoke cleared at noon, every Spanish ship was resting on the bottom in the shallows off Cavite, six sunk by gunfire, the two small Armstrong cruisers scuttled to avoid capture. The latter were raised, repaired, and commissioned as gunboats in the American navy. Along with one of the *Velascos*, they served in the Philippines after the islands were annexed by the United States. Dewey's decisive victory surprised everyone, including his own government, which did not have troops ready to occupy the Philippines until August. Until then he blockaded Manila, receiving as reinforcements two double-turret monitors and the protected cruiser *Charleston*. The latter stopped to shell the old Spanish fort on Guam, en route to its new station.[43]

Meanwhile, in the Atlantic, a week after the declaration of war Rear Admiral Pascual Cervera left the Cape Verde Islands with Spain's four armored cruisers, escorted by three destroyers. The battleship *Pelayo* and the armored cruiser *Emperador Carlos V*, the latter nearing completion, were held back along with the remaining destroyers to form the nucleus of another squadron under Admiral Manuel de la Cámara.[44] The newest Spanish armored cruiser, the Italian-built *Cristóbal Colón*, delivered in May 1897, almost did not join Cervera's squadron because its three heaviest guns still had not been delivered when war was declared. The Spanish navy had enough faith in the ship's secondary armament of fourteen 6-inch guns to send it into action anyway.[45] Cervera eluded two American naval forces, the North Atlantic squadron under Rear Admiral William T. Sampson and a "flying squadron" under Commodore Winfield S. Schley, and anchored at Santiago, Cuba, on 19 May. Schley arrived there nine days later to blockade him and was joined on 1 June by Sampson's force. The combined squadrons included almost every American warship except those sent to the Philippines. To ensure a clear superiority over the Spanish in armored ships, the US navy ordered its lone west-coast battleship, the *Oregon*, to steam from San Francisco via Cape Horn to Key West, a cruise of 15,000 miles completed in sixty-seven days. After its arrival the blockaders had five battleships and two armored cruisers, more than a match for Cervera's four armored cruisers. Within a month the Spanish situation in Santiago became desperate, as 17,000 American troops were landed to lay siege to the city. Around 9:30 on 3 July Cervera broke out of the harbor and ran to the west, along the southern coast of Cuba. For four hours the blockaders gave chase, led by the *Oregon* and the armored cruiser *Brooklyn*. One by one the four Spanish cruisers were hunted down, set ablaze by gunfire, then beached by their own captains to avoid further loss of life. One destroyer accompanying the cruisers was sunk, another driven aground. The Americans scored around 120 hits against Cervera's ships, which returned fire but did little damage to their pursuers. The beaching of the cruisers held down casualties for the Spanish, who nevertheless lost 474 men, 323 killed and 151 wounded. Of the Americans, one man was killed and no more than ten wounded.[46]

Meanwhile, in Spain, two transatlantic liners purchased from Germany were armed as the *Patriota* and *Rápido*, and joined the battleship *Pelayo* and armored cruiser *Emperador Carlos V* in Admiral Cámara's squadron. Ordered to retake the Philippines, Cámara left Cadiz for the Far East via the Suez Canal, only to be recalled when Madrid received word that the United States planned to deploy a battleship squadron under Sampson to attack the coast of Spain. When the Spanish government sued for peace, Sampson's squadron remained in the Caribbean.[47]

The two principal naval battles of the Spanish–American War confirmed the lessons of the Sino-Japanese War. Quick-firing guns of medium caliber had scored all the hits at Manila Bay, where no heavy guns were present, and most of the hits at Santiago. The ranges were similar to the previous war and the fire control even worse. By one account American gunners at Manila Bay registered 141 hits out of some 6,000 shells fired (2.3 percent), against an enemy for the most part fighting at anchor. Their counterparts at Santiago scored just 122 out of 9,433 (1.3 percent), against an enemy they were pursuing, but the 12- and 13-inch guns of the battleships were responsible for 42 of the hits, out of around 1,300 shells fired (3.2 percent).[48] There are no accurate estimates of the number of shells expended by Spanish forces at the two battles, but their ratio of success certainly was under 1 percent. Navies continued to build their pre-dreadnought battleships with a mixed armament of heavy guns and medium-caliber quick-firing guns, and began to pay more attention to range-finding technologies and the need to improve fire control. In the only significant change in naval construction resulting from the war, shipbuilders in all countries took note of the fiery demise of the Spanish cruisers at Manila Bay and Santiago, and in the future used far less wood in the decks and interiors of their steel-hulled warships.[49]

When an armistice ended the fighting on 12 August, the Spanish army still held the cities of Manila and Havana, but with the enemy commanding the sea, their garrisons had no hope of being reinforced or resupplied. Like the Japanese navy against China three years earlier, the US navy had achieved an almost total victory. Of the Spanish warships engaged in either the Caribbean or the Philippines, only the few detached to defend Puerto Rico survived to return to Cadiz at war's end.[50] The Treaty of Paris (10 December 1898) gave the United States the Philippines, Guam, and Puerto Rico, adding to a colonial empire that already included Hawaii and Midway Island, annexed earlier in the year. Cuba became an independent republic, dominated by American business interests and hosting an American naval base at Guantanamo Bay. The war also intensified American interest in completing a canal across the Colombian province of Panama, the voyage of the *Oregon* around Cape Horn at the start of the war having underscored the strategic significance of such a waterway to the US navy.[51] A French company had been working on a Panama canal since 1879, but engineering problems and financial scandals plagued the project. In 1902 the French canal company agreed to sell its concession to the United States. The following January the Colombian government approved the transfer, only to have the Colombian senate refuse to ratify the transfer treaty. President Theodore Roosevelt responded by sponsoring a Panamanian independence movement. In November 1903 a small party of marines landed by the 1,370-ton steel gunboat *Nashville* sufficed to deter Colombian troops from crushing the Panamanian rebellion. Within the month the new Republic of Panama agreed to a treaty granting the United States control over a "canal zone" ten miles wide, which became a *de facto* American colonial possession. Work on the canal resumed in 1904 and the first ship passed through in August 1914, during the week in which the First World War began in Europe.

The naval power of the United States, though modest compared with what was to come, more than sufficed to dominate the Western hemisphere at the turn of the century. During the 1890s the three leading South American countries suffered divisive civil wars, and in each case the navy sided with the rebel movement. In Argentina the navy shelled the presidential palace in Buenos Aires in July 1890, supporting the overthrow of President Juárez Celmán, who resigned the following month. In Chile's eight-month civil war of 1891, President José Manuel Balmaceda countered Captain Jorge Montt's rebel fleet with a torpedo flotilla led by the 710-ton torpedo gunboats *Almirante Lynch* and *Almirante Condell*, delivered by Laird shortly after the conflict began. On 23 April, leading a raid on the port of Caldera, the *Almirante Lynch* sank the 3,370-ton *Blanco Encalada*, the first battleship ever to fall victim to a torpedo attack. The Argentinian and Chilean navies benefited from the victories of the factions they supported. During the 1890s the Argentinians added two 2,330-ton coastal battleships, four protected cruisers, four destroyers, and 23 torpedo craft of various types, most purchased in Britain. As the future centerpiece of the fleet, six *Garibaldi* class armored cruisers were ordered in Italy. Meanwhile, in Chile, Montt became president after Balmaceda's defeat, and the navy took delivery of the 6,900-ton French-built battleship *Capitán Prat* (more than compensating for the loss of the *Blanco Encalada*) as well as two armored and five protected cruisers, most built by Armstrong. British firms provided another ten torpedo boats and four destroyers. A territorial dispute in the Andes fueled a naval rivalry between Argentina and Chile, but in May 1902, after signing a new border treaty, they agreed to limit their naval armaments.[52]

In Brazil the navy did not fare as well, supporting a failed revolt in 1893–94 against Marshal Floriano Peixoto, president of the republic established in 1889. Like Balmaceda in Chile, Floriano Peixoto purchased torpedo craft abroad, the 480-ton torpedo gunboat *Gustavo Sampaio* from Armstrong and five first-class torpedo boats from Schichau. On the night of 16 April 1894 these forces attacked the rebel stronghold at Desterro (Florianopolis) and torpedoed the flagship *Aquidaba*, which ran aground in shallow water. The rest of the navy soon surrendered, after which the *Aquidaba* was refloated and sent to join Brazil's other battleship, *Riachuelo*, for renovation in Europe. Another armored warship, the 3,540-ton double-turret monitor *Javary*, was a total loss after being sunk in November 1893. The navy suffered the effects of its defeat for the next decade, during which it added just two 3,160-ton coastal battleships, two protected cruisers, and a torpedo gunboat.[53]

With war clouds gathering elsewhere, the South American naval powers found it difficult to reject offers to purchase some of the warships they had ordered in foreign shipyards. The trend began with the sale of Chile's *Esmeralda* to Japan in 1894, during the Sino-Japanese War, and Brazil's two Armstrong-built protected cruisers to the United States in 1898, on the eve of the Spanish–American War. With hostilities between Russia and Japan looming and the border dispute between Chile and Argentina resolved, in 1903 Argentina sold to Japan the last two of the six *Garibaldi* class armored cruisers it had ordered in Italy. Meanwhile, Russia attempted to buy the 11,800-ton battleships *Constitución* and *Libertad*, which Chile ordered in 1901 from Armstrong and Vickers, respectively, only to be foiled by Japan's ally, Britain, which purchased the two battleships after they were launched in 1903.[54] From the onset of the twentieth century Latin American countries would resent the increasing intervention of the United States in their affairs, but the leading naval powers among them made no attempt to match the growing strength of the American navy. The warship sales reinforced the Latin American tradition of maintaining naval forces great enough to defend interests against peers within the region, but no greater.

William II, Tirpitz, and the German Navy Laws of 1898–1900

In the spring of 1897, frustration with the political ineptitude of Germany's leading admirals prompted William II to appoint Rear Admiral Alfred Tirpitz state secretary of the Imperial Navy Office. Tirpitz had been a rising star within the German naval officer corps for years, an opportunist who embraced the Jeune École in the 1880s (rising to the top of the navy's torpedo service), then Mahan and the battleship in the early 1890s. Known for his anti-British sentiments, he had failed in a premature attempt to gain the navy's top administrative post in January 1896, amid the international furor over William II's "Kruger telegram," supporting the Boer republics against British aggression from the Cape Colony of South Africa. Thereafter Tirpitz spent 1896–97 as commander of the German cruiser division in the Far East before finally taking control of the Imperial Navy Office in June 1897.[55]

In his initial imperial audience, Tirpitz presented William II with a memorandum describing Britain as Germany's "most dangerous enemy . . . against which we most urgently require a certain measure of naval force as a political power factor." He then presented his proposal for a Navy Law, calling for an armored fleet of nineteen high sea battleships and eight coastal battleships, with twelve large cruisers, thirty small cruisers, and twelve divisions of torpedo boats. The goals would be met by 1905, at a cost of 58 million marks per year over the seven-year period 1898–1905. Because the Reichstag had already conceded 58 million for construction for 1897–98, the estimate appeared reasonable enough. Of course, the adoption of such a program would mark a dramatic change in Germany's official posture *vis-à-vis* Britain. Throughout his long tenure Bismarck had never viewed British naval power as a threat to German interests; as recently as 1889 the old chancellor had praised the British fleet as "the greatest factor for peace in Europe."[56]

Tirpitz's nineteen battleships included the four 7,600-ton *Sachsens* (commissioned between 1878 and 1883), the 5,200-ton casemate ship *Oldenburg* (1886), four 10,000-ton *Brandenburgs* (1893–94), and the first three battleships of the 11,100-ton *Kaiser Friedrich III* class (under construction at the time), leaving him seven short of his goal. The eight coastal battleships of the 3,500-ton *Siegfried* class (1890–96) already were in service, and Tirpitz planned to build no more of that type. In the category of large cruisers, Tirpitz counted the renovated old battleships (armored cruisers) *König Wilhelm*, *Kaiser*, and *Deutschland*, the protected cruiser *Kaiserin Augusta* (1892), and six warships then under construction – the five vessels of the 5,700-ton *Hertha* class and the 10,700-ton armored cruiser *Fürst Bismarck* – leaving just two to be built. The small cruisers included nineteen vessels already with the fleet, commissioned between 1883 and 1896, as well as four 2,650-ton *Gazelle* class warships then under construction, leaving seven to be built. The new warship projects, which represented a 30 percent expansion in the size of the fleet, naturally attracted the most attention at the time, obscuring the key to the Tirpitz plan: the provision for the automatic replacement of battleships after twenty-five years, large cruisers after twenty years, and smaller cruisers after fifteen years. The new state secretary's Reichstag speech of 6 December 1897, marking the formal onset of the battle for passage of the Navy Law, employed the ominous language of the social Darwinism then in fashion, characterizing the construction of the fleet as a "question of survival" for Germany.[57] The bill finally became law on 10 April 1898. The last two battleships of the 11,100-ton *Kaiser Friedrich III* class were laid down later in 1898, followed by the five vessels of the 11,800-ton *Wittelsbach* class in 1899 and 1900. The new large cruisers were the 8,900-ton armored cruiser *Prinz Heinrich* (laid down in 1898) and the 9,100-ton *Prinz Adalbert* (1900). Most of the small cruisers were additions to the *Gazelle* class.

In June 1900 Tirpitz took advantage of an international situation including the Anglo-Boer War in South Africa and the Boxer Rebellion in China to secure passage of the Second Navy Law. The new legislation expanded the fleet to thirty-eight battleships (including the 3,500-ton *Siegfried*s), fourteen large and thirty-eight small cruisers. As in the 1898 law, the ships were to be replaced automatically after a fixed number of years. Construction began on the five battleships of the 13,200-ton *Braunschweig* class in 1901 and 1902, and the five battleships of the 13,200-ton *Deutschland* class between 1903 and 1905. In primary armament the two classes reverted to the 11.1-inch gun used earlier in the *Brandenburgs*, an improvement over the 9.4-inch gun which left the *Kaiser Friedrich III* and *Wittelsbach* classes too weakly armed. The 11,600-ton armored cruisers *Scharnhorst* and *Gneisenau* were the new large cruisers, and work began on another three armored cruisers to replace the renovated old battleships counted as large cruisers in Tirpitz's 1898 plan. By 1906, Tirpitz had all but one of his thirty-eight battleships built or building; that year, he secured passage of a new supplementary law which authorized another six large cruisers, increasing the total in that category to twenty, and raised the tonnage ceilings for new battleships.[58]

The automatic replacement provision – twenty-five years for battleships, twenty for large cruisers, fifteen for small cruisers – gave Tirpitz the ultimate insurance policy. In an industrialized Germany in which the Social Democratic Party was making gains in every election, it would be unconstitutional for a more left-wing Reichstag of the future to reject the construction estimates.[59] In addition to guaranteeing the size of the fleet, the Reichstag, in effect, also gave the navy *carte blanche* to "replace" small old ships with larger new ships, because it was taken for granted that replacement ships would have to reflect the state of the art of their future era. As luck would have it, the oldest existing battleships counted in the Tirpitz plan, the four 7,600-ton *Sachsens*, came due for replacement just after the British *Dreadnought* revolutionized battleship design. The four 18,900-ton dreadnoughts of the *Nassau* class "replaced" them. The newer but smaller *Siegfried* class coast defenders, 3,500-ton vessels counted as battleships under the Second Navy Law, ultimately were "replaced" by dreadnoughts of the 22,800-ton *Helgoland* class and 24,700-ton *Kaiser* class. Initially armored cruisers filled the quota of new and replacement cruisers in the "large" category; eventually these gave way to battle cruisers that rivaled the dreadnoughts in size. In his calculations of 1897, Tirpitz categorized as "large" cruisers ships as small as the 5,700-ton *Herthas*. The *Ersatz Hertha*, when finally built, was the 27,000-ton battle cruiser *Hindenburg*.

France and Britain at the turn of the century

Tirpitz's navy laws set Germany on a course to become the second naval power after Britain. Whereas France made an effort in the early 1890s to match the British Naval Defence Act of 1889 and the eight *Royal Sovereigns*, the "Spencer program" of 1893 and the nine *Majestics* brought the French navy to abandon all hope of competing with its traditional rival. As the last of the battleships begun in the 1890s were completed, France laid down just six more: the two 14,605-ton *Républiques* and the four 14,490-ton *Libertés*. All carried four 12-inch guns paired in two centerline turrets fore and aft, and followed the general trend toward a heavier secondary armament, culminating in the ten 7.6-inch guns of the *Libertés*. Unfortunately they were obsolete by the time they entered service, between 1906 and 1908. In utility and longevity they were surpassed by the seven armored cruisers France laid down between 1901 and 1906, ranging in size from the 12,350-ton *Léon Gambetta* to the 13,995-ton *Waldeck-Rousseau*.[60]

The Fashoda crisis of 1898 produced the last war scare between Britain and France, after which the two countries affected a rapprochement culminating in the Entente Cordiale of 1904. The French Naval War College (*École supérieure de guerre de la Marine*), established in 1895 under the direction of Admiral Gabriel

Darrieus, helped lead France's turn away from the Jeune École. As a strategy wedded to a single scenario of war against Britain, the Jeune École further lost its appeal as relations with Britain improved.[61] Nevertheless, French construction policies continued to reflect a strong commitment to warship types associated with the Jeune École. Between 1890 and 1905 the navy added another thirty-seven seagoing torpedo boats, displacing 100–150 tons, and another 165 smaller torpedo boats, displacing less than 100 tons. An additional seventy-five torpedo boats of 100 tons were added by 1908.[62] During the same years France established itself as the world leader in submarine technology, further developing the electric battery-powered submarine after the groundbreaking *Gymnôte* of 1888. The *Narval*, commissioned in June 1900, served as a model for most of the seventy-six submarines built for the French navy by the outbreak of the First World War.[63]

The prohibitive cost of international isolation drove Britain to conclude the Entente Cordiale and, before then, an alliance with Japan in 1902. In the meantime, turn-of-the-century British naval policy reflected panic as much as prudence. In the eight years between the revision of the Mediterranean war plans in 1896 and the conclusion of the Entente Cordiale in 1904, Britain laid down twenty-eight battleships and thirty-five armored cruisers, reflecting the need for continued vigilance against France and Russia, at a time when Germany had committed to a long-term battleship program and Japan was rising in the Far East. The last of the battleships were the eight 15,585-ton vessels of the *King Edward VII* class, funded in the 1901–2 estimates and the two subsequent budgets. Like their predecessors they carried four 12-inch guns paired in two centerline turrets fore and aft, but with a mixed secondary armament of four 9.2-inch guns and ten 6-inch guns. In the estimates for 1904–5 Parliament funded another pair of battleships, the 16,090-ton *Lord Nelson* and *Agamemnon*, the last laid down before the *Dreadnought*. They had four 12-inch guns and a uniform secondary armament of ten 9.2-inch guns. The same budget included the three 14,600-ton armored cruisers of the *Minotaur* class, the last and largest of twenty-five British armored cruisers laid down between 1900 and 1905. The purchase of the 11,800-ton Chilean battleships *Constitución* and *Libertad* in 1903, to block their potential transfer to Russia, increased the British advantage. The two battleships, second class by British standards, entered service as *Swiftsure* and *Triumph*.[64]

While France could not match Britain in battleship construction, until 1904 Britain remained concerned about the French or Franco-Russian naval threat to its global interests through a revival of the Jeune École strategy, in a new and more lethal form. Such fears were hardly irrational, for France's best larger ships were its armored cruisers, and at least for the moment France was the world leader in the development of the submarine, which could join the torpedo boat as a means of delivering torpedoes which now had an extended range and accuracy. While the effective range of battleship guns, estimated roughly at 2,000 yards since early in the ironclad age, during the 1890s doubled to 4,000 yards, after the 1896 invention of the torpedo gyroscope (by the Austro-Hungarian naval officer Ludwig Obry) the effective range of self-propelled torpedoes more than doubled. Thereafter, the gap in range between the heaviest guns and the latest torpedoes continued to narrow. By 1904 the range of Whitehead torpedoes had reached 3,000 yards, and Britain's Admiral Fisher predicted that torpedo ranges would soon reach 7,000 yards.[65]

Better known for his promotion of the dreadnought and battle cruiser designs after becoming First Sea Lord in 1904, at the turn of the century Fisher was most concerned about the emergence of the submarine. As British commander in the Mediterranean (1899–1902) he kept a close watch on Toulon, main base for the growing French submarine force. His next posting, as commander in Portsmouth (1903–4), gave him the opportunity to observe the growth of his own navy's undersea force. The British were slow to embrace the submarine, and launched their first in 1901, built by Vickers after the American Holland design. Britain had not pioneered any aspect of submarine technology up to that point, but Captain Reginald Bacon is credited with introducing the periscope, fitted to the first British submarine. By the outbreak of the First World War the British had commissioned more submarines – eighty-nine – than any other navy.[66] Fisher was impressed by the power of the submarine, not so much as an offensive weapon but as a defender of harbors that would make it impossible for navies of the future to impose close blockades. Yet the advances in submarine and torpedo technologies were matched after 1900 by further breakthroughs favoring big battleships. Improved gun sights and range finders enhanced fire control, widening the gap between the effective range of heavy artillery and torpedoes, while new boilers by Yarrow and Babcock (fitted in British warships laid down after 1901) proved to be superior to the Belleville boilers of the 1890s, further enhancing speed. Experiments leading to the adoption of oil as a cleaner-burning alternative fuel for capital ships began in 1898, in smaller warships.[67]

In the years before 1914, the rising German naval threat ultimately compelled the British navy to scale down its presence around the globe in order to concentrate its battle fleet in home waters. Even before that, the deployment of battleships reflected the German, and general European, practice of organizing the fleet in peacetime in order to train it for war. By 1906 sixteen of thirty-two active battleships were in the Channel squadron, eight in the Mediterranean, and eight in the Atlantic. Sixteen of twenty-two active armored cruisers were under the same three commands, and another three were on the north Atlantic station. Aside from three British armored cruisers on the China station, protected and unarmored cruisers defended British interests in the rest of the world. These included Britain's last masted warships, the six 1,070-ton steel-hulled sloops of the *Cadmus* class, completed in 1902–4.[68]

Especially as it became clear that Japan would soon clash with Russia in the Far East, Britain chose to follow a policy of accommodation and ultimately, in 1902, alliance with Japan. The Anglo-Japanese treaty confirmed the end of the Pax Britannica. Britain conceded that it could no longer defend its interests as a great power on its own resources alone, and thus concluded an alliance, purely for strategic reasons, with a country that did not share its overall values or international outlook. Anglo-French strategic arrangements made during the ten years after the Entente Cordiale of 1904, to facilitate the concentration of British naval power in home waters, further underscored the fact that the British navy no longer was the world's policeman.

Italy and the revival of the Austro-Hungarian navy

Italy embraced the Jeune École later than other navies, built more torpedo boats in the 1880s than anyone else, then abruptly turned away from the strategy, ordering no more torpedo boats between 1888 and 1897. Between 1893 and 1904 Italy laid down another eight battleships: two of the 10,080-ton *Ammiraglio di Saint Bon* class, two of the 13,215-ton *Regina Margherita* class, and four of the 12,550-ton *Regina Elena* class. Improvements in Italian shipyards reduced the construction time of the latter two classes to an average of just under six years per ship. Six armored cruisers begun during the 1890s included three of the very successful 7,230-ton *Garibaldi* class.[69]

From the Italian strategic perspective, in the best of all possible worlds Britain would have joined the Triple Alliance or at least formed an Anglo-Italian Mediterranean pact. Italian leaders were disappointed when the Franco-Russian Alliance failed to push the British in their direction, and when Germany and Austria–Hungary rebuffed their appeals for a Triple Alliance naval convention. Italian naval materiel was first rate but its personnel were not, and the navy failed to impress foreign visitors at its maneuvers and reviews. In 1896 the first Italian attempt to conquer Ethiopia met with humiliating defeat at Aduwa, ending the political career of Prime Minister Francesco Crispi, the greatest francophobe and staunchest friend of the Triple Alliance among Italy's leaders. Thereafter, growing Anglo-German tensions caused many Italians to question the wisdom of their German alliance, and during the Crete crisis of 1897–98 Italy actively sought to cooperate with countries other than its allies. After the Italian navy committed the most ships to an international demonstration designed to force the Greeks to leave Crete under Turkish rule, Admiral Felice Canevaro was named overall commander. A compromise solution ultimately left Crete under Turkish sovereignty but with a Greek prince as governor. The outcome pleased Germany and Austria–Hungary less than the other powers, and in a sign of dissatisfaction they withdrew their ships early, in March 1898. The Italians, hedging their bets, stayed on until the end of the demonstration, alongside British, French, and Russian forces. In 1900 the Italians concluded a secret treaty giving the French a free hand in Morocco in exchange for an Italian free hand to annex Libya. That same year the first Triple Alliance naval convention was finally concluded, ironically just as Italian navy leaders again began to view Austria–Hungary, rather than France, as their most likely future enemy.[70]

During the same years Austria–Hungary emerged from the Jeune École era to resume a battleship program of its own, a build-up justified initially by the Franco-Russian Alliance, later by fears of an Italian defection from the Triple Alliance. Britain's concession that it could no longer stop the Russians at the straits raised the specter of the Black Sea fleet deploying in support of a future Russian offensive in the Balkans. Austria–Hungary also shared Britain's concern for the security of the Suez Canal and trade routes in the eastern Mediterranean, reflecting the fact that Trieste had become Mediterranean Europe's leading port for trade with South and East Asia. In 1893 work began on three 5,600-ton coast defenders of the *Monarch* class, followed by three 8,300-ton *Habsburgs* and three 10,600-ton *Erzherzogs*, the last of which was laid down in 1904. Three armored cruisers also joined the fleet, the largest of which was the 7,400-ton *Sankt Georg*. The Stabilimento Tecnico Triestino built all but one of the battleships and one armored cruiser, which were built in the Pola navy yard. Construction times averaged just over four years per ship. Starting with the armored cruiser *Maria Theresia* (completed 1894) the navy ordered all of its armor plate from Witkowitz of Moravia, and in 1901 Krupp guns were abandoned in favor of ordnance from the Skoda works of Bohemia. That same year the navy leadership took a decisive step to allay Hungarian anti-navy sentiment by committing to spend in Hungary a share of its budget equivalent to the Hungarian contribution to the joint-budget of the Dual Monarchy. In a very fragmented domestic arena a broad pro-navy coalition began to evolve, representing nationalities far from the Adriatic. The navy also gained a valuable ally in Francis Ferdinand, heir to the Habsburg throne, after the archduke traveled to Japan in 1892–93 aboard the protected cruiser *Kaiserin Elisabeth*. In the years that followed he promoted the naval cause in Austria–Hungary with a vigor matched only by William II in Germany.[71]

The Boxer Rebellion (1900)

The Boxer Rebellion occasioned the last great exercise in "gunboat diplomacy" by the great powers, bringing even Austro-Hungarian warships to the waters off China.[72] In the late 1890s the Boxers began lashing out against foreigners (especially missionaries) and Chinese Christians, actions which only guaranteed further foreign intervention. In November 1897 the murder of two German Catholic missionaries provided the pretext for Germany to seize Tsingtao with Kiaochow Bay, an action endorsed by the Chinese government in a long-term lease granted in March 1898. Russia promptly demanded, and received, a similar lease of the Liaotung peninsula, including Port Arthur, while France received a port in Kwangtung. Britain insisted upon Weihaiwei, which it pledged to evacuate as soon as the Russians left Port Arthur. During the same years (1897–99) the same four powers established formal spheres of influence covering most of the rest of China. During the first months of 1900 foreign pressure led to official Chinese attempts to suppress the Boxer movement, which instead only grew larger and bolder, in May 1900 attacking the railway that linked Beijing and Tientsin to the coast at Taku. After the foreign legations in the Chinese capital requested reinforcements from their warships stationed off Taku, the senior officer on the station, Britain's Vice Admiral Sir Edward Seymour, organized an international relief operation which, as a first step, secured the Taku forts. While impressive warships such as Russia's 13,675-ton armored cruiser *Rossia*, Britain's 14,200-ton protected cruiser *Terrible* and the 10,500-ton battleships *Centurion* and *Barfleur*, and France's 7,995-ton protected cruiser *D'Entrecasteaux* stood well offshore, a flotilla of nine much smaller vessels negotiated the shallow waters to attack the Taku forts: one gunboat apiece from Germany, France, and Japan, three from Russia, and two destroyers and a steel screw sloop from Britain. The forts fell on 17 June, after which Seymour led a force of 2,000 men – assembled from each of the six European powers, and Japan and the United States – up the railway toward Beijing. Chinese troops joined the Boxers to block their way, forcing them back to Tientsin, where they were besieged. In Beijing the mob put further pressure on the ill-defended legations, and on 20 June the German ambassador was murdered. Riding the wave of anti-foreign sentiment, the Chinese government formally declared war on the foreign powers the following day.

The Boxer Rebellion inspired an unprecedented degree of cooperation among the governments and navies of the great powers, against the common threat to their citizens and their interests in China. On 13 July reinforcements from Taku arrived to relieve the siege of Tienstin, and on 4 August a force of 20,000 men, half of them Japanese, left Tientsin for Beijing. Ten days later they entered Beijing, relieving the legations and, afterward, looting the city. Britain remained the strongest naval power off Taku but, with its army bogged down in South Africa fighting the Boers, ultimately let others take the lead on land. A German expeditionary force dispatched by William II in response to the murder of his ambassador arrived in September, and its commander, Field Marshal Alfred von Waldersee, served as head of an international force which conducted punitive operations around Beijing until April 1901. Under the terms of the "Boxer Protocol," signed in September 1901, China agreed to pay an indemnity, permit the destruction of the Taku forts, and allow larger foreign garrisons in Beijing and along the rail line to the coast.

The destruction of the Chinese navy in the Sino-Japanese War left it in no position to challenge the international force off Taku. After 1895 it had added five protected cruisers, two unarmored cruisers, one torpedo gunboat, and four destroyers, some built at Foochow but most purchased abroad. All were kept safely out of harm's way in 1900 except the four destroyers, which were anchored in the Peiho River upstream from the Taku forts. They were captured on 17 June 1900 after the forts fell, and were recommissioned – all with the name *Taku* – in the navies of Britain, France, Germany, and Russia. Between 1900 and 1914 China attempted to rebuild its naval forces yet again, ordering seven cruisers, five destroyers, four torpedo boats, and several small river gunboats from shipyards in six different foreign countries. The outbreak of the First

World War prevented delivery of five of the cruisers and two of the destroyers.[73] The humiliation of the Chinese empire in 1900 paved the way for the establishment of a republic a dozen years later, but a half century passed before a government emerged that was strong enough to restore the country's sovereignty. No one would have imagined that a century which began in such a humbling defeat would end with China as the world's third-strongest naval power.

The Russo-Japanese War (1904–5)

Japan's victory against China in 1894–95 added a sense of urgency to the Russian navy's quest to secure a warm-water Pacific port, linked by rail to the rest of Russia. Vladivostok, founded in 1860, was to be the eastern terminus of the Trans-Siberian Railway, begun in 1891, but every winter ice limited its utility as a naval base. After France and Germany joined Russia in pressuring Japan to return the Liaotung peninsula and Port Arthur to China in 1895, the Chinese granted the Russians a concession in 1896 to build the Trans-Siberian Railway across Manchuria, shortening the route to Vladivostok by hundreds of miles. Two years later Russia leased the Liaotung peninsula from China and began building a spur of the Trans-Siberian Railway from Harbin to Port Arthur. Assessing the situation in 1898, a British observer, Colonel George Sydenham Clarke, remarked that Port Arthur had "immense advantages" over Vladivostok as Russia's Pacific naval base, and predicted that "in less than ten years the Russian position [there] will be unassailable, and Port Arthur . . . will be quite as strong as Cronstadt or Sevastopol."[74]

Against the growing Russian threat the Japanese navy, between 1897 and 1904, commissioned an entire new fleet of six pre-dreadnought battleships, eight armored cruisers, and eight protected cruisers. The battleships, all built in Britain, were improved versions of the British *Royal Sovereign* and *Majestic* classes, ranging in size from the 12,320-ton *Yashima* (1897) to the 15,140-ton *Mikasa* (1902). The armored cruisers were somewhat smaller than their turn-of-the-century counterparts in other navies, the largest being the 9,700-ton *Asama* (1899), the smallest the 7,630-ton *Kasuga* (1904). Four were built in Britain, one in Germany and one in France; the remaining two, laid down in Italy for Argentina, were purchased in 1902 just before their completion. Another eight protected cruisers commissioned between 1896 and 1904 ranged in size from the 2,660-ton *Suma* to the 4,900-ton *Kasagi*. Two were built in the United States and one in Britain, the remainder in Japanese shipyards.[75]

Dependence on foreign industry cast doubt over Japan's claim to naval great power status. Owing to the limitations of its steel industry, seventeen of the newest warships in the fleet of 1904 were built abroad, and the five built in Japan were relatively small protected cruisers. The Japanese first manufactured their own armor in 1901, albeit in quantities so limited that imports remained essential. Assistance from Vickers and other British firms improved steel production, but until 1914 most steel for shipbuilding continued to be imported from

Europe. Britain also provided the latest Barr and Stroud optical range finders, leaving Japanese fire control at least equal to that of the Russian navy. Japan's lack of high quality domestic coal left the navy vulnerable in the event of a long war, especially as the fleet grew in size, but after the Anglo-Japanese treaty of 1902 the navy stockpiled over a million tons of British coal. The Japanese took some consolation in the fact that, by 1904, they were producing their own medium- and light-caliber naval artillery, gun mountings, shells, torpedoes, mines, shipboard machinery, boilers, and radio telegraph equipment.[76]

Counting ships commissioned since 1880, in 1904 the Russian navy had twenty-seven battleships, eight armored cruisers, and fourteen protected cruisers. The Japanese navy had seven battleships, including the *Chin Yen* (ex-Chinese *Chen Yuan*), ten armored cruisers, including the small *Chiyoda* and *Hei Yen* (ex-Chinese *Ping Yuan*), and seventeen protected cruisers. In January 1904 the two navies were roughly equal in capital ships in the Pacific theater, where the Russians had seven battleships with an eighth on the way. Of course Russia had an even larger force in European waters and, aside from warships trapped in the Black Sea by the terms of the Straits Convention of 1841, could send these to the Pacific as reinforcements. Russia also had the money to buy additional warships abroad, while in recent years Japan had spent so much on foreign-built warships that no funds were left for emergency wartime purchases. The commander of the Japanese fleet, Admiral Heihachiro Togo, entered the conflict keenly aware that he would have to win the war with the ships already on hand, and tailored his strategy accordingly.[77]

After years of increasing tension over their competing designs on Manchuria and Korea, Japan broke diplomatic relations with Russia on 6 February 1904. On the night of 8 February ten destroyers led a surprise torpedo attack against the Russian Pacific squadron at Port Arthur, which damaged the battleships *Tsesarevich* and *Retvisan* and a cruiser. Togo followed up with a more conventional attack on 9 February, led by six battleships, five armored and four protected cruisers, but did not attempt a close action. Neither side lost a ship on either day, and the Russian units damaged in the torpedo attack all were repaired. Coinciding with Togo's sortie against Port Arthur, the remaining units of the fleet supported a successful landing at Chemulpo (Inchon) by the Japanese army, in the process damaging the Russian protected cruiser *Variag* so badly that it had to be scuttled by its crew. In March the Russian navy's morale recovered with the appointment of Vice Admiral Stepan Makarov as commander in the Far East. The former dashing torpedo boat commander of the 1877–78 war led a number of sorties from Port Arthur, but the aggressive campaign came to an abrupt end on 13 April, when the flagship *Petropavlovsk* struck a mine and sank while returning to base. The dead included Makarov and all but 80 of the 715 men aboard.[78]

As the Japanese army secured Korea and advanced into Manchuria, the Russian navy gained revenge for the loss of the *Petropavlovsk* when a minefield sowed by the minelayer *Amur* claimed two of Japan's Armstrong-built battleships, the *Hatsuse* and the *Yashima*, both sunk on 15 May. Thereafter the Russian cruiser squadron (the armored cruisers *Rurik*, *Gromoboi*, and *Rossia*, and the protected cruiser *Bogatyr*) conducted a series of sorties from its base at Vladivostok, sinking three Japanese transports and eighteen merchantmen in the Sea of Japan. The Japanese finally deployed four armored cruisers which engaged the cruiser squadron on 14 August in the Battle of the Sea of Japan (also known as the Battle of Ulsan), sinking the armored cruiser *Rurik*. Afterward the rest of the cruiser squadron returned to Vladivostok, where it remained inactive for the balance of the war.[79]

Meanwhile, the Japanese army laid siege to Port Arthur, prompting Makarov's successor, Rear Admiral V. K. Vitgeft, to attempt a breakout with the entire Russian Pacific squadron. On 10 August Togo intercepted him, and in the Battle of the Yellow Sea (also known as the Battle of Shantung) foiled his planned run for Vladivostok. The first fleet-scale high seas action of the war opened at an unprecedented distance. The Japanese began firing at 11,000 meters, and warships on both sides were fully engaged at between 8,000 and 9,000 meters. At such distances, the 12-inch guns did all the damage, and the quick-firing 6-inch and 8-inch guns played no role. In the battle Togo first tried "crossing the T," a tactic tested during British maneuvers in 1901 and introduced at the Japanese naval staff college the following year. When Vitgeft turned his column away to avoid the concentration of fire against his leading ships, Togo maneuvered his column into a position to cross the "T" once more, forcing Vitgeft again to turn away. The Russians continued to checkmate the Japanese move until Vitgeft finally managed to get past Togo's force, which then had to give chase as the Russians headed southeast for the Korea strait. After two hours the superior speed of the Japanese put them back to within 7,000 meters of the tail of the Russian column, where their gunners again registered hits, resuming the battle. As the Japanese closed, their shells struck the bridge of the flagship *Tsesarevich*, killing Vitgeft and most of his staff. The Russian column then dispersed, the *Tsesarevich* and three destroyers steaming for the German base at Tsingtao, two protected cruisers and a destroyer seeking refuge in other neutral ports. All were interned for the duration of the war. The protected cruiser *Novik* came closest to making Vladivostok but was forced aground and scuttled off Sakhalin. As the remaining Russian ships straggled back to Port Arthur with night falling, Togo chose not to risk his battleships and armored cruisers in a bid for a decisive victory. Japanese destroyers and torpedo boats pursued them, capturing one destroyer. Afterward Togo reimposed the blockade of Port Arthur.[80]

After the Battle of the Yellow Sea, the guns and men of the surviving Russian warships at Port Arthur were put ashore to reinforce the land defenses. The Japanese army continued to tighten the siege, and on 5 December installed a battery of 11-inch howitzers on high ground overlooking the harbor, which soon sank most of the larger Russian units. Just one battleship, the *Sevastopol*, went down in water deep enough to foil later Japanese efforts to raise her, and only after being deliberately scuttled there by the Russians. The garrison surrendered on 2 January 1905. In the final weeks of the siege five battleships, one armored cruiser, and one protected cruiser were sunk at Port Arthur, bringing total Russian losses in the war to six battleships, two armored cruisers, and four protected cruisers, not counting the units interned in neutral ports. The minelayer *Yenisei* sank after striking one of its own mines shortly after the war began, on 11 February, and its sister-ship *Amur* was sunk by Japanese siege guns at Port Arthur in December. In addition to the two Japanese battleships destroyed by mines on 15 May, Japan's only other losses in 1904 (or in the entire war) were the protected cruiser *Yoshino*, accidentally rammed and sunk by the armored cruiser *Kasuga*, ironically also on 15 May; the small armored cruiser *Hei Yen* (ex-Chinese *Ping Yuan*), mined off Port Arthur on 18 September; the protected cruiser *Sai Yen* (ex-Chinese *Chi Yuan*), mined on 30 November; and the protected cruiser *Takasago*, mined on 13 December.[81]

By the time Port Arthur fell, relief was on the way. On 15 October 1904 Admiral Zinovy Rozhestvensky left Libau for the Far East with the "second Pacific squadron," actually most of the Russian Baltic fleet. A week later in the North Sea, the lively imagination of Russian gunners led them to mistake British fishing trawlers for Japanese torpedo boats; in the Dogger Bank incident of 21–2 October, one trawler was sunk and six damaged. France, which hoped eventually to bring the British and Russians together in an anti-German bloc, intervened diplomatically to restrain an outraged Britain from declaring war. The Russian battleships reached the Indian Ocean by rounding the Cape of Good Hope while the cruisers and destroyers used the Suez Canal; the squadron reunited in January 1905 off Madagascar, where Rozhestvensky learned of the fall of Port Arthur. To compensate for the ships lost at Port Arthur, the Russians dispatched Rear Admiral N. I. Nebogatov with the so-called "third Pacific squadron," older or smaller battleships and cruisers initially left behind in the Baltic because of their limited speed and fighting ability. The third squadron caught up with the second squadron in April 1905, at Camranh Bay on the coast of Vietnam, having made the passage from the Baltic via the Suez Canal. Together they steamed for Vladivostok and a planned rendezvous with the Russian cruiser squadron.[82]

Rozhestvensky approached Japanese waters with a fleet of thirty-eight units, including eleven battleships, three armored cruisers, and five protected cruisers, but among the battleships were three coast defenders of the 4,970-ton *Admiral Ushakov* class, and the three armored cruisers were, in fact, armored frigates dating from the early 1880s. The four 13,520-ton *Borodinos* and the 12,680-ton battleship *Osliabia* were the only truly formidable Russian warships. Breaking with his cautiousness of the past fifteen months, Togo steamed out with all four of his battleships and all eight armored cruisers, accompanied by a flotilla of destroyers and torpedo boats, intent on stopping the Russian column in the straits of Tsushima.[83] The Japanese had two fewer armored warships than the Russians but the oldest had been commissioned in 1897; three of their four battleships were larger than any ship in the Russian fleet, and their smallest armored cruiser displaced 7,630 tons. The encounter began on 27 May 1905 at 13:40, when Togo crossed the Russian "T" from east to west, then reversed course to recross the "T" from west to east. Rozhestvensky turned away and attempted to outrun the Japanese, steaming to the northeast and putting the two fleets on parallel courses. The first shots were fired at ranges somewhat shorter than at the Battle of the Yellow Sea. At 14:08 the Russians hit Togo's flagship, the 15,140-ton *Mikasa*, from a distance of 7,000 meters. The Japanese began returning fire at 6,400 meters. As at the Yellow Sea, long-range fire by 12-inch guns dominated the action. With Togo's column steaming at 15 knots and Rozhestvensky's at 9 knots, the Russians had no hope of getting away. Superior Japanese gunnery soon took its toll; the *Osliabia* was the first to succumb, sinking at 15:00. After the Japanese line gradually pulled ahead of the Russian line, Rozhestvensky doubled back for a run to the northwest, toward Vladivostok. Togo countered by doubling back to the west, cutting him off and forcing him to turn away to the south. As the Russian fleet fell into disorder, the Japanese closed for the kill. By nightfall some warships were dueling at 2,500 meters, incredibly close range for the heavy and middle artillery of the day. Several Russian warships were disabled long before they were in danger of sinking, owing to serious fires fueled by the large stocks of coal they carried into the battle. Three of the four *Borodinos* sank between 18:30 and 19:30; Rozhestvensky, severely wounded, was rescued from his flagship *Suvorov* just before it sank. Over the night of 27–8 May the Japanese armored cruisers, destroyers and torpedo boats hunted down most of the rest of the Russian fleet. The following morning Nebogatov surrendered the 13,520-ton *Orel* and three smaller battleships that had survived the disaster.

Tsushima was the largest naval battle since Trafalgar a century earlier, and equally decisive. In addition to the four battleships captured, the Russians lost six battleships, one armored cruiser, and one protected cruiser to Japanese fire, and scuttled another battleship, two armored cruisers, and one protected cruiser to prevent their capture. The three remaining protected cruisers ran for Manila, where they were interned by the Americans. (One of the three, the *Aurora*, was later made into a museum ship by the Soviet Union in commemoration of its role in the Bolshevik Revolution.) Of the nineteen smaller units only the armed yacht *Almaz* actually made it through to Vladivostok; the rest were either sunk, scuttled, or captured. Russian casualties included 4,830 men killed and 5,917 captured. In contrast, the Japanese lost three torpedo boats, and three of their armored warships sustained moderate damage. Their casualties included 110 men killed and several hundred wounded. The Japanese captured Rozhestvensky aboard a Russian destroyer which had taken him aboard when he left the *Suvorov*. After the war he assumed complete responsibility for the defeat but was acquitted by a Russian court martial. Nebogatov and the captains of the ships that had surrendered received death sentences, later commuted to life imprisonment by Tsar Nicholas II.

Peace talks opened in the wake of the Battle of Tsushima, as Russia, since

January 1905 wracked by revolution, and Japan, running out of money, both sought an end to the war. In September 1905 the Treaty of Portsmouth gave the Japanese the southern half of Sakhalin Island and a free hand in Korea, which they annexed in 1910. Both Russia and Japan agreed to restore Manchuria to Chinese sovereignty except for the Liaotung peninsula and Port Arthur, where the Japanese assumed the Russian lease of 1898. The victory established Japan as the world's sixth naval power, while Russia's fleet collapsed to a level barely stronger than that of Austria–Hungary. In addition to the battleships captured at Tsushima, the Japanese navy raised and repaired several sunken or scuttled enemy warships, most of them at Port Arthur, bringing their total number of prizes to eight battleships, one armored cruiser, and three protected cruisers, more than compensating for the two battleships, one small armored cruiser, and three protected cruisers lost during the war. The Russian navy emerged with just ten battleships, three armored cruisers, and eight protected cruisers, of which eight battleships and one armored cruiser were in the Black Sea fleet, which succumbed to mutiny one month after Tsushima. The largest of the Black Sea battleships, the 12,580-ton *Potemkin*, supported a revolutionary uprising at Odessa before steaming for Constanza, Romania, where its crew scuttled the ship and sought asylum. Within months the Russians raised and repaired the *Potemkin*, which served in the imperial navy until 1917 under the name *Panteleimon*. During 1905 mutineers also seized an armored cruiser, a protected cruiser, and four destroyers; like the *Potemkin*, they were renamed afterward to erase the stain of revolution.[84]

Conclusion

By the autumn of 1905 Britain had in service or under construction sixty-six battleships, including all those commissioned since the *Dreadnought* of 1879. France remained second, with forty battleships, the oldest dating from 1878. Germany now ranked third with thirty-seven, the oldest likewise in service since 1878. The United States had thirty-six, the oldest commissioned in 1891. Britain's superiority appears even more impressive if one subtracts from these totals the smaller battleships or large monitors designed for coastal operations only, of which Britain had two, France seven, Germany eight, and the United States ten. In the second tier of naval powers Italy had eighteen battleships built or building, including the *Duilio* of 1880. Japan had sixteen, including three under construction and eight captured Russian vessels not yet repaired; its oldest battleship, the *Chin Yen* (ex-Chinese *Chen Yuan*), dated from 1885. Russia ranked next, with its ten survivors of the Russo-Japanese War (including the *Ekaterina II* class battleships, in service since 1889) joined by another five on the stocks. Austria–Hungary ranked eighth, with twelve battleships commissioned since 1882. A combination of diplomacy and warfare had rendered Britain's two-power standard meaningless, as France was no longer an enemy and Russia no longer a great naval power, while Japan was an ally and war with the United

States was highly unlikely. Britain's most likely future naval adversary, Germany, as yet was not a serious threat; indeed, as of 1905 the British navy surpassed in strength the combined fleets of the Triple Alliance.

Over the fifteen years between 1890 and 1905, the battle fleet once again assumed center stage in naval warfare. Protected cruisers of a type popular in the era of the Jeune École played significant roles in the Sino-Japanese and Spanish–American wars, but the Russo-Japanese War and, in particular, the Battle of Tsushima – a decisive high seas encounter between battle fleets led by large armored warships – validated the vision of naval warfare promoted by Mahan and his followers. One month after the Treaty of Portsmouth ended the war between Russia and Japan, the British navy laid down a new *Dreadnought*, a battleship of unprecedented size and speed with an all big-gun armament. Some fifteen years after the emergence of the standard pre-dreadnought design, all existing battleships would be considered obsolete, creating a clean slate and a new challenge for all navies.

Notes

1   Marder, *The Anatomy of British Sea Power*, 7, 120–35.
2   Beresford to House of Commons, 13 December 1888, quoted in Charles William de la Poer Beresford, *The Memoirs of Admiral Lord Charles Beresford*, 2 vols (Boston, Mass., 1914), 2: 360.
3   Marder, *The Anatomy of British Sea Power*, 105–6.
4   Jon Tetsuro Sumida, *In Defence of Naval Supremacy: Finance, Technology, and British Naval Policy, 1889–1914* (Boston, Mass., 1989), 13–16; Roberts, "The Pre-Dreadnought Age, 1890–1905," 116; Brown, *Warrior to Dreadnought*, 124–32; *Conway, 1860–1905*, 32–3, 76–7, 66, 82.
5   Jon Tetsuro Sumida, *Inventing Grand Strategy and Teaching Command: The Classic Works of Alfred Thayer Mahan Revisited* (Baltimore, Md, 1997), 22–5.
6   Sumida, *Inventing Grand Strategy and Teaching Command*, 99–103.
7   Marder, *The Anatomy of British Sea Power*, 30; Sondhaus, *The Naval Policy of Austria–Hungary*, 126, 150–1; idem, and "The Imperial German Navy and Social Democracy, 1878–1897," *German Studies Review* 18 (1995): 51–64; Cooling, *Gray Steel and Blue Water Navy*, 85–109.
8   Sondhaus, *Preparing for Weltpolitik*, 223–4.
9   Sumida, *Inventing Grand Strategy and Teaching Command*, 45, 72.
10 Still, *American Sea Power in the Old World*, 94–101.
11 Sondhaus, *Preparing for Weltpolitik*, 189, 193, 196–8. Tirpitz quoted from "Relation über die Herbstmanöver der Marine im Jahre 1893," Bundesarchiv–Militärarchiv, RM 4/62, 104–84.
12 Lambi, *The Navy and German Power Politics*, 66; Evans and Peattie, *Kaigun*, 24.
13 Tritten, "Doctrine and Fleet Tactics in the Royal Navy," 21.
14 Thomas W. Harvey, comp., *Memoir of Hayward Augustus Harvey* (New York, 1900), 62–3; *Krupp: A Century's History, 1812–1912* (Essen, 1912), 289; Günther Leckebusch, *Die Beziehungen der deutschen Seeschiffswerften zur Eisenindustrie an der Ruhr in der Zeit von 1850 bis 1930* (Cologne, 1963), 35; Cooling, *Gray Steel and Blue Water Navy*, 96–7.
15 Richard Owen, "Military–Industrial Relations: Krupp and the Imperial Navy Office," in Richard J. Evans, ed., *Society and Politics in Wilhelmine Germany* (London,

1978), 75; *Krupp: A Century's History*, 288–89; Leckebusch, *Eisenindustrie*, 36n; Gröner, *Die deutschen Kriegsschiffe*, 1: 36–7. Gary E. Weir, *Building the Kaiser's Navy: The Imperial Navy Office and German Industry in the von Tirpitz Era, 1890–1919* (Annapolis, Md, 1992), 30, dates the Krupp–Dillinger alliance from 1893.

16 Owen, "Military–Industrial Relations," 75; *Krupp: A Century's History*, 289–91; Leckebusch, *Eisenindustrie*, 36–7; Gröner, *Die deutschen Kriegsschiffe*, 1: 36; Brown, *Warrior to Dreadnought*, 151; Weir, *Building the Kaiser's Navy*, 31, 224n.

17 Harvey, *Memoir of Hayward Augustus Harvey*, 65–79; Roberts, "The Pre-Dreadnought Age, 1890–1905," 116; Campbell, "Naval Armaments and Armour," 162; *Conway, 1860–1905*, 34, 142–9, 180–2, 221–2, 294–7, 343–4.

18 Brown, *Warrior to Dreadnought*, 150–1.

19 Campbell, "Naval Armaments and Armour," 162–3; *Conway, 1860–1905*, 34, 142, 182, 221, 273, 293, 343; Sondhaus, *The Naval Policy of Austria–Hungary*, 153, 180.

20 Roberts, "The Pre-Dreadnought Age, 1890–1905," 118–19; *Conway, 1860–1905*, 292–6, 303–5.

21 George F. Kennan, *The Fateful Alliance: France, Russia, and the Coming of the First World War* (New York, 1984), 97–115, 220–3, and *passim*; Roberts, "The Pre-Dreadnought Age, 1890–1905," 120–1; Clarke, *Russia's Sea-Power*, 117; Tomitch, *Warships of the Imperial Russian Navy*, 25–75, and *passim*; Watts, *The Imperial Russian Navy*, 172; Wilson, "Early Submarines," 153, 157.

22 Brown, *Warrior to Dreadnought*, 143–6; Roberts, "The Pre-Dreadnought Age, 1890–1905," 117; *Conway, 1860–1905*, 34–7.

23 Brown, *Warrior to Dreadnought*, 137–41; *Conway, 1860–1905*, 90–1, 157, 205, 237–8, 264, 326, 355.

24 Ropp, *The Development of a Modern Navy*, 205; see British naval intelligence office memorandum of 28 October 1896: text in Marder, *The Anatomy of British Sea Power*, 578–80.

25 Marder, *The Anatomy of British Sea Power*, 263.

26 Evans and Peattie, *Kaigun*, 19–20.

27 Ibid., 40, 524, 536.

28 Ibid., 38; *Conway, 1860–1905*, 228, 236, 400.

29 Evans and Peattie, *Kaigun*, 41–2; Richard Hough, *The Fleet that Had to Die* (London, 1958), 148; *Conway, 1860–1905*, 217, 399.

30 Evans and Peattie, *Kaigun*, 45; *Conway, 1860–1905*, 217.

31 Sondhaus, *The Naval Policy of Austria–Hungary*, 97.

32 Evans and Peattie, *Kaigun*, 42, 44, 46, 128; *Conway, 1860–1905*, 217, 219–20.

33 Evans and Peattie, *Kaigun*, 46–47; *Conway, 1860–1905*, 217, 220, 229, 395–9.

34 Evans and Peattie, *Kaigun*, 47–8; Charles H. Fairbanks, Jr, "The Origins of the *Dreadnought* Revolution: A Historiographical Essay," *International History Review* 13 (1991), 261; Brown, *Warrior to Dreadnought*, 167.

35 Patrick J. Kelly, "Strategy, Tactics, and Turf Wars: Tirpitz and the Oberkommando der Marine, 1892–1895," paper presented at the Thirteenth Naval History Symposium, Annapolis, Md, 2–4 October 1997, 10; Gröner, *Die deutschen Kriegsschiffe*, 1: 37–40.

36 *Conway, 1860–1905*, 223.

37 Ibid., 35; Fairbanks, "The Origins of the *Dreadnought* Revolution," 267.

38 Evans and Peattie, *Kaigun*, 50; *Conway, 1860–1905*, 395–400, and *passim*.

39 A. B. Feuer, *The Spanish–American War at Sea: Naval Action in the Atlantic* (Westport, Ct, 1995), 1–28.

40 Alden, *The American Steel Navy*, 265.

41 *Conway, 1860–1905*, 140–1, 145–8, 160, 163–6; Canney, *The Old Steam Navy*, 2: 75–88.

42 Rodríguez González, *Política naval de la Restauración*, 233–305, and *passim*; *Conway, 1860–1905*, 380–4.

43 Beach, *The United States Navy*, 343–9; *Conway, 1860–1905*, 150–64, and *passim*, 383–6; Brown, *Warrior to Dreadnought*, 167; Evans and Peattie, *Kaigun*, 128; Alden, *The American Steel Navy*, 322; Tritten, "Doctrine in the Spanish Navy," 86.

44 Jaime Pérez-Llorca, *1898: La estrategia del Desastre* (Madrid, 1998), 56.

45 *Conway, 1860–1905*, 351, 382.

46 Beach, *The United States Navy*, 354–64; Alden, *The American Steel Navy*, 322–9; Pérez-Llorca, *1898*, 125–35; Feuer, *The Spanish–American War at Sea*, 169–79; Brown, *Warrior to Dreadnought*, 167–8.

47 Pérez-Llorca, *1898*, 56, 167–70; Alden, *The American Steel Navy*, 322; Still, *American Sea Power in the Old World*, 135.

48 Beach, *The United States Navy*, 394.

49 Brown, *Warrior to Dreadnought*, 168.

50 Pérez-Llorca, *1898*, 138.

51 Gordon Carpenter O'Gara, *Roosevelt and the Rise of the Modern Navy* ([1943] reprinted New York, 1969), 5.

52 Araya, "Situación estratégica naval," 2: 460–72; Rodríguez González, *Política naval de la Restauración*, 339–45; *Conway, 1860–1905*, 402–4, 410–15; Lyon, "Underwater Warfare and the Torpedo Boat," 136.

53 Carvalho, *Nossa Marinha*, 114–42, and *passim*; *Conway, 1860–1905*, 407–10.

54 Araya, "Situación estratégica naval," 2: 471–3; *Conway, 1860–1905*, 39, 226, 403, 409, 411; Watts, *The Imperial Russian Navy*, 23.

55 Unless otherwise noted, the sources for this section are Sondhaus, *Preparing for Weltpolitik*, 220–5, and Gröner, *Die deutschen Kriegsschiffe*, vol. 1.

56 Tirpitz quoted in Jonathan Steinberg, *Yesterday's Deterrent: Tirpitz and the Birth of the German Battle Fleet* (New York, 1965), 126. Bismarck quoted in Beresford, *Memoirs*, 2: 363. See also Tirpitz, "Allgemeine Gesichtspunkte bei der Feststellung unserer Flotte nach Schiffsklassen und Schiffstypen" [July 1897], in Volker R. Berghahn and Wilhelm Deist, *Rüstung im Zeichen der wilhelminischen Weltpolitik: Grundlegende Dokumente, 1890–1914* (Düsseldorf, 1988), 122–7.

57 Tirpitz quoted in Holger H. Herwig, *The German Naval Officer Corps: A Social and Political History* (Oxford, 1973), 11.

58 Alfred von Tirpitz, *Erinnerungen* (Leipzig, 1919), 100n, notes that the coast defenders of the *Siegfried* class formed a separate category under the First Navy Law but were "rechristened, on paper, as battleships (*Linienschiffe*)" in the Second Navy Law of 1900.

59 Volker R. Berghahn, "Naval Armaments and Social Crisis: Germany before 1914," in Geoffrey Best and Andrew Wheatcroft, eds, *War, Economy, and the Military Mind* (London, 1976), 66.

60 Roberts, "The Pre-Dreadnought Age, 1890–1905," 119–20; *Conway, 1860–1905*, 297.

61 Tritten, "Navy and Military Doctrine in France," 55–8.

62 *Conway, 1860–1905*, 332–3.

63 Tritten, "Navy and Military Doctrine in France," 55; Wilson, "Early Submarines," 154.

64 Brown, *Warrior to Dreadnought*, 146–9; Roberts, "The Pre-Dreadnought Age, 1890–1905," 117–18; *Conway, 1860–1905*, 38–40, 70–3; Nicholas Lambert, "Admiral Sir John Fisher and the Concept of Flotilla Defence, 1904–1909," *Journal of Military History* 59 (1995): 651.

65 Lambert, "Admiral Sir John Fisher and the Concept of Flotilla Defence," 647–51; Roberts, "The Pre-Dreadnought Age, 1890–1905," 113. On Ludwig Obry, see Sondhaus, *The Naval Policy of Austria–Hungary*, 48, 72 note 42.

66 Lambert, "Admiral Sir John Fisher and the Concept of Flotilla Defence," 651; Wilson, "Early Submarines," 155–7; *Conway, 1906–21*, 86–9.

67 Lambert, "Admiral Sir John Fisher and the Concept of Flotilla Defence," 650–3; Roberts, "The Pre-Dreadnought Age, 1890–1905," 113; Griffiths, "Warship Machinery," 177.

68 Brown, *Warrior to Dreadnought*, 204; *Conway, 1860–1905*, 60.

69 Franco Bargoni, *Corazzate italiane classi Re Umberto – Ammiraglio di Saint Bon, 1893–1901* (Rome, 1978), *passim*; *Conway, 1860–1905*, 343–44, 350–1.

70 Baratelli, *La marina militare italiana*, 148; Marder, *The Anatomy of British Sea Power*, 171–2; Sondhaus, *Preparing for Weltpolitik*, 195, 220; idem, *The Naval Policy of Austria–Hungary*, 132, 156–57, 210, 236; Christopher Seton-Watson, *Italy: From Liberalism to Fascism, 1870–1925* (London, 1967), 181–3, 212.

71 Sondhaus, *The Naval Policy of Austria–Hungary*, 124–9, 147–56.

72 Unless otherwise noted, the sources for this section are Henry Keown-Boyd, *The Boxer Rebellion* (New York, 1991); E. M. W. Norie, *Official Account of the Military Operations in China, 1900–1901* ([1903] reprinted Nashville, Tn, 1995); Paul A. Cohen, *History in Three Keys: The Boxers as Event, Experience, and Myth* (New York, 1997), 14–56.

73 *Conway, 1860–1905*, 397, 400–1; *Conway, 1906–21*, 396–9.

74 Clarke, *Russia's Sea-Power*, 149–53.

75 *Conway, 1860–1905*, 221–2, 224–6, 229–30.

76 Evans and Peattie, *Kaigun*, 63–4, 67, 79–81.

77 Evans and Peattie, *Kaigun*, 93; Watts, *The Imperial Russian Navy*, 19.

78 Watts, *The Imperial Russian Navy*, 20; Woodward, *The Russians at Sea*, 122–5, 131; Evans and Peattie, *Kaigun*, 100.

79 Watts, *The Imperial Russian Navy*, 21, 172; Woodward, *The Russians at Sea*, 133, 137–8; Evans and Peattie, *Kaigun*, 109.

80 Watts, *The Imperial Russian Navy*, 20–1; Woodward, *The Russians at Sea*, 135–7; Evans and Peattie, *Kaigun*, 75, 77, 103, 105.

81 Woodward, *The Russians at Sea*, 138–42; *Conway, 1860–1905*, 204, 220, 228–9.

82 Hough, *The Fleet That Had to Die*, 32–144, and *passim*; Woodward, *The Russians at Sea*, 139–44.

83 On the Battle of Tsushima and its aftermath, see Hough, *The Fleet that Had To Die*, 156–86, 206–7; Watts, *The Imperial Russian Navy*, 22–3; Woodward, *The Russians at Sea*, 151–3; Evans and Peattie, *Kaigun*, 119–24; Brown, *Warrior to Dreadnought*, 173.

84 Woodward, *The Russians at Sea*, 156–9; see also Richard Hough, *The Potemkin Mutiny* (London, 1960).

CHAPTER EIGHT

The dreadnought and the origins of the First World War

The great battleship-centered build-up in naval materiel that started in the 1890s drew considerable support from writers such as Mahan and Colomb, whose historical accounts validated the battle fleet. Yet by the eve of the First World War, the next generation of navy men – creatures of the build-up – tended to scoff at such notions. The principal British writer on naval doctrine after Colomb, Sir Julian Stafford Corbett, author of *Some Principles of Maritime Strategy* (1911), like his predecessors drew "principles of maritime warfare" from history, only to have the sea officers of his day argue that technological and material superiority were far more important than "lessons" predating their own era.[1] A parallel development occurred during the same years within the armies of Europe, reflected in Germany's "Schlieffen plan" and other war plans of the great powers. On land as well as at sea, strategy prevailed over tactics amid an obsession with technology and the rapid mobilization of superior force. Appreciation of the past reached an unprecedented low.

Those seeking to learn from the naval warfare of their own era found the study of the Russo-Japanese War frustrating indeed, as it had featured such a variety of action by ships of so many types that it yielded no universally recognized lessons. The fighting opened with a torpedo attack, yet submarines played no role in the war. Destroyers were used in combat for the first time, employed effectively by both sides. Mines claimed three new battleships – two Japanese and one Russian – and fear of mines influenced operations throughout the conflict. International attention ultimately focused on the fact that the quick-firing guns in the secondary armament of battleships and armored cruisers – the guns that had inflicted the most damage on the enemy in the major battles of the Sino-Japanese and Spanish–American wars – had done little damage at the Battle of the Yellow Sea or at Tsushima, engagements in which the big guns of the Russian and Japanese navies had opened fire at unprecedented distances. Even the Russians, not known for their expertise in fire control, hit the Japanese flagship *Mikasa* from 7,000 meters in the opening exchange at Tsushima. While some historians draw a direct connection between Tsushima and the subsequent popularity of all big-gun battleships (modeled after the British *Dreadnought*) and battle cruisers, others see the dreadnought era as a new departure that rendered meaningless any potential lessons of the Russo-Japanese War, a conflict fought in the pre-dreadnought era.[2]

Accidental revolution

If the "lesson" presented in 1904–5 by long-range fire of unprecedented accuracy helped accelerate the rush to build dreadnoughts, it played no role in the actual genesis of the all big-gun battleship. In 1903 *Jane's Fighting Ships* published an article proposing "An ideal battleship for the British navy," authored by Vittorio Cuniberti, chief engineer of the Italian navy. At first Cuniberti had offered the all big-gun design to his own navy, only to have it rejected as impractical. The Japanese navy was the first in the world to order all big-gun battleships, contracting for two in late 1904, months before Tsushima and a year before the *Dreadnought* was laid down. The ships were designed to displace 19,370 tons and carry twelve 12-inch guns, but at the time Japan still imported all of its heavy naval ordnance from Britain, and with the Russo-Japanese War still underway the cost and importation of the guns posed serious difficulties. The first of the battleships, the *Satsuma*, was laid down at the Kure Navy Yard in May 1905, five months before work began on the *Dreadnought*, but the vessel and its eventual sister-ship were completed with a mixed armament of 12- and 10-inch guns, and would hold the distinction of being not only Japan's last pre-dreadnoughts, but the largest pre-dreadnoughts ever built by any navy.[3] The man behind the construction of the revolutionary *Dreadnought*, Admiral Sir John Fisher, likewise developed the idea long before Tsushima. He came to the post of First Sea Lord in October 1904 already convinced of the need for a new type of capital ship dominated by a single caliber of gun. His analysis of the wars of the 1890s led him initially to advocate the largest possible quick-firing gun; at least one historian believes that Fisher's preference, as of 1904, was for a large armored cruiser with 9.2-inch guns.[4] If the Russo-Japanese War had any impact on Fisher's thinking, it was in his adoption, by 1905, of the 12-inch gun as the uniform armament for his new capital ships.

In October 1905, twelve months after Fisher became First Sea Lord, the *Dreadnought* was laid down at Portsmouth. Upon entering service in December 1906, the new battleship was hailed as the most powerful ever built, and well before the outbreak of war in 1914 all battleships that were not "dreadnoughts" were considered obsolete. For decades naval historians, influenced by the works of Arthur J. Marder, considered Fisher a disciple of Mahan and a visionary who foresaw the way of the future pointing inevitably toward the fast, all big-gun battleship. It was Fisher who made sure that Britain pioneered the new type, in the process gambling away the pre-dreadnought battleship superiority his country had built up since the Naval Defence Act of 1889 and touching off a new international naval arms race. But in recent years the studies of Jon Tetsuro Sumida and his supporters have led to a new understanding of Fisher as an unorthodox strategist who scoffed at the lessons of naval history touted by

Mahan, and thus a man at odds with the theoretical premises that shaped the overall naval discourse of his age.[5]

When Fisher became First Sea Lord he did, indeed, push for an entirely new type of capital ship, not a battleship but a "fusion" of a battleship and armored cruiser, eventually known as a battle cruiser. Fisher's formative experiences as a naval officer in the last decades of the nineteenth century left him with firm convictions that Britain's long-term naval interests were global, not European; that the threats to British security at sea would come from France or the Franco-Russian combination; and that the conditions which had made the anti-British Jeune École plausible in the 1880s could, and probably would, return. Fisher feared that the accurate range of torpedoes would outstrip the range of accurate battleship gunfire, and saw great potential in the destroyer and especially the submarine as new delivery platforms for torpedo attacks against larger warships. These factors, combined with his reading of Britain's global strategic situation, led Fisher to conclude that the ideal British capital ship of the future would be larger and more heavily armed than any existing battleship or armored cruiser, and also faster, thanks to turbine engines and weight saved by reduced armor protection. The combination of superior speed, a uniform battery of guns, and improved fire control systems would give Fisher's battle cruiser the ability to catch and sink any armored cruiser, and to outgun any battleship from a distance at which its own relatively weak armor would not be a liability. From the perspective of 1904, Fisher envisioned a future in which battle cruisers would gradually replace pre-dreadnought battleships, as the latter neared the end of their service lives, defending British interests worldwide while flotillas of destroyers and submarines, backed by old battleships of the reserve fleet, protected the British Isles from enemy attack. After letting others take the lead in early submarine development, thanks to Fisher the British navy by 1914 had more submarines than any other navy. While the capital ship program attracted the most attention, on Fisher's watch the share of the construction budget devoted to flotilla craft rose from less than one-tenth in 1904 to almost a quarter in 1909.

Planning for his first program of capital ships, to be laid down in 1905–6, Fisher proposed three battle cruisers (17,370 tons, 567 feet long, eight 12-inch guns, 6-inch armor, with a speed of 25 knots) and, to placate battleship proponents, one battleship (18,110 tons, 527 feet long, ten 12-inch guns, 11-inch armor, with a speed of 21 knots). The battleship (the *Dreadnought*) was laid down first, in October 1905, to be completed as quickly as possible in order to serve as a test platform for the combination of unprecedented size, all big-gun armament, and turbine engines. The three battle cruisers (the *Invincible* class) were laid down in the early months of 1906, to be completed late enough to incorporate any lessons derived from the sea trials of the *Dreadnought*.

There is evidence that Fisher hoped the *Dreadnought* would be the last British battleship ever built, and that all subsequent capital ships would be battle cruisers. But in December 1905, when planning the program for 1906–7, Fisher could

Plate 8.1 HMS *Dreadnought* (laid down October 1905, completed December 1906)
Naval Historical Center, Basic Collection

find no support for his strategic vision even among his own protégés, thanks to changes in the international arena. By then, the Anglo-French entente of 1904, greeted with skepticism by most British navy men, had survived the test of the Moroccan crisis of 1905, and the Russo-Japanese War had all but destroyed the Russian navy. The growing German navy now appeared to be the likely future adversary, and by 1907 a common fear of Germany would motivate an Anglo-Russian rapprochement, completing the Triple Entente. Britain's grow-ing friendship with France and Russia invalidated Fisher's strategic premises, and the battle cruiser, with its global reach for a war against those powers now unnecessary, lost out to the battleship, which would be needed for a future confrontation with Germany in the North Sea. Much to Fisher's dismay, the *Dreadnought* – which he had never intended to replicate – became the model capital ship rather than the *Invincible*. After being completed in an unprecedented fourteen months, a building time never since matched for a capital ship, the *Dreadnought* impressed all critics during its trials. The ship's improved 12-inch guns proved capable of firing two rounds per minute, a rate three times faster than that of the 12-inch guns of *Majestic*, completed just a decade earlier. Its powerful Parsons turbine engines, of a type first installed experimentally in the destroyer *Viper* six years earlier, also did not disappoint, and had the added advantage of weighing hundreds of tons less than reciprocating engines with similar power. The program for 1906–7 included the three dreadnoughts of the 18,800-ton *Bellerophon* class, and for 1907–8, the three dreadnoughts of the 19,560-ton *St Vincent* class. All had the *Dreadnought's* layout of ten 12-inch guns paired in five turrets, three on the centerline and two amidships, abreast of the superstructure, and all were powered by Parsons turbine engines. Fisher had to wait until the 1908–9 program for another battle cruiser, the 18,500-ton *Indefatigable*, authorized along with an eighth dreadnought, the 19,680-ton *Neptune*.

The completion of the *Dreadnought* had an immediate impact on the ship-building programs of every other significant navy in the world. Throughout the evolution of the seagoing armored warship – the replacement of the broadside ironclad with the casemate ship, and the casemate ship with the various barbette and turret ships of the pre-dreadnought generation – old types had continued to be built alongside the new in overlapping years of transition. But December 1906 brought the sudden death of the pre-dreadnought battleship; indeed, not since the first ironclads spelled the end of the wooden screw ship of the line, forty-five years earlier, had a new type of capital ship so completely doomed its predecessor. Only eight pre-dreadnought battleships were begun after the completion of the *Dreadnought*: the last five ships of France's *Danton* class, and the three of Austria–Hungary's *Radetzky* class. Within seven years those countries and the other great powers of Europe – Germany, Russia, and Italy – all had dreadnoughts in service or nearing completion, as did the non-European great powers, the United States and Japan. By 1913 even Spain had built a dread-nought, and Greece and Turkey had ordered dreadnoughts in foreign shipyards, as had the three leading naval powers of South America – Argentina, Brazil, and Chile. Like nuclear weapons in the latter decades of the twentieth century, possession of dreadnoughts meant that a country counted for something in global or regional balances of power, and the ability to build them from one's own domestic resources became the measure of true great power status.

Fisher failed to realize his dream of having the battle cruiser replace the battleship; instead, the emergence of the battle cruiser all but killed the armored cruiser, a very popular ship type in the quarter-century preceding 1905. After the first of the *Invincibles* was laid down in February 1906, work began on just four armored cruisers: the French *Waldeck–Rousseau* later in 1906, and the German *Blücher*, Italian *San Marco*, and Greek *Georgios Averof*, all in 1907. Meanwhile, the gap in tonnage between capital ships (dreadnoughts and battle cruisers) and other units continued to widen. Between 1905 and 1914 no navy laid down an unarmored or protected cruiser larger than 5,500 tons, and construction of these types all but ceased except in Britain, which laid down forty-one, and Germany, which began twenty-six. Japan and Italy laid down six each, Austria–Hungary and Russia four, the United States and France none at all. Significant cruiser construction did not resume until the Washington Naval Treaty of 1922 placed limitations on warships of over 10,000 tons with more than 8-inch guns, after which navies again ordered large numbers of armored and protected cruisers, many of them "treaty cruisers" built up to the new tonnage limit.[6]

While countries were quick to abandon the pre-dreadnought battleship in favor of the dreadnought, ultimately only Germany and Japan copied the battle cruiser. In the case of either capital ship type, much time was lost in the preparation of new designs and the development of capacities to copy the British achievement in building ships of such size, with so many heavy guns and capable of such speeds. The United States, which laid down the dreadnought *Michigan* in May 1906, was the only country other than Britain with an all big-gun battleship under construction as of December 1906, and the only other country not forced into a hiatus in its building program. Ironically, in a time of universal faith in big battleships, many navies experienced their longest lapses in battleship construction since the Jeune École of the 1880s. In its quest to narrow the margin of Britain's naval superiority Germany welcomed the clean slate but did not lay down its first dreadnoughts until June 1907, after having begun its last pre-dreadnought in 1905. In Japan the gap between construction starts of the last pre-dreadnought and first dreadnought lasted from March 1906 to January 1909, in Russia, from April 1904 to June 1909, and in Italy, from October 1903 to June 1909. Decisions by Austria–Hungary and France to proceed with pre-dreadnought programs already approved before the end of 1906 delayed the onset of work on their first dreadnoughts to July 1910 and September 1910, respectively.

Britain and Germany

Germany's four *Nassau* class dreadnoughts were begun between June and August of 1907. The design of 18,900 tons was over 40 percent larger than the last pre-dreadnoughts of the *Deutschland* class, but like the last two classes of German pre-dreadnoughts the *Nassau*s mounted 11.1-inch guns and were powered by triple-expansion engines, the latter leaving them capable of just 19.5 knots compared to the 21 knots of the first British dreadnoughts. They carried their twelve heavy guns paired in six turrets, two fore and two aft on the centerline and two on either beam; thus, like the first British dreadnoughts, they could not train all of their guns for a broadside. The *Nassau* entered service in October 1909, by which time Britain already had commissioned its first five dreadnoughts and three battle cruisers.[7]

But by early March 1909 Germany had laid down the last of four dreadnoughts of the *Helgoland* class, larger (at 22,800 tons) and more heavily armed (with 12-inch guns) than the *Nassau*s, though still powered by triple expansion engines. The 15,800-ton armored cruiser *Blücher* (counted by the British as a battle cruiser), the 19,400-ton battle cruiser *Von der Tann*, and the 23,000-ton battle cruiser *Moltke* also were under construction; the battle cruisers were the first German capital ships with turbine engines. Tirpitz, unlike Fisher, had no great love for the battle cruiser design, but Germany began building them because he could count them under the "large cruiser" category of the navy laws already passed, and thus eventually have a battle fleet of fifty-eight capital ships (thirty-eight dreadnoughts and twenty battle cruisers). Furthermore, through a supplementary navy law in 1908, Tirpitz had secured Reichstag approval to accelerate future battleship construction. Meanwhile, Britain's Liberal government had approved only two capital ships (the dreadnought *Neptune* and battle cruiser *Indefatigable*) in the naval estimates for 1908–9, giving Britain a total of twelve built or building at a time when Germany had ten. Thus Tirpitz was on track to achieve much better than the 3:2 ratio of inferiority which he felt would give the German High Sea Fleet a chance of defeating the British in the North Sea.

The Anglo-German naval arms race was on, and by the first months of 1909 the projected pace of German construction had caused a near panic in Britain. At the end of March 1909 Parliament approved the naval estimates for 1909–10, including three dreadnoughts and one battle cruiser to be laid down before the end of 1909, with another three dreadnoughts and one battle cruiser to be laid down no later than April 1910 unless Germany agreed to negotiate a settlement with Britain to end the naval race. Navalist political circles in Britain were arguing for a "two-German" standard, which Germany would never accept, but the Admiralty in April 1909 quietly dropped the traditional two-power standard and was willing to negotiate on the basis of a 60 percent capital ship superiority over Germany. In the first months of 1909, however, Tirpitz's best offer was to concede a 4:3 ratio of British superiority. With no prospect for an Anglo-German treaty, in July 1909 Parliament authorized the navy to lay down the four conditional capital ships in the spring of 1910. The "four-plus-four" program was to be funded through sweeping tax increases, mostly at the expense of the wealthy, a fact which delayed approval in the House of Lords for several months. By May 1910 Britain had under construction two 20,225-ton *Colossus* class dreadnoughts, four 20,220-ton *Orion* class dreadnoughts, and two 26,270-ton *Lion* class battle cruisers. The British advantage would be qualitative as well as quantitative, as the *Orion*s and *Lion*s had 13.5-inch guns rather than 12-inch guns, and the *Lion*s would be capable of a remarkable 27 knots. Peoples of the empire soon did their share as well. In June 1910 British shipyards laid down another two battle cruisers, copies of the 18,500-ton *Indefatigable* named *Australia* and *New Zealand*, paid for by those two dominions.

Tirpitz miscalculated terribly in assuming the British would not have the will to construct enough dreadnoughts and battle cruisers to remain safely ahead of the German build-up. During the months when the British laid down their ten new capital ships, the Germans started work on just three: the first two dreadnoughts of the 24,700-ton *Kaiser* class and the 23,000-ton battle cruiser *Goeben*, a sister-ship of the *Moltke*. The construction starts of June 1910 left Britain with twenty-two battleships or battle cruisers built and building, compared to thirteen for Germany. Shortly after Parliament passed the naval estimates for 1909–10, Tirpitz all but admitted to the chief of the naval cabinet, Admiral Georg von

Müller, that the race was lost. Within a year he agreed to negotiate a settlement based on a 3:2 (15:10) ratio of British capital ship superiority, very close to the Admiralty's new 60 percent (16:10) standard of superiority over Germany. But Tirpitz wanted to count "dominion ships" such as the *Australia* and *New Zealand* in the British total, and Germany's new chancellor, Theobald von Bethmann Hollweg, wanted to link any German ratification of British superiority at sea to a British recognition of the status quo on land in Europe, including Germany's possession of Alsace–Lorraine. Such conditions eliminated any possibility of a deal, as the Admiralty considered ships paid for by the dominions a non-negotiable supplement to the British program, and Britain's foreign secretary, Sir Edward Grey, had no intention of destroying the Anglo-French entente by guaranteeing a German Alsace–Lorraine.

In their budgets for 1910–11 Germany laid down three more *Kaiser* class dreadnoughts and the 25,000-ton battle cruiser *Seydlitz*, but Britain countered with the four dreadnoughts of the 23,000-ton *King George V* class and the 26,770-ton battle cruiser *Queen Mary*. In the following fiscal year the Germans began the first three dreadnoughts of the 25,800-ton *König* class and the 26,600-ton battle cruiser *Derfflinger*, but the British once again laid down four dreadnoughts, the 25,000-ton *Iron Duke* class, along with the 28,430-ton battle cruiser *Tiger*, at 704 feet the longest capital ship begun before the outbreak of the First World War. Further attempts at a negotiated end to the naval race hinged on informal contacts between British banker Sir Ernest Cassel and German steamship magnate Albert Ballin, which led, in February 1912, to a visit to Berlin by Lord Richard Haldane, the British secretary for war. The "Haldane mission" ultimately failed, as Germany sought broader assurances of British neutrality in any German war against a continental European power, while the British would only pledge not to support a war of aggression against Germany. Winston Churchill, recently appointed First Lord of the Admiralty, proposed a one-year "naval holiday" later in 1912, but Germans better remembered his derisive characterization of the German navy as a "luxury" fleet. Tirpitz soon secured passage of another supplementary navy law which added three dreadnoughts to the numbers previously approved. Thus the Reichstag raised the authorized strength of the fleet to sixty-one capital ships, to be built as forty-one dreadnoughts and twenty battle cruisers, but the triumph was Tirpitz's last. The navy's budget had grown to consume more than one-third of Germany's total defense outlay, a trend finally reversed in 1913, when legislation provided for a dramatic expansion of the German army. The German naval estimates for 1912–13 included construction starts for just two capital ships (the last dreadnought of the *König* class and the 26,700-ton battle cruiser *Lützow*) and for 1913–14, three (the first two dreadnoughts of the 28,500-ton *Bayern* class and the 27,000-ton battle cruiser *Ersatz Hertha*).

In Britain, meanwhile, the naval estimates for the same two years provided for nine dreadnoughts, with a tenth, the *Malaya*, funded by the subjects of that British colony. Five of the warships were of the 27,500-ton *Queen Elizabeth* class, and five of the 28,000-ton *Royal Sovereign* class. They were the first British capital ships with 15-inch guns (eight, paired in four centerline turrets). The *Queen Elizabeth*s were the first battleships fitted to burn oil only; from 1912 the Admiralty would be the primary customer of the newly-established Anglo-Persian Oil Company.[8] As for the battle cruiser, Fisher's retirement in 1910 appeared to spell the end of the type in Britain. The Admiralty laid down none after the *Tiger* (June 1912), but more would be ordered during the First World War, after Fisher returned to the office of First Sea Lord in October 1914.

The increasing size of warships naturally drove up their cost. The *Dreadnought* had been built for just under £1.73 million, but the *Queen Elizabeth*s – laid down seven years later – cost just over £2.68 million. On the German side, the *Nassau* had been built for just under 37 million marks, while the *Ersatz Hertha* – commissioned during the war with the name *Hindenburg* – cost 59 million.[9] At the end of July 1914, Britain had forty-two of the new capital ships (thirty-three dreadnoughts and nine battle cruisers) built or building, of which twenty-nine (twenty-one dreadnoughts and eight battle cruisers) were in service. Germany had twenty-six (nineteen dreadnoughts and seven battle cruisers) built or building, of which eighteen (fourteen dreadnoughts and four battle cruisers) were in service. The British advantage, slightly better than 3:2, would suffice to keep the German High Sea Fleet in port for much of the war. Faced with the hopelessness of defeating the British navy in a surface fleet action, after the outbreak of war Tirpitz executed another of the opportunistic philosophical about-faces that had characterized his rise to power within the German navy before 1897, emerging as an advocate of submarine warfare. Ironically, before the outbreak of war in 1914 Germany had completed just thirty-six submarines, fewer than each of the three navies of the Triple Entente.[10]

The United States and Japan

Only the United States came close to keeping pace with the construction programs of Britain and Germany, even though the American navy, like the British and German, had just spent a fortune on several classes of pre-dreadnoughts. By 1908 the US fleet included twenty-six battleships and fifteen armored cruisers completed within the past fifteen years. During the decade 1899 through 1908 the five battleships and two armored cruisers in commission over the course of the Spanish–American War were joined by ever-larger classes of battleships: the two vessels of the 11,540-ton *Kearsarge* class, three of the 11,565-ton *Illinois* class, three 12,850-ton *Maines*, five 14,950-ton *Virginias*, and six 16,000-ton *Connecticuts* and *Vermonts*. These were followed by the two ill-conceived *Mississippis*, a 13,000-ton design approved by the US Congress over the objections of President Theodore Roosevelt and Admiral Dewey. All carried a typical pre-dreadnought armament of four heavy guns paired in two centerline turrets fore and aft. The *Kearsarge* and *Illinois* classes copied the 13-inch guns of the earlier *Indiana* class, but all others carried 12-inch guns. Experimentation with numbers and calibers of secondary armament ended with the adoption of a standard layout of eight 8-inch guns for the *Virginia*s, *Connecticut*s, *Vermont*s, and *Mississippi*s. The battleships of the *Kearsarge* and *Virginia* classes carried four of their secondary guns paired in superposed turrets atop the turrets of their primary guns. The unique arrangement eliminated the weight and space of two sets of turret-turning machinery, but the stacked turrets could not turn independently. Armored cruisers completed during the same years included six 13,680-ton *Pennsylvania*s, four 14,500-ton *Tennessee*s, and three ships of the 9,700-ton *St Louis* class. The four *Tennessee*s were the most heavily armed warships of their type in any navy, their primary armament of four 10-inch guns making them the practical equivalent of second-class battleships. In the decade after the Spanish–American War the United States commissioned just nine more protected cruisers, all displacing between 3,000 and 4,000 tons, and added four new monitors to placate coast-defense advocates. During the same years the first twenty destroyers and another twenty torpedo boats entered service. Irish-born John Philip Holland designed the first submarine commissioned by the US navy, the USS *Holland* of 1900. While the American submarine designs of Holland and Simon Lake were copied worldwide, the US navy added just thirty-one more by the outbreak of the First World War, to rank fifth in the world in numbers of submarines.[11]

The navy prospered in no small measure thanks to the enthusiastic support of Roosevelt, a former assistant secretary of the navy and author of a naval history of the War of 1812. In his 1907 State of the Union address he reflected the extent to which his staunch navalism had been influenced by the works of Mahan, remarking that "in time of war the navy is not to be used to defend harbors and sea-coast cities. . . . The only efficient use for the navy is for offense. The only way in which it can efficiently protect our coast against the possible action of a foreign navy is by destroying that navy."[12] Later that year, Roosevelt ordered a world cruise by his navy's newest battleships as a demonstration of American naval power. The "Great White Fleet," or "Battle Fleet," as it was officially known, consisted of sixteen battleships, escorted by destroyers and auxiliary ships. The fleet covered 42,000 miles in a westward circumnavigation of the globe between December 1907 and February 1909, visiting the major ports of Latin America, the western United States and Hawaii, the western Pacific, the Indian Ocean, and the Mediterranean. It was fitting that the American battleships made their cruise wearing coats of archaic Victorian-era peacetime white. The fleet of pre-dreadnoughts was already obsolete by the time it left Hampton Roads, twelve months after the completion of the *Dreadnought* in Britain. The first American dreadnought, the 16,000-ton *Michigan*, had been laid down in May 1906, just one year after work began on the last pre-dreadnought, the *New Hampshire*. Some attribute this rapid transition to the future admiral William S. Sims, an innovative thinker and personal friend of Roosevelt, being briefed unofficially by British navy contacts on the advantages of Fisher's *Dreadnought* design, then still under construction in great secrecy.

In any event, the *Michigan*'s sister-ship *South Carolina*, and the 20,380-ton *Delaware* and *North Dakota*, all were on the stocks by the time the "Great White Fleet" returned home. All four were completed in 1910.[13]

The US Congress refused to support a long-term program of dreadnought construction, but until the outbreak of the First World War it became the norm for two of the ships to be laid down every year. Thus the navy continued to build all of its dreadnoughts in pairs: the 21,825-ton *Florida* and *Utah* (built 1909–11), the 26,000-ton *Wyoming* and *Arkansas* (1910–12), the 27,000-ton *New York* and *Texas* (1911–14), the 27,500-ton *Nevada* and *Oklahoma* (1912–16), and the 31,400-ton *Pennsylvania* (1913–16) and *Arizona* (1914–16). The *Michigan* and its sister were not only small but relatively lightly armed, with eight 12-inch guns paired in four turrets. The next four had ten 12-inch guns in five turrets, and the *Wyoming* and *Arkansas* twelve in six turrets. The *New York* and *Texas* pioneered the 14-inch gun, with ten paired in five turrets. In the *Nevada* and *Oklahoma*, the same primary armament was arranged in two turrets of three guns and two of two guns, while the *Pennsylvania* and *Arizona* carried twelve 14-inch guns in four triple-gun turrets. In contrast to the early British and German designs, all American dreadnoughts mounted all of their heavy guns in centerline turrets. The *Michigan*, *South Carolina*, and four other American dreadnoughts had triple-expansion engines, the rest turbine engines. The *Nevada* and *Oklahoma*, like their British contemporaries of the *Queen Elizabeth* class, were designed to burn oil only, as were subsequent American dreadnoughts. The United States never embraced the battle cruiser design and laid down no cruisers of any type between 1905 and 1918. At the end of the First World War six battle cruisers were ordered but four were broken up on the stocks under the Washington Naval Treaty of 1922 and two (the *Lexington* and *Saratoga*) completed as aircraft carriers.[14]

The US naval build-up alarmed the Japanese, who considered the Americans their most likely enemy at sea after the defeat of the Russians. After Theodore Roosevelt mediated the Treaty of Portsmouth (5 September 1905), formally ending the Russo-Japanese War, the antagonism gradually worsened. At the Naval Staff College in 1907–9, Japanese theorist Tetsutaro Sato developed the notion that, to have any chance of victory, Japan must have a navy at least 70 percent the strength of the US navy. For the next three decades the 70 percent standard remained an article of faith for the Japanese navy. The friendly reception given the "Great White Fleet" at Yokohama in the autumn of 1908 hardly reflected the true state of the relationship between Japan and the United States.[15] Japan's growing naval strength likewise concerned the United States, whose Pacific empire stretched from Hawaii to the Philippines. Nevertheless, under Roosevelt's presidency the peacetime deployment of the fleet reflected the continued, if not increased, primacy of the Atlantic in American naval strategy. In 1901 the United States had seven battleships dispersed among five stations worldwide, along with its armored and protected cruisers. During Roosevelt's presidency the stations were abolished in favor of an Atlantic and a Pacific fleet, each organized and trained in peacetime for service in wartime, as were the principal European fleets. In 1909, the Atlantic fleet consisted of twenty battle-ships and two armored cruisers – including all the battleships of the recently returned "Great White Fleet" – while the Pacific fleet, formally established during 1908, had as its largest warships eight armored cruisers of the *Pennsylvania* and *Tennessee* classes. In the event of war with Japan, Roosevelt planned to withdraw the Pacific fleet to California, temporarily sacrificing the Philippines and even Hawaii while marshalling a force with sufficient superiority to ensure decisive victory in a counterattack.[16]

While the United States had commissioned a fleet of soon-to-be-obsolete pre-dreadnoughts by 1908, after its victory in 1905 the Japanese navy focused its attention on refitting the eight battleships, the armored cruiser, and the three protected cruisers captured from the Russians. Except for one battleship, all were in service by 1908, but some were woefully obsolete by then: the battleship *Iki* (ex-*Nikolai I*) displaced just 9,700 tons, two others were coastal battleships of under 5,000 tons, and the armored cruiser *Aso* (ex-*Bayan*) displaced just 7,800 tons. In 1906 the Japanese took delivery of their last foreign-built battleships, the 16,400-ton *Kashima* (from Armstrong) and *Katori* (from Vickers), improved versions of the *King Edward VII* class ordered just before the outbreak of the war in 1904. Their four 12-inch guns were backed by a formidable secondary arma-ment of four 10-inch guns. Japan's first projected all big-gun battleships, the 19,370-ton *Satsuma* (laid down in May 1905) and its sister-ship *Aki* (March 1906), were completed with a similar mixture of 12- and 10-inch guns. The largest pre-dreadnoughts ever built by any navy, they were obsolete by the time they entered service in 1910–11.[17]

The 21,440-ton *Settsu* and *Kawachi*, laid down in 1909 and completed in 1912, were Japan's first dreadnoughts. Their twelve 12-inch guns were imported Armstrongs, but their Brown–Curtis turbine engines were made in Japan, under license by Kawasaki. Their armor, too, was manufactured in Japan, which had first produced Krupp armor under license for the two 13,750-ton armored cruisers of the *Tsukuba* class, laid down in Kure early in 1905 as replacements for the battleships *Hatsuse* and *Yashima*, lost to Russian mines earlier in the war. These warships, and the two 14,640-ton armored cruisers of the subsequent *Ibuki* class, eventually were re-rated as battle cruisers, owing to their large size and heavy primary armament of four 12-inch guns.[18] After laying down the *Settsu* and *Kawachi*, Japan waited three years to begin another dreadnought. The 30,600-ton *Fuso* (built 1912–15) and *Yamashiro* (1913–17) were the only other Japanese dreadnoughts under construction when war broke out in the summer of 1914. The first true Japanese battle cruiser, the 27,500-ton *Kongo*, was ordered from Vickers in 1911 and delivered in 1913. By then, three sister ships had been laid down in Japanese shipyards, all of which were in service by 1915. To match the guns of the newest American dreadnoughts, the Japanese adopted the 14-inch gun for the *Fusos* (which mounted twelve, paired in six centerline turrets) and the *Kongos* (eight, in four centerline turrets). The last two *Kongos* were the first capital ships built by private Japanese shipyards: the *Haruna* by Kawasaki at Kobe, and the *Kirishima* by Mitsubishi at Nagasaki.

Ever since 1910, the Japanese navy had as its goal an "eight–eight" fleet of eight battleships and eight battle cruisers. Counting the four large pre-dreadnought battleships commissioned after the Russo-Japanese War and the four large armored cruisers re-rated as battle cruisers, Japan had its "eight–eight" fleet built or building when the First World War began. But the core of the Japanese battle fleet fell far short of 70 percent of the strength of the US navy, which had ten dreadnoughts in service and another four under construction by 1914. Six dreadnoughts and four battle cruisers begun after 1915 gave Japan an "eight–eight" fleet of dreadnought battleships and true battle cruisers built or building by 1921, just in time for the Washington Naval Treaty to cancel part of the program.[19] Like the US navy during the same years, Japan laid down few smaller unarmored warships between 1905 and 1918. The Japanese had no submarines in service until shortly after the end of the Russo-Japanese War, when five Holland-type boats were commissioned. Another seven were added by 1914.[20]

The delivery of the battle cruiser *Kongo* after its completion by Vickers in August 1913 bore witness to the fact that the Anglo-Japanese alliance was alive, if not altogether well, on the eve of the First World War. The alliance of 1902 had lost its *raison d'être* with the virtual elimination of the Russian threat in the Far East, and in the post-1905 naval rivalry between Japan and the United States British sympathies clearly lay with the Americans. At Britain's insistence, in 1911 the Anglo-Japanese treaty was amended to stipulate that neither party ever would be obligated to fight the United States. This revision disappointed the traditionally anglophile Japanese navy and prompted its leaders to place far less value on their British connection.[21]

Italy and Austria–Hungary

While Germany measured its naval progress against that of Britain, and Japan against that of the United States, in the years before 1914 a naval race broke out in the Adriatic between Italy and Austria–Hungary. Though members of the same alliance, their mutual animosity ran deep. Italian claims against the Dual Monarchy's territory and the Italian threat to its coastline gave Austro-Hungarian naval leaders a strong case for a battle fleet deterrent, indeed, one resting on a more solid foundation than Tirpitz's argument against Britain, which by no stretch of the imagination posed a threat to the German coast in the North Sea. By 1906 Austria–Hungary had developed first-rate shipyards and supporting industries, and its navy enjoyed the patronage of Archduke Francis Ferdinand and the support of a broad domestic political coalition. Yet the fleet lagged far behind its Italian rival in the number, size, and strength of capital ships. Like Germany in its contest with Britain, for Austria–Hungary the dreadnought era erased Italy's quantitative advantage, and gave the pursuing power the opportunity to catch up.

Even before the construction of dreadnoughts became an issue, the passage of time promised to erode the Italian advantage. At the end of 1905 Italy had eighteen battleships, counting those under construction and all others completed since 1880, while Austria–Hungary had twelve, but in battleships laid down since 1893, Italy had eight to Austria–Hungary's nine. The Italian navy still enjoyed a qualitative advantage, however, as the Austro-Hungarian total included the three 5,600-ton *Monarchs* and no warships larger than the three 10,600-ton *Erzherzogs*, while all of Italy's newer battleships displaced 10,000 tons or more. By 1905 Italy had six armored cruisers to Austria–Hungary's three, with four more (ranging in size from 9,800 to 10,700 tons) laid down by 1907. Austria–Hungary built no armored cruisers after completing the *Sankt Georg* in 1905.[22]

Even though the Italian navy's chief engineer Cuniberti had advocated the all big-gun battleship as early as 1903, Italy did not lay down its first dreadnought until June 1909, almost six years after work began on the last Italian pre-dreadnoughts of the *Regina Elena* class. In the meantime, a scandal over armor contracts with the Terni steelworks had led to a parliamentary investigation that paralyzed naval construction until 1906; thereafter, Italian shipyards focused on completing the program of armored cruisers.[23] Meanwhile, in Austria–Hungary the naval estimates for 1907, including construction starts for the three 14,500-ton *Radetzky* class battleships, won parliamentary approval in November 1906, a month before the completion of the *Dreadnought*. The *Radetzkys* were roughly the equivalent of the British pre-dreadnoughts of the *Lord Nelson* class, with a primary armament of four 12-inch guns and a secondary battery of eight 9.4-inch guns, a caliber as heavy as the primary armament of the previous three classes of Austro-Hungarian battleship. When the first of the class was laid down in September 1907, it caused a sensation in Italy, which at the time had no battleships as large or as formidable.[24]

Italian navy leaders sought to counter the threat the *Radetzkys* would pose upon their completion, and included funding in their estimates for the fiscal year 1907–8 to start a dreadnought program. The cost of such ships, at a time when Italy's regional naval rivals, Austria–Hungary and France, were still building pre-dreadnoughts, caused enough controversy in the Italian parliament to postpone the project. A new sense of urgency followed Austria–Hungary's annexation of Bosnia–Hercegovina in September 1908, which touched off a European war scare. Italian public and political opinion turned strongly anti-Austrian, the Triple Alliance appeared to be a dead letter, and by the end of the year panicky Italian admirals were calling for a 2:1 ratio of superiority over the Austro-Hungarian navy, a standard their government rejected on financial grounds. Meanwhile, citing the danger of war with Italy, in January 1909 the Austro-Hungarian naval commander Admiral Count Rudolf Montecuccoli sent a memorandum to Emperor Francis Joseph calling for a new fleet plan to include four 20,000-ton dreadnoughts. Three months later the plan was reported in the press, long before anything had been done to implement it. By then the furor over Bosnia had subsided, but the prospect of Austria–Hungary having four dreadnoughts in addition to the three *Radetzkys* finally moved the Italian parliament to authorize a dreadnought. In June 1909 the 19,550-ton *Dante Alighieri* was laid down at Castellammare. The ship's twelve 12-inch guns were to be carried in four triple-gun centerline turrets, the first use of the triple-gun turret in any dreadnought design.

By then, the long-rumored Austro-Hungarian dreadnought program had fallen victim to a constitutional crisis in Hungary. During a thirteen-month interregnum in Budapest starting in April 1909, no legislation affecting the common institutions of the Dual Monarchy (including the naval estimates) could be approved. Faced with a hiatus in their lucrative relationship with the navy, in July 1909 the Stabilimento Tecnico Triestino shipyard, Skoda gun factory, and Witkowitz armor works offered to construct dreadnoughts "at their own risk" with the understanding that the government would purchase them once the Hungarian crisis ended. Admiral Montecuccoli accepted the offer and Archduke Francis Ferdinand intervened with the Rothschild bank to arrange financing. By the time the press first reported the illegal arrangement in April 1910, materials for two dreadnoughts were being assembled in Trieste.

In Italy, meanwhile, there was no shortage of political will to remain ahead of Austria–Hungary in the incipient dreadnought race. The three 22,990-ton dreadnoughts of the *Cavour* class were laid down in June, July, and August of 1910. Upon completion they would be even more powerful than the *Dante Alighieri*, mounting thirteen 12-inch guns in three triple-gun and two double-gun turrets. In late July, a week after work began on the second *Cavour* (the third Italian dreadnought overall), the 20,000-ton *Viribus Unitis* was laid down in Trieste. The *Tegetthoff*, for which the class was named, followed in September. Like the *Dante Alighieri*, the *Tegetthoffs* were designed to carry twelve 12-inch guns in four triple-gun turrets on the centerline. With four Italian dreadnoughts already on the stocks, Montecuccoli had no trouble persuading the politicians of the need for the first two Austro-Hungarian dreadnoughts, which were approved retroactively in October 1910 along with the rest of the naval estimates for 1910. The following year's budget was not passed until March 1911, but with it came authorization to start two more dreadnoughts and parliamentary approval of a fleet plan including sixteen battleships, twelve cruisers, twenty-four destroyers, seventy-two torpedo boats, and twelve submarines, with ships to be replaced automatically after fixed terms of service as under Tirpitz's German navy laws.

In January 1912 work began on the third and fourth Austro-Hungarian dreadnoughts, the *Prinz Eugen* at Trieste and the *Szent István* at Fiume, the latter a "Hungarian" port whose shipyard had to be used for political reasons. Italy followed with its fifth and sixth dreadnoughts, laid down in February and March 1912. The 22,960-ton *Andrea Doria* and *Duilio* were considered a new class but were virtual copies of the *Cavours*, featuring the same layout of thirteen 12-inch guns. Owing to the greater efficiency of the Trieste shipyard, Austria–Hungary's *Viribus Unitis* entered service in October 1912, three months before Italy's *Dante Alighieri*, which had taken sixteen months longer to complete. Thus the Austro-Hungarian navy became the third in Europe to commission a dreadnought and the first to have one in service with triple-gun turrets. The *Tegetthoff* entered service in July 1913, followed by the first two *Cavours* in May 1914 and the *Prinz Eugen* in July 1914, giving both navies three dreadnoughts in service when the war began. Ironically, the tensions accompanying the onset of the Austro-Italian dreadnought race had disappeared by the time these ships were completed, as the Italo-Turkish War of 1911–12 temporarily poisoned Italy's relations with the countries of the Triple Entente and led to an unexpected renewal of the Triple Alliance in December 1912.

With German encouragement, in June 1913 Italy and Austria–Hungary negotiated a stronger Triple Alliance naval convention, which went into effect that November after all three allies ratified it. Because the British already were concentrating their fleet for a clash with the Germans in the North Sea, war plans drafted under the convention focused on the French navy in the western Mediterranean. In the event of war against the Triple Entente, Admiral Anton Haus (Montecuccoli's successor as Austro-Hungarian naval commander) would command a battle fleet consisting of the newest Italian and Austro-Hungarian warships, supplemented by whatever German units happened to be in the Mediterranean. Messina, on the coast of Sicily, was designated as the port of rendezvous, after which the allied fleet would advance westward, seeking battle with the French navy and to disrupt convoys of North African colonial troops to France. Despite ongoing mistrust between the Austro-Hungarian and Italian navies, the convention remained alive until 31 July 1914, when the Italian foreign minister characterized the Austro-Serbian war (then three days old) as an act of aggression by the Dual Monarchy, the consequences of which would not activate the *casus foederis* of the Triple Alliance. Italy's neutrality became official on 2 August. Nine-and-a-half months later, Italy entered the war on the side of the Entente.

In October 1913 the Austro-Hungarian council of ministers approved four 24,500-ton dreadnoughts, and in May 1914 parliamentarians included in a multi-year special credit of 426.8 million kronen the funds to lay down the first two warships of the new class. The sums now being spent on the fleet amounted to one-quarter of the entire defense outlay, and the amount of the special credit was staggering compared to the navy's pre-dreadnought budgets (as recently as 1907 the navy had received just 63.4 million). For political reasons Admiral Haus promised two of the contracts to Trieste and two to Fiume, even though the Stabilimento Tecnico Triestino completed its first three dreadnoughts in an average of thirty-one months – rivaling British and German shipyards in its efficiency – while Fiume's "Hungarian" shipyard would take forty-seven months to build the *Szent István*, which was finally ready in December 1915. With the onset of the First World War the four contracts were cancelled. Meanwhile, in Italy, four dreadnoughts of the 31,400-ton *Caracciolo* class were laid down after October 1914, but in the wake of Italy's declaration of war in May 1915 work was suspended and the ships were never completed. During the First World War the Austro-Hungarian and Italian dreadnoughts never met in action, the former spending the war as a fleet-in-being at Pola, the latter guarding the mouth of the Adriatic at Taranto (where Italian units were reinforced by British and French warships). Austria–Hungary's most active warships were the four 3,500-ton scout cruisers of the *Admiral Spaun* class and submarines operating out of Cattaro (Kotor) at the southern tip of Dalmatia. Seven submarines in service in 1914 were joined by another twenty during the war. Italy had three times as many submarines in service by the summer of 1914 and likewise made good use of undersea boats during the war, along with cruisers, destroyers, and high-speed motor torpedo boats.

Russia and France

By the end of 1905, losses in the war against Japan had reduced the active strength of Russia's navy, in the Pacific, the Baltic, and the Black Sea combined, to barely more than what Austria–Hungary had afloat in the Adriatic alone. Defeat at the hands of Japan brought great changes within Russia, affecting the navy along with other institutions. The Revolution of 1905 prompted Nicholas II to grant constitutional reforms, including an elected Duma which first met in the spring of 1906. The tsar abolished the position of "general admiral," a joint operational commander-in-chief and navy minister, in favor of a true navy minister, and in April 1906 created the Naval General Staff, which in 1909 drafted a construction program including Russia's first four dreadnoughts.[25]

During the hiatus before work began on the dreadnoughts, Russia's shipyards completed five pre-dreadnought battleships already on the stocks when the Russo-Japanese War ended: the 13,520-ton *Slava*, the 12,840-ton *Evstafi* and *Ioann Zlatoust*, and the 17,400-ton *Andrei Pervosvanni* and *Imperator Pavel*, all of which were in service by 1910. Two protected cruisers were completed in 1905, and the same year Russia laid down the 15,190-ton *Rurik* and three smaller armored cruisers, all of which were in service by 1911. In the meantime, the old battleships *Ekaterina II* and *Tschesma* were stricken in 1907, and the mutinous armored cruiser *Pamiat Azova* became a training ship. The net result by 1911 was an active fleet of thirteen battleships, six armored cruisers, and ten protected cruisers. Russia laid down no protected cruisers after 1902, but launched thirty-seven submarines and eleven large destroyers by 1914.[26]

The four dreadnoughts of the 23,360-ton *Gangut* class were laid down in June 1909 in St Petersburg; all would serve in the Baltic fleet after being commissioned in the last weeks of 1914. Influenced by the Italian designer Cuniberti, the final plan included twelve 12-inch guns in four triple-gun turrets on the centerline, with turbine engines capable of 23 knots. The Russian experience at Tsushima led to modifications in the design, including a near-complete armor plating of the hull above the waterline. After the four dreadnoughts were launched in 1911, four 32,500-ton battle cruisers of the *Borodino* class were laid down in the same slips, but none was ever completed. In 1911 the Duma approved an expansion of the Black Sea fleet, leading to three dreadnoughts of the 22,600-ton *Imperatritsa Maria* class being laid down at Nicolaiev. All three were commissioned in time to serve in the First World War, but a fourth Black Sea dreadnought, the 27,300-ton *Imperator Nikolai I*, was not begun until 1915 and never completed. The Black Sea dreadnoughts had the same layout of guns as the *Ganguts* but were even more heavily armored.[27]

The construction of so many dreadnoughts and battle cruisers in Russian shipyards consumed tremendous sums of money. Expenditure on the Russian navy rose from 87 million rubles in 1908 to 247 million in 1913,[28] resources perhaps better spent on the tsar's army or on civilian concerns. The Russian navy never had a clear strategy of how to use the new capital ships; indeed, after 1905 it seemed to have no strategy at all, other than to stand on the defensive. In 1909 the advance base of Libau on the Latvian coast, developed in the 1890s, was practically abandoned in favor of a strengthening of the Baltic bases at Reval, Vyborg, and Kronstadt. A 1912 plan drafted by the Naval General Staff confirmed that the Baltic fleet would remain on the defensive, protected by minefields and under the guns of powerful coastal batteries. Meanwhile, after the loss of Port Arthur to Japan, the Russian base at Vladivostok was expanded but only light warships were stationed there. Nothing was done to strengthen installations on the Black Sea.[29]

France, like Russia, approved a naval construction program in 1909. Vice Admiral Augustin Boué de Lapeyrère, newly-appointed minister of marine, devised and secured passage of the plans for the build-up, to be completed in 1919. The naval estimates for 1910 included construction starts for the first two dreadnoughts of the 22,190-ton *Courbet* class; another two were laid down in 1911. But the French navy paid dearly for its decision to proceed with the *Danton* class of six 18,320-ton pre-dreadnoughts, even though only the *Danton* itself had been laid down by the time the *Dreadnought* was completed. The last five *Danton*s were laid down between August 1907 and July 1908, and all six were commissioned in 1911.[30] By the time the *Courbet* was laid down in September 1910, ten other countries had dreadnoughts built or building (the other seven naval powers plus Spain, Argentina, and Brazil) and four had dreadnoughts already in service (Britain, Germany, the United States, and Brazil).

The *Courbet*s were followed by eight more dreadnoughts, the three 23,230-ton *Bretagne*s, laid down during 1912, and five 25,230-ton *Normandie*s, laid down by January 1914. The *Courbet*s carried their twelve 12-inch guns paired in six turrets, two fore and two aft on the centerline and two on either beam. The *Bretagne*s mounted ten 13.4-inch guns in five centerline turrets, while the *Normandie*s were designed with a revolutionary layout of twelve 13.4-inch guns in three centerline turrets of four guns each. The first of the *Courbet*s – the *Jean*

Bart – was completed in June 1913, the last of the class on 1 August 1914, giving France four dreadnoughts with another eight under construction when the war began. The three *Bretagnes* entered service during the war, but the *Normandies* were still on the stocks when the conflict ended. Four were never completed and the fifth, the *Béarn*, eventually became France's first aircraft carrier.[31]

Between 1905 and 1914, the expense of the French army's build-up against Germany, the decision to complete the program of *Dantons*, and an overall tight budget combined to cause France to drop rapidly from second to fifth place among the world's navies. Nevertheless, during the First World War the seven French dreadnoughts, backed by the six *Dantons*, more than sufficed to dominate the Mediterranean, which the British had all but conceded to the French after the failure of the "Haldane mission" to Berlin in 1912. First Lord of the Admiralty Winston Churchill shifted the battleships of the Mediterranean squadron to Gibraltar and subsequently ordered that all British dreadnoughts be available for action in the North Sea against Germany, reducing the force at Malta to a few battle cruisers and smaller warships. British public denials notwithstanding, Anglo-French naval commitments made during 1912 transformed the entente into an alliance, in which the British navy took responsibility for defending the French Channel and Atlantic coast against the German navy in exchange for the French navy defending Anglo-French interests in the Mediterranean against the possible combination of Italy and Austria–Hungary.[32]

Spain and Latin America

With a fleet a fraction the size of that of Austria–Hungary, Spain did not figure in the pre-1914 naval balance of power, even in the Mediterranean. The destruction of most of the Spanish navy in 1898 left the 9,745-ton pre-dreadnought *Pelayo* (commissioned in 1888) and 9,090-ton armored cruiser *Emperador Carlos V* (1898) as the largest warships. In the depressed postwar years no new warships were begun, and the three 6,890-ton armored cruisers of the *Princesa de Asturias* class, laid down in 1890, were not completed until 1902–4. Adding to the prevailing gloom, shipwreck claimed the last of the class, the *Cardinal Cisneros*, after just one year in service.[33] Revitalization finally began in 1908, when the Cortes passed a navy law calling for the construction of three dreadnoughts in the main Spanish naval shipyard at Ferrol. The Spanish government, neutral but with strong pro-entente sympaties, established a consortium with four leading British armaments manufacturers to oversee the necessary improvements in the shipyard and supporting industries, and the eventual construction of the warships themselves. The 15,450-ton *España* class were the smallest dreadnoughts ever built and, with just eight 12-inch guns, also the most lightly armed. The *España* was laid down in 1909 and completed in 1913, followed by the *Alfonso XIII* (1910–15). The First World War revealed the extent to which the program depended upon materials from Britain, which suspended such exports to neutral Spain from 1914 to 1919. The third dreadnought, *Jaime I*, took nine years to complete (1912–21). In 1914 the Cortes approved another naval program including a class of three 21,000-ton dreadnoughts, but the war forced the project to be abandoned.[34]

The coming of the First World War also affected the naval programs of the leading South American countries, which, like Spain, remained neutral during the conflict. Brazil, which had fallen to third in the region in naval strength, in 1905 instigated a new naval arms race. Argentina, which had ended its turn-of-the-century naval race with Chile in the treaty of May 1902, felt compelled to respond to the Brazilian challenge. When Argentina placed orders for new warships a suspicious Chile followed suit, but both countries waited until the expiration of a five-year construction moratorium stipulated in their naval treaty.

By 1906 the 3,160-ton coast defenders *Marshal Deodoro* and *Marshal Floriano* were the only operational armored warships in the Brazilian navy, but better times were soon to come. A coffee boom coincided with a rubber boom, and Brazil established itself as the world leader in both areas. Amid the prosperity the navy's early opposition to the republic was forgotten. A program including three battleships and three armored cruisers was approved in 1905. The dreadnought revolution delayed orders for the three battleships, all of which were eventually laid down as dreadnoughts in British shipyards: the 19,280-ton *Minas Gerais* (Armstrong) and *São Paulo* (Vickers) in April 1907, and the 27,500 *Rio de Janeiro* (Armstrong) in September 1911. Thus Brazil became the first country after Britain and the United States to have a dreadnought under construction, beating even Germany by two months. The *Minas Gerais* was completed in January 1910, the same month as the much smaller USS *Michigan*, preceded into service only by the first British and German dreadnoughts. The *Minas Gerais* and *São Paulo* arrived in Brazilian waters before the end of 1910, just in time to participate in a naval mutiny in November. The incident discredited the navy, which would fare worse under the presidency of Hermes da Fonseca, a general who won election in 1910 with the support of the Brazilian army. As early as 1911 Fonseca called the third dreadnought project a colossal waste of money, and the ensuing collapse of coffee and rubber prices on world markets compelled Brazil to sell the *Rio de Janeiro* to Turkey just months after the ship was launched in January 1913. The three armored cruisers authorized in the 1905 program were never ordered but in 1910 Armstrong delivered the two 3,100-ton scout cruisers *Bahia* and *Rio Grande do Sul*, ships whose speed of over 27 knots made them the fastest of their type in the world. Meanwhile, Yarrow delivered ten destroyers and two river gunboats, and Fiat completed Brazil's first three submarines in 1913.[35]

In 1907 the Argentinian navy responded to the Brazilian dreadnought orders with a plan of its own including three dreadnoughts. The government authorized the program the following year but signed no dreadnought contracts until 1910, the delay caused by failed attempts to secure the right design at the right price from the leading European warship builders. Argentina instead turned to the United States, where the Fore River Shipbuilding Company laid down the *Rivadavia* and *Moreno*, the former in its own shipyard at Quincy, Massachusetts, the latter contracted out to the New York Shipbuilding Company and laid down at Camden, New Jersey. The 27,940-ton ships were similar in design to the American dreadnoughts *Arkansas* and *Wyoming*, laid down the same year. They were armed with twelve 12-inch guns and had turbine engines capable of 22.5 knots. The *Rivadavia* was ready in December 1914 and the *Moreno* in March 1915; each ship arrived in Argentinian waters two months after its completion. Argentina cancelled its projected third dreadnought after Brazil sold its third, the *Rio de Janeiro*, to Turkey. German and British shipyards each built four destroyers for Argentina in 1911–12, but another four laid down in France were purchased by the French navy upon their completion in 1914. On the eve of the war Argentina rejected an overture from Russia to buy the *Rivadavia* and the *Moreno*. Brazil likewise rejected Russian offers for the *Minas Gerais* and *São Paulo*.[36]

Chile answered Argentina's dreadnought orders with an ambitious program of its own later in 1910, including dreadnoughts, destroyers, and submarines. Armstrong laid down the 28,000-ton dreadnoughts *Almirante Latorre* and *Almirante Cochrane* in November 1911 and January 1913, but both were still under construction when seized by the British navy at the outbreak of the First World War. The *Almirante Latorre* served from 1915 as HMS *Canada* and was delivered to Chile in 1920, resuming its original name. Britain kept the *Almirante Cochrane*, which entered service in the early 1920s as the aircraft carrier *Eagle*. Of six destroyers ordered in Britain two were delivered before 1914, another three in 1920 after wartime service in the British navy. In 1917 Britain gave Chile five American-built submarines in partial compensation for the warships seized in 1914, and Chile bought a sixth boat of the same class.[37]

Thus the naval race touched off by Brazil gave that country South America's first dreadnoughts by 1910, but a decade later the Brazilian navy was arguably the region's third-strongest. The selection of an American dreadnought builder proved to be a lucky decision for Argentina; in the summer of 1914 the United States was a fellow neutral, and the ships, then still under construction, were in no danger of being seized by a belligerent government. The Argentinian navy emerged from the race as the clear winner, with two dreadnoughts both newer and significantly larger than Brazil's pair. Chile paid dearly for its dependence on British shipyards, but eventually emerged with South America's largest dreadnought and also the most submarines (six), at a time when Brazil had half that number and Argentina none.

The Ottoman empire, the Italo-Turkish War (1911–12), and the Balkan Wars (1912–13)

In the early twentieth century, as in the early twenty-first, the degree or complexity of great-power interests at stake in the Near East (and, by extension, the whole of the Middle East), the Balkans (and, by extension, the whole of eastern Europe), and Northeast Asia (in particular Korea and Manchuria), made regional conflicts in these areas far more dangerous than troubles elsewhere, and more likely to escalate into warfare involving the great powers. In the years since 1815 naval power had been brought to bear on a number of occasions in the Near East and Northeast Asia, either to defuse a conflict on land or bring it to a hasty conclusion; even in the Balkans, if only in matters pertaining to Greece, the naval might of the great powers had some coercive or deterrent effect. On the eve of the First World War, as the Russo-Japanese conflict in Northeast Asia subsided, the beleaguered Ottoman empire faced threats from Italy in the Near East and an alliance of small states, including Greece, in the Balkans, but at a time when arms races in the North Sea and the Adriatic, combined with Russia's weakened naval condition, precluded the effective application of great-power naval force as a mediating factor in either area. In the Italo-Turkish War of 1911–12 no one intervened to prevent the Italian navy from achieving an easy victory, while in the First Balkan War of 1912–13 the Greek navy enjoyed a similar free hand against the Turkish fleet.

The Young Turk revolt of 1908 brought constitutional government, and political chaos, to the Ottoman empire. In the first three years of constitutional rule the navy ministry changed hands nine times. A British naval mission established before the revolt left in 1910, after which German influence increased, reflected in the Ottoman purchase of the two 10,000-ton pre-dreadnoughts *Weissenberg* and *Kurfürst Friedrich Wilhelm*, commissioned in September 1910 as *Barbaros Hayreddin* and *Torgud Reis*, respectively. They joined a fleet of warships renovated or acquired in the wake of the Greco-Turkish War over Crete in 1897, of which the best units were the former casemate ship *Mesudiye*, rebuilt in Italy as a 9,190-ton pre-dreadnought, the 3,485-ton American-built protected cruiser *Mecidiye*, the 3,900-ton Armstrong protected cruiser *Hamidiye*, seven destroyers, and fifteen modern torpedo boats.[38]

After declaring war on the Ottoman empire in late September 1911, Italy deployed a fleet under the Duke of the Abruzzi which landed troops at Tripoli and other cities on the Libyan coast during October. The Turkish battleships *Barbaros Hayreddin*, *Torgud Reis*, and *Mesudiye* had gone on a summer cruise in the eastern Mediterranean from July to September and were ready for action, but remained at anchor throughout the war. During an attack on Beirut in January 1912, shellfire from the Italian armored cruisers *Francesco Ferruccio* and *Giuseppe Garibaldi* sank the stationary harbor watch *Anvillah*. This 2,360-ton casemate corvette, in commission for forty-two years, was the only armored vessel lost in the conflict. In April 1912 the *Giuseppe Garibaldi* and the armored cruiser *Varese* shelled the Dardanelles forts; the Turks responded by closing the straits with a minefield. In May 1912 diplomatic pressure from the great powers led Italy to lift its blockade of Constantinople in exchange for an Ottoman commitment to clear the minefield. Ironically the only ships sunk by the mines in April–May 1912 were an Ottoman navy minesweeper and two Turkish steamers operating as neutrals under the American flag. In addition to the old *Anvillah*,

Ottoman navy losses during the war included three torpedo boats, two armed yachts, and seven gunboats either sunk in action or scuttled with battle damage. The Italian navy emerged entirely unscathed. With trouble brewing in the Balkans, the Ottoman empire agreed to cede Libya to Italy in exchange for an Italian evacuation of the Dodecanese Islands, which the Italians had seized in May. After signing the Treaty of Lausanne (18 October 1912), Italy refused to give up the Dodecanese Islands.[39]

Greece, Bulgaria, Serbia, and Montenegro attacked the Ottoman empire on the same day that the Italo-Turkish War formally ended. In the first naval action of the First Balkan War, on 19 October 1912, the battleships *Barbaros Hayreddin* and *Torgud Reis* shelled Bulgarian forts near Varna. The protected cruisers *Hamidiye* and *Mecidiye* returned within days to shell these and other Bulgarian Black Sea targets. In November the old ironclads *Necm-i Şevket* and *Iclaliye*, unable to move under their own power, were towed into place to supplement the bombardment of Bulgarian positions. On the night of 21–2 November 1912 Bulgarian torpedo boats attacked and torpedoed the Ottoman navy's best ship, the British-built *Hamidiye*. The ship survived but was out of action over a month while being repaired at Constantinople. From November 1912 through February 1913, Ottoman warships not otherwise engaged in the Aegean or the Black Sea remained in the Sea of Marmara, providing long-range artillery support for defenders against the Bulgarian army's advance toward Constantinople and the straits.[40]

Among the Balkan countries only Greece had warships larger than torpedo boats or river gunboats. On paper the Greek navy was much smaller than the Ottoman, but it entered the war with a core of new or recently renovated warships. The flagship was a 9,960-ton armored cruiser completed by Orlando of Livorno in 1911 and named after Georgios Averof, a Greek million-aire who donated £300,000 toward its purchase. The 4,810-ton French-built armored cruisers *Spetsai*, *Hydra*, and *Psara*, completed in the early 1890s, had been rearmed in 1908–10, and Germany and Britain each had delivered four small destroyers in 1906–7. In 1910 the Greeks negotiated unsuccessfully for two French pre-dreadnoughts to offset the Turkish purchase of the two German pre-dreadnoughts.[41] Even with no battleships, their navy was strong enough to keep the Aegean Sea practically a Greek lake throughout the war.

In the war's first Aegean action, on 31 October 1912, a Greek torpedo boat sank the Salonika harbor watch, the 2,760-ton casemate corvette *Feth-i Bülend*. On 16 December, in its first high seas action since 1877, the Ottoman navy sent the battleships *Barbaros Hayreddin*, *Torgud Reis*, and *Mesudiye*, the renovated battery frigate *Asar-i Tevfik*, and an escort of torpedo boats and destroyers on a sortie into the Aegean. The Ottoman warships encountered the four Greek armored cruisers off the Dardanelles, and opened fire at 9,000 meters. The action continued sporadically for six hours, and neither side lost a ship before the Turks withdrew to the safety of the straits. Turkish battleships were involved in two other inconclusive sorties, on 18 January and 11 April 1913, in each case returning to the straits after engaging the Greek armored cruisers in the Aegean. Throughout the brief conflict, the superior speed of Greek warships and the skill of their crews contributed to the timidity of the Ottoman fleet. The Greeks also had the war's only submarine, the French-built *Delfin*, which became the first undersea boat to fire a self-propelled torpedo in action. In the attack, on 22 December 1912, the *Delfin* targeted the Ottoman cruiser *Mecidiye* from a distance of 800 meters, but the torpedo missed the mark.[42] The largest Turkish warship lost in the war, the 4,870-ton *Asar-i Tevfik*, ran aground after being detached from the Ottoman battleship division in February 1913 for a raid on the Bulgarian port of Podima. Other Turkish losses at the hands of the Greeks included two torpedo boats and one wooden-hulled armed merchant steamer. The Ottoman navy failed to sink or damage any enemy warships during the war.[43] The Second Balkan War (June–July 1913) broke out after Bulgaria emerged from the First Balkan War with the lion's share of the spoils. Former Bulgarian allies Greece, Serbia, and Montenegro joined Romania and Turkey in attacking Bulgaria, which promptly sued for peace. The brief renewal of fighting featured no action by naval vessels.

After the purchase of the two German pre-dreadnoughts in 1910, the Ottoman navy attempted to purchase or build dreadnoughts abroad. The subsequent poor showing in the Italo-Turkish War and First Balkan War intensified Turkish efforts to acquire state-of-the-art capital ships. In August 1911 Vickers began work on the 23,000-ton *Reşadiye*, and in June 1914 Vickers laid down the *Fatih Sultan Mehmed*, another dreadnought of the same design. The Ottoman government also purchased the 27,500-ton Brazilian dreadnought *Rio de Janeiro*, laid down in 1911 by Armstrong, which was completed as the *Sultan Osman-i Evvel*. The outbreak of the First World War brought an end to all three projects: on 1 August 1914 the British government seized the *Reşadiye* and the following day the *Sultan Osman-i Evvel*, commissioning them in the British navy as *Erin* and *Agincourt*, respectively, while the *Fatih Sultan Mehmed* was broken up on the slipway. The Turks finally got their capital ship just two weeks after the outbreak of the war, when the 23,000-ton German battle cruiser *Goeben*, trapped in the Mediterranean, steamed for Constantinople and on 16 August became the *Sultan Yavuz Selim*. Its escort, the 4,570-ton protected cruiser *Breslau*, became the *Midilli*. The battle cruiser, eventually renamed *Yavuz* after the fall of the Turkish monarchy, survived longer than any other capital ship of the First World War. It was sold for scrap in 1971 and broken up between 1973 and 1976.[44]

Greece responded to the Turkish quest for dreadnoughts by ordering one of its own, the 19,500-ton *Salamis*, from the German shipbuilder Vulcan. When the ship was laid down in July 1913, Greece became the fourteenth and last country to order a dreadnought. The *Salamis* was launched in November 1914 but never completed. Meanwhile, in June 1914 the St Nazaire shipyard laid down the 23,500-ton *Basileos Konstantinos*, a virtual copy of the French dreadnoughts of the *Bretagne* class. The project was suspended shortly after the outbreak of war and never resumed. The Greeks had to settle for two pre-dreadnoughts, the 13,000-ton *Mississippi* and *Idaho*, purchased from the United States at the end of June 1914 and named *Kilkis* and *Limnos*, respectively. In 1914 the New York Shipbuilding Company sold to Greece the 2,600-ton cruiser *Helle*, laid down in 1910 for the Imperial Chinese Navy but not wanted by the new republic of China. Smaller units added between the First Balkan War and the First World War included the submarine *Xifias*, a sister-ship of the *Delfin*.[45]

Naval aviation

By the mid-1920s Britain, France, the United States, and Japan all had completed as aircraft carriers warships originally laid down as dreadnoughts or battle cruisers, seeking to capitalize on a technology that, for practical purposes, had not existed when the dreadnought era began in 1906. The initial boom in aviation began after the Wright brothers conducted their first public aircraft demonstrations in the United States and Europe during 1908, five years after their first successful flight. France took the early lead in European aircraft development; there, the army monopolized the arming of airplanes, in 1910 conducting the first maneuvers to include aircraft. Meanwhile, Frenchman Louis Bleriot's pioneering flight across the English Channel in 1909 had a sobering effect in Britain, which in 1912 set up army and navy air services. In May 1914 the British navy began converting an unfinished merchantman into the 7,080-ton seaplane tender *Ark Royal*, the world's first warship built to carry aircraft. The United States did little to develop naval aviation before the First World War, ironically so, for in 1910–11 the American navy staged the first aircraft take-off from a warship (the cruiser *Birmingham* at Hampton Roads) and the first landing on a warship (the armored cruiser *Pennsylvania* at San Francisco), in each case using a temporary platform constructed over the afterdeck. The next deck landing occurred during the First World War; in the meantime, in most countries, armies dominated the military use of aircraft, and where navies operated planes they did so from coastal air stations or, for aircraft fitted with floats rather than wheels, from naval harbors. In 1911 the German navy conducted its first experiments with dirigibles and airplanes but Tirpitz was skeptical of their value; thanks to the influence of Count Ferdinand von Zeppelin, prewar Germany focused more on airships than on planes. In Italy and Russia, as in France, the army monopolized air power. Airships were more popular than planes with the Italian armed forces, although the Italians were the first to use airplanes in combat, in their conquest of Libya. Russian army pilots subsequently saw action against the Turks in the Balkan Wars. Austria–Hungary put its faith in the airplane rather than the dirigible and developed a naval air arm; the first naval air station opened at Pola in 1912. The same year, the Japanese navy imported its first airplanes from the United States and France.[46]

In July 1921 Colonel "Billy" Mitchell of the US Army Air Corps choreographed a demonstration of the effectiveness of air power over battleships, sinking the former German dreadnought *Ostfriesland* near the mouth of Chesapeake Bay with bombs dropped from the air. Even though the ship was an undefended stationary target, Mitchell's detractors in the US navy had argued that aircraft alone could not sink a battleship under any circumstances. The demise of the *Ostfriesland*, scripted though it was, became a watershed event, inasmuch as it put proponents of the battleship on the defensive *vis-à-vis* proponents of military and naval aviation, a position from which they would never recover.[47] The battleship had survived the invention of the steam engine, the shell gun, and armor plate by incorporating these breakthroughs, to face down the later threats from the self-propelled torpedo and its delivery systems, the torpedo boat and the submarine, but it would not survive the threat from the air. During the Second World War air power transformed naval warfare dramatically and established the aircraft carrier, rather than the dreadnought or battle cruiser, as the capital ship of the second half of the twentieth century.

Conclusion

In 1914 the navies of the world counted their strength in dreadnoughts and battle cruisers alone. During the First World War the leading navies would assign their pre-dreadnoughts to peripheral theaters of action; the pace of technological change in capital ship construction became so rapid that even the *Dreadnought* itself was considered a reserve battleship less than a decade after its launching. It was a far cry from the situation at the Battle of Trafalgar just over a century earlier, when Lord Nelson had commanded the best fleet in the world from a ship of the line then four decades old.

Counting the battleships *Erin* (ex-*Reşadiye*), *Agincourt* (ex-*Sultan Osman-i Evvel*), and *Canada* (ex-*Almirante Latorre*), seized or purchased in August 1914, Britain entered the First World War with forty-five new capital ships (dreadnoughts or battle cruisers) built or building, compared to twenty-six for Germany, fourteen for the United States, twelve for Japan, twelve for France, eleven for Russia, six for Italy, four for Austria–Hungary, and three for Spain. In ships actually in service by August 1914, Britain had thirty-one, Germany eighteen, the United States ten, Japan seven, France four, Italy three, Austria–Hungary three, Spain one, and Russia none. The seizures, sales, and cancellations at the onset of the war left Brazil, with two in service, and Argentina, with two under construction, as the only other countries whose navies had dreadnoughts.

Notes

1 Tritten, "Doctrine and Fleet Tactics in the Royal Navy," 22–3.
2 Cf. Evans and Peattie, *Kaigun*, 128; Roberts, "The Pre-Dreadnought Age, 1890–1905," 124.
3 *Conway, 1906–21*, 228; Evans and Peattie, *Kaigun*, 159.

4 Fairbanks, "The Origins of the *Dreadnought* Revolution," 262.

5 Unless otherwise noted, sources for the remainder of this section are Lambert, "Admiral Sir John Fisher and the Concept of Flotilla Defence," 641–60; Sumida, *In Defence of Naval Supremacy*, 50–61; idem, "Sir John Fisher and the *Dreadnought*: The Sources of Naval Mythology," *Journal of Military History* 59 (1995): 620, and *passim*; Conway, *1906–21*; Campbell, "Naval Armaments and Armour," 165; Griffiths, "Warship Machinery," 178.

6 James L. George, *History of Warships: From Ancient Times to the Twenty-First Century* (Annapolis, Md, 1998), 120–1.

7 Unless otherwise noted, sources for this section are Arthur J. Marder, *From the Dreadnought to Scapa Flow: The Royal Navy in the Fisher Era, 1904–1919*, 5 vols (London, 1961), 1: 136–79; Holger H. Herwig, *"Luxury" Fleet: The Imperial German Navy, 1888–1918*, rev. edn (Atlantic Highlands, N.J., 1987), 59–80; Conway, *1906–21*, 25–33, 145–55; Gröner, *Die deutschen Kriegsschiffe*, 1: 46–54, 80–5.

8 Sumida, *In Defence of Naval Supremacy*, 192; Herwig, *"Luxury" Fleet*, 80.

9 Sumida, *In Defence of Naval Supremacy*, 358; Herwig, *"Luxury" Fleet*, 273–9.

10 Conway, *1906–21*, 174–6.

11 O'Gara, *Roosevelt and the Rise of the Modern Navy*, 65; Conway, *1860–1905*, 141–62, and *passim*; Wilson, "Early Submarines," 153; Conway, *1906–21*, 126–8.

12 Quoted in O'Gara, *Roosevelt and the Rise of the Modern Navy*, 70.

13 Ibid., 112; Alden, *The American Steel Navy*, 333–46; Conway, *1906–21*, 112–13; Beach, *The United States Navy*, 407.

14 Conway, *1906–21*, 112–16, 119.

15 Evans and Peattie, *Kaigun*, 143, 186; Alden, *The American Steel Navy*, 344.

16 O'Gara, *Roosevelt and the Rise of the Modern Navy*, 6, 81; Alden, *The American Steel Navy*, 157.

17 Evans and Peattie, *Kaigun*, 159; Conway, *1906–21*, 226–8.

18 Evans and Peattie, *Kaigun*, 159–60; Conway, *1906–21*, 229, 233.

19 Evans and Peattie, *Kaigun*, 159–60; Conway, *1906–21*, 229–35.

20 Conway, *1906–21*, 245–6.

21 Evans and Peattie, *Kaigun*, 186.

22 Sondhaus, *The Naval Policy of Austria–Hungary*, 173.

23 Seton-Watson, *Liberalism to Fascism*, 242, 265, 358–9; Baratelli, *La marina militare italiane*, 327.

24 The source for the remainder of this section is Sondhaus, *The Naval Policy of Austria–Hungary*, 180–3, 191–8, 203–4, 231–47, 274.

25 René Greger, *The Russian Fleet, 1914–1917*, trans. Jill Gearing (London, 1972), 9–10.

26 Tomitch, *Warships of the Imperial Russian Navy*; Conway, *1906–21*, 309, 312–15.

27 Woodward, *The Russians at Sea*, 160–1; Greger, *The Russian Fleet*, 10; Conway, *1906–21*, 302–4.

28 Greger, *The Russian Fleet*, 10.

29 Ibid., 11–12.

30 Paul G. Halpern, *The Mediterranean Naval Situation, 1908–1914* (Cambridge, Mass., 1971), 54–57; Tritten, "Navy and Military Doctrine in France," 58.

31 Conway, *1906–21*, 196–98.

32 Halpern, *The Mediterranean Naval Situation*, 13–46, 86–110; Samuel R. Williamson, Jr, *The Politics of Grand Strategy: Britain and France Prepare for War, 1904–1914* (Cambridge, Mass., 1969), 264–83.

33 Conway, *1860–1905*, 381–2.

34 Halpern, *The Mediterranean Naval Situation*, 280–95; Conway, *1906–21*, 374–5, 378.

35 Araya, "Situación estratégica naval," 2: 606–7; Conway, *1906–21*, 403–7.

36 Araya, "Situación estratégica naval," 2: 607; Guillermo Montenegro, "U.S. Battleships for Export: The Argentine Dreadnoughts," paper presented at the Thirteenth Naval History Symposium, Annapolis, Md, 2–4 October 1997; *Conway, 1906–21*, 400–3; Greger, *The Russian Fleet*, 10.
37 Araya, "Situación estratégica naval," 2: 607–8; *Conway, 1906–21*, 407–9.
38 Langensiepen and Güleryüz, *The Ottoman Steam Navy*, 9–17, 152–7, 161–6.
39 Ibid., 15–16; Donolo, "The History of Italian Naval Doctrine," 109.
40 Langensiepen and Güleryüz, *The Ottoman Steam Navy*, 20–1, 25.
41 Halpern, *The Mediterranean Naval Situation*, 323–4; *Conway, 1906–21*, 383–7.
42 Langensiepen and Güleryüz, *The Ottoman Steam Navy*, 20–5; *Conway, 1906–21*, 387.
43 Langensiepen and Güleryüz, *The Ottoman Steam Navy*, 20–5.
44 Ibid., 17–18, 142, 151; *Conway, 1906–21*, 391.
45 *Conway, 1906–21*, 384–7.
46 Ibid., 64; John Buckley, *Air Power in the Age of Total War* (London, 1999), 31–9; Herwig, *"Luxury" Fleet*, 84–5; Evans and Peattie, *Kaigun*, 155, 180; Sondhaus, *The Naval Policy of Austria–Hungary*, 200.
47 Buckley, *Air Power*, 91.

CHAPTER NINE

Reflections on deterrence

A study of the evolution of naval warfare from 1815 to 1914, leading ultimately to the focus on the battle fleet and the dreadnought, provides an excellent opportunity for a discussion of the nature of deterrence in sea power. Analysis of the concept of deterrence itself poses rather unique difficulties. As Louise Arbour, prosecutor for the International War Crimes Tribunal for the former Yugoslavia, remarked in 1999, in assessing the success or failure of any policy of deterrence we face the task of "measuring what did not occur."[1] The utility of the large armored warship came under attack at its birth in the early 1860s, during the era of the Jeune École, and again after 1918, with the emergence of air power and in light of the fact that battleships had spent most of the First World War rusting at anchor, while smaller vessels did the bulk of the fighting at sea. Twentieth-century critics of battleship construction have argued that most countries could have done without them. Their judgements have been harsh for the pre-1914 naval programs of every country except Britain, the United States, and Japan, on the grounds that for the others some less expensive combination of cruisers and lighter craft would have provided a better actual fighting force.[2]

This sort of argument overlooks the fact that deterrence always has been largely psychological, and that the force which best deters is not necessarily the same as the force which, in actual warfare, would best attack or defend.[3] Regardless of their relevance to modern naval warfare, the works of Mahan quite correctly emphasized the importance of the British battle fleet in the early modern period and the Napoleonic era. A *guerre de course* could make life miserable for the British, but without a battle fleet able to command the seas France had no hope of dislodging Britain from its pre-eminent position. The same essential fact remained unchanged after 1815, eventually applying to Germany's challenge to Britain. Indeed, beyond 1914, German submarine campaigns in two world wars inflicted serious damage but not of the catastrophic sort that would have followed the loss of the battle fleet, opening the way to the invasion and defeat of Britain. The only other modern naval powers with overseas trade of sufficient importance to tempt opponents to adopt a *guerre de course* strategy – the United States and Japan – likewise have withstood the challenge. The

United States won the American Civil War despite the damage done by the commerce raiders of the Confederacy, and Japan lost the Second World War for reasons other than the unrestricted submarine warfare of the American navy, costly though it was for the Japanese. For continental European powers such as Germany, Russia, and Austria–Hungary, navies consisting of smaller units perhaps could defend a limited stretch of coastline or break a blockade, but each learned that by building battleships they could challenge general or regional balances of power *and* deter the attacks of potential enemies, so build battleships they did.

The great powers of 1815–1914 also came to appreciate the utility of naval force in conflicts farther from home, where the survival of the state and its vital interests were not at stake. With battleships or cruisers, competent navies could deter or decide conflicts at a far lower cost, with far less disruption to the civilian societies of their countries, and inflicting far fewer casualties, than by calling up and deploying troops. In the age of "gunboat diplomacy," sending a respectable squadron, with or without an exercise in bombardment, was the equivalent of the late twentieth-century air strike with laser-guided ordnance and cruise missiles: using state-of-the-art technology to coerce or deter, without causing broader damage or great numbers of casualties, and without the prohibitive cost and domestic social consequences of mobilizing an army. Naval force also afforded the luxury of proportionality, a measured response ranging from sending a battle fleet to dispatching a lone cruiser, from standing offshore and showing the flag to imposing a blockade, to shelling coastal installations or cities. Naval forces fully exploited the luxury of sailing or steaming away as soon as the punishment inflicted fit the crime, or when the exercise had outlived its usefulness or become politically unpopular at home. The force of armies simply could not be brought to bear in anything approaching the same range of situations, or with the same range of strength. It has never been possible for an army to successfully "invade a little bit." Countries could use armies only to intimidate their immediate neighbors, or the colonies of countries bordering their own colonies. Once an army crossed a border, extrication was far more problematic than weighing anchor and leaving for home. Mobilization without resort to war could be used to support a diplomatic position, but in the age of mass armies such measures were extremely expensive as well as politically and socially disruptive (for example, the Austrian army's mobilizations in the German crisis of 1850, during the Crimean War in 1854–55, and much later, during the Balkan Wars immediately preceding the First World War.) The universal conviction of 1914 that "mobilization meant war" in no small measure reflected the general appreciation of the great financial, political, and social consequences of mobilizing a modern army and *not* fighting. Of course, along with its advantages, "gunboat diplomacy" had the same limitations as modern air strikes in situations where troops on the ground were indispensable to resolve or stop a conflict.

Faith in the well-ordered battle fleet was reinforced by the fact that navies seldom enjoyed success with makeshift forces, even in conflicts far from home waters, where vital interests were not at risk. There were notable exceptions to the rule – the Wars of Latin American Independence, the American Civil War, and the Russian effort against the Turks in 1877–78 – where improvised navies achieved victories even when the stakes were high, but in each case the victorious forces, by their very nature, were not capable of projecting power and thus were soon largely disbanded by governments which recognized that they had no lasting value. The Russian torpedo launches shared the fate of all unconventional challenges to conventional sea power, which throughout modern history have brought incomplete or ephemeral success, in part because the navies mounting such challenges did not fully believe in them. In the 1820s the Greeks had some success with fireships against the Turks while, more conventionally, hiring the veteran Lord Cochrane and buying a big frigate abroad. As early as the 1820s the French hoped steam power would overturn British naval supremacy, but their challenge took on serious dimensions only around 1850, when the screw propeller was introduced to the ships of the line of the conventional battle fleet. During the American Civil War the Confederacy sent out commerce raiders and deployed a submarine which carried out the first successful sinking of a warship with a spar torpedo, but the Confederate navy, like the leading navies of the 1860s, pinned its hopes (and spent much of its budget) on ironclads. Meanwhile, the monitors that helped ensure the rebel defeat were of little use when the postwar US navy reverted to its traditional blue-water focus. In 1877–78, against the Ottoman navy in the Black Sea, the Russian navy demonstrated that torpedo attacks by small craft could prevent the superior battle fleet of an opponent from asserting command of the sea, but the lack of a Russian battle fleet in the Black Sea left them unable to support their army's march on Constantinople and compelled them to back down when the British sent a fleet to the Turkish straits. While the experience of 1877–78 spurred other navies to further develop torpedo warfare capabilities, the Russians responded with their conventional naval build-up of the 1880s and 1890s. In 1894–95 the Japanese navy defeated the Chinese with protected cruisers built under the influence of the Jeune École, but was impressed enough by the performance of Chinese battleships to build an armored battle fleet of its own, which a decade later defeated the Russian navy.

Japan was more fortunate than the other naval powers that embraced the Jeune École sufficiently to temporarily stop building battleships. France, Germany, Austria–Hungary and, belatedly, Italy, all clearly hurt themselves by doing so, weakening the capacity of their fleets to serve their deterrent function. Each of these navies included significant factions of officers that did not believe in the Jeune École, and in each case their dissent was vindicated in the long run. From 1815 to 1914, through the series of dramatic changes in technology that repeatedly revolutionized naval warfare, the battle fleet remained a constant, in no small measure because even its opponents, their own advocacy of unconventional naval warfare notwithstanding, conceived of naval supremacy in terms of the traditional battle fleet. During that century, the technological changes that mattered most – in propulsion, armament, and armor – were those eventually applied to the battleship. By incorporating new technologies in capital ships, the navies of the world ensured that the paradigm would survive even the challenge of the self-propelled torpedo. Even after the aircraft carrier superseded the battleship and battle cruiser to become the capital ship of the second half of the twentieth century, any navy that mattered felt that it had to have a surface fleet of capital ships. During its Cold War challenge to the United States, the Soviet Union spent enormous sums on the *Kiev* and the *Kuznetsov* class aircraft carriers, as did the dramatically downsized navies of Britain, France, and Italy in their quests to keep smaller carriers in service. The further evolution of the submarine eventually culminated in the US navy's *Ohio* class of Trident submarines – underwater units with displacements rivaling those of the dreadnoughts of the First World War, symbolically named for the states like American battleships of the past – yet the carriers and their battle groups remained the core of the American fleet and the key to its projection of global power. For all the potentially destructive firepower of the missiles of a Trident submarine, as a deterrent or an instrument of diplomacy the type could not match surface capital ships.

A dozen years after Hiroshima, prominent West German Social Democrat Fritz Erler remarked that "atomic weapons are the mark of a world power, as battleships were for Tirpitz and the Kaiser."[4] Over the decades prior to the First World War, battleships provided a deterrent that mattered in the balance of power; cruisers, torpedo boats, and other smaller warships did not. They were the most lethal weapons systems created to date and could project a country's power far beyond its borders, even when anchored in its home ports. As with nuclear weapons at the dawn of the twenty-first century, the possession of such instruments of destruction made a country count for something in the world, and the ability to build them at home, with domestic engineers and workers, from domestic resources, was the hallmark of great power status. Most dreadnought battleships were destined not to be used in the war for which they had been built, and after international conditions changed they became the focal point of disarmament and arms limitation efforts. Owing to their limited operational value during the First World War, they became emblematic of the folly of the time, obscuring the complex conjunction of factors which caused their construction in the first place. Because the force which best deters is not necessarily the force which has the greatest practical value in warfare, the historian has all the more reason to seek to understand the conditions and circumstances which gave rise to the naval deterrents of yesterday.

Notes

1 Louise Arbour, International War Crimes Tribunal, news conference aired on CNN, 30 April 1999.
2 E.g. Herwig, *"Luxury" Fleet*, 222–25, indicating his views of the German battle

fleet, and O'Connell, *Sacred Vessels*, Chapters 3–12, and *passim*, criticizing all armored warships as folly, from the time of their emergence through the Persian Gulf War of 1990–91.

3 O'Connell, *Sacred Vessels*, 6–7, accepts the premise that deterrence is psychological but lampoons the dreadnought battleship all the same for its "shortcomings as a weapon," failing to appreciate the fact that the actual combat performance of battleships was irrelevant to their deterrent function.

4 Quoted in Gordon D. Drummond, *The German Social Democrats in Opposition, 1949–1960: The Case Against Rearmament* (Norman, Okla., 1982), 199. O'Connell, *Sacred Vessels*, especially 7, 290, makes the comparison between battleships and nuclear weapons but draws very different conclusions from it.

Bibliography

Memoirs, published documents, and contemporary (1815–1914) publications

Beresford, Charles William de la Poer. *The Memoirs of Admiral Lord Charles Beresford.* 2 vols. Boston, Mass., 1914.

Bianchini, Lodovico. *Della storia delle finanze del regno di Napoli.* Naples, 1859.

Bonner-Smith, D., ed. *Russian War, 1855, Baltic: Official Correspondence.* London, 1944.

Bonner-Smith, D., and Dewar, A. C., eds. *Russian War, 1854, Baltic and Black Sea: Official Correspondence.* London, 1943.

Busk, Hans. *The Navies of the World; Their Present State, and Future Capabilities.* London, 1859.

Camerani, Sergio, and Arfè, Gaetano, eds. *Carteggi di Bettino Ricasoli.* Vol. 22: *20 giungno–31 luglio 1866. Fonti per la storia d'Italia,* no. 81. Rome, 1967.

Clarke, George Sydenham. *Russia's Sea-Power Past and Present, or the Rise of the Russian Navy.* London, 1898.

Conner, Philip Syng Physick. *The Home Squadron under Commodore Conner in the War with Mexico.* Philadelphia, Penn., 1896.

Dewar, A. C., ed. *Russian War, 1855, Black Sea: Official Correspondence.* London, 1945.

d'Orléans, François Ferdinand [Prince de Joinville]. *De l'état des forces navales de la France.* Frankfurt, 1844.

—— *Essais sur la marine française.* Paris, 1853.

Dundonald, Thomas [Cochrane], Earl of. *Narrative of Services in the Liberation of Chili, Peru, and Brazil, from Spanish and Portuguese Domination.* 2 vols. London, 1859.

Gerloff, Wilhelm. *Finanz- und Zollpolitik des Deutschen Reiches.* Jena, 1913.

Hall, W. H. *Narrative of the Voyages and Services of the Nemesis, from 1840 to 1843.* 2nd edn London, 1845.

Harvey, Thomas W., comp. *Memoir of Hayward Augustus Harvey.* New York, 1900.

Jane, Fred T. *The Imperial Russian Navy.* 2nd edn London, 1904. Reprinted London, 1983.

Krupp: A Century's History of the Krupp Works, 1812–1912, Essen, 1912.

Lütken, Otto Georg. *Søkrigsbegivenhederne i 1864.* Copenhagen, 1896.

Norie, E. M. W. *Official Account of the Military Operations in China, 1900–1901.* 1st end 1903. Reprinted Nashville, 1995.

Randaccio, Carlo. *Le marinerie militari italiane nei tempi moderni, 1750–1850.* Turin, 1864.

Sterneck zu Ehrenstein, Maximilian Daublebsky von. *Admiral Max Freiherr von Sterneck: Erinnerungen aus den Jahren 1847 bis 1897*. Ed. Jerolim Benko von Boinik. Vienna, 1901.

Tirpitz, Alfred von. *Erinnerungen*. Leipzig, 1919.

Books, articles, and papers

Alden, John D. *The American Steel Navy*. Revised edn Annapolis, Md, 1989.

Araya, Francisco Ghisolfo. "Situación estratégica naval." In *El Poder Naval Chileno*, 2 vols. Valparaíso, 1985. Vol. 1: 271–312; vol. 2: 401–72, 605–44.

Bade, Rodrigo Fuenzalida. *Marinos Ilustres y Destacados de Pasado*. Concepción, 1985.

Baratelli, Franco Micali. *La marina militare italiana nella vita nazionale, 1860–1914*. Mursia, 1983.

Bargoni, Franco. *Le prime navi di linea della marina italiana, 1861–1880*. Rome, 1976.

—— *Corazzate italiane classi Duilio–Italia–Ruggiero di Lauria, 1880–1892*. Rome, 1977.

—— *Corazzate italiane classi Re Umberto – Ammiraglio di Saint Bon, 1893–1901*. Rome, 1978.

Battesti, Michèle. *La Marine au XIXe siècle: Interventions extérieures et colonies*. Paris, 1993.

Baxter, James Phinney. *The Introduction of the Ironclad Warship*. Cambridge, Mass., 1933.

Beach, Edward L. *The United States Navy: 200 Years*. New York, 1986.

Beeching, Jack. *The Chinese Opium Wars*. New York, 1975.

Beeler, John F. *British Naval Policy in the Gladstone–Disraeli Era, 1866–1880*. Palo Alto, Calif., 1997.

Berghahn, Volker R. "Naval Armaments and Social Crisis: Germany before 1914." In Geoffrey Best and Andrew Wheatcroft, eds, *War, Economy, and the Military Mind*. London, 1976. Pages 61–88.

Berghahn, Volker R., and Deist, Wilhelm. *Rüstung im Zeichen der wilhelminischen Weltpolitik: Grundlegende Dokumente, 1890–1914*. Düsseldorf, 1988.

Billingsley, Edward Baxter. *In Defense of Neutral Rights: The United States Navy and the Wars of Independence in Chile and Peru*. Chapel Hill, N.C., 1967.

Black, Shirley J. "Napoléon III et le Mexique: un triomphe monétaire." *Revue historique* 259 (1978): 55–73.

Boris, Ivan. *Gli anni di Garibaldi in Sud America, 1836–1848*. Milan, 1970.

Brown, David K. "The Era of Uncertainty, 1863–1878", in Robert Gardiner, ed., *Steam, Steel and Shellfire: The Steam Warship 1815–1905*. London, 1992. Pages 75–94.

—— *Paddle Warships: The Earliest Steam Powered Fighting Ships, 1815–1850*. London, 1993.

—— *Warrior to Dreadnought: Warship Development, 1860–1905*. London, 1997.

Buckley, John. *Air Power in the Age of Total War*. London, 1999.

Bulnes, Gonzalo. *Resumen de la Guerra del Pacífico*. Santiago, 1979.

Campbell, John. "Naval Armaments and Armour." In Robert Gardiner, eds, *Steam, Steel and Shellfire: The Steam Warship 1815–1905*. London, 1992. Pages 158–69.

Canney, Donald L. *The Old Steam Navy*. 2 vols. Annapolis, Md, 1993.

Carvalho, Trajano Augusto de. *Nossa Marinha: Seus Feitos e Glórias, 1822–1940*. Rio de Janeiro, 1986.

Casali, Antonio, and Cattaruzza, Marina. *Sotto i mari del mondo: La Whitehead, 1875–1990*. Rome, 1990.

Ceva, Lucio. *Le forze armate*. Turin, 1981.

Cohen, Paul A. *History in Three Keys: The Boxers as Event, Experience, and Myth*. New York, 1997.

Conway's All the World's Fighting Ships, 1860–1905. London, 1979.

Conway's All the World's Fighting Ships, 1906–21. London, 1985.

Cooley, Benjamin Franklin. *Gray Steel and Blue Water Navy: The Formative Years of America's Military–Industrial Complex, 1881–1917*. Hamden, Ct, 1979.

Dakin, Douglas. *British and American Philhellenes during the War of Greek Independence, 1821–1833*. Thessaloniki, 1955.

—— *The Greek Struggle for Independence, 1821–1833*. Berkeley, Calif., 1973.

Daly, John C. K. *Russian Seapower and "the Eastern Question," 1827–41*. Annapolis, Md, 1991.

Donolo, Luigi. "The History of Italian Naval Doctrine." In James J. Tritten and Luigi Donolo, eds, *A Doctrine Reader: The Navies of United States, Great Britain, France, Italy, and Spain*. Newport, R.I., 1995. Pages 91–123.

Dupont, Maurice, and Taillemite, Étienne. *Les guerres navales françaises: du Moyen Age à la guerre du Golfe*. Paris, 1995.

Eller, E. M. *The Texas Navy*. Washington, D.C., 1968.

Evans, David C., and Peattie, Mark R. *Kaigun: Strategy, Tactics, and Technology in the Imperial Japanese Navy, 1887–1941*. Annapolis, Md, 1997.

Fairbanks, Charles H., Jr. "The Origins of the *Dreadnought* Revolution: A Historiographical Essay." *International History Review* 13 (1991): 246–72.

Feuer, A. B. *The Spanish-American War at Sea: Naval Action in the Atlantic*. Westport, Ct, 1995.

Field, James A., Jr. *From Gibraltar to the Middle East: America and the Mediterranean World, 1776–1882*. Revised edn Chicago, 1991.

Gabriele, Mariano. *La politica navale italiana dall'unità alla viglia di Lissa*. Milan, 1958.

George, James L. *History of Warships: From Ancient Times to the Twenty-First Century*. Annapolis, Md, 1998.

Giorgerini, Giorgio. *Almanacco storico delle navi militare italiane: La Marina e le sue navi dal 1861 al 1975*. Rome, 1978.

Gogg, Karl. *Österreichs Kriegsmarine, 1848–1918*. Salzburg, 1967.

Greger, René. *The Russian Fleet, 1914–1917*. Trans. Jill Gearing. London, 1972.

Griffiths, Denis. "Warship Machinery." In Robert Gardiner, ed., *Steam, Steel and Shellfire: The Steam Warship 1815–1905*. London, 1992. Pages 170–8.

Gromov, F. N., Gribovskii, Vladimir, and Rodionov, Boris. *Tri Veka Rossiiskogo Flota*. 3 vols. St Petersburg, 1996.

Gröner, Erich. *Die deutschen Kriegsschiffe, 1815–1945*. 8 vols. Coblenz, 1989.

Halpern, Paul G. *The Mediterranean Naval Situation, 1908–1914*. Cambridge, Mass., 1971.

Hamilton, C. I. *Anglo-French Naval Rivalry, 1840–1870*. Oxford, 1993.

Harbron, John D. *Trafalgar and the Spanish Navy*. London, 1988.

Harding, Richard. *Seapower and Naval Warfare, 1650–1830*. London, 1999.

Hawkey, Arthur. *Black Night Off Finisterre: The Tragic Tale of an Early British Ironclad*. Annapolis, Md, 1999.

Hearn, Chester G. *Admiral David Dixon Porter: The Civil War Years*. Annapolis, Md, 1996.

—— *Admiral David Glasgow Farragut: The Civil War Years.* Annapolis, Md, 1998.

Herwig, Holger H. *The German Naval Officer Corps: A Social and Political History.* Oxford, 1973.

—— *"Luxury" Fleet: The Imperial German Navy, 1888–1918.* Revised edn Atlantic Highlands, N.J., 1987.

Holcombe, Robert. "Types of Ships." In William N. Still, Jr, ed., *The Confederate Navy: The Ships, Men, and Organization, 1861–65.* Annapolis, Md, 1997. Pages 40–68.

Hough, Richard. *The Fleet that Had To Die.* London, 1958.

—— *The Potemkin Mutiny.* London, 1960.

Kelly, Patrick J. "Strategy, Tactics, and Turf Wars: Tirpitz and the Oberkommando der Marine, 1892–1895." Paper presented at the Thirteenth Naval History Symposium, Annapolis, Md, 2–4 October 1997.

Kennan, George F. *The Fateful Alliance: France, Russia, and the Coming of the First World War.* New York, 1984.

Kennedy, Paul. *The Samoan Tangle: A Study in Anglo-German–American Relations, 1878–1900.* New York, 1974.

Keown-Boyd, Henry. *The Boxer Rebellion.* New York, 1991.

Kjølsen, F. H. "The Old Danish Frigate." *The Mariner's Mirror* 51 (1965): 27–33.

Lambert, Andrew. *Battleships in Transition: The Creation of the Steam Battlefleet, 1815–1860.* Annapolis, Md, 1984.

—— *The Crimean War: British Grand Strategy against Russia, 1853–56.* Manchester, 1991a.

—— *The Last Sailing Battlefleet: Maintaining Naval Mastery, 1815–1850.* London, 1991b.

—— "The Introduction of Steam." In Robert Gardiner, ed., *Steam, Steel and Shellfire: The Steam Warship 1815–1905.* London, 1992a. Pages 14–29.

—— "Iron Hulls and Armour Plate." In Robert Gardiner, ed., *Steam, Steel and Shellfire: The Steam Warship 1815–1905.* London, 1992b. Pages 47–60.

—— "The Screw Propeller Warship." In Robert Gardiner, ed., *Steam, Steel and Shellfire: The Steam Warship 1815–1905.* London, 1992c. Pages 30–46.

Lambert, Nicholas. "Admiral Sir John Fisher and the Concept of Flotilla Defence, 1904–1909." *Journal of Military History* 59 (1995): 639–60.

Lambi, Ivo Nikolai. *The Navy and German Power Politics, 1862–1914.* Boston, Mass., 1984.

Langensiepen, Bernd, and Güleryüz, Ahmet. *The Ottoman Steam Navy, 1828–1923.* Ed. and trans. James Cooper. Annapolis, Md, 1995.

Leckebusch, Günther. *Die Beziehungen der deutschen Seeschiffswerften zur Eisenindustrie an der Ruhr in der Zeit von 1850 bis 1930.* Cologne, 1963.

Long, David F. *Nothing Too Daring: A Biography of Commodore David Porter, 1780–1843.* Annapolis, Md, 1970.

Luraghi, Raimondo. "Background." In William N. Still, Jr, ed., *The Confederate Navy: The Ships, Men and Organization, 1861–65.* Annapolis, Md, 1997. Pages 1–20.

Lyon, David. "Underwater Warfare and the Torpedo Boat." In Robert Gardiner, ed., *Steam, Steel and Shellfire: The Steam Warship 1815–1905.* London, 1992. Pages 134–46.

Marder, Arthur J. *The Anatomy of British Sea Power: A History of British Naval Policy in the Pre-Dreadnought Era, 1880–1905.* New York, 1940.

—— From the Dreadnought to Scapa Flow: The Royal Navy in the Fisher Era, 1904–1919. 5 vols. London, 1961.

Marzalek, John F. Sherman: A Soldier's Passion for Order. New York, 1994.

Montenegro, Guillermo. "U.S. Battleships for Export: The Argentine Dreadnoughts." Paper presented at the Thirteenth Naval History Symposium, Annapolis, Md, 2–4 October 1997.

Naval Historical Foundation. The Russian Navy Visits the United States. Washington, D.C., 1969.

O'Connell, Robert L. Sacred Vessels: The Cult of the Battleship and the Rise of the U.S. Navy. Oxford, 1993.

O'Gara, Gordon Carpenter. Roosevelt and the Rise of the Modern Navy. 1st edn 1943. Reprint ed. New York, 1969.

Owen, Richard. "Military–Industrial Relations: Krupp and the Imperial Navy Office." In Richard J. Evans, ed., Society and Politics in Wilhelmine Germany. London, 1978. Pages 71–89.

Pappas, Paul Constantine. The United States and the Greek War for Independence, 1821–1828. Boulder, Colo., 1985.

Pérez-Llorca, Jaime. 1898: La estrategia del Desastre. Madrid, 1998.

Radogna, Lamberto. Storia della Marina Militare delle Due Sicilie, 1734–1860. Turin, 1978.

Ritchie, Pedro Espina. El Monitor Huáscar. Santiago, 1969.

Roberts, John. "The Pre-Dreadnought Age, 1890–1905." In Robert Gardiner, ed., Steam, Steel and Shellfire: The Steam Warship 1815–1905. London, 1992a. Pages 112–33.

—— "Warships of Steel, 1879–1889." In Robert Gardiner, ed., Steam, Steel and Shellfire: The Steam Warship 1815–1905. London, 1992b. Pages 95–111.

Roberts, William H. USS New Ironsides in the Civil War. Annapolis, Md, 1999.

Rodríguez González, Agustín Ramón. Política naval de la Restauración, 1875–1898. Madrid, 1988.

Ropp, Theodore. The Development of a Modern Navy: French Naval Policy, 1871–1904. Ed. Stephen S. Roberts. Annapolis, Md, 1987.

Sandler, Stanley. The Emergence of the Modern Capital Ship. Newark, Del., 1979.

Seton-Watson, Christopher. Italy: From Liberalism to Fascism, 1870–1925. London, 1967.

Shaw, Stanford J. "Selim III and the Ottoman Navy." Turcica 1 (1969): 212–41.

Sondhaus, Lawrence. "Die österreichische Kriegsmarine und der amerikanische Sezessionskrieg 1861–1865." Marine–Gestern, Heute 13 (1986): 81–4.

—— The Habsburg Empire and the Sea: Austrian Naval Policy, 1797–1866. West Lafayette, Ind., 1989.

—— The Naval Policy of Austria–Hungary: Navalism, Industrial Development, and the Politics of Dualism, 1867–1918. West Lafayette, Ind., 1994.

—— "The Imperial German Navy and Social Democracy, 1878–1897." German Studies Review 18 (1995): 51–64.

—— Preparing for Weltpolitik: German Sea Power before the Tirpitz Era. Annapolis, Md, 1997.

Spencer, Warren F. The Confederate Navy in Europe. Tuscaloosa, Ala., 1983.

Steensen, Robert Steen. Vore Panserskibe, 1863–1943. Copenhagen, 1968.

—— Vore Krydsere. Copenhagen, 1971.

Steinberg, Jonathan. *Yesterday's Deterrent: Tirpitz and the Birth of the German Battle Fleet*. New York, 1965.

Still, William N., Jr. *American Sea Power in the Old World: The United States Navy in European and Near Eastern Waters, 1865–1917*. Westport, Ct, 1980.

—— "The American Civil War." In Robert Gardiner, ed., *Steam, Steel and Shellfire: The Steam Warship 1815–1905*. London, 1992. Pages 61–74.

—— "Operations." In William N. Still, Jr, ed., *The Confederate Navy: The Ships, Men and Organization, 1861–65*. Annapolis, Md, 1997. Pages 214–38.

Stolz, Gerd. *Die Schleswig–Holsteinische Marine, 1848–1852*. Heide in Holstein, 1978.

Sumida, Jon Tetsuro. *In Defence of Naval Supremacy: Finance, Technology and British Naval Policy, 1889–1914*. Boston, Mass., 1989.

—— "Sir John Fisher and the Dreadnought: The Sources of Naval Mythology." *Journal of Military History* 59 (1995): 619–38.

—— *Inventing Grand Strategy and Teaching Command: The Classic Works of Alfred Thayer Mahan Revisited*. Baltimore, Md, 1997.

Tomitch, V. M. *Warships of the Imperial Russian Navy*. London, 1968.

Tritten, James J. "Doctrine and Fleet Tactics in the Royal Navy." In James J. Tritten and Luigi Donolo, eds, *A Doctrine Reader: The Navies of United States, Great Britain, France, Italy, and Spain*. Newport, R.I., 1995a. Pages 1–36.

—— "Doctrine in the Spanish Navy." In James J. Tritten and Luigi Donolo, eds, *A Doctrine Reader: The Navies of United States, Great Britain, France, Italy, and Spain*. Newport, R.I., 1995b. Pages 77–90.

—— "Navy and Military Doctrine in France." In James J. Tritten and Luigi Donolo, eds, *A Doctrine Reader: The Navies of United States, Great Britain, France, Italy, and Spain*. Newport, R.I., 1995c. Pages 37–75.

—— "Revolutions in Military Affairs, Paradigm Shifts, and Doctrine." In James J. Tritten and Luigi Donolo, eds, *A Doctrine Reader: The Navies of United States, Great Britain, France, Italy, and Spain*. Newport, R.I., 1995d. Pages 125–51.

Vale, Brian. *Independence or Death! British Sailors and Brazilian Independence, 1822–25*. London, 1996.

Valenzuela, Ricardo. *Cochrane: Marino y Libertador*. Valparaíso, 1961.

Verchau, Ekkard. "Von Jachmann über Stosch und Caprivi." In Herbert Schlottelius and Wilhelm Deist, eds, *Marine und Marinepolitik im kaiserlichen Deutschland, 1871–1914*. Düsseldorf, 1972. Pages 54–72.

Watts, Anthony J. *The Imperial Russian Navy*. London, 1990.

Weir, Gary E. *Building the Kaiser's Navy: The Imperial Navy Office and German Industry in the von Tirpitz Era, 1890–1919*. Annapolis, Md, 1992.

Wiley, Peter Booth. *Yankees in the Land of the Gods: Commodore Perry and the Opening of Japan*. New York, 1991.

Williamson, Samuel R., Jr. *The Politics of Grand Strategy: Britain and France Prepare for War, 1904–1914*. Cambridge, Mass., 1969.

Wilson, Michael. "Early Submarines." In Robert Gardiner, ed., *Steam, Steel and Shellfire: The Steam Warship 1815–1905*. London, 1992. Pages 147–57.

Wong, J. Y. *Deadly Dreams: Opium, Imperialism, and the Arrow War (1856–1860) in China*. Cambridge, 1998.

Woodward, David. *The Russians at Sea: A History of the Russian Navy*. New York, 1966.

Internet sources

http://www.uss-salem.org/danfs/frigates. Accessed May 1999.
http://www.uss-salem.org/danfs/line. Accessed May 1999.
http://www.uss-salem.org/danfs/sail. Accessed May 1999.
http://www.uss-salem.org/danfs/sloops. Accessed May 1999.

Index